The Complete Golfer

PETER THOMSON

'Those whose work
and pleasures are one
are fortune's favourites.'

SIR WINSTON CHURCHILL

The Complete Golfer

PETER THOMSON

A biography

Peter Mitchell

LOTHIAN BOOKS

For Geoff, Philippa, Amelia, Ben and Valmai

A Lothian book
Lothian Publishing Company Pty Ltd
11 Munro Street, Port Melbourne, Victoria 3207

First published 1991

National Library of Australia
Cataloguing-in-Publication data

Mitchell, Peter.
The complete golfer: Peter Thomson.

Includes index.
ISBN 0 85091 474 4.

1. Thomson, Peter, 1929– . 2. Golfers — Australia — Biography. I. Title.

796.352092

Designed by Tom Kurema
Typeset in 11/13 Garamond by Typeset Gallery, Malaysia.
Printed in Singapore

Contents

Acknowledgements

IN my late teens, I was a novice in golf (and journalism). My enthusiasm for golf led me to research as much as I could about the game and those who could play it well. As an Australian, I read all I could about the lives of local heroes, but to my frustration I was to discover one glaring omission: there was no detailed, substantial work on Peter Thomson. Thomson has always had the idea of writing his autobiography and had always discouraged requests to write his life, but his many business and private interests have so far kept him too busy. When we finally met after much correspondence, he said, 'I guess I can't stop you doing what you want to do. I'll happily answer any questions you have, but I want to make it clear it won't be an authorised biography. It's your project. I don't want a cent from it.' Peter Thomson finally gave me the green light for this book when I sat down with him at Royal Melbourne during the Coca-Cola Classic of early 1989. If there was one restriction placed on me it was that I not contact his elderly mother: 'Mother is getting on a bit and I'd rather you left her alone,' he said. In every other way I had his full co-operation and I am extremely grateful to him for sparing time for lengthy interviews, for answering my hundreds of questions and for his generosity in allowing me full use of all his features in the *Sun, Melbourne Herald* and the *Age*, and the revealing pages of *The Wonderful World of Golf* which he wrote with Desmond Zwar in 1968.

I thank Peter's brother Anthony (Tony), Peter's children Andrew, Peta-Ann and Fiona, and especially his wife Mary who encouraged me in the project with very practical help, yet in no way sought to influence what I was writing in her husband's favour, or indeed anyone else's. The photographs, letters and private cuttings Mary provided were invaluable.

I must also acknowledge the considerable help of Michael Wolveridge: to know Peter Thomson well is one thing, but also to be able to describe the friendship in detail is quite another and Mike was able to do this with great relish and eloquence.

Another extremely helpful source was the marvellous Mrs Lorraine Young, widow of Harry, who remained courteous and delightful company despite health problems.

My thanks are also due to the following who consented to being interviewed for this book: Deidre Alexander, Peter Alliss, Doug Bachli, Ian Baker-Finch, Richie Benaud, Fred Brooks, Jimmy Buchanan, Jack Campbell, Bruce Crampton, Claude Crockford, Tom Crow, Bruce Devlin, Billy Dunk, Bill Edgar, Don Galbraith, Terry Gale, John Gordon, David Graham, Neil Harvey, Andrew Hay, Brian Huxtable, Brian Jones, Don Lawrence, Sam Loxton, Ranald McDonald, Lois McKay, Bob Miller, Kel Nagle, Jack Newton, Peter Norris, Frank Phillips, Gary Player, Adrian Quist, Bill Richardson, Eric Routley, Frank Sedgman, Neville Selway, Dr Ken Sheperd, Sam Snead, Lindsay Thompson, Peter Toogood, Norman von Nida and Ben Wright. I also acknowledge the services generously given at the State Library and Museum of Victoria.

I thank the Herald and Weekly Times, the *Age*, the staff at Thomson Wolveridge and Associates, Victoria Golf Club, Royal Melbourne Golf Club, Huntingdale Golf Club and the Brunswick City Council.

Our thanks to the following for permission to reproduce the photographs:

The Melbourne *Herald-Sun* for 'The look of a champion', 'Harry and Lorraine Young', 'Arthur and Grace', 'Friends for more than 40 years', 'Destined for defeat', 'A toast to Peter' and 'A public showing'; AP/AAP for 'I'll never forget'; the Bettman Archive for 'Ready for another lesson'; Lawrence Levy for 'Past and future Open champions'; *News of the World* for 'Inspired by ghosts' and 'On the way to victory'; the Royal and Ancient Golf Club for '31 Open Championships'; Johannesburg *Star* for 'Thomson tees off' and 'More fruit'; Time Inc. for 'Immersed in the life' and 'Building an empire'; Victoria Golf Club for 'VGC winners'. Other photographs from the private collections of Mary and Peter Thomson and Mrs Lorraine Young. Jacket photographs: colour photograph of Peter Thomson, 1965, courtesy Australian Picture Library; British Open trophy pictures, the Bettman Archive.

The author and publisher have made every effort to trace sources of photographs in this book; if there are any unwitting errors or sources not properly acknowledged they would be grateful to have this information.

Preface

GOLFING is an all demanding endeavour that has no beginning and no end. It can devour a man with its insatiable appetite, or slowly torture and destroy him as surely as a disease. And there is no cure. Some say a man must have a goal and it must be the highest or it is not a goal at all. Others have another god that beckons them further and further from home. Golf is different things to different people, and if you don't watch out it becomes all things before you know it. It is a good servant but a bad master.

A young man starts out in golf with no accurate picture of what it involves, except that he knows by observation and newspaper reading that somewhere at the end of the rainbow is a pot of gold. He adopts an idol who is wealthy by now, beyond his wildest dreams. If he emulates him he thinks he might end up with the same opulence. So he sets about copying him in practice, trying to swing like him, adopting the same rhythm, wearing the same clothes and shoes. If he makes progress he is full of praise for the great man and attributes every advancement to him. He may even draw close to him. If he does, familiarity will more than likely destroy his image of his benefactor. He will realise his god is merely human with human failings that might even be repulsive. At that stage he takes off on his own, flushed with a strong ego that tells him he is as good or better than his rivals. Success is likely to come fast and free at that point. Events fall into his lap. He becomes a new 'find'. His scrap-book fills up. He is wooed by manufacturers, magazines and hangers-on. Now he may be sponsored, ending his financial problems. No longer will he have to worry about money. It will always be available if he runs short. He may even be able to afford a manager. If he doesn't quite make it, however, if his ego gets a rude deflation at the hands of an experienced veteran, he is in for a bad time. Nobody woos him. Manufacturers feed him with the barest minimum of balls and equipment, magazines never mention him and no one hangs around.

Loneliness is his worst enemy. It saps his confidence and drains his spirit. His life becomes an aimless wandering in search of a purpose only he can remember. He becomes resentful and morose and his road to the top now takes detours in the opposite direction. The successful ones can almost become unbearable, shouting advice, philosophising and generally building up an unpopular image. It would be inconceivable that all the spoiling, writing up, following, and hysterical adulation would not have some effect on the strongest make-up. It is understandable if a young man leaves the ground and starts floating up in the clouds. The hangers-on will do their best to keep him up there, keep his image polished, hoping some of the reflection will hit them. It would all be revolting except that once in a while you see a young man who goes through it all and comes out unscathed. If you enter into big races you have big hurdles to jump. Some get over the first lap then crash the second time around. It takes a big man to finish.

Boredom is another enemy. It takes about four hours to play a round of golf and maybe one hour to be shod, practised and ready to tee off. That leaves another 19 hours to be filled. Assuming one sleeps for nine hours (my own figure) there are ten vacant hours to fill every day. It is enough for some to spend two hours or more of this time on the practice tee training the muscles to respond to trigger mechanisms. Very satisfying, I'm sure, to those that find it fills their needs but boring beyond words for others. It is dangerous to read too much. It might tire the eyes. One mustn't do anything too athletic, at least before tee-off time. Better by far to save every ounce for the real thing. So what is there to do? The ones who solve this problem best are the most consistent winners. Boredom is the curse of intelligent man. It destroys interest, incentive, concentration, and eventually application. It wrecks a golfer. There is a strong temptation to waste time; fill it with trivia, comic company or just plain twiddling thumbs. Even this becomes mentally unbearable. Drink, make fun, play cards, matches, dice, anything to pass the awful waiting time. Count your money, dream of riches, think up schemes to get more, plan your pleasures, indulge until it too becomes a colossal bore. Go to church, pray, read the Bible, talk about it, preach until someone tells you to keep your problems to yourself. Try everything in turn. The truth is it can't be done for long, for months on end. It palls. The mind collapses under the weight.

It must surely dawn on even the dumbest in time that golf playing, demanding as it is, is not the whole of life or even an adequate substitute for some creative, satisfying occupation. Those who try to make it so end up disappointed if not a little disillusioned. The professional's life is an odd mixture of maestro and virtuoso. Not so long ago he was a teacher and a club maker, a servant of the game. Now it is possible to be an actor, an entertainer, an entrepreneur and manufacturer all at once. Played year in and year out it is not a game but a profession, a life-supporting craft with the richest spoils going to the craftiest. And if you're lucky — very, very lucky — you can turn your back on it early enough to enjoy living a life like a normal citizen and live to a ripe old age watching your children grow.

But you'll learn things along the way. You'll learn about life and human frailty, and wickedness and cunning and craft and all the other short cuts social man has contrived. If you're lucky you'll learn about honour and trust and other high levels of behaviour. Most of all you'll learn about yourself. At the end you might have something to show for it, something to pass on, something to share. And if you succeed, you will have, above and beyond all that, a warm and healthy respect for life and love for your family.

P. W. THOMSON, 1968

Prologue

IT was a sight the Melbourne golf enthusiast had seen many, many times before, but until now, for the majority of them at least, only on television. That solid frame, long since slimmed down from the body that once earned the nickname 'Ohio Fats', strode out with accustomed purpose and confidence. Normally scenes of vivid colours and sheer beauty such as those found at Augusta National, Baltusrol or Pebble Beach would have provided the backdrop, but on this occasion the gentle waves of Port Phillip Bay lapped up to the shores of Black Rock in the distance. The man voted by a knowledgeable group as 'Golfer of the Century', Jack Nicklaus, 48, was making his debut at Australia's acclaimed golf course, Royal Melbourne, and the Australian Bicentennial Classic was his first tournament appearance in the Victorian capital for more than two decades.

Organisers had guaranteed a mammoth turnout that day by pairing Nicklaus with the current No. 1 golfer in the world, Greg Norman, and quite a few patrons became hot under the collar anticipating that the following mob would limit their chances of a clear vantage point. For the golfing spectator it was far from the traditional orderly peaceful stroll but those in charge were entitled to do exactly as they pleased after paying an astonishing A$500,000 for both men to play in the championship. In the end it mattered little to the hordes of people who swarmed over the composite course — a rare glimpse of the Bear and the Shark, golf's most popular exhibits.

The par-4 12th on the wonderful composite course is the one members recognise as the 18th on the club's West course. Its green is situated near the clubhouse and when Nicklaus pulled his second shot well short and left into a greenside bunker, people wandering past took advantage of the grandstand provided and settled down to watch the 'Golden Bear' extricate himself from this little mess. The gallery ropes were full once those who'd been walking the previous holes arrived. The moment the famous thatch of golden hair settled over the ball the snapshots ceased and the entire gallery focused on the 'Golfer of the Century'. The shot was no piece of cake. With very little green to work with, Nicklaus had to fly the ball high over the steep lip of the bunker, long enough to carry a 15-metre crater of short grass, yet soft enough to pitch on the mound at the front of the green and roll down within reasonable range of the flag. It was all touch and finesse and Nicklaus played it brilliantly. From a cloud of sand the ball floated onto the mound, bit into the surface of the green and caressed the edge of the hole, finishing within 'gimme' distance to enthusiastic applause. Norman gave a smile of genuine warmth.

A few years before he was given the daunting title of golf's man of the century, the name Jack Nicklaus was one of more than a hundred fed into a computer. Attempting to settle the endless debate about who have been the greatest golfers of the 20th century, a British author and his researchers gathered all the statistics on the leading contenders and the computer eventually printed out the following top tens:

Pre-war era (1900–45)			Modern era (1945–83)		
1	Bobby Jones	USA	1	Jack Nicklaus	USA
2	Walter Hagen	USA	2	Ben Hogan	USA
3	Harry Vardon	Brit.	3	Tom Watson	USA
4	Gene Sarazen	USA	4	Arnold Palmer	USA
5	Byron Nelson	USA	5	Gary Player	S. Af.
6	Henry Cotton	Brit.	6	Lee Trevino	USA
7	Tommy Armour	USA	7	Sam Snead	USA
8	James Braid	Brit.	8	Seve Ballesteros	Spain
9	J. H. Taylor	Brit.	9	Peter Thomson	Aust.
10	Ted Ray	Brit.	10	Bobby Locke	S. Af.

Of the twenty players the computer selected, eleven were American and, as the project was completely handled by British interests, it at least proved dispassionate. Only four players came from countries outside the USA or Britain, and only one from Australia; Jack Nicklaus may have attracted the lion's share of the publicity at Royal Melbourne in 1988, but it was only fitting that the name of Peter Thomson be included in the exclusive field of fifty players celebrating a milestone in Australian professional golf. Indeed, during those early days of December, a great many people recognised that, in terms of ability, reputation and popularity, Peter William Thomson was Australia's answer to Jack William Nicklaus.

He too was instantly recognisable as he strode jauntily down the fairway, constantly surveying all around him. At 59, he retained his characteristic 'waddle' and seemed contented, relaxed and sure of his ability. He may not have given himself any chance of winning the tournament, but that didn't mean he wasn't going to give his utmost. This was no novelty appearance for the sake of old times. His reputation was on the line and anyone who thought otherwise simply had to scan the first round scores. Thomson had a 74 — one behind Greg Norman, equal to Jet Ozaki, Bob Shearer, Wayne Grady, Gordon Brand jr, Wayne Riley, Terry Gale, Johnny Miller, Jeff Woodland and Ossie Moore, and one stroke better than his companion in the top twenty of all time, Jack Nicklaus. Two shots behind was the newly crowned Australian Open champion, Mark Calcavecchia.

Thomson did many things that day to suggest that here was a man who knew how to play golf. In another age there were few better at the game in the world. It would not be an exaggeration to say his rightful place in the history of Australian sport ranks right alongside those of Bradman, Dawn Fraser, Lindrum and Opperman. He won the British Open (the unofficial world championship) five times and remains the only man to have won the 72-hole version three years in succession. In fact, he was either first or second in the event for seven consecutive years. He won a string of other tournaments around the globe, including three Australian Opens and nine New Zealand Opens and virtually singlehandedly established the Far East circuit, now a multi-million-dollar tour boasting some of the world's finest players. He twice paired with Kel Nagle to win the Canada (World) Cup. Awarded a CBE and MBE for his contribution to golf, he is also an honorary member of the Royal and Ancient Golf Club of St Andrews, a foundation member of the Sport Australia Hall of Fame, an inductee into the United States Golf Association Hall of Fame, was named Victoria's No. 1 sporting hero in an Australian bicentennial newspaper poll, and in 1990, was ranked in first place ahead of twenty-four others in a 'Vicstar' survey of the state's top sports stars since the second world war. He is without question Australia's greatest golfer.

Like many successful people, Thomson has sacrificed and suffered a great deal to climb to the top of the heap. Born into a working class family during the Great Depression, times were extremely tough when he chose to abandon the chance of a solid career as an industrial chemist to become a professional golfer. For a time, there was much anxiety expressed by his parents. Later there was the death of his first child only twelve days after his birth, a failed marriage, a daughter with whom he had virtually no contact for almost a decade, and months on end away from his second wife and young children following the itinerant lifestyle of the touring professional. There have also been serious health problems. As a young boy Thomson was diagnosed as suffering from asthma and later, when he first began to walk the pollen and dust filled fairways of the world, discovered his breathing difficulties were compounded by acute bouts of hay fever. When battling the combined effects of these two illnesses good golf seemed almost impossible, yet it was during these times that Thomson recorded some of his most famous victories. Then there has been disappointment from a couple of business ventures as well as much criticism of him in his multiple roles of golfer, journalist, critic, broadcaster and administrator.

Norman von Nida, the pioneer of Australian golf in Europe and the man who contributed so much to Thomson's first tentative steps as a professional, admits that he could never completely come to terms with the man's intellect. 'We were on a plane out of Australia once and he pulled out a book and buried his face into it. It was the life story of Mahatma Gandhi. That sort of stuff was too deep for me, but I could see that Peter was terribly interested in everything; hellbent on learning as much as he could.' Others haven't been quite so understanding. 'Pompous', 'living in the past', 'provocative to the point of obsession', 'arrogant', 'pre-historic', 'a snob', 'trouble maker', 'pure pest', ... these are some of the terms used to describe Thomson. Despite the broadsides fired his way, not once has Thomson ever responded in kind. He remains calm, cool and completely rational — some say he has the instincts of a cat; able to react and deal with situations at an instant. 'The way he plays golf is the way he is. He is splendidly "balanced",' says Michael Wolveridge, his partner in their golf course architecture business for the last quarter of a century. It remains a salient feature of Thomson's play that he is not bothered by a terrible shot or a terrible hole. No one can remember seeing him display anything remotely like anger on a golf course: he does not throw clubs, bend them over his knee or toss putters back into the bag, nor does he curse or swear. Experience has taught him a patient, almost fatalistic attitude. He accepts both good and bad bounces with the same mocking smile.

Once in the British Masters when he was in contention he pulled his tee shot at a long par-4 into heavy rough. Hitting out with a wood, he scuttled the ball across the fairway into a grove of trees. His third shot plopped into a fairway bunker. He then caught the sand shot thin and sailed it across the green and behind a small operations hut. His fifth was also too strong, bouncing back across the front of the green. He chipped on with his sixth and two-putted for an eight. With not a visible trace of emotion he went on to birdie the next hole and win the tournament. 'My attitude doesn't change,' he has maintained.

Thomson is the first to admit he has made many mistakes in his time and has trodden fairly and squarely on many toes, some of them eminent people, but through it all his remarkable balance and a strong sense of humour are not far beneath the surface. 'I fancy that the key to Peter's life lies in his humour,' says Wolveridge. 'It is this which makes him such delightful company. Slightly whimsical with a strong sense of the fancifully ridiculous, he is quick to acknowledge the funny side with never a hint of malice. It's all part of playing down the importance of it all. Lightening it up, achieving consistency. It mightn't produce a round of 63, which that McEnroe side of anybody's character might permit, but it doesn't produce an 83 either.'

Thomson's face retained that trademark smile as he made his way around Royal Melbourne, carried along by those famous white shoes. He loved Royal Melbourne. Of all the hundreds of courses he'd played all over Australia, this was the one he favoured most. More than any other it reminded him of the famous courses he found in Britain, because the West course, comprising the majority of holes on the composite layout, was the acknowledged masterpiece of Dr Alister Mackenzie, a Scotsman who turned his hand from medicine to golf course design after the first world war. Mackenzie also had a striking sense of humour. Once told the story of the constructor who was praised for his natural-looking undulations, Mackenzie retorted that 'he simply employed the biggest fool in the village and asked him to make them flat!' To this day the West course remains almost one hundred per cent Mackenzie, virtually the only true example of his work world-wide.

From the time he first played Royal Melbourne as a teenage amateur, Thomson realised it was a special place. He once concluded in an article, 'It is to the enduring honour of the Scots that they provided man with the most popular of his outdoor pastimes. Other outdoor games tend to belong to a common castle, the essential principles being those of attack and defence. The ball is common to both sides and is dealt with mostly in motion. Golf, on the other hand, is unique. From the time the first upright bi-ped began to wield sticks as weapons, the mind of man has devised no other game of similar structure or purpose and none so free and simple … the dispatching of a ball into a hole in the ground appropriately small. There is no one to oppose or interfere with you, no one to make a counter-move against you and, where in other games you have to reckon with a mortal antagonist, in golf it is your solitary self versus the nature in you and around you.'

Thomson understands this perhaps better than most. It was a major factor behind his warm smile and jaunty step during the Bicentennial Classic. Combined with the fact that it was to be his last major professional tournament over the historic layout, he was entitled to indulge in a little reminiscing. His thoughts, though, were also with his family, his wife of nearly forty years, Mary, and his children, daughter Deidre, from his first marriage, son Andrew and daughters Peta-Ann, better known as Pan, and Fiona. His entire professional golfing career had been for them. It was only fitting now, as he strode along the final steps towards the end of a remarkable playing career, that he spare a thought for the people who had inspired him when he was homesick and motivated him and helped preserve his golfing momentum when he reached his lowest ebb. 'The most important thing in my life is trying to do two things at once,' he'd said twenty years earlier. 'That is to perform my family obligations and be abroad where the golf tournaments are as much as possible. I know some other players seem to overlook this and perhaps the penalty will be paid later on, but I am very anxious to be a good father and husband. Three times a year I say goodbye and my small son weeps and says he doesn't want to go to school. He doesn't know why and it tears my heart so that I wonder why I am doing it to him, and whether it is worth the anguish.'

Now his children were no longer youngsters. They were all mature, well educated and pursuing their own careers far removed from golf. It must have seemed like only yesterday that he was walking down the final few holes at the Commonwealth club, only a few miles away along the sandbelt, and Andrew, then six, had run under the ropes and out on the fairway to greet his father, who was only a few shots away from winning the 1967 Australian Open. It could well have been one of the most heartfelt moments in golf, and it remains vivid in the memory of Andrew Thomson. 'I know it was interpreted by some as a pretty cheeky sort of thing to do, but for me it just seemed normal. I remember walking alongside him, talking, and in between him hitting shots, asking him things like, "Dad, is Superman real?" and "What's that over there?" You can imagine some kid all of six, tagging along while his father is trying to win the Australian Open. It seemed to me that everybody there was interested in what my father was doing, and while I had no idea of the importance of it all then, he didn't push me back to Mother. I felt ten feet tall.'

In future, there would be plenty of chances for pleasant rounds with his son and daughters and, for that matter, his grandchildren. The following year he would be 60, a time when most men think of putting their feet up, easing back on the throttle and living the good life.

As the temperature began to rise and the carparks began to swell in anticipation of an absorbing day's golf to conclude the Bicentennial Classic, Thomson pulled his driver out of his bag and characteristically hit a clean, crisp final tee shot to the fairway's middle. He waited for his partner and friend to hit, and watched the snarling, impatient cars banking up on Cheltenham Road. A small crowd of enthusiasts followed him and his pal Kel Nagle as they walked the final hole.

People imagine a sporting superstar like Thomson must be very rich, and, indeed, following wise investments and remarkable success on the United States Seniors tour, he was. At his Toorak home and at the Mt Eliza office of Thomson Wolveridge, there were bulky blueprints for the design and construction of golf courses throughout Australia, Europe and Asia. Thomson had decided to channel his energies into this business, and business was booming. Yet Peter Thomson never stopped to count his riches. Some have claimed he chose to play on the US Seniors circuit solely for the money. He'd seen the professional game grow from the paltry purses of his era to the obscene figures of commercial corporate golf in the 1980s. Having missed the boat in the 1950s and 1960s, they claimed, Thomson simply wanted a slice of the action.

Nothing could be further from the truth. 'I love sport,' he says, 'but the commercialism of it bothers me, and that is different from professionalism. There are people involved in the periphery who are not there for the enjoyment but to make money out of it.' The influence of commercialism was everywhere as he walked up that final fairway, but it was easy to block it from his mind — he only had to look over at his close friend of forty years, dear Kel Nagle. Afflicted by arthritis in his legs, and struggling to gain length from the tee, Nagle hobbled along, also retaining a warm smile. He had rejoiced in Thomson's excellent shots, just as Thomson had rejoiced in his. Together they lifted each other and floated along the fairways on a tide of mutual inspiration. Even Nicklaus and Norman were temporarily forgotten as the veteran pair came up the 18th, side by side. 'We were pleased and proud to be amongst them during the Bicentennial Classic,' recalls Thomson. 'At our age it's a big effort to play and stride all those holes for four days to keep the score respectable, but I enjoyed it. I chose to play because it was our festival and I suppose we should have played if we were capable, and I'm glad I did.'

The 59-year-old with the white shoes stepped up to his ball, resting in the short grass in front of the massive grandstand at the rear of the 18th green. His second shot had been overclubbed and he now found himself with a challenge. Up and down and he would have his best round for the championship, a 73. It would have been a great shame to see him finish with a bogey, but with Nagle looking on and with a huge audience watching from the stands and on national television, a finishing bogey was out of the question. He stalked around that shot as though it was for all the marbles. The final putt in a British Open or a pennant match with Victoria Golf Club, it was the same story. Judging the speed of the green superbly, Thomson ran his ball smoothly up to the hole from a difficult position to leave a putt of a metre. Much to the delight of all those watching, the putt was negotiated without fear. 74-75-74-73 for 296 and outright 44th placing ahead of Johnny Miller, Brian Jones, Jeff Woodland, Bruce Devlin, Mike Ferguson and Kel Nagle. Fourteen years earlier in the Chrysler Classic, over the same course, Thomson's total had been ten shots worse.

As Thomson and Nagle shook hands amidst the generous applause, just as they had done on the same spot twenty-nine years before, there was a little joke and broad grins as they made their way to the scorers' hut. There was no public show of relief that it was all over, no throwing of the ball into the crowd, no prolonged acknowledgement of the gallery's ovation, just a grateful doffing of the visor. As always, grace, dignity and the strongest belief that the game itself is the most important thing. With the bonus of this being a valedictory performance, it was a moment for Australian sport, not just for golf, to savour. The fact was not lost on many of the people who had come to watch Peter Thomson play. An old gent whispered his reason for traipsing the fairways of Royal Melbourne: 'He's still the best we've ever had and I just wanted to see him one more time. Never mind the rest!' An elderly woman perched on her shooting stick a few metres away was also enjoying herself: 'It's nice to know that some of the good things from the 1950s are still giving us pleasure,' she said. Then there was the young father in shorts and T-shirt with his son, similarly attired: 'I brought my 9-year-old along today so that he can grow up saying he actually saw the great Peter Thomson play.'

Although he has warmly embraced the trappings of success, Thomson has never relinquished the absence of pretension that has won him firm and loyal friendships from Wellington to Washington, Blackpool to Bombay. He floats around the scene at Australian tournaments, always on the move. One minute he's at an outdoor table with a group of young professionals, eating an ice-cream and chatting about experiences during overseas tours, the next, he's heading for the media tent, stopping on the way as he bumps into old friends. Soon he can be spotted out on the course, following a promising junior or a local hero.

He was once watching a round of the Australian matchplay championship at Kingston Health between Sydney's Jeff Wagner and Brett Ogle, when Wagner had an argument with his caddy and ended up carrying the bag himself. When the match became tight and Wagner began to wilt from lumping his bag for several kilometres, Thomson stepped in and offered his services. A startled Wagner gratefully accepted, and with the most famous caddy on the course took the match to a fifth extra hole, where a birdie from Ogle ended proceedings. Thomson offered his commiserations to Wagner, congratulated him on a fine match, gave him back his bag, and melted into the crowd. It was no stunt for publicity, rather a spontaneous gesture. 'I just couldn't bear to watch him carry the bag any longer,' said Thomson.

Judged in his multiple roles of player, administrator, writer, broadcaster and designer, history must see him as one of the game's true greats. Long after he is gone, the legacy of his remarkable contribution will continue to be felt wherever and whenever a person wields a club in fun or competition. Of few players indeed may it be said, as of Peter William Thomson, that golf has been greatly uplifted by his presence.

CHAPTER 1

The Wilds of Royal Park

SCORES of weather-beaten golf balls yet to be discovered, a modest set of hickory shafted clubs and an unpretentious 9-hole golf course with a flattering name — to a keen young boy in short pants they were a heavenly combination. And feeling on top of the world, he marched confidently down the fairway. The lad was on the brink of a personal best round and, with another stylishly executed tee shot, he wondered what his father might say on hearing his good news. Just float this approach onto the green, jot down another par, and he was almost done.

He stood over his ball. He gave the club a customary waggle. He slowly drew it back and made his swing ... and it had more lumps than last night's porridge. The shot bore absolutely no resemblance to the ones taken previously on the round. It felt awful. Where were tempo and direction, that familiar sweeping blow as smooth as velvet? The hacker's bread-and-butter shot, a sickening slice, had sent the treasured golf ball way down to the bottom of the railway cutting.

The youngster's reaction was as sudden as it was uncharacteristic. He felt he wanted to snap the club in his hands like a piece of chalk. Instead, he flung it violently into a clump of trees. Fortunately for him, nobody saw him do it — fortunately for the future world of golf, nobody needed to. Twelve-year-old Peter Thomson learned something about himself and the game. It was a lesson he never forgot. He did not wonder why golf wasn't an especially popular game; why it appeared exclusive to slow, old men; why he seemed to be the only child on the course; why his friends preferred the more glamorous pursuits of cricket and football; and why he'd spent just about every spare moment chasing a little white ball around a field. He did wonder why his reaction to the stroke he'd just played was such a shameful one.

Already a mental attitude that was to become the very core of his play and the success that followed had taken seed. 'I was filled with remorse,' says Thomson of that club-throwing episode, 'and I made up my mind never, ever to do it again.' He was quick to perceive that the only bruises to be suffered in golf were to the spirit; it was a game that tested the mind more than the muscles. From an early age he regarded the act of striking a golf ball as essentially a natural, simple exercise and has since stated many times that it is not the swing but golfers themselves who make the game seem so difficult. 'It is at least 50 per cent a mental game: if you recognise that it is the mind that prompts us physically, then you can almost say that golf is entirely a mental effort,' says Thomson. 'The most important facets of golf are careful planning, calm and clear thinking, and ordinary commonsense.'

Herein lies a key to the man himself, if you include the qualities that are abundant in golf more than any other game: honour and integrity. It is a sport in which there is no umpire or referee. Writer and humorist P. G. Wodehouse captured this aspect superbly when he wrote:

> The only way of really finding out a man's true character is to play golf with him. In no other walk of life does the cloven hoof so quickly display itself. I employed a lawyer for years, until one day I saw him kick his ball out of a heel-mark. I removed my business from his charge next morning. Golf is the infallible test. The man who can go into a patch of rough alone, with the knowledge that only God is watching him, and play his ball where it lies, is a man who will serve you faithfully and well. The man who can smile bravely when his putt is diverted by one of those beastly worm-casts is pure gold right through. But the man who is hasty, unbalanced, and violent on the links, will display the same qualities in the wider field of everyday life.

Thomson is a stickler for simplicity and honesty. His ultra-logical approach to the game, particularly in the tense, heady and often dramatic world of professional golf, can be traced back to a similarly simple, no-frills childhood — and perhaps to that early club-throwing incident. Like many of the game's greatest players, he grew up in far from affluent circumstances with a nearby golf course providing an obvious distraction for a broadening mind. Such golfing legends as Gene Sarazen, Walter Hagen, Ben Hogan, Sam Snead, Lee Trevino and Seve Ballesteros all emerged from humble beginnings — Peter Thomson was no different.

His father, Arthur, was a lover of sports but, surprisingly, golf wasn't one of them. Cricket and Australian Rules football were his favourites. He was a successful wicketkeeper and batsman for the Brunswick City XI, based at Royal Park. A little further down the road was Princes Oval, home of his favourite Victorian Football League club, Carlton, 'the mighty Blues'. Golf in the late 1920s was mainly for the middle to upper-class and, although popular with small groups at established private clubs, the game could hardly compete with the major participation and spectator sports. Yet golf did have an illustrious ally in the prime minister of the day, Stanley Bruce, whose father J. M. Bruce was instrumental in the foundation of Royal Melbourne Golf Club in 1891. In May 1927 the nation's leader belted a drive down the 1st fairway to open Victoria Golf Club's new 18-hole course at Cheltenham. Twenty-seven years later Bruce would play a far greater role in the game, coinciding with a remarkable year for Australian golf and Peter Thomson in particular, but in late 1929 there were far more pressing matters on the prime minister's agenda.

Growing industrial unrest and uncertainty led to defeat for Bruce's Nationalist government in the October elections, and Stanley Bruce went down in history as the only prime minister to lose his seat, that of Flinders on Victoria's Mornington Peninsula. Australia, desperate for stability, was to suffer from the stockmarket crash in the US which heralded the start of the Great Depression of the 1930s. Those who borrowed could not pay their loans, banks were forced to close, companies went broke, and financial chaos crippled families worldwide. In Melbourne, a third of the workforce was suddenly unemployed and thousands lined up outside emergency soup kitchens or begged door-to-door.

One of the unemployed was Arthur Thomson. Born into a less than prosperous family in the northern inner-city suburb of Brunswick, he left school in his early teens soon after the end of the first world war and, having shown a talent for sketching, painting and drawing, obtained qualification as a signwriter. At the time there was little demand for billboards and advertisements, and Arthur had to work at a series of jobs, which included a road building gang. Like many caught in the grip of tough times, Arthur was keen to escape the despondency and pessimism by making the most of his leisure hours. One of the most eagerly anticipated events of the week for a young man was the popular Saturday night dance at the Brunswick Town Hall, and during one memorable waltz an attractive young lady caught his eye. Her name was Grace Watson, a dress maker, born at Kyneton, 50 miles north-west of Melbourne, who had moved to Parkville, immediately to the south of Brunswick, as a toddler with her parents. Arthur and Grace began to see each other regularly and within a few months the young man proposed. To the young lady's amusement, she was about to become a Thomson, the maiden name of her mother. It was not a long engagement. Despite financial hardship and lack of solid employment the couple were married and eventually found enough money to set up a modest, happy home in a small, rented flat above the business premises and petrol station of a motor mechanic in West Brunswick. Here Arthur, at age 24, and Grace 19, welcomed their first child, Peter William, born at a West Brunswick maternity nursing home on 23 August 1929.

It was, as things turned out, a productive period in the district for Australian sport. Two other notables sprang from the same kind of solid, respectable working-class background: tennis player Frank Sedgman, born eighteen months earlier, also in West Brunswick, and cricketer Neil Harvey, born just eight months before in Fitzroy, a few miles to the east. Both men offer, in their careers and personalities, parallels to Thomson: fierce patriotism and competitiveness combined with easy cosmopolitanism, outstanding achievements in international sport, and financial and social success whilst retaining the simple values and standards drummed into them in their youth.

Sedgman was one of the dominant figures in world tennis during the early 1950s, resplendent in the all-white colours of the club as he crisply served and volleyed his way to memorable victories at Wimbledon, in the Davis Cup, and the Australian and United States Opens. Never a doubt was expressed over a line call. Harvey was second only to Donald Bradman on the list of total runs and centuries in Australian first-class cricket. A diminutive but punishing left-hander, he scored 21 centuries in 79 Tests for his country between 1948–63. When fielding in the slips cordon he took no part in leg before wicket appeals, and never a pause marked his acceptance of the umpire's raised finger. Though their paths did cross, the trio were never to become close friends.

Brunswick at this time was an eight-square-mile working-class suburb with a distinctly lean and hungry look about it. Mostly light industry and low-income housing, it could have passed for any other impoverished and uninspiring inner-city locale except for a massive oasis of parkland along its southern edge, conveniently only a minute's walk from the Thomson home. Royal Park had acres of playing fields, gardens, ovals, even a zoo … and 'the' golf course. Its historical claim to fame was as starting point for the ill-fated Burke and Wills expedition to cross the continent from south to north in 1860. The only place for miles that offered relief from the rows and rows of neat but drab houses and factories, the grey roads and cobblestoned alleys, Royal Park attracted children as a porchlight does moths on a balmy summer night. To youthful eyes it seemed a vast, lush, green adventure world, with huge trees, hills, fences, a tram line, trains and a cavernous railway cutting.

'It was a time of great fun,' Peter Thomson recalls. 'Children don't know what a depression is — parents do. To me it was really all one great lot of fun because Royal Park was my playground and that's where we spent endless hours. We used to play our games to the roar of the lions at the zoo. That's one strong memory. When it came feed time for them we'd hear their roars waft across the park. Even before I started playing golf I spent my happy childhood roaming the wilds of Royal Park.'

There was also much happiness at school. An extremely quick learner and enthusiastic student, Thomson attended Brunswick southwest primary (again a short walk from home). He was not a complicated boy, but his teachers remarked many times that he was mature for his years. Young Peter relished his first regular contact with children of his age. He was hardly introverted, but away from the classroom, schoolyard or playing field he was a rather solitary child. There were a few close schoolfriends but it seemed a great deal of his boyhood was spent in the company of adults — his parents and their friends, his aunts and uncles and grandparents. Peter was almost seven before the next Thomson child, Anthony, was born. There was a further six-year gap to the third boy, Roger, and the youngest Thomson lad, Michael, was born when his eldest brother was 18.

For siblings such age differences seemed unbridgeable. As one American critic once observed of him: 'There is about Thomson, beneath the articulateness and the worldly sophistication and the distantness, a very real shyness that goes back to his youth.' 'I was a bit of a loner,' Thomson says. 'One reason I played golf so much was to be by myself.' Another reason was that his brothers were much younger. 'I was almost a generation older,' he says, 'so I was at different schools and being much older I didn't get down to playing with my brothers the way brothers do. They did, because they were close.' As a consequence, Thomson's maternal grandfather, Anthony Watson, became one of his closest friends. A strong character whose background was a hardworking combination of life in the city and on the land, Anthony Watson was a popular member of the community. He was nicknamed 'Castles of Kyneton' after his birthplace and, after marrying locally, he and his young wife set about raising a family of four girls and two boys. His work buying and selling horses, the then predominant mode of transport, took his family to Melbourne, and a small stables alongside the Flemington race course. They eventually moved to the more salubrious locale of Parkville, and later, once the children were into their adult years, retired to a farm at Blackwood, several miles south of Kyneton.

Ironically it was the terror of the infamous 'Black Friday' bushfires of January 1939 that cemented the bond between Grace Thomson's father and her young boy. The blaze devastated large areas of Victoria, claimed seventy-six lives and left its scar on the countryside and many hundreds of families. The tiny town of Blackwood was all but wiped out, and Thomson's grandparents fled the charcoal hills to rent a dwelling in West Brunswick, almost opposite that of their daughter and son-in-law.

Of all his children, Mr Watson felt a close bond to his girl Grace, a strong personality in the mould of her father. 'Mother was always the strict disciplinarian of the family and the teacher,' says Peter's brother Tony. 'Mother believed in doing the right thing by other people and we were brought up to do the same. Her concern was never to be a bother to other people. She went to great lengths to teach us that sort of thing.' Much closer to his daughter than he had been for many years, Anthony Watson was now able to take a much keener interest in his grandson. 'Peter was like his grandfather in many ways,' recalls his Aunt Marge, Grace's sister. 'Peter was very sure of himself from an early age and no one had to worry about disciplining him at all. He got on very well with my father and they became very close. They were like each other in looks and all.' With Peter's father busy working and his mother taking care of young Anthony, the lad was taken for many walks by his grandfather through Royal Park, and inevitably though not an enthusiast himself, Mr Watson and Peter were to discuss golf. The lad was only aware of the game as played by 'old people' on land that was strictly off-limits to him.

There is no doubt Thomson had a close relationship with his father, and through his formative years it was his father who instilled in him an appreciation of sport and an attitude that suggested life was never anything to be taken too seriously but, in the typically working-class ethic, 'a man still had to do what a man had to do'. When he could afford the time, Arthur Thomson deliberately encouraged Peter's competitive instincts with the mandatory bat and ball games, 'bowling down a few spinners' in the nearby park or backyard. During these brief 'test matches' Peter Thomson first received praise for a good shot, and criticism when he failed to stick to instructions. Much later, basking in the summer sun on the dry, brown grass of Royal Park with drink or icy-pole in hand, he would watch his father bat or keep wickets for Brunswick City. An excellent cricketer, Arthur Thomson was a character and a happy-go-lucky type, but if there was a mate to help, a point to make or a belief worth preserving, he was never one to shirk the fight. Tony Thomson often remembers the rough days watching Carlton play at Princes Park, when his father was quick to display his aggressiveness: 'I vividly recall those times when I would find father getting into a punch-up after an argument with some opposition supporter, and I would be there standing by his side. He would often end up with a blood nose or a black eye, but no matter how badly father had been injured you could bet that the other fellow was no better off.'

Arthur had precisely the same attitude to cricket. He loved the sport with a passion. Young Peter would stare out into the middle and see his father darting quickly between the stumps, shouting encouragement to his batting partner, or bellowing from behind the stumps a vigorous appeal. While it was a great outlet for Arthur, it meant that whenever his son played cricket, he tried to be like his dad, enthusiastic, determined, competitive. He was learning the thrill of competing, and without really understanding the meaning of it all he became sullen when he lost and cheerful when he won, which was more often than not. While other boys of his age would approach their sport with all the innocence and awkwardness expected of them, 'Thommo', as he became known, was already displaying an exceptional mentality. 'He was very, very sure of himself at a young age, but he was not an objectionable kid,' says his Aunt Marge. 'He fended for himself a lot. I remember when one of his brothers had been in a fight and had said to the boy, "I'll tell my brother on you," so he ran up to Peter and said so-and-so just hit me, and Peter said, "You got yourself into the trouble, you get out of it."'

The worst of his financial struggles were over when Arthur Thomson found a steady job as a dairyman, delivering milk by horse-drawn wagon to the nearby suburbs of Ascot Vale and North Melbourne. It was a demanding job, particularly in the depths of winter, but the family's horizons had brightened considerably. This didn't mean that steak replaced tripe on the dinner table, but it allowed a couple of 'luxuries' that are to this day among Peter Thomson's favourite pastimes: reading and radio. His parents realised the importance of reading to partner a good education and books like *David Copperfield*, *Treasure Island*, *King Solomon's Mines*, and *The Adventures of Robinson Crusoe* became well-leafed at home. Magazines were devoured (the popular publication *Smith's Weekly* was a favourite) and a creditable knowledge of the dictionary resulted from a love of crossword puzzles. There were also plenty of newspapers to read. At one stage Thomson earned pocket-money selling papers outside the local hotel just a few doors from home and in moments of quiet trade had a chance to catch up on the news.

Then there was the staple form of evening entertainment for most families of the era, the wireless. On winter nights the Thomsons would gather around the radio in the kitchen where the wood stove provided the warmest room in the house. Otherwise it was the lounge room where Peter, like any other youngster, 'tuned in' before bed to the large number of serials bombarding the airwaves, 'Betty and Bob', 'Mittens',

'Dad and Dave', 'Dr Fu Manchu', 'Mrs 'Olmes and Mrs Hentwistle', 'Biggles', 'The Lone Ranger', 'The Air Adventures of Jimmy Allen', 'Secret Diary', and many more.

On the night of 3 September 1939 Prime Minister Robert Menzies's broadcast attracted the biggest ever audience in Australian radio history:

> Fellow Australians ... It is my melancholy duty to inform you officially that in consequence of the persistence of Germany in her invasion of Poland, Great Britain has declared war on her ... We are therefore as a great family of nations involved in a struggle which we must at all times win.

A boy in West Brunswick just eleven days past his tenth birthday couldn't see what all the fuss was about: 'I was too young to be excited or frightened by the war. Again, like the depression it all seemed perfectly natural to me. I didn't especially notice any anxiety or worry. I was simply a young boy growing up in Melbourne on the edge of a great park.'

And for most Melburnians it was all utterly normal. The postman still came twice a day; the butcher, baker and grocer home-delivered; people put out billies to collect their milk from Arthur Thomson. Ice chests greatly outnumbered refrigerators and vacuum cleaners had just come on the market. And it cost £1,250 for an average house, most of which would be advanced by a building society at a 5 per cent interest rate. As if endorsing the illusion that life was for the most part unchanged, the prime minister applauded 'a spontaneous movement among Australian businessmen to carry on as usual. It is only another example of the calmness with which you would expect a British community to face a tough situation,' he said. It was left to the postponement of Test cricket to provide the biggest jolt to a happy existence. While most of the boys his age considered the more flamboyant Stan McCabe or Sid Barnes to be the pin-up boys of the Australian Test team, Peter directed his adulation firmly towards the unimpeachable talent and demeanour of Donald Bradman — after all, their birthdays were only days apart. Thomson was just an infant when 'The Don', at 21, made his first tour of England in 1930, but young Peter grew to learn of that Test series win and Bradman's astonishing 309 in a day's play at Headingley, Leeds, and his series tally of 974 at an average of 139. For thousands of youngsters 'The Don's' place in the public eye was immutable. It seemed sacrilegious to allow such skills to lie dormant and, more than the mounting casualties, Bradman's enforced retirement brought home to many the enormity of the European conflict. 'That was a great shame,' says Thomson. 'Everybody that one came across was a big fan of Bradman. He was the great figure and I suppose every young boy aspired to be as good at whatever he took up as Don Bradman was at cricket. Through my father, I was encouraged to emulate such a man.'

And Thomson did his best to comply.

He won a scholarship to Brunswick technical school, where administrators held a firm belief that physical education was the equal of arithmetic and English and where his sporting ability blossomed. Brunswick tech. was an all-boys school renowned as progressive and innovative. Working-class students were introduced to Shakespeare, Ibsen and Shaw, and the music of Beethoven, Schubert and Tchaikovsky. Its image as the antithesis of the rough, raw trade school was further cultivated by speech nights, performances of community singing and a school orchestra. Activities associated with the war effort, such as training 650 RAAF fitters, were also scheduled at night and weekends.

The year 1941 was Thomson's first of three in the junior school aiming for his 'intermediate technical certificate'. In Form 1A with twenty-four boys Thomson's academic abilities in a range of subjects; social studies, science, solid geometry, modelling, free drawing, woodwork, sheetmetal work and the compulsory English and arithmetic were immediately noticeable. A sharp intellect was coming to the surface in both the classroom and the field of sport.

Cricket and football remained his obsessions.

He represented the school with distinction at both and also played cricket with the Brunswick Presbyterian XI in the local churches competition. As a footballer he played centre and although not a big boy for his age was solid and skilful enough to earn more than his share of attention. Cricket, though, was his first love. If he hadn't eventually proved his exceptional hand-eye co-ordination in golf, he may well have made his name hitting a swinging, spinning or seaming ball instead of a stationary one. Neil Harvey, no less, then a student at rival Collingwood tech., was a respectful opponent in those inter-school clashes at Royal Park. 'Every time we played Brunswick, Peter stood out,' recalls Harvey. 'The first thing you'd notice about the opposition was who'd be good at footy and cricket and who'd be bad. We all knew Peter was pretty handy at both sports. I would say he was close to the best cricketer at Brunswick tech.' Harvey's assessment was underlined when Thomson, a left-hand top order batsman and leg-spin bowler, compiled an unbeaten 150 for the Presbyterian XI — a huge score in junior ranks. Later he was invited to practise with Carlton in the Victorian Cricket Association's district competition, the breeding ground for State and, ultimately, Test cricket. The CCC officials felt they had come extremely close to persuading the young lad to choose cricket as his sporting priority, but Thomson refused to neglect his golf.

Much later a fashionable canard within sports writing circles was that Thomson decided to take up golf only after instructions from the family doctor to exercise his legs with plenty of walking. And that he was given a 2-iron by his grandfather for Christmas and immediately took it to the golf course where he could satisfy the doctor's demands. It is true his parents were concerned about Peter's legs but this was much earlier, in his days growing from a toddler. 'There was nothing seriously wrong,' he explains. 'But there were misguided notions and someone suggested putting my legs in irons to straighten them. I'm not sure what the problem was — it could have been that I was knock-kneed or bow-legged or something — but fortunately good sense prevailed and my legs were quite normal once I'd developed further.'

And the story of a club for Christmas is false. Anthony Watson was indeed the catalyst, but his support came in the form of encouragement. Thomson's start in golf was typically low-key: 'One day some old hickory sticks surfaced in the family,' he says. 'Honestly I can't be sure how or from where they turned up — my grandfather may well have obtained them from somewhere — but suddenly they were there and something prompted me to start using them.' It was not a full set: the basic few irons, a wood and a putter. And they were a right-handed set, which proved to be a complete coincidence. Thomson's father was a left-handed batsman in cricket and, although a natural right-hander, Peter deliberately copied his Dad by batting left-handed. Luckily Arthur was not a golfer, for his son would have grown up using left-handed clubs and 'would never have been any good'. Once he started using the right-handed clubs he suddenly had the feeling he was doing something right. It almost felt comfortable, as if he was meant to be doing it. Yet these were frustrating times for him. His introductory forays in golf were very much 'hit and run' missions and not particularly memorable. Thomson had problems concentrating and it wasn't difficult to understand why. 'It was never a regular thing for me to go out and play golf at first because I had no business being on the Royal Park course. I didn't belong. I certainly couldn't afford the green fees, so occasionally I would sneak on and play a few holes.' Constantly on the lookout for fear of being discovered, Thomson put himself under a great deal more pressure than there ought to have been. His ball hooked left and sliced right; he hit it fat and he hit it thin. When it did fly straight, it was either way too short or over the back of the green. It was certainly not love at first smite!

That wartime summer of brown, dry grass, of scorching days, of men in singlets drinking beer on suburban verandahs, of cicadas singing their staccato song and of children frolicking under garden hoses, was the summer when Peter Thomson and the game of golf came to know each other.

In December 1941 an air attack by the Japanese on Pearl Harbor in Hawaii brought the war nearer home than ever before. Two months later Singapore had fallen, the Japanese had bombed Darwin on Australia's north coast and had put submarines into Sydney Harbour. In Melbourne, invasion seemed imminent and hundreds of digging squads tore up parks and gardens to build hideous air-raid shelters. In March 1942 a contingent of American servicemen arrived to 'help defend' Melbourne and all available land, schools and large buildings were taken over. Even that sporting holy of holies, the Melbourne Cricket Ground, was given to the United States air force and renamed Camp Murphy. Thomson clearly remembers 'the Yanks coming' and the transit base they built on Royal Park called Camp Pell. With the eerie wailing of practice sirens, the sight of public servants filing out of their offices for air-raid drills, and the rows of trenches blotting the landscape, it became indeed a gloomy winter in Melbourne. There were coupons for food, clothing and petrol. People were ordered to cover their windows and turn down their lights.

Through all this gloom the youngster from Brunswick was far from dejected. He would finish his day at school, grab his modest set of clubs and walk briskly down the short street that separated his home from the golf course. And he was often late to the dinner table.

'The winters didn't seem so cold or so wet that one couldn't practise after school,' recalls Thomson. 'Something drew me to this long before there was any incentive and I learned a love of practice which has never been far beneath the surface. I can even remember playing in the moonlight and thinking it dangerous because I'd heard you could be moonstruck if exposed too long to the rays of the moon! Everything that happened to me at that time seemed so natural. I had no great ambition to achieve this or that — I simply went along on the tide that carried me. My greatest memory of those times is that they were fun and very enjoyable.'

One day he was nearing the end of another solo round and about to play his chip to the green when a youth on a bicycle burst through the trees forming the course boundary and rode right over the green. Thomson was incensed. 'Hey, you,' he yelled at the boy, 'What do you think you're doing?' The lad wheeled the bike around and cheekily replied, 'What do you mean?' Thomson strode up to him as bold as brass and recognised him as a youngster of his age that had been in his year at primary school and was now at University High. 'You don't ride bikes across golf greens,' said Thomson forcefully. Jimmy Buchanan knew of Peter Thomson and, although he saw he was not a big boy, had heard that he was not someone to lock horns with. 'I realised I'd done the wrong thing and said I was sorry,' says Buchanan. 'Peter accepted that straight away and then we chatted about his golf and the club he was holding in his hand and he asked me if I was keen on having a hit. The next morning at five o'clock we were out there and he gave me an old hickory-shafted club and I duffed my way around. All the way though, he was terribly encouraging.' It was the start of a solid friendship. Over the next several years Thomson and Buchanan became as close as brothers. 'Peter was the cleverest kid out of the ones I knew in the area,' says Buchanan. 'He was very, very good at just about everything he did. He was above average intelligence I always felt, and he could put words together better than most of us in that age bracket. He definitely displayed leadership qualities. When we were playing in the park or the alley and made up sides for football, cricket, basketball or whatever, Peter would just about always be captain of one of those sides. He had a good, quick-thinking brain and was a real leader. His ability with a golf club meant that he was suddenly surrounded by men much older than he was. As a result he developed more quickly than the rest of us, who stayed around boys our own age.'

This was a crucial period in the development of Thomson's game for two major reasons. The war meant a loss of members to the services, a deterioration of courses, a general lack of incentive and resources to play so that courses lay idle. Very few people were at Royal Park to prevent a young boy from sneaking on at the 4th tee and playing a few holes. The second influence was the complete lack of expense for the young lad: he didn't need to buy clubs or shoes; there was no green fee, and the old law of 'finder's keepers' applied to golf balls. The only snag was finding enough to play with. Rubber was an essential war material and the manufacture of balls ceased soon after conflict began. Such was the extent of the shortage the Victorian Golf Association found it necessary to obtain permission from the state government for sporting goods company Spalding, established in the western suburbs of Sunshine in the 1930s and a future employer of one Mr P. Thomson, to collect used golf balls and recover them with a rubber-substitute compound called balata. For his private searching, Thomson was aided mainly by his grandfather, and together the pair covered the golf course and surrounding area in a desperate but ultimately successful search. 'Balls were very scarce at the time and if I wanted to play, which I did, I simply had to find some,' he says. 'I found them in the railway cutting and in hedgerows. I looked everywhere for them and that was how I managed to keep on playing.' Hardly recognisable compared with the gleaming missiles of today, they were old, weather-beaten and battle-scarred, but they served their purpose.

Royal Park GC was founded in 1903 and originally consisted of eighteen holes surrounding the Melbourne Zoological Gardens. It was a far from prosperous beginning and play progressed intermittently for two years before a clubhouse was built. In 1909 the membership slumped to just fifteen and finances were stretched to such a limit that it was sometimes not possible to pay £1 a week for the greens to be cut! Facing drastic cutbacks, even possible extinction, the club's controlling body, the Royal Park trustees, made the momentous decision to halve the number of holes. It seemed a logical move, but at the time many members alleged that those in charge were unsympathetic towards golf and could have easily retained the original course had they not considered the game an unpopular one. This view from the membership carried some weight a few years later when the club's first full-time professional, Walter Spicer, arrived from the renowned Royal Cinque Ports Club at Deal in England but, due to lack of staff, found himself tending the greens and performing custodial duties around the clubhouse instead of making clubs and balls and helping members lower their handicaps. Further, the trustees regularly granted permission for church picnics to be held on the 8th fairway on Saturdays, reasoning that 'a tap provided a convenient place for water'. Much to the anger of the membership this pushed the club competition onto the seven holes north of the railway line. It was the last straw when the trustees notified the club of an increase in rent from £25 to £100!

Understandably there was much rejoicing when control of the entire park and golf course transferred to the Melbourne City Council in 1934. Major improvements followed immediately. Sprinklers were introduced (a tap was provided for church picnics away from the course); fairways and greens were mown regularly; a system of bunkers and mounds were added to toughen the course, and play was initiated on Sundays. Another innovation was admission of junior members, between the ages of 15–21.

A boy not yet in his teens was often caught red-handed playing illegally. Far from deterred he would be back next day. Even when he felt he might be pushing his luck a little too far he would go and grab Jimmy Buchanan and tell him to get his clubs ready. 'We used to hit balls from the front yard of my parents' place in Park Street to the 7th tee of Royal Park,' Buchanan recalls. 'It was only about 150 yards, but it was a little dangerous I suppose with the cars going past. Often we used to practise together — he'd get up one end of the park and I'd get up the other and we'd hit our few balls to each other, back and forth. He was incredibly accurate even then. Most of his hits would end up near my feet and he'd go crook if I sprayed mine all over, which I usually did.' On other occasions the pair would retreat to the small yard behind the Thomson home and practise chip shots, where Peter recalls 'breaking plenty of windows!' Fortunately for his parents' still slender budget and unfortunately for the local glazier, young Peter's trips to Royal Park Golf Club were soon to become more frequent. Legend has it that Thomson started his 'official' golf as a caddy, earning a few pence in his leisure time, but this is not the case. 'I was never a caddy for anybody, not at Royal Park or anywhere,' he says. 'There was no caddying at Royal Park because there were not enough active players and those few who were playing were not the sort of affluent people who would engage caddies. Besides, I wanted to play golf, not watch it.'

A prominent member at the club was Joe Andrew, who lived opposite the Thomsons and who came to learn of young Peter's surreptitious journeys onto his home course. Thomson knew full well who Andrew was. 'He was a former Carlton footballer [he played just a handful of games for Carlton in 1911 when the team finished fourth in the VFL competition] and that set him up on a pedestal as far as I was concerned.' One afternoon he stopped the young lad in the street, but not to talk football. The topic of a certain boy's illegal rounds was raised and Thomson immediately thought his golfing days were about to come to an abrupt end. On the contrary, his fledgeling career was to strengthen as the first of many reassuring souls came forward to offer assistance. 'Here was the situation of a boy stealing his golf by way of a few holes here and there, mostly after school and, instead of being kicked off the course, I was encouraged by a kind Joe Andrew to play more,' says Thomson. 'He gave me great help and sponsorship in the way of nominating me for the club and clearing the path for me.'

Joe Andrew and his younger brother Walter, a club committeeman, played a few rounds with the boy and after watching his prodigious natural talent began lobbying for his induction as a member. Turning 13 in August 1942, Thomson was still well short of the required age for junior membership, but the committee realised their layout hadn't been inundated during the war and here was a lad who would, at least, put it to good use. They also recognised a character that suggested something special and changed the Royal Park Golf Club rules to admit Peter Thomson.

The boy from Brunswick had set his first golfing record, and with the burden of illegality lifted he could concentrate on improving his game rather than keeping his eye out for a rapid exit. His trips twice around the layout were still mostly played in his own company.

'It's like the way they teach it now,' he says. 'A golfer is set goals and targets. Back then, I set my own targets and the main one was the experience and accomplishment of getting my handicap down. When I first started playing golf it seemed like just another sport to me, but then I started to get a thrill out of making a good score. There wasn't such a thing as a practice fairway at Royal Park, so I played holes and kept a score. Of course the only way I could lower my handicap was by shooting good scores or by winning Saturday competitions.' Thomson wasted no time submitting cards and after averaging 92 over five rounds received a debut mark of 20. Proving just how quickly he'd mastered the game, and more importantly the mental pressures associated with winning, he took out his first competition at Royal Park playing off 18. It was the middle of the war and most of the vanquished that day were elderly men, but Thomson's victory created quite a stir — he was still only 13!

Arthur and Grace Thomson were delighted with their boy's success and thrilled that he was thoroughly enjoying himself, and while they trusted him completely and gave him plenty of freedom, they were mindful not to see Peter swept off his feet. They refused to let golf interfere with his schooling and the importance of a good education was hammered home by Grace. Those around him at the time say that, although he had his father's determination and strong-willed spirit, Peter was very much like his mother — Grace was a tranquil, relaxed type of person and very firm without being overly strict. After watching her husband stumble through a series of jobs, Grace had definite ambitions for Peter, and Peter adored his mother and had no intention of letting her down and unlike many sporting prodigies did not show any inclination to put sport before schooling. Ranked the No. 1 pupil in the class order-of-merit during his third and final year at Brunswick tech. in 1943, Thomson was beginning to think of a profession. At year end he took home a report card that included 97 for algebra, 94 for trigonometry and geometry, and 93 for English. His parents were delighted and with another scholarship Peter was bound for Footscray technical school, a few miles away in the western suburbs. And now he knew what he wanted to be. 'My goal at that stage was to become a geologist and discover all of Australia's minerals. That appealed to me immensely, but to be a geologist one had to obtain a diploma of chemistry. The only school of geology at that time was the Melbourne University and after finishing my diploma that's where I thought I would end up.' His course in analytical chemistry meant three years at Footscray and a year at the Royal Melbourne Institute of Technology to complete the diploma. Travelling by train from Royal Park station to Footscray, making new friends and discovering further independence from the rather insular life in Brunswick, Thomson was maturing quickly.

'Peter became a very independent youngster,' says his old friend Jimmy Buchanan. 'He could make decisions like a much older person. His voice broke and he reached the age of manhood before all of his friends. He seemed to be ahead of us all the way and his parents knew that their boy was particularly bright and, although he wasn't a big fellow by any means, they knew he could handle himself very well. He was a very confident lad and a super-quick learner. I can remember him saying to me one day, "Do you want to make some money?" I said "sure", and he said "well give me four bob and I'll double it for you". So while I was forced into going to church with my parents on a Sunday morning, Peter would be out there on the golf course gambling with my money. I didn't lose too much though — I think he knew he was a gifted golfer.'

He kept the details of his modest winnings away from his parents, who didn't mind what Peter was getting up to as long as he didn't get into any trouble and continued to bring home sparkling report cards. And he did. And while the figures on his report card remained high, those on his golf card continued to drop.

'I used to caddy for him in some of his competitive rounds,' says Buchanan, 'and I'd get worried when blokes would hit it much further than Peter but he'd say, "don't panic" and sure enough, would still win the matches. He was just such a relaxed, unflappable guy.'

Though he has never, ever had an official golf lesson, Thomson was greatly influenced at this time by the club professional at Royal Park. As a slim, blond caddy at Royal Melbourne after the first world war, Jimmy Grace attracted plenty of attention and in 1922 he journeyed to America with his club colleague, J. Victor East, and Australia's international golfing pioneer, Joe Kirkwood. Grace made and broke records on a number of courses in the US but became an epileptic, returned home ill in 1925, and dropped out of tournament golf. He was never able to fulfil the promise of his early years, but his effortless swing was put to good use in a series of club jobs. During his stint at Royal Park he found a young lad fascinated by stories of the world of professional golf and its shining lights. 'Grace was a beautiful player and, as I learned later, had a marvellous reputation,' says Thomson. 'He was a beautifully mannered person and was always perfectly dressed. He didn't really play all that much because he was there to teach members and repair their clubs but I played a few rounds with him and naturally had a close look at the way he hit the ball. He wasn't a very big man but he had a solid, very smooth swing and superb balance all the way. I never had a lesson from him, or anyone, but Grace gave me an occasional word here and there. He had sense enough to know that a young boy is a sensitive pupil and the trick is to bring out the natural gift, and I think that's what he did.'

Thomson developed a copybook swing that had his handicap plummeting. It was also a swing that stood up remarkably well to the big occasion. If there were any doubts about his future in the game they were conclusively rebuffed when barely 16 he played excellent golf 'against men old enough to be my grandfather' to become Royal Park's 1945 club champion. Now his name was in the papers: 'Schoolboy wins club championship,' said the headlines. It was his first big golfing triumph and he looks back fondly on taking the plaudits of the membership as the youngest-ever club champion. It gave his golfing aspirations a wonderful boost. 'That championship gave me tremendous satisfaction and it added to that whole feeling of being a winner,' says Thomson. 'Who knows? If I'd lost I may well have lost interest in the game and given it away. But I found out then that I got a great thrill out of winning — the taste of it is without doubt what kept me going all my life.'

Late 1945 was a turning point in his life. All at once the air over Royal Park smelled sweet, heavy with the scent of success and free from the stench of war. The world had finally come to its senses with the war's end and Peter Thomson looked to the horizon with anticipation, excitement and optimism. On the day he won his club championship it so happened that among the many fascinated onlookers was wealthy Fitzroy hotelier, Harry Young. On the recommendation of some of his friends, who were members at Royal Park, Young had gone along to watch this boy playing in a man's final. He fancied himself as a spotter of future talent; a self-made sporting entrepreneur, and he was considered everyone's favourite uncle. This thick-set, non-drinking, non-smoking, blond but balding man with a face that spoke a thousand words was the next great influence in Peter Thomson's life. Harry Young loved sport and sporting people to the point of obsession.

An adopted child raised by a methodist woman, Young began his official involvement in sport as a raw teenager at Diamond Creek, north-east of Melbourne, playing football with the famous Coventry brothers before they began their illustrious careers at VFL club Collingwood. After leaving school in his early teens, sport became his lifeblood. He tried to earn a little money competing in country gifts as a sprinter, was a one-time professional boxer and wrestler, played sub-district cricket with Yarraville and Footscray, became a professional tennis coach, played competitive billiards and snooker, tried lawn bowls with Fitzroy and Sunshine and into his late 40s became one of Victoria's finest trap-shooters, once scoring a record 28 consecutive hits at a Stawell Easter meeting. Finally, he took up golf and became a member of the senior pennant winning team at Victoria Golf Club playing from a one handicap ... and all this after suffering serious injuries in his youth when struck by a train at Albury!

'Harry was widely respected for his energy and his ability to conduct himself admirably,' says his wife Lorraine. 'During the war both the Australian and American air forces were staying at the Exhibition Building across the street from our hotel [the Carlton Club Hotel, Fitzroy]. They'd always end up having a few jars and inevitably, tempers would become strained. That's when Harry would step in and handle the situation brilliantly. He didn't have much of an education, but he was very smart. Harry taught himself everything; by listening to people, observing people. He had an excellent ear and his grammar was superb. He was truly an astonishing personality — an unashamed extrovert, quick with a story or joke, and very, very popular.'

The countless friendships forged through a wealth of activity in sport and the hotel/catering industry became the Youngs' life — they were never to have children. When Harry first saw 'this Thomson kid with loads of potential', he liked the look of him; the lad seemed sure of where he was heading. Harry knew Peter's parents weren't exactly rolling in clover, but it was not a case of 'stick with me and you'll wear diamonds'. Young's primary thought was purely to help the boy realise his quite obvious potential. When Thomson first met Young he was taken by the wealthy publican's friendliness and enthusiasm: 'Harry was a very good golfer himself but it was in the practical side of things that he was of enormous value,' he recalls. 'He was a tremendous morale-booster and was a great help to me and my career by way of super-encouragement in countless ways. Harry Young took me under his wing and was like an uncle to me.'

Indeed, Young came to look on Thomson as the son he had never had. He treated him accordingly, clearing the path for membership at the renowned Victoria Golf Club, providing transport, caddying for him in competitions, helping financially, and for a little more independence, having him over to stay with him and Lorraine at the Carlton Club.

Several weeks after the club championship win and a call at the family home by Young, Thomson was taken to play at Victoria, a course to this day widely regarded as one of the finest in Australia. Situated alongside the more famous Royal Melbourne, Victoria resides in the heart of a stretch of real estate known throughout the golfing world as simply, 'the sandbelt'. A dozen miles south of Melbourne, the belt travels south-east from the shores of Port Phillip Bay and, concealed among the many thousands of homes, factories, market gardens and playing fields, are courses such as Kingston Heath, Metropolitan, Huntingdale, Yarra Yarra, Commonwealth, Woodlands and Kingswood. The sandbelt is held in such high regard that more than a third of the 75 Australian Open championships to 1991 have been played within its boundaries, and the world's greatest players have paid the highest compliment by visiting and playing its courses.

It was largely the sandbelt that transformed Peter Thomson into a golfer of world class. He remains extremely grateful for the start Royal Park gave him, but its 9-holes could never have progressed beyond a role of proving ground, and in early 1946 it was time for a more stringent test of the boy's ability. Victoria had not the subtlety of its neighbour Royal Melbourne, but was adequately compensated with length and bunkering. The greens were not nearly as fast but were smaller than Royal Melbourne's. They placed a premium on the approach shot, particularly long irons (it is no coincidence that the long iron became Thomson's major golfing weapon). Like all good courses Victoria's holes aimed to the four points of the compass and demanded a proficiency in all shots. Young Peter was told of all this before arriving at Victoria, but nothing could have prepared him for those crucial first impressions. He cast his eyes out over the rolling hills and hollows; he marvelled at the sheer beauty of it all; every blade of grass lovingly cared for; every bunker superbly manicured. The monolithic clubhouse capped it all off. At first the lad could only stand and look; Royal Park was a million miles away. 'There I was out in the big, wide world and it was very exciting,' remembers Thomson. 'I never imagined that Victoria would be so striking. It was a giant step forward for me.'

While the lad was falling in love with the golf course, Harry Young was mustering support, the best available. The young club champion from Royal Park was introduced to his counterpart at Victoria, Harold Edward Richard Payne. Before he died in 1960, 'Dick' Payne was one of the club's most respected figures and one of the state's best amateurs. He was a class act. From the time he joined Victoria as a 17-year-old, just a few months before Thomson was born, his appearance and manners were never less than impeccable, and he proved he had the game to match. In matchplay, the bread-and-butter contest in amateur golf, Payne earned a fearsome reputation and the nickname, 'The Tiger'. Runner-up to Jim Ferrier in the Australian Amateur Championship, he was to win the state amateur crown in 1947 and was five times club champion at Victoria between 1935–50. The Thomson lad was immediately impressed and so was Payne.

The wheels of membership were set in motion. Not without coincidence, Payne was also serving on the club's board of directors, and on the evening of 12 March 1946 he met with his colleagues for a routine monthly meeting. The application for junior membership marked Peter William Thomson — proposer: H. R. Payne; seconder: H. Young, was passed without demur. The directors had unknowingly given the green light to a career that would change the face of Australian golf.

Inter-club pennant matches resumed after their wartime hibernation a few weeks after this meeting and, showing their faith in Thomson's ability, Victoria's selectors slotted him straight into the senior team at No. 6. Gone were the days of restrictive medal matches twice around Royal Park. It was priceless experience for a wide-eyed 16-year-old.

'In those days pennant matches were played between twelve clubs all on one course on one occasion and, really, it was an assembly of the

Left: The depression years behind them, Thomson (age 5 and with cravat) poses with mother Grace in a studio portrait.

Below: The look of a champion. Thomson, 15, soon after becoming Royal Park Club Champion, 1945.

Above: Harry and Lorraine Young entertain the Thomson family at their Fitzroy hotel the night before Peter's trip to the USA, 1950.

Left: Arthur and Grace, with Michael, 7, proudly receive another telegram after Peter's 1954 Open Championship triumph.

Left: 'Harry Young was like an uncle to me.' With the Victorian Amateur Championship trophy at Victoria GC, 1948.

Below: Victoria Golf Club, winners of the VGA's 'A' pennant in 1948. Thomson sits front right, next to his captain Dick Payne. Behind Payne is Doug Bachli.

Thomson in 1951, home from Britain and America and displaying a dress sense more in tune with big-time golf. The cap was bright green.

very best amateur players in the state,' says Thomson. 'Yarra Yarra had marvellous players like Laurie Duffy, Alec Ray and Hartley Mitchell; Royal Melbourne had its stars like John Baillieu; Metropolitan had a good list; Kingswood were always formidable with Bill Higgins and John Hood; Commonwealth had a few beauties like Billy Edgar and Eric Routley; Medway had Harry Papworth; Northern's Bobby Brown was one of the most graceful players I ever saw, and Huntingdale had Barry West. Then there was our own strong contingent (with names like Payne and Doug Bachli), so it was tremendous competition and I was amongst all those greats.'

The tight, demanding layout at Metropolitan was the venue for post-war resumption of the senior pennant competition and the air was full of expectation that Saturday in 1946 as Victoria was pitted against the team from Commonwealth. Thomson stood on the first tee and later admitted to feeling as nervous as he ever has playing golf; his opponent, the vastly experienced 38-year-old left-hander, Jack Campbell. The Commonwealth team fully expected their man to chalk up a point to their side of the scoreboard. 'I remember that I was banging along nicely and managed to get a few good putts in for an early lead of 2-up,' Campbell says. 'But he fought back like a demon towards the end and after the 18th we were all square and had to head back up Metropolitan's 1st to decide it. The kid didn't seem too nervous at all and unfortunately I three-putted and he won at the 19th. He struck me as an extremely polite young fellow, but he sure was determined. When I shook his hand I had this feeling he was going to be on the scene for a while.'

For the remainder of the season Thomson held his place in the senior team and performed admirably. In a fierce battle for the pennant Victoria was beaten by Yarra Yarra, but the club was confident it had unearthed a future star in Peter Thomson.

'Pete was completely consumed by the game,' says Jimmy Buchanan. 'He used to invite me down to Victoria on Sundays and one day he told me to bring money. I brought money and thanks to his play, we won, but I thought we were playing for shillings when all along we were playing for pounds. I was shaking afterwards when I found out we'd been playing for quids, but Peter's manner didn't change one bit. He was exactly the same if we were playing for two pounds, two bob, or nothing. He was just happy to be playing golf.'

On the home front, Peter's parents continued to marvel at their boy's ability with a golf club, but they still insisted he place his education first. The youngster proved he could cope with anything that came his way. Whilst enveloped by the game of golf and the club atmosphere of Victoria, he was still able to enjoy a busy social life and able to complete his final year at Footscray tech. with excellent results.

The writing was now on the wall: complete his diploma at the Royal Melbourne Institute of Technology and continue on the path to geology. But his desire to discover Australia's minerals was beginning to wane. After constant sub-par rounds and still only 17, Thomson earned a scratch handicap and his position on the pennant team was no longer 'down the bottom' at No. 6. All the senior pennant clubs knew of the key role played by the teenager in the line-up from Victoria, but one man from Royal Melbourne took particular interest. Ivo Whitton was one of the most respected men in Australian golf. A brilliant player, he won the Australian Open five times, the first as an 18-year-old in 1912, and the last, nineteen years later. He had the greatest tournament record of any Australian amateur — two National championships, five Victorian titles, three Queensland amateurs and one New South Wales championship. He was renowned for his 'perfect' match temperament, based on cheerful acceptance of all adversity. He was club champion of his beloved Royal Melbourne nine times and captain from 1947–50, but he felt his highest honour came in 1951, when he was invited as Australia's representative to London's House of Lords to reframe the Rules of Golf. Whitton had started his business life as a wool salesman but his sporting connections won for him the position of Australian managing director of A. G. Spalding sporting goods manufacturers. It was in this capacity that the 53-year-old chatted to the remarkable youngster after watching him in a pennant match one Saturday. The conversation quickly turned to the boy's plans of becoming an industrial chemist and eventually a geologist. Whitton, a vehement campaigner for amateur ideals in sport, was impressed by Thomson's manner and offered the lad a job as a rubber technologist at Spalding's Sunshine laboratory. The Spalding company had a long and intimate association with golf, dating back to 1898 when it made advertising history by contracting the British Open champion of that year, the legendary Harry Vardon, to endorse its golfing equipment. This was the first time that a professional athlete had been paid to promote a commercial product. Almost half a century later the Spalding company was again assisting one of the world's greats, only this one had yet to prove himself.

Thomson knew that a position so close to the technology of the game, and with such a reputable firm, could only help his golf. Australia's minerals could stay where they were. Golf was taking over his life. He knew that he had an incredible natural talent for the game and in the back of his mind he thought of earning a living from playing golf.

'The work at Sunshine gave me great interest in golf ball manufacture, an interest I still have. At that time I used to make my own personal golf balls, injecting a few drops of fluid into the centre of the ball with a hypodermic needle. The idea, which was patented, was to increase the internal tension and add weight. I thought I had made the perfect golf ball but there was one snag. The injection created a weak spot which invariably burst under extra tension. The idea was a failure but it certainly enlivened the ball.

'There was a very kindly man at the time, Don Galbraith, who was Spalding's chief chemist and he was doing remarkable research into golf balls. The company's way of manufacturing a ball was really a formula from the United States and Don thought there must have been a better way to do it, so we used to vary the centre of the ball in tests. We used silicone, water, honey, even strawberry jam! Then we'd make the ball by winding it up with rubber, covering it, painting it, then testing it. It became absolutely clear that no matter what you put in the middle the performance of the ball was always the same. In that job I also did routine tests on golf clubs and tennis balls, but I certainly learned all there was to know about making golf balls.'

Thomson loved the work. 'Peter was a very enthusiastic young fellow,' says Don Galbraith. 'He was very interested in sport and enormously keen about what he was doing in the laboratory. There was an enormous amount to be learned in rubber technology and Peter threw himself into it. He often did far more than he was asked to. Work with Spalding was of invaluable assistance to his game and there were ample opportunities for him to practise.'

Thomson agrees: 'On several occasions Ivo Whitton took me to a factory near Royal Melbourne ostensibly to test balls and clubs, but we only spent a few minutes at the factory. The reason for the journey was so that we could hop across to his club and have a game of golf! Whitton was very lenient towards my golf and was a very kind man. I had access to every club in the factory if I wanted it and there were thousands of them. There was a mechanical driving machine that did all the testing of balls, but there was also an artificial tee and a net and we were required to hit quite a few ourselves.'

Don Galbraith clearly recalls Thomson's change of heart in the battle between chemistry and golf. 'I remember we had to take a load of balls down to Royal Melbourne one day for them to be tested by Ossie Pickworth,' says Galbraith. 'Ossie [the reigning Australian Open champion and eventual four-times winner] was on the Spalding payroll as the professional who would test our golf balls for us on the practice ground. We took this batch of balls down there and Ossie started hitting them, while Peter and I were up the other end marking the distances and checking that the balls had retained their shape. As we were picking them up, Peter said out of the blue, "Pickworth will be picking up balls for me one day!"'

The biggest influence on Thomson's game at this stage was Dick Payne. The 36-year-old pennant captain led his team to the very brink of winning the 1947 competition, tying with Yarra Yarra on top of the table at season's end. In the play-off to decide the 'A' Division champion team, Yarra Yarra won an absorbing contest four matches to three. Payne more than accounted for any personal disappointment when he won the state amateur title soon after, defeating Bill Edgar 3 & 2 over Edgar's home course of Commonwealth. For all his success though, Payne was considered a team specialist, particularly in foursomes, the curious battle where two players use one ball and hit alternately. One of his favourite events was the grandly titled 'Australasian foursomes shield', a matchplay knockout event keeping the name of the now defunct newspaper that was once its sponsor. Each pennant club nominated its pair, and on consecutive weekends they battled it out until one team was left standing. Payne was victorious three times (1935 and 1939 with Harry Williams and 1938 with Ian Rhodes) and was confident of a fourth triumph in 1947 when the club selectors named him in tandem with Doug Bachli. A few days before the first round though, Bachli was affected by hepatitis and reluctantly had to withdraw. Payne did not ruminate over a replacement — he insisted on Peter Thomson — and, with his young companion providing the support and strokeplay of a seasoned veteran, Payne had his fourth shield.

In partnership with a man he greatly respected, Thomson gained enormous confidence and satisfaction from that foursomes win. 'It was a marvellous experience,' he says. 'I hardly made a stroke without instruction from Dick. He was by no means an elegant player, but he was very tall with a look of aloofness and a strong demeanour. He was a complete master of all that went on and this had a lot to do with his success. Few of Dick's opponents could match his personality — he was a natural leader and a very impressive man. He taught me a vast amount about tactics, manners and what competition is all about. He coached or advised me in many ways, but he didn't interfere. I was given invaluable golf advice and I'm sure that without Dick's help I would not have obtained the success I have.'

The significance of that triumph in tandem with Payne was evident when Thomson's parents discovered that their boy was considering quitting his RMIT studies. Immensely proud of Peter's scholastic achievements and having paid good money to see their lad take positive steps to a worthwhile career, Arthur and Grace Thomson were far from impressed with his decision and it led to much anxiety within the family. Ultimately they placed their faith in Peter's commonsense and his ability to make his own decisions. Thomson knew it was an enormous gamble. 'By the time I was 18 golf was luring me,' he says. 'I began to dislike the smells of the laboratory and much preferred the aroma of the golf course. I dropped out of the RMIT course because I had chosen golf to be my career and my work at Spalding was principally for the golf, not the chemistry.'

The year 1948 began with the pennant season at Victoria. Yarra Yarra had won the two pennants after the war, but the star-studded combination from Victoria dominated the competition. They had an outstanding season and were never toppled from top position on the 'A' division ladder. They met 'B' division winners, Northern, in the pennant final and trounced them six matches to one. Thomson, the youngest member of the team, played a crucial role in the victory and his form continued into the club championship, eliminating many of his more senior pennant colleagues before scoring a wonderful victory over his captain and mentor Dick Payne in a semi-final. Prominent members recall the impact of Thomson's win around the club and the brilliance of his play, but the winner was hardly overjoyed: 'I felt very sorry about it,' he says. 'To beat one's own teacher is to break up one's world. In the final I was beaten by [Doug] Bachli. I felt I should have won — Dick surely would have done if he'd beaten me.' Such defeats were expected by many to have a pernicious effect on the youngster's master plan for a career in professional golf, but they always seemed to work to his benefit.

The 1948 Australian Open was set down for Kingston Heath, on the sandbelt, and the pre-tournament publicity centred on the return to Australia of Jim Ferrier and his inevitable clash with the man hoping for an unprecedented hat-trick of Open titles, the popular 30-year-old chain-smoking ex-army cook, Ossie Pickworth. The battles between these two went back to the days before the war when Ferrier was the favoured son of the club secretary-manager at Manly, and Pickworth was the hardworking 'boy in the shop'. The assistant's duties often included picking up Ferrier's practice balls. They made no secret of the fact they weren't the best of buddies.

After the outbreak of war Ferrier had gone to America where he continued to play golf. When he lost his amateur status for writing a golf instructional book, he turned professional and then became a US citizen in 1944. A former Australian amateur and Open champion from the Manly Golf Club in Sydney, he was the first Australian-born golfer to win one of the world's four 'major' titles, and his 2 & 1 victory over Chick Harbert (the PGA became a strokeplay event in 1958) at Plum Hollow in Michigan made headlines thousands of miles away in Melbourne. In all, he won twenty-one tournaments in the United States to cap two Australian Opens, four Australian amateur championships and two Canadian Opens. With six holes to play in the 1950 US Masters at Augusta, Ferrier led the field by three shots, but took bogey at all but one of the remaining holes to finish two strokes behind the winner, Jimmy Demaret. In

1960 he came close to winning a second US PGA championship, but lost by a stroke to Jay Hebert. He was one of the most successful golfers Australia has produced, forging a remarkable record that began back in the early 1930s as a 16-year-old in Sydney.

'At Kingston Heath Ferrier was not a very popular figure, mainly because he wasn't here during the war,' says Thomson. 'Ossie Pickworth, of course, was a fellow who had done his war service and he was one of those people very resentful of Ferrier having gone to the United States. Before the US became involved in the war, Jim Ferrier was apparently playing golf over there while his contemporaries here, were in the desert.' So there was plenty of tension in the air as the 33-year-old United States PGA champion set out to shake loose the Open trophy from Pickworth's grip, and prevent him from taking it home for the third successive year. The galleries loved every minute of the battle and didn't take much notice of the young amateur who was slowly working his way towards the lead. Peter Thomson was playing in only his second 72-hole tournament. His first, the previous month, was the inaugural Victorian Close championship at Huntingdale where he carded 80–79–73–78 for sixth place, seven strokes behind the winner, Pickworth. At the Heath, the field was a much stronger one and, while the big guns took centre stage, Thomson settled back away from the spotlight and approached the event as the biggest test of his ability to date.

After his closing 36-holes on Saturday it seemed Ossie Pickworth was headed for Open history when he made his way back into the clubhouse with a total of 289. His arch-rival Ferrier was making a determined finish and needed a birdie at the final hole to win. He played a mighty tee shot down the centre of the fairway and chose a 6-iron for his crucial second shot. It was far too much club and his approach sailed past the 18th green, took a cruel bounce and ended up on the fringe of the 6th green, 30 metres away! Faced with a near impossible shot over a tall row of trees, Ferrier took several minutes to plan his attack, and then under colossal pressure lofted the ball high over the trees. The roar of the crowd told him it was close. He jogged through the trees to see just how close. His ball finished little more than two yards below the hole and he made the putt. With play disallowed on Sundays the duo had to wait two days for the play-off and the huge crowd returned to watch the climax to a marvellous championship when Pickworth covered the front nine in 33. He stumbled with a few bogeys near the end to give Ferrier some hope but after the expatriate dragged his second shot into bushes at the long 17th, it was all over. Pickworth 71, Ferrier 74, and the crowd absolutely delighted. Among them was the young lad who'd finished the Saturday as the Open's leading amateur,

Peter Thomson. With George Holland, his uncle, following dutifully, Thomson played a wonderful final 36-holes to leapfrog numerous players and, with rounds of 75–79–73–72, was one of only five players to break 300. He ended up in fifth place, ten strokes behind Pickworth and Ferrier, with only Queensland's Reg Want and New South Wales's Eric Cremin in front of him.

'It was easily the biggest tournament I'd played in and I was very happy to finish in such a high place,' Thomson recalls. 'Uncle George made the observation that on the 36-holes of the last day I was not off the fairway once. It did indicate to me that if Pickworth and Ferrier were world-class players, well, if I persisted I could get there too.' Pickworth and Ferrier dominated the headlines but Thomson's performance hadn't gone unnoticed. During his trip to Melbourne, Ferrier was to play an exhibition match at Kew Golf Club, but when the local pro was unable to play, and Pickworth had already declared himself unavailable, an invitation was hastily despatched to the wonder boy. In blustery conditions a crowd of nearly a thousand turned up to watch Thomson and the Kew champion, E. H. Anderson, pitted against Ferrier and W. Richardson. Although he and his partner lost the match on the 18th green, Thomson stole the show with a round of 70 to Ferrier's 72. The boy from Brunswick, just six days past his 19th birthday, made the reigning USPGA champion sit up and take notice. 'Well,' said Ferrier, when asked his thoughts of the boy's ability, 'Thomson has excellent prospects. He has a nice, smooth action, a fine personality and temperament, and is the only young golfer I have seen in Australia who looks as if he might have learned his game in America. He comes in well from behind and goes through after it. This is the style made famous by Walter Hagen.'

Thomson now fixed his sights on Metropolitan and the Australian Amateur championships starting with the interstate series. After his attractive performances at Kingston Heath and Kew, the state selectors named Thomson in the seven-man Victorian team, along with clubmates Dick Payne and Doug Bachli. The rest of the line-up comprised Laurie Duffy and Hartley Mitchell (Yarra Yarra), Bill Edgar (Commonwealth), and Bob Brown (Northern). They formed a superb combination and comfortably finished on top of the table. In the national individual title the following week, Thomson breezed through to the semi-finals where he was again outwitted by Doug Bachli, who triumphed one-up. Bachli went on to win the first of his two Australian Amateur titles with a convincing 7 & 6 win over his former Canberra schoolchum, Peter Heard, while the lessons continued for Thomson. He was to learn from the loser's corner. To him it was never failure. It was sometimes not succeeding.

By now the sportswriters were saying Bachli 'had the wood' on Thomson and within a month were again trotting out the tired bogeyman angle when the clubmates from Victoria once more found themselves facing each other, in the final of the state amateur championships at nearby Woodlands. On a bright November day Harry Young was adamant his lad was ready for a big one, but inspiration was to come from another friendly face looking on. Incredibly, Arthur Thomson had never before watched his son in competition. For some time he'd harboured a fear of putting his son off his game should he tag along, but he finally succumbed to Peter's urging. Some have said his reticence stemmed from a lack of confidence under the spotlight; that he felt he didn't belong amongst the sort of people attracted to golf. To his mates, Arthur was known as 'Catsy' or 'Cats-eye' Thomson, the one who was out all night and the one who loved nothing more than a convivial beer with his pals most nights at the local pub. With a severely disfigured nose, broken many times courtesy of battles both on and off the cricket field and unable to afford the sort of clothing synonymous with golf, it was said that Arthur Thomson, the battler from Brunswick, was uncomfortable amongst the people that were now praising and helping his son. That day at Woodlands, any unease was completely blown away by his son. Always a person to keep his emotions under constant restraint, Peter felt he was out there for himself and his father. A broad smile broke across Arthur Thomson's face when he later founded out he had had far from a debilitating effect on his son's game; rather, he was a good luck charm. Witnessing for the first time his boy's remarkable talent, Arthur's chest swelled with pride and Peter, duly inspired, began the final as though he had an afternoon plane to catch. He scorched around the front nine in 31, five-under, and eventually carding a morning 67, happily sat down to lunch with a lead of five-up.

The afternoon was expected to be a stroll in the park for the youngster, but his control had evaporated. Some thought he'd been 'nobbled' — his lemonade must have been tampered with while he wasn't looking. Bachli needed only par figures to win four of the first six holes and, with Thomson's lead slashed to just one hole, more than a few onlookers were wondering if these predictions of stardom weren't just a little premature. But the lad's 'spokesman' Harry Young provided an explanation: 'Peter is a growing boy [5ft 9in and 10st 9lbs] and how he can eat! I warned him during the luncheon interval to go light on the victuals, but he doesn't know how to do that. He had to work off that lunch before he got back to balance!' Indeed, when the going really did get tough, Thomson had the balance of a cat. He was back to two-up heading to the long 10th (28th) and then the scales tipped dramatically in his favour when Bachli's approach caught a bunker and the youngster, safely on in two, holed a 7-yard roller-coaster putt for eagle! The next was halved in three, Thomson won the 12th when Bachli missed a sitter, and the lad went five-up at the 13th with a birdie putt that rolled into the hole like a well-cued billiard ball. At the next it was all over when another 7-yard putt went in, and Thomson, with a grin the size of a split watermelon signalled to all at Woodlands that he had more than enough credentials to turn pro. An eagle-par-par-birdie-birdie finish for a 6 & 4 win over the national amateur champ was startling proof.

'That win was phenomenal,' says Thomson. 'I had a great day with the putter and it was easily the best I'd ever played in my life. For the whole championship everything seemed to click and it felt great.' Bachli could merely tug his forelock and acknowledge a remarkable performance. 'Peter blitzed me with 13 threes in the 32 holes we played,' he says. 'That would beat anybody. He played fantastic golf to get back on me.' In the Melbourne *Herald* veteran golf writer Jack Dillon wrote: 'Young Peter has tremendous possibilities as a golfer. With one of the most fluent, easy and artistic swings he is efficiency personified. Perhaps the most pleasing possession, in addition to his grand temperament, is a most disarming and intriguing modesty. To a greater degree, probably, than any former champion, Peter "plays" golf ... It's his fun — not work.' It was perhaps this attitude more than any other that was eventually to strike a chord with spectators the world over and was later summed up by the British golfing personality Peter Alliss, in his autobiography (*Peter Alliss An autobiography*, Collins, 1981), when he wrote: 'I think I have known only four players who have said in a manner which I could believe that they actually enjoyed the competitiveness of it all. Palmer, Nicklaus, Nagle and Thomson.'

At only 19, Thomson had earned his wings on the sandbelt. It had been quite a year and his life was turning about-face. He had a full-time job, a flourishing career in golf ... and a girlfriend. At Hamilton on a golfing trip to Victoria's western district Thomson was introduced to Lois Brauer, the young daughter of a distinguished Warrnambool family. Her father was a prominent doctor. The friendship blossomed a few weeks later when they met again at an exhibition match in her home town. With her mother Reta, the club champion at Warrnambool, Lois was destined to become a golf enthusiast and renewing acquaintances with the young man from Melbourne the couple fell into chatting. The attractive, short-haired Lois was only 16 and a trainee nurse, but she was a girl who liked to enjoy herself. Peter, for his part, was energetic, humorous, keen on the girls and hardly a shrinking violet. Although he came from a family of four boys and devoted a large slice of his time to studies and golf, Thomson admits he 'had no problems getting to know girls' and he was curious about the opposite sex well before reaching his mid-teens. Later, regular Saturday nights were spent taking girlfriends to the pictures at the Moonee Ponds Town Hall or the Waratah Theatre in Ascot Vale, but none was anything more than a harmless flirtation. It was only when Peter returned from his country trip that his friends detected a note of seriousness about his latest romance. He spoke of 'this pretty *gal* — the doctor's daughter' from Warrnambool and many of the people around him at that time have remarked that, despite his furious pursuit of golf and a completely different career path, he always found time to visit young Miss Brauer. It suggests that he was able to retain a remarkable balance during a period of great change. Soon after, the lady fortuitously started work at the Royal Melbourne hospital in Parkville, less than a minute's drive from the Thomson residence. As Peter was frequently staying over at the Youngs' hotel in Fitzroy, the young couple were able to meet regularly, often late at night when Lois had finished her shift. While they became inseparable, and their relationship rapidly progressed, Peter still had his gaze firmly fixed on his golf and the enormity of what lay ahead. There were trips during the summer months with Lois and his friends to the beach at Point Lonsdale as the guests of Harry and Lorraine Young at their holiday residence, and often the journey continued to Warrnambool for time with the Brauer family, but again golf was never far away, and numerous practice rounds filled the time between work at the Spalding factory and the trips away. Then came the invitation he was waiting for. It was addressed to the amateur champion of Victoria, and requested his company in the select field for a brand-new event scheduled for late March of 1949; the £2,500 McWilliams Wines tournament at the Australian Golf Club, Kensington, Sydney. Promoted as 'the biggest and richest golfing championship ever staged in Australia', the McWilliams was the first event in the country to offer prizemoney comparable with events in the US, and its shopping list included the country's finest professional and amateur names, including the man who was missing from the 1948 Australian Open at Kingston Heath, Norman von Nida.

It would be Thomson's first trip outside Victoria and immediately Harry Young stepped forward with the overwhelming offer to drive the lad to Sydney and caddy for him during the event. Underneath the surface Peter was terribly excited, but he refused to show it publicly. The new year began with renewed vigour. He worked on his game even harder, and it showed. In the space of three weeks he strung together a series of incredible rounds: a 69 on the nation's longest championship course at Huntingdale, a 64 at Croydon and an amazing nine-under 63 at Northern. Of the last effort his playing partner, local pro, Martin Smith said: 'I doubt if anyone in Australia has played more perfect golf than this boy played in his 63.' The back-nine was played in an incredible five-under 30, with birdies at 12, 17 and 18, and an eagle at the par-4 15th, where Thomson watched his approach hit the front of the green, bite hard and roll straight into the cup! The round was four shots better than any other score on the Glenroy course and incredibly did not include a holed putt of more than four metres. It didn't stop there. The following week he carded 72–70 to win his home club's 36-hole Open Amateur event, against the state's top professionals and amateurs, including triple Australian Open champion Ossie Pickworth.

His confidence was soaring with every round and it was after this series of spectacular scores that Thomson was convinced his future lay in professional golf. He handed in his chemistry books, quit his job at Spalding and set his sights on the McWilliams Wines tournament in Sydney.

Tony Thomson, Peter's younger brother recalls a definite period of concern within the Thomson household at Brunswick and his mother seemed to be the biggest stumbling block. Arthur, of course, was an eye-witness to his boy's ability, but Grace was not a sporting person and was far from convinced. 'My mother was very apprehensive when Peter decided to turn professional,' says Tony. 'She had scrimped and saved all her life, watching every penny carefully, and she wasn't sure that playing golf was the right way to be making a living. My parents had paid hard-earned money to put Peter through his chemistry course and obviously there were reservations that it would be of no effect if he chose to pursue golf.' Some years later Grace Thomson, not a superstitious person, revealed what eventually brought about her change of heart: 'I hoped he would [become an industrial chemist], but a fortune teller told me that my eldest son would be going for long walks over green grass and that he would travel all over the world.'

In truth, her son had already made up his mind and was prepared to be dogmatic about his future. It was almost as if he was taking offence at those, not just his parents, who thought he wasn't mature enough to be making such a decision. He felt he was more than capable of coming to grips with the situation — he knew that he alone would have to shoulder the responsibility. Peter was no doubting Thomson. He was extremely self-possessed, and comfortable in the knowledge that he had a natural gift. Understandably, a lot of this was interpreted as big-headedness but, as he himself later said, 'I came to find that most champion golfers were like that. Of course I couldn't be anything but myself, but I saw the benefit of behaving that way, and the benefit was that it was easier to concentrate totally on playing golf and achieving my goals.'

One of his first requirements for the Sydney trip was to have Lois come along. With permission from the Brauers they climbed into Harry and Lorraine's car and headed north to the harbour city, stopping on the way to pick up friends of the Youngs at Deniliquin. They spoke of young Peter's biggest golfing test to date, but at no stage did he appear nervous or lose his sense of humour.

In the practice rounds Thomson refused to be distracted. 'I was concentrating on the job ahead and on what I had to do. I don't think I even saw the Sydney harbour. I remember I was taken by the course. The old Australian course was a marvellous piece of work and I thought it was very difficult.' On tournament eve Thomson, watched by Harry Young, was practising his putting in front of the clubhouse when Norman von Nida, the established star of Australian golf, walked over and renewed his acquaintance with Young, whom he'd met in Melbourne many times before. 'The Von' introduced himself to Thomson and, more or less as a favour to Young, suggested he and the boy play a few holes together. By the time they reached the 6th tee, von Nida realised the youngster was prodigiously gifted. He walked across to Young and with his voice shrill with excitement said, 'Harry, this boy is much better than I was at his age. What are you going to do with him?' Young replied that Thomson was seriously considering turning professional. Von Nida merely nodded and continued his play. That evening the draw for the first round was announced at a club dinner, and tournament organisers revealed the names of von Nida and Thomson in the same group, with West Australian Neville Johnston. Some members of the press said the Von had deliberately requested to play with Thomson and, as the best player in the country, was granted his wish. Johnston may as well not have been there when their 10.15 hit-off time arrived; the huge gallery that had turned out seemed interested only in the peppery campaigner

The Australian Golf Club
OPEN
CHAMPIONSHIP
1949

Honorary Member
(Competitor)
ISSUED TO
Mr P. Thomson.
NOT TRANSFERABLE

Thomson's player's pass for his second appearance at the Australian in 1949 after the McWilliams Wines event, his country's Open Championship, won by Eric Cremin.

and the teenage challenger. Von Nida, dressed in canary yellow shirt, mustard slacks and trademark black beret, shook Thomson by the hand and said, 'Don't worry too much about the crowd, just enjoy yourself ... good luck.' He needn't have bothered — if anyone was unsettled over those opening holes it was himself! The boyishly handsome, quietly-clad and quietly-smiling Thomson made an impressive start and the crowd rapidly warmed to the lad from Melbourne and his bulky, baldheaded caddy. While Thomson displayed his brilliance, Harry Young entertained the gallery. Every time his youthful charge holed a putt of reasonable length, Young clapped his hands, cheered, and shouted: 'You beaut!' If his boy missed a putt or his tee shot found a bunker, the publican slapped his head and groaned aloud in anguish — he was more boxing trainer than golf caddy. The crowd soon felt for him and cheered or agonised accordingly. The noisy background would have upset many a golfer, but it didn't worry Thomson. One writer said he had 'ice in his veins'. Another scribe, a visiting American, wrote: 'This inseparable combination which has already captured the Victorian Amateur Championship and boasts victories over Jim Ferrier, Ossie Pickworth and other top professionals, performed with typical brilliance in its Sydney debut ... My guess is that if and when the Thomson-Young team decides to turn pro, the rest of the play-for-pay boys had better look around for new jobs!' Among the gallery watching the first round were cricketing heroes Sid Barnes and Keith Miller, and Davis Cup tennis star Adrian Quist. They saw at the 14th, the boy was two shots up on von Nida, but he then double-bogeyed the 15th. The Von was utterly convinced of the lad's ability when he then knocked his approach to a metre at the 16th, and holed the birdie putt. Another at the last and, fittingly, both players finished with 72. 'I sensed he had that indefinable "something" when I first set eyes on him,' says von Nida. 'His swing was probably the simplest of any player I had seen with the possible exception of Byron Nelson. There were no frills so virtually nothing could go wrong. When he teed it up with me in the McWilliams Wines, I'm sure he thought he could beat me. He was so composed.' Harry Young echoed those sentiments when asked by a local reporter after the round how his young charge had coped. 'He was not the least bit worried by being drawn in the first round with von Nida, even though it meant a huge gallery,' said the burly caddy with a customary grin. 'Peter was glad to have the chance to play with Von. Nothing ever scares him.' Thomson was remarkably calm after the round when a bunch of reporters crowded around him: 'I accept galleries with golf,' he said matter-of-factly. 'After all, it wouldn't be much of a tournament without them.' Ossie Pickworth carded a course record 68 and was the only player to break par that day, but he couldn't sustain the brilliance and

1949 McWilliams Wines Tournament, Australian GC, Sydney

Total	Player	Rounds
281	Norman von Nida (NSW)	72–71–70–68
287	Ossie Pickworth (Vic.)	68–73–73–73
289	Peter Thomson (Vic. a.)	72–73–72–72
291	Eric Cremin (NSW)	74–71–72–74
294	Dennis Denehy (S. Aust.)	75–75–71–73
	Bill Holder (NSW)	70–73–72–79

ultimately buckled under the pressure from von Nida, who improved with each round to finish with a marvellous 68 for a three-under total of 281 and victory in the inaugural McWilliams by six strokes. Thomson finished eight shots behind, but his role was far from a cameo. After 72 in the morning on the last day, he was in devastating form after lunch, holing long birdie putts at the 1st, 2nd and 8th for an outward nine of 33, the best of the championship. He stumbled a little coming home with a 39, but finishing outright third he was ten strokes ahead of the next amateur, Kep Enderby. He would have picked up £200 if he'd been professional, twenty times his father's weekly wage.

If it hadn't dawned on any of the Sydney crowd that the youngster on 289 was headed for stardom, von Nida made sure of it when he stepped up to speak at the trophy presentation. 'In Australia,' he said, 'we have a future champion of the world in Peter Thomson. He is a magnificent player; very unassuming, not like myself [laughter]. He can do more for golf in Australia than either Ossie Pickworth or myself because he is a better player now than either of us were at his age. He is the greatest golfing prospect Australia has produced. Greater than Joe Kirkwood, greater than Ferrier, greater than I am. He would be crazy not to turn professional for I believe given a fair go he could make big money in golf. In three years I'll be done and he could treble whatever I've done. He can rely on me for any help I can give.' The crowd was silenced by the frank, surprising admission from the golfer who'd tangled with Hagen and Sarazen and was widely recognised as the country's finest pro golfer.

The next day von Nida invited Thomson and Young to lunch at his Sydney hotel and the Von urged the youngster to turn pro immediately. 'All that we discussed was Peter's future,' he says. 'He said if he was to turn pro he needed a job and I said I'd get in touch with someone. But I wanted him to come away overseas with me there and then, because I thought he would have been an instant success.'

It had been a hectic week in the harbour city, enough to make a young lad's head spin with excitement and anticipation. Yet Thomson was characteristically calm, relaxed and unhurried; many have said he simply knew it was all going to fit neatly into place. Over the next few weeks he saw a great deal of the Von. The nuggety player came down to Melbourne to meet and reassure Thomson's family that their boy had nothing to worry about.

'Norman von Nida, then in his controversial prime, was the man who led me out of the amateur ranks like a farmer leads a donkey out of the barn with a carrot in front of his nose,' Thomson says. 'In my case the carrot was money and at 19, as I was then, nothing looked sweeter. I remember von Nida showing me, in his room in Aarons Hotel, Sydney, a wardrobe so full of slacks of all colours that you couldn't see past them. I am sure he had more slacks at that time than Myer's department store. "You've got to dress so that people know you are better than everyone else," he said. "It's good for you and bad for the people you play against," and that was the first of many lessons in the art of climbing up the ladder.

'He even took me to the barber's shop to make sure my hair was cut properly, and told me never to wear a hat. "A head of hair like yours will be priceless where you're going," he said.'

C • H • A • P • T • E • R 2

Locke Provides a Key

ON 21 April 1949, in the eastern Melbourne suburb of Glen Waverley the Riversdale Golf Club's newest employee walked the short distance from the nearby railway station and through the stately clubhouse entrance to begin his new life as a golfing professional. Waiting in the pro shop was a man by the name of Naismith. An experienced campaigner, George Naismith was twice Victorian PGA champion in the 1930s, his record climaxed with victory in the 1937 Australian Open at Kensington, when Thomson was eight. George Naismith came from a famous golfing family — his brother Ted was Australian PGA champion in 1939, George the man he defeated 7 & 5 in the final at Royal Melbourne.

Naismith was part of the furniture at Riversdale; he'd been based in the pro shop for two decades when he received a call from his old friend Norman von Nida. The Von was close to the Naismith family and before the war had played an exhibition against Ted over a testing 72-holes — 36 at Riversdale and 36 at Victoria. It was reputed to be the biggest 'money' match ever staged in Australia with both men putting up £850, a colossal sum pre-war. Naismith had backers to help him raise the money, while von Nida claimed he pawned his car. At Victoria the nuggety Queenslander played superlative golf, carding 66–67 for an incredible lead of 15-up with 36 to play. But the drama was far from over. 'That night, after the match, I was shaving in the shower,' says von Nida. 'I slipped over and the razor gashed my thumb badly. It needed five stitches and I could hardly hold a golf club at all. Teddy, the good sport that he was, wanted to call the match off but I insisted we play on. I reckon a bet's a bet. If you bet on a horse that falls and breaks its leg then it's your bad luck. Anyway, my hand was worse than I realised.' The next day his left hand was almost numb, and although he inevitably lost the match and his money, a bond of friendship was forged with the Naismiths. It meant that von Nida knew George well enough to speak to him openly about this young Thomson fellow, the one the press had dubbed 'Placid Pete'. Naismith had been among the field in the McWilliams Wines event, finishing 24 strokes behind Thomson, and he knew all about the boy from Brunswick. At the Von's request and with a convenient vacancy in his pro shop Naismith decided to take Thomson on as an assistant.

The day after he started at Riversdale, Thomson was invited by his boss to join him in showing two members how best to attack the course at Kew, in preparation for the next day's pennant matches. The youngster took the instructions literally to scorch around the layout in a brilliant 66, equalling the course record. Naismith later admitted to complete astonishment at Thomson's demeanour that day, particularly at the 7th, where he hit a shot out of bounds. 'Now we'll see what he's made of,' thought the wily old pro. Thomson merely tut-tutted to himself, teed his ball again and proceeded merrily on his way as if nothing had happened. Two days later he joined Naismith and another two club members for his debut round at 'home' and had the entire clubhouse buzzing when word quickly spread that the young assistant had come in with a 65. The official course record stood at 68.

Another pro shop employee at the time was a graduate from the caddy school who eventually became a pro, Brian Huxtable. 'After just walking onto the course and playing a round like that we all knew Peter was heading for big things,' says Huxtable. 'George told me afterwards that Peter had made that 65 seem so easy, and that he was a player blessed with phenomenal talent. His swing didn't need to be tampered with at all, and it's my opinion that George was contacted for good reason because Peter's game could well have been ruined under someone keen to interfere with, or dominate his thinking and approach to golf. George's help came in the form of encouragement and support to play in certain events, and that cannot be underestimated.'

It didn't take long for Thomson to be deeply impressed by Naismith's method and manner. 'George Naismith was as big an influence on my career as anybody,' he says. 'He was a most generous and very likeable man who always had a nice smile on his face. He didn't have an easy time as a club pro by any means because club jobs were not often lucrative. As I observed, it was far from an easy life, with long hours, six days a week, for not a lot of profit. Then he had to answer to a committee, so he certainly wasn't his own boss.' Thomson didn't exactly relish the chores of the pro shop; he would rather have been out there like the members, matching his wits against the course and conditions and improving his game, but he soon realised that rules were rules and that he had two years of the life of an assistant to serve before he could hope to rival golf's big names.

In those days the role played by an assistant was different from what it is now. Very few clubs were purchased 'off the rack' and it was up to the men in the pro shop to produce a set tailor-made to the buyer's measurements. It was the art of making a club; assembling the head, the shaft, then the leather grip. And when there were no orders for new clubs, such tasks as repairing or cleaning members' sets, retrieving balls from the practice fairway, helping out with requests, serving behind the shop counter, or organising the time-sheet for competitions took up most of Thomson's time. As much as he desperately wanted to spend his hours playing golf and honing his game, the youngster knew that such a knowledge of the mechanics of golf — combined with his study of balls at the Spalding factory — would one day work to his benefit. 'Once, not so long ago, the professional was fixed to a position on the fringe of the game,' he has written. 'He was the maker and repairer of clubs, the tutor to beginners and the others with 'breakdowns'. He was the keeper of the little shop detached from the clubhouse. Even then he was by no means the best player in the land or even in the club and a good deal of his 'knowledge of the game' may have been theories and guesswork handed down. Then someone offered a small purse to set these men at each other's throats, rather like emperors setting gladiators. And the professional tournament was born ... It wasn't long before a professional realised that if he gave up his teaching and other onerous duties he could earn more money at winning purses. So then the specialist arrived on the scene — not the golf professional, but the professional golfer — the money player. Naturally he was a different breed — one who had to concentrate on his own problems to the exclusion of all else. He became a wanderer with a suitcase in one hand and a golfbag in the other. The smartest of them became showmen as well. Now because a golfer carries his tools with him and requires no other incentive except a prize to play for, it has become possible for him to play almost continuously. Tournament follows tournament in city after city. Newspapers carry results, however brief, from wherever they go and by constant repetition the best of them have become household names.'

Although Thomson's journey into professional ranks was a smooth one it wasn't entirely without controversy. A Victorian PGA rule stipulated that before an amateur could be accepted as a full member and be allowed to compete in all tournaments, he was required to serve two years as an apprentice under a PGA member or serve as a professional at a recognised club for five years. During this time the golfer would be permitted to play only in the Australian Open championship or the Victorian Close, an event closed to all professionals and amateurs other than those living in the state. The official PGA reason was that such a rule protected the carefully nurtured name of professional golf, protected the public from coaching by inexperienced teachers, and prevented the professional ranks outgrowing the available purses in Australia. Those who inevitably failed would not have teaching or club-making skills to fall back on for their livelihood.

Several golf writers, and Norman von Nida in particular, were incensed by this rule. Von Nida slammed it as 'a bloody farce' and implored the Victorian PGA to make an exception in Thomson's case and waive its two-year rule to allow him to compete in Britain, 'where he could fly our flag and do much more for Australian golf than he could sitting at Riversdale twiddling his thumbs!' But the PGA refused to budge.

While the youngster concentrated on learning his new craft it was expected that von Nida, after receiving a slap in the face from the PGA over the apprenticeship debate, would head off for another crack at the British tour. To the surprise of many he chose to stay in Australia to play a series of exhibitions, but he later claimed this was done for Thomson's benefit. The Von spent June 1949 in transit around Victoria, leap-frogging from Albury to Bendigo, Mildura to Traralgon, Shepparton to Ballarat. He invited Thomson to play a role in the series. With permission from Naismith and with Harry Young again at his side toting his bag, the assistant competed against von Nida at Geelong, determined to make a good showing in his first public appearance as a pro. The result was another spectacular round and a 4 & 3 victory to the youngster. Von Nida refused to bite his tongue. Again he slammed the Victorian PGA for 'living in the past', ironically, an accusation levelled at Thomson himself years later. Again the PGA refused to release the boy from his apprenticeship.

In July, as a three-week train and tram strike brought Melbourne to a standstill, and while a tubby South African named Arthur 'Bobby' Locke was winning the first of his four British Open titles on the other side of the planet, Thomson carded a record-equalling 76–73–72–72 (293) over the newly lengthened Yarra Yarra course to win the Victorian Close Championship, one of the two 'legitimate' tournaments in which he was allowed to compete. He finished eight shots ahead of his nearest rival, Jack Harris, and 14 strokes clear of Ossie Pickworth. The same story followed; vigorous lobbying for him to be allowed to play in the West Australian Open the next month, and another PGA refusal. He was not even allowed to compete as a 'marker' with no claim to title or prizemoney. 'Rules are rules,' their statement said. 'If we open the door for Peter Thomson we must open it to everyone and that would be chaotic.'

In August, just before his 20th birthday, Thomson partnered von Nida in a sellout exhibition against Pickworth and Eric Cremin at his former club, Victoria. It was to raise funds for an Australian women's team travelling to Britain and was a huge success. Three thousand people watched von Nida and Thomson win 3 & 2, the lad carding a brilliant 70.

For his part, Thomson was largely unaffected by the campaign to win him early membership. 'As far as I knew I was assistant to George Naismith for two years and that was that. A rule change was never possible and in retrospect Norman should have realised that, but he is not the sort of person to back off. These days that rule no longer applies. Now, we must provide events in which assistants can play. There's not always prizemoney for them but at least events are arranged and the best of the trainees are invited to play the big events. But back then I was quite content to serve my time. I was enjoying it, because I was able to start travelling overseas.' While the rule applied in his homeland and in Britain, there was nothing to stop him from competing in other countries.

The reputation of the boy from Brunswick was quickly spreading. In November came an invitation to play a tournament in the Philippines with the rather lofty title of the 'World Open'. Thomson's supporters quickly rallied. Naismith gave permission for him to defer his pro shop duties and von Nida, well versed in the ways of South-East Asia, chose to overlook the £1,000 Ampol tournament at Woodlands to act as Thomson's official chaperone. The Philippines opened Thomson's eyes to big-money golf. The championship, over Manila's Wack Wack Country Club course, carried prizemoney of almost £8,000 with the colossal sum of £2,230 scooped up by the winner. In addition the organisers announced they would include 75 per cent of the gate takings in the overall prizemoney for the first dozen places. Thomson couldn't help thinking of the Ampol event back home, and the £250 cheque for first prize.

Von Nida and Thomson spent a great deal of time together in Manila and the veteran came to realise that the youngster was different. Several times he called at the boy's hotel room, fully expecting him to tag along and see the sights, join in practice, head out for a meal or meet some of the Von's influential friends. More often than not Thomson politely refused. At first, von Nida was upset. He thought it was a display of outrageous impertinence, especially after what he'd done for him — why, he'd almost come to blows with Ossie Pickworth one night in Tasmania when Pickworth, after a few too many beers, said that von Nida was showing a little too much interest in the boy from Brunswick — and now, here he was virtually ignoring him. After giving the matter a great deal of thought, the Von came to the conclusion the lad didn't need a chaperone at all. He was distant all right, even aloof, but that was all part of what made him a champion. 'I'd say he was the hardest person to get to know that I've ever met,' says von Nida. 'I think the only bloke who knows Peter Thomson is Peter Thomson. Peter knew he was going to be a great player one day — he knew that greatness was his destiny. I came to understand that blokes like him are from their own mould, but back then, I suppose in the interests of Australian golf and for him, I just wanted Peter to get there quicker.'

In the first round of the World Open, amongst some big names from America, Thomson began with an even-par 73 and was tied for 4th, two strokes behind the leaders, 'Dutch' Harrison and Dicky Metz, both from the USA. Von Nida could only manage a 76. Interestingly, it was during the first round that a sports commentator from the local radio station broadcasting from the course said: 'I'm afraid I don't know much about Peter Thomson's golfing background, but I can tell you he is the best dressed man I can remember seeing on this course.' He was becoming a showhorse as well as a workhorse.

Over the remainder of the tournament, von Nida helped him out with introductions to many of the big name players in attendance and, while Peter came home in a creditable tie for fifth, the Von improved with each round and displaying his guile and cunning on the difficult couch greens, climbed the pack to finish a worthy runner-up to American Ed 'Porky' Oliver. Keen to make the most of his slick finish, he challenged the leading Americans to three four-ball matches using any combination they wanted — he would partner his 20-year-old countryman. Together, mentor and protégé won all the money and dropped in at Singapore on the way home for another exhibition arranged by von Nida. When Thomson finally touched down on home soil at Essendon Airport he proudly clutched his biggest paycheque, a whopping £500.

'That trip really came about through von Nida's generosity,' says Thomson. 'He was enormously generous, almost to a fault. He had no reason to do generous things for me but he was that sort of man. He just had to do it. I never really got close to the Von — we were two entirely different people — and in this I am sure he was disappointed. He had to help people, especially young people, and he's been doing it ever since. After me, he helped other young aspiring golfers who gave him much more satisfaction. But in Manila I came up against a bunch of Americans who were marvellous players. Lloyd Mangrum, Jack Burke, 'Dutch' Harrison, Johnny Bulla — it was my first look at players of that calibre.

It was a big surprise to me to finish with such a high placing amongst that lot, but it was terribly exciting to win that amount of money. Of course I had never seen such a sum before and I immediately decided to use it to further my golfing education.'

So at the age of 20, technically still an assistant and with just one professional title to his credit, Thomson made a monumental decision ... he was attracted to the bright lights of golf's 'big time', the United States tour. This trip is examined more closely in the following chapter, but originally Thomson planned a three-month tour of America, again with the blessing of George Naismith, and he wanted to make the most of the contacts he had made in Manila. It ended with him returning home after just three weeks with not a penny of prizemoney to show for his efforts.

It was the first real setback to his grand plan, but Thomson was far from discouraged. He had too much strength, too much springback, to be destroyed the way countless other young hopefuls had been. There was no 'if' — he vowed to himself that he would one day return to America, and when that time arrived he would be ready.

Soon after arriving home from America he moved out of his family's Brunswick house. He wanted to be out on his own and took a room for £3 a week at the old Menzies Hotel in the heart of Melbourne. By now he'd purchased his own car, a 1936 Buick, which was the envy of all of his friends. But Peter was a kind-hearted soul; he let his mates drive the car whenever they wanted. Often the entire mob would squeeze into the vehicle and take it for trips to the beach, but Thomson was always in control; he would never tolerate speeding or reckless driving. The Buick, nicknamed the 'Monster', proved a popular mode of transport and Peter was never short of enthusiastic 'chauffeurs', all of them to discover that a familiar destination was the Royal Melbourne hospital around the time that Lois Brauer came off duty. It was obvious to many that despite his love affair with the game, Peter kept his feet very firmly on the ground and set out to enjoy himself. He preferred the unpretentious company of his mates on Friday nights at a city hotel but, unlike them, he was hardly a heavy drinker. At this time the newspapers often described him with catch-phrases such as 'wonder boy', 'the find of post-war golf', 'our best prospect ever', and 'future British Open champion', but still he retained a remarkable stability. Thomson continued to show a maturity far beyond his years. He never uttered a boastful word or took a swaggering step.

While Thomson travelled between Riversdale and Warrnambool the prospect of a brief tour of New Zealand was raised. The golf tour in the land of the long white cloud was not particularly strong, rich or popular, but it did provide the one thing Thomson couldn't get in his own country, competition. Again, George Naismith gave his approval and young Peter headed off alone for the New Zealand Masters at Hamilton, near Auckland. 'George came in for a lot of criticism from his peers about my trips,' says Thomson, 'because it wasn't an accepted thing for an assistant from your shop to be allowed to go and play in anything, let alone be allowed to play abroad. George knew what he was doing though, and there were no rules against it. As long as he trained me in the way the PGA required, which he did, well then that was enough.'

Starting the NZ Masters with two solid rounds of 72, Thomson found himself out in the lead by three strokes at the halfway mark. On the final day he never once looked like faltering, and calmly and calculatingly closed with a pair of 71s for a 286 total and his first overseas victory by a mammoth ten strokes! 'The little money I earned there was most welcome and although the weather along the Waikato River in the peat country of the North Island was grim, I thoroughly enjoyed the trip. The New Zealanders made quite a fuss of me. This was at once surprising and very pleasant and did a lot for my ego, which is a great help in making a champion.' There is no doubt Thomson had a healthy ego. He liked the attention. From an impoverished background it was only natural for him to delight in taking the plaudits of a wide cross-section of golf fans. The newspapers and indeed the whole of Australian golf wanted to know just exactly what it was that made him so good. What was it? There had been plenty of brilliant youngsters on the scene in the past, but this one showed more than simple promise. He was a ready-made champion; he showed the winner's smile. But why?

There is no doubt he was exceptionally gifted and had some crucial and crafty backing along the way, but more than this, his outlook was the reason for his early success. It was his ultra-logical, commonsense approach to the game. He kept the ball in play from the tee, hit the greens (or if he missed them he made sure it wasn't by much), holed a few long putts and didn't miss any short ones. Simple. But how? By using an economical, conservative, unspectacular, straightforward and mechanically frill-free swing, coupled with a clear, happy mind 'free from the poison of worry'. He stood out from the pack. Thomson adhered to the famous dictum of the great American, Walter Hagen, who said he 'didn't want to be a millionaire, only live like one'. Hagen also thought the key to success on the golf course lay with an ability to never hurry, never worry; always smell the flowers. Thomson agreed with this, and added: 'Sport is for pleasure, for amusement, for exercise, for fun. Golf is my sport as much as it is my business. The great fight in golf is not with the course, or the conditions, or your clubs. It is with yourself. This is the battle that is never won. I would say, very seriously, that if you want to play the game with the maximum pleasure and if you want to play it well, the first thing to do is to get to know yourself.' Thomson, a self-possessed young man, played the game with maximum pleasure and he knew himself very, very well.

A month after his return from New Zealand, Thomson blitzed around Adelaide's Kooyonga course on the final day of the 1950 Australian Open with a 66, a round which included one of the most spectacular front nines in the history of Australian golf. His 29 was two shots better than the course record, yet it was all in vain as he failed by a shot to catch Norman von Nida, who won his first Open. Again, Thomson was far from disappointed. He knew the future held plenty of chances to make amends.

After a small, but hearty 21st birthday celebration with family and friends at the Menzies Hotel, more travel loomed on the horizon. New Zealand again beckoned, this time for the Open championship at the Shirley Golf Club in Christchurch. Once more Thomson flew out of Melbourne alone, and arrived to find an eager press and public following his every move. After his 10-shot win in the Masters he was now officially accorded star billing across the Tasman and he enhanced that reputation with a brilliant display at Shirley, again completely outclassing the field for his first national open title. Consistency was once more the key: 70–69–71–70 (280) gave him victory by a handsome nine strokes over local pro A. E. Guy. He became the first Australian since Joe Kirkwood (coincidentally also attached to Riversdale GC) in 1920 to win the NZ Open, but claims he 'was the first Australian to win it since Kirkwood because I was the first Australian in the event since Kirkwood,' a statement to be taken, like much of what he says about himself, with a pinch of salt.

Thomson has a unique, some say peculiar, sense of humour. Its style can be easily misinterpreted and some believe he is devoid of a funny bone; an old sourpuss. Those who know him well simply laugh at such a misconception. His humour is just like everything else about him — pointed, succinct and, like one of his 4-irons, delivered crisply with a perfectly straight face. On the outside his lips might curl ever so slightly at the edges, but inside he's belly-laughing like everyone else. In the early 1960s when Thomson was responsible for blazing a tournament trail in the Far East, he holed-in-one during an event at Wack Wack in Manila. The local press, still feeling their way in the not entirely familiar world of professional tournaments, but obviously eager for any possible insight into this remarkable feat, rushed up to Thomson like a bunch of excited schoolboys as he came off the final green. 'Oh, you had a hole-in-one! Fantastic! Well done! What club did you use?' Thomson merely gave a look of mild surprise and said: 'Oh well, I can't tell you that. If I told you what club I'd used, they'd all be doing it!' It wasn't until he'd almost reached the clubhouse that Thomson looked over his shoulder at them and gave a little grin. The penny dropped, and the group burst out laughing.

It was this brand of humour that had quite a say in the way he played his golf, and along with many other tricks of the trade, he learnt a great deal about it from the legendary South African, Arthur D'Arcy Locke, or to his legion of admirers, simply 'Bobby'. In late 1950 their healthy rivalry developed, eventually to become a strong friendship. While Thomson was streeting the field in the New Zealand Open, an event Locke had won at Otago in 1938, the South African was taking the plaudits on the other side of the Tasman Sea for his part in what was described as 'the most spectacular golfing match ever seen in Australia'. The reigning British Open champion fired a 65 over Royal Melbourne's West course, but amazingly lost his exhibition against Ossie Pickworth 2 & 1. The clash was arranged exclusively for RMGC members, who could hardly quibble about value for money: Pickworth three-putted the 18th for a phenomenal round of 63 which included 10 birdies before that closing blemish. An incredulous Locke shook his head on the 18th tee and muttered: 'Here I am needing a par on a top class championship course for a 65 and I'm beaten!' The sheer quality of that match pushed news of Thomson's debut Open victory out of the golfing headlines. They didn't know it at the time, but it was the beginning of a wonderful decade of competition, Thomson v. Locke.

The South African first visited Australia in 1938 as a slender, good-looking, fair-haired gentleman of 21. Returning in 1950 he was tubby and jowly, and despite the torment of piloting more than a hundred missions over enemy territory during the war, still hit the golf ball with superb skill. The star players in the United States could testify to that — they watched him win fifteen tournaments there between 1947–9. Part of his Australian tour involved a series of exhibitions and after his remarkable clash with Pickworth, the next on the itinerary was a fourball contest against Pickworth and von Nida. His partner? None other than the lad fresh home from abroad and returning to his 'old' club, Peter Thomson.

The youngster compiled a 72 and along with the crowd of 3,000 that turned up to watch, was fascinated to have the chance of watching closely the winner of the two previous British Opens. It had been twelve years since Locke last played Victoria, yet he carded a course record 67 and the boy from Brunswick marvelled at his play. It was Thomson's first real look at a foreigner of world class and he noticed immediately that while he was a most gracious partner and visitor, underneath there lurked an unmistakable self-confidence and belief that he was the one under the spotlight. Locke was a good player all right; at that time only Ben Hogan rivalled him as the world's greatest, but as Thomson soon discovered, no one knew this better than Locke. 'I was absolutely delighted when I found out I'd be playing with him when I got back from New Zealand,' says Thomson. 'I remember his very striking personality and he had a superb game to match. I didn't understand a lot of what he said, for he had a very strange sense of humour, but I was deeply impressed by his manner and of course, his golf.'

Afterwards, away from the crowds and in the more informal setting of the clubhouse, Locke, as comfortable with a scotch in his hand as with a 7-iron, chatted to his young professional colleague about his experiences in Britain and America. In 1949, when he'd won the first of his British Opens, Locke had received an immediate boost in contractual commitments with his sponsors in Europe, so he had no alternative but to send two cables to the United States, withdrawing from two tournaments. The US PGA had a rule requiring 30 days notice of withdrawal and many were deeply shocked when Locke was banned from the tour for life. Gene Sarazen said it was 'the most disgraceful action by any golfing organisation in the past 30 years'. The ban was lifted without explanation the following year, but Locke thought the Americans took the action because he was winning too many tournaments. He told Thomson he thought 'the Yanks were out to get him'. Soured by the experience he turned his attention to the British tour and never saw America or Americans in the same light again. Shortly before bidding Thomson farewell at Victoria, and wishing him good luck, he told the young lad that he ought to get himself over to Britain as soon as his apprenticeship was over. Thomson hardly needed prompting.

Finally in April 1951 Peter Thomson's work under George Naismith came to an end. He left the Riversdale pro shop, having broken all records as an assistant. There can be no underestimating George Naismith's contribution to Thomson's career and there is no doubt he helped shape the lad's future by allowing him to compete overseas whilst still an assistant. Many claim Naismith gave Thomson too much latitude but the 1937 National Open champion was a shrewd judge and realised his assistant was a unique specimen. Seventeen years later another gifted youngster came before him and he reacted in the same manner. 'George Naismith was one of the very, very special people of this world,' says David Graham, who in 1981 became the first Australian to win the US Open, his second major after the 1979 USPGA Championship. 'I spent about four years with him and one of his strong points was that he was able to detect skill in a player, and more importantly teach that player manners and how to grow up right. Peter and I were both very fortunate to have a deep association with the man in the early stages of our careers. He couldn't have had a better boss.'

A day before he left, and after several weeks as the guest of von

Nida at his Sydney home playing and practising almost every day, Thomson appeared before the Victorian PGA executive and told them of his intention to leave the next day for England. Eleven days later they cabled a brief message to a London hotel, informing him that he'd been admitted to 'full membership of the Victorian Professional Golfers' Association' and was free to compete for prizemoney in any tournament he wished. They would immediately cable their British counterparts advising that 'Peter Thomson's credentials are in order'.

At last it was official. He was no longer bound to the life of a club pro and no longer an amateur. It made no difference to his game. Every shot had always been played as though his life depended on it: he remained, in the true sense of the word, an amateur, that French word that has its origins from the Latin *amat*, meaning 'he or she loves'. Thomson's love for the game has never, ever wavered. Of course he was delighted to win a big cheque, particularly in his early days; indeed he has been able to build his empire from an astute use of his healthy earnings on the golf course but, unlike many of his professional brethren, his career has never revolved around money. He knew that if he entered tournaments to play his best golf, money would look after itself.

Thomson touched down in post-war Britain with Norman von Nida and soon joined the other members of the Australian contingent, Eric Cremin and Kel Nagle. They were there to play individually and not as a team but, beginning a tradition and camaraderie that has lasted to this day with Australian golfers, the men toured, lived, worked and played together, each encouraging the other if anyone hit a low patch along the way.

Thomson's debut British tour was memorable for many reasons, not the least the immediate affinity he felt with the land and its people. He struck up many friendships, and cemented two in particular that were to have a lasting effect on his play and his character. One was with Kel Nagle, the other with Bobby Locke, who immediately recognised the advantage of associating with a group of men who were not only charming and outstanding company, but who were also fellow tourists coming to terms with playing golf for money in a strange land. When he wasn't winning tournaments, Locke often mingled with the party from the antipodes and Thomson came to know him well. The bridge between them in years (Locke was then 32 and Thomson 21) was hardly noticeable and, as he'd done at Victoria several months before, the South African took a shine to the young Australian. As someone who clearly enjoyed a good time and a hearty laugh, he was greatly impressed by the youngster's subtle sense of humour, forthright personality and distinct belief in his own ability. For Thomson, one of the most significant things to happen on that tour was to have Locke invite him to

South Africa for the summer. Locke raised the possibility of the lad furthering his education in 'tournament toughness' on his home circuit in early 1952 and, out of the kindness of his heart, offered himself as chief guide.

Home again, and with time to reflect on the first five months of his new life as a jet-setting professional golfer, Thomson, now 22, had already come to the conclusion that it had all been thoroughly exhilarating. He told his parents his future success was guaranteed; his gamble had worked. He told Lois that the world was out there just waiting to be explored and that golf would be his passport. He was totally enamoured of the lifestyle; he wanted more. Another trip to New Zealand would quench his thirst, but before that he could squeeze in the Victorian Close championship at Commonwealth. The timing seemed ideal. A week after Frank Sedgman trounced Vic Seixas in straight sets to become the first Australian to win the US Open tennis championship, another Brunswick boy broke through — Peter Thomson won his first professional title in Australia. Ossie Pickworth had led the field by three strokes at the halfway mark, but faded badly on the final day. Thomson, again with aggressive yet controlled play, finished eight-under par and victor by a healthy eight strokes.

He was now living life at a furious pace and this was reflected in his rush to the airport two days after the victory at Commonwealth. He arrived at Essendon with 20 minutes to spare before leaving for Sydney where he was to connect with the Trans-Tasman flying boat for New Zealand. He unloaded his suitcase and his bag of clubs, slipped his hand into his coat to produce an airline ticket, and came up with precious little. He had left it at his parents' home in Brunswick. Thomson made it quite clear to airline officials that if he missed his connecting flight the New Zealand Open would be left with no one to defend it, but the airline was firm: no ticket, no trip. Thomson jumped into a car and raced off to Brunswick, dodging traffic with all the skill of a Juan Fangio; he raced back to the airport, ticket in hand, to arrive 15 minutes after the scheduled departure time. To his relief, the plane was still waiting with engines running: the pilot was a golf fan. Along with the successful defence of his New Zealand Open, this time at the Dr Alister Mackenzie designed Titirangi Golf Club on Auckland's Manukau Harbour, there was an eight stroke victory in the 'Pacific and Regent Radio Golf Tournament' at Middlemore, also in Auckland. Thomson won the latter event with a closing round of 65 to 'add more fruit for the sideboard'.

It could not have been a better grounding for his country's premier event, the Australian Open, a few weeks later at Metropolitan. With several victories under his belt, and on a course he knew well from his amateur days, Thomson felt ready. Harry and Lorraine Young, whilst retaining their interest in the Carlton Club hotel, had by now moved into a palatial home in the affluent suburb of East Hawthorn and Thomson was invited to live with them in an atmosphere free from distractions so he could concentrate fully on the task ahead. Though no longer intimately involved in Thomson's game, Young remained the boy's staunchest supporter and continued to volunteer his support in whatever role the youngster wished, but Thomson was stubborn. He had to do it his way and his way alone.

The pre-tournament speculation concentrated on the 'conquering quad' of Pickworth, von Nida, Cremin and Thomson — one scribe was bold enough to state that the winner could only come from this group. On the eve of the championship came news from Brisbane of the death of von Nida's father. The defending champion agonised whether he should withdraw from the event and leave for home, but he chose to play on, hoping the memory and inspiration of his father would carry him to victory.

Fine weather greeted the field for the opening round on Thursday and Thomson proved he was the form player by jumping from the blocks brilliantly to be five-under after just nine holes. He'd started as if half his name was already engraved on the trophy but then three-putts at the 10th and short 13th halted his momentum and he came home in 36. Despite the blemishes, it was a fine start of 68 and, matched only by his one-time pennant teammate and former Australian Amateur champion, Doug Bachli, it was worthy enough to lead the Open. Ossie Pickworth was well placed a stroke behind, joined on 69 by the little known pro from the Peninsula club, south of Melbourne, Bill Clifford, who credited his impressive start to an impromptu putting lesson from Eric Cremin on the practice green before he set out. Surprisingly, Cremin couldn't buy a putt during his round and was six strokes from the lead after a 74. On the same mark were Kel Nagle and Jack Harris, while von Nida displayed typical determination to return a 71 under the strain of his personal tragedy.

Thomson was delighted with his excellent start, but like most of the field he found Metropolitan a not so gentle lady the following day. A fearsome northerly wind lashed the course in the afternoon and the early starters had a clear advantage. One of them was the young pro from Newcastle who'd played in every Open since the war, Syd Cowling. With a gallery consisting of his opponent, a friend and two caddies, Cowling holed a mammoth 12-metre putt at the 5th and one of seven metres at the 17th, both for birdies. Arriving at the clubhouse just as the trees around Metropolitan were beginning to bend in the wind, Cowling found himself in the tournament lead after a pair of 71s. 'I've never played better golf than this week,' he said. 'My putter is my best friend.' Jack Harris and amateur Harry Berwick were able to match the day's best score, but behind them came a string of hard luck stories. Von Nida had trouble finding the fairways and netted a 74. Cremin, Clifford and Nagle could only manage 75s. Pickworth, out in a scratchy 37, fumbled his way home and bogeyed the last for a 76. It was exactly the same for Bachli. Of all the afternoon casualties though, it seemed Thomson would be dealt with the harshest. Appearing to suffer from nerves, wayward tee shots and tentative putting crept into his game and eventually he scribbled an ugly 40 on his card for the front nine. Chinks were beginning to show in the wonder boy's armour. Even his supporters feared that his spell of brilliant form was about to come apart at the seams. But it was at times like this when Thomson proved his abilities. Most 22-year-olds would never have recovered from such a demoralising start; indeed, most professionals will testify that one of the toughest tasks in golf is not simply to halt a string of bogeys, but to turn about face and retrieve those lost strokes before the round finishes. Thomson, digging deep into his reserves, shrugged off the disappointment with absolute contempt, his face masked with the same 'mocking' smile throughout, as he fired a remarkable closing sequence of birdie-birdie-birdie-par. If there was ever such a thing as a 'good' 75, this was it.

The importance of that finish quickly surfaced next morning. As Cowling began a dramatic free-fall down the leader's board, eventually destroying his chances with a 78, Thomson came in at lunch with a solid 70 and found himself leading the Open. But the big guns were set to pounce should the lad slip up. Von Nida, back to his best with a 69 was only a stroke behind, and Pickworth was within three after a 71. Of the remainder, only Jack Harris seemed a threat, trailing Thomson by five shots. In glorious afternoon conditions the players set out for the final round, Pickworth aiming for his fourth Open, von Nida a second and Thomson his first.

From the outset it was clear Pickworth would be the first to fall by the wayside. His working relationship with his putter was less than harmonious and, as the big man began uttering a few expletives, his major strength, his driving, disappeared too. In the early stages it seemed only von Nida was capable of preventing a popular Thomson triumph. Playing three groups ahead, the Queenslander holed a marvellous putt at the 4th which dramatically perched on the hole's edge before dropping in to give him a share of the lead. The large crowd anticipated a thrilling finish, but for the Von the closing stretch was a disaster. 'Of course I was most upset at the death of my father before the tournament, but that was no excuse for my performance,' he recalls. 'During that final round I remember joining Peter in the lead and at the 6th hole the gallery was getting in a bit close. My drive hit a fellow flush in the temple and I thought I'd killed him. The poor bloke got up and was okay, but I three-putted that hole and did the same at the next three and I really didn't know if I was Arthur or Martha! That didn't take anything away from Peter's performance though ... he fully deserved to win.'

By now a huge gallery was following Thomson's every move. He knew he had the luxury of being able to play the final three holes in one-over par and still win. Concentrating on nothing but hitting the ball he reached the long 16th in two and although his eagle putt slipped past he made the one for birdie coming back. At the 440-yard par 5 17th he put his second in a bunker 20 yards from the flagstick. After carefully studying the lie of his ball in the shallow trap he flipped it up gently and watched with great delight as the ball pitched a few yards from the pin, bit hard, and rolled straight into the cup for an eagle 3! 'The roar from the big crowd that followed that shot sounded in my ears as though I had kicked the winning goal in the grand final at the MCG!' Thomson could not hide his broad smile and knew he had his first Open in the bag. At the final hole he needed a birdie to equal Gene Sarazen's tournament record set on the same course in the 1936 Australian Open. Feeling as if he could do no wrong, he cracked one of his best drives for the day down the 18th and with the gallery swarming around the green (there were no such things as grandstands then), he played an approach to within three metres of the pin. His bold putt lipped out, but to thunderous applause he sank the return and the Open was his. 'Nearly all tournaments are half-won and half-lost,' he says, typically understating. 'And on that occasion I did my half properly by scoring 283. Von Nida and Pickworth, who were better players than I at the time, obliged on the losing side and left me high and dry the winner.'

1951 Australian Open, Metropolitan GC, Melbourne		
283	P. Thomson (Vic.)	68–75–70–70
287	N. von Nida (Qld)	71–74–69–73
288	H. Pickworth (Vic.)	69–76–71–72
292	J. Harris (Vic.)	74–71–73–74
296	K. Nagle (NSW)	74–71–73–74
	K. Pix (NSW a.)	78–73–73–72

The second youngest winner to the 18-year-old Ivo Whitton in 1912, the Open was Thomson's fourth tournament win in succession. If that was not proof enough of his ability, Thomson had showed conclusively he could cope with the tension of such a prestigious event as the Open. Par for the closing three holes at Metropolitan was then

5–5–4. The first three rounds he finished 4–4–4, and finally, 4–3–4. He'd gained Australia's top golfing honour with a blistering sequence of seven birdies and an eagle over 12 of the tournament's most important holes.

He took his success, as always, modestly, paying tribute at the presentation to the help he'd received from von Nida, Naismith and other Australian professionals. He spoke quietly, slowly and politely, without a trace of self-satisfaction, yet underneath the relaxed exterior there was a racing heartbeat. 'Winning that Australian Open was an enormously proud moment for me,' he says. 'It was really thrilling. I remember holing that bunker shot towards the end and having a chuckle to myself because I knew I wasn't a very good bunker player. Every time I go back to Metropolitan it stirs something inside me because that win was a huge stepping-stone ... it took me on to much bigger things.'

Now the offers came pouring in. Sponsorship contracts to promote equipment, balls and clothing. The *Argus* newspaper wanted him on staff as a permanent golf writer and so began the pursuit of excellence in another field. 'I always thought it would be something to fall back on if the golf didn't work out,' he says. But his future success on the course was assured. Although mature enough to deal with any person he came across, Thomson was wise enough to appreciate that the world of bartering in business contracts was best left to the experts. Despite an age difference of 15 years Peter Thomson became close friends with Peter Norris, a solicitor and long time member of Victoria Golf Club and any contract that was placed before the youngster was not signed before Norris, as legal adviser, had given it his approval. 'He left everything to me,' says Norris. 'Like most people at the club when he first arrived, I was struck by Peter's intelligence and remarkable ability to handle people; knowing people, understanding people and liking people. He appreciated that I was interested in his well being and he was prepared to accept whatever advice I gave him along the way.'

Victory in his country's Open championship was the ideal promotion for his South African tour which began a few months later, and doubtless one of those to delight in the news of his triumph was Bobby Locke. As much as the Open made Thomson's name in his home country and elevated him to world class, his trip to South Africa was to add another dimension to his game and to his personality.

Thomson had proved he was ruthless in his quest for knowledge and experience; this was one reason he surrounded himself with people much older than he was. It was so with Bobby Locke. Separated by an age difference of twelve years they were as unlike as they could be: Thomson a youthful, boyishly handsome Australian with a quick, jaunty step; Locke a vastly experienced, jowl-faced South African with hardly a suggestion of fitness. He moved his portly frame around the golf course at a speed once described as 'akin to the progress of an Archbishop up the aisle of a church.' Another South African golfing legend, Gary Player, was a fresh-faced youngster of barely 16 when he 'watched very move' made by Locke and Thomson during their exhibition matches in Johannesburg. Player went on to forge one of the most successful playing records in the history of golf and it all started for him with his first big tournament win in Australia in 1956, largely at Thomson's urging. In describing Locke as his earliest hero and a major influence on his career, Player tells a story he once heard from Locke about his childhood which bears a striking resemblance to the experience of a young boy growing up in Australia. 'Bobby had a very bad temper as a boy,' says Player. 'And when he was a young lad in his early teens he threw a club in anger. What Bobby didn't know was that his father was watching and he immediately took Bobby's clubs away from him and said he was going to keep them for a month. It was the making of Locke. It taught him a marvellous lesson. Bobby told me that he resolved there and then never to lose his temper when it came to golf. He was never angry on a golf course again.'

So Arthur D'Arcy Locke outgrew that habit, but not his childhood nickname, invented by the family nurse, amused at the way he 'bobbed' up and down in his pram. Locke was born on 20 November 1917, into a family living on the boundary of the Germiston Golf Club near Johannesburg, but in later years he always considered himself to be British, by the grace of parents who'd emigrated from Northern Ireland. He once said: 'When I was 13, my dear old dad gave me Bobby Jones's book of golf, and said to me, "Son, here is the finest golfer in the world. I want you to learn how to play from this book. A lot of people are going to try to help you, but you just let it go in one ear and out the other. You model your game on Bobby Jones and you will be a fine player." So that's what I did when I started and what I've done all my life.' At the age of 15 Locke's handicap plummeted from five to plus two and less than two years later he won his country's Amateur and Open championships in successive weeks. Like Thomson, Locke also had a two-year wait before becoming eligible for PGA membership in South Africa, and a staggering five years, as it was then, for the same in Britain. The problem resolved itself with the outbreak of war. Locke joined the South African Air Force and was out of golf for five years. It was during this time, while Thomson was learning his basic golf at Royal Park, that Locke's swing underwent a complete transformation. Through his experiences in Britain, on long and often heavy courses and into strong headwinds, Locke was convinced that he needed another forty yards on his drives. Refusing to hit the ball harder, therefore sacrificing control, he employed the same lazy tempo based on his view of the Jones swing, but he tried to 'draw' the ball. The most individualistic swing of the era was born. At address he would point himself in the direction of the deep rough out to the right, often frightening the spectators. With a stroke resembling a high, controlled hook, he bent his ball over the heads of the gallery and back to the centre of the fairway. Locke had his extra forty yards.

In early 1947 the legendary Slammin' Sam Snead arrived in South Africa for a sixteen match exhibition against Locke. The pair had met at the previous year's British Open at St Andrews, where Snead won and Locke came second. Upon offering his congratulations the South African was told: 'Thanks Bob, but it was just another tournament.' Snead's response affected him deeply and convinced Locke that a tournament temperament was as important as technique if he was to become a champion.

'That man had about as much control of himself on a golf course as anybody I ever saw,' recalls Snead. 'He was without doubt the best putter I've ever played with. It didn't matter what surface we were playin' on ... he could hole a putt down a cobblestone road!' Snead also remarked that Locke never seemed to care where the pin was positioned. 'He'd just slop it up there onto the green and didn't care where it ended up. All he wanted was a good run at the hole and, by God, from there he was the best.' Locke annihilated Snead in that exhibition series, winning twelve matches and drawing two. He'd been advised by the great Walter Hagen in the 1930s to try the American tour and, with Snead adding his voice, Locke made up his mind. He arrived in time for the 1947 US Masters, where he finished a creditable 14th. He then went on to win four of the next five tournaments. When he left in August, he'd won seven events, finished second twice, third once, and was in the top seven on four occasions. Only Jimmy Demaret, who played the full twelve-month tour, finished ahead of him on the money list, by a mere US$3,600. America could not believe Locke. On the practice tee he would stand in front of the usually large gallery, all eager to see this novelty from South Africa, and he would deliberately hit his shots with severe hook so the crowd would think he was in for a terrible day. Then he'd say to his caddy in a loud voice, 'Okay, I'm happy now,' and would then trot off to the practice green where he never had more than three putts and said the same thing. American fans were convinced that Locke could not play a fade to save himself. A golf writer was playing alongside him in a pro-am once and tackled him on the subject. 'Mawstah,' Locke said (to Locke almost every other male, including Thomson, went by the name Master), 'Let me show you how it's done.' He then proceeded to play an immaculate shot that started way left and flew back gloriously to pepper the flagstick — and this from his normal 45-degrees-right stance! To prove his point Locke casually played a carbon copy.

Locke did not appear to be more talented than most of the players he defeated and in many ways less so. Irritating to the American players were his obvious lack of athleticism, his fiercely competitive demeanour, and his individualistic 'uniform' of white cap and shoes, navy plus-fours, a white dress shirt with the sleeves rolled up, and a club tie tucked beneath the third button below the neck. 'It was a most impressive outfit; to his fingertips he always looked the complete professional,' says Thomson. One US pro summed it up in *The Masters of Golf* (by Dick Aultman and Ken Bowden, Century Hutchinson, 1988) when he said: 'The guy gets to me before we ever hit a shot. I look at that nutty outfit and I'm one down. I listen to that accent and I'm two down trying to figure out what he said. I watch that crazy swing and I go three down trying to work out why he doesn't flat whiff it. Then he starts hooking those 50-foot putts into the cup and I'm done — cooked to a turn!' Particularly in the USA, Locke took the greatest delight in defeating those who least admired him. Yet he was a kind, modest man, who bore little if any malice. His idiosyncratic outfit, his highly unorthodox swing, his measured pace, his unflappable disposition and complete lack of self-consciousness were not, as some Americans bluntly suggested, calculated competitive ploys. Thomson believes they were more simply the guileless expressions of a unique and unusual character but, whatever it was, it had a big influence on the young Australian.

If anyone indulged in gamesmanship, it was the Americans. They tried to upset Locke by attacking him in the press for his slow play or his lack of distance from the tee, or by ignoring him, or even by sending a strange woman to his hotel room late at night — but these crude attempts always failed. 'He had a skin like a rhinoceros,' says Thomson. 'He was completely impervious to any suggestion of criticism. He would just give a wry grin, dismiss the words as though they'd never happened, and then walk off with his head held high. He had incredible self-confidence.' Once in America, Locke was being consistently outdriven by his playing partners, each of whom were becoming quite vocal about the foreigner having to play fifty yards behind them on every hole. Locke ignored the niggling, but after the locals had boomed out their drives at the next hole, he pulled out his driver and belted his ball thirty yards past the others. Still saying nothing he marched past them down the fairway. Another incident, more publicised, took place in a locker room before the final round of a big tournament. Locke was sitting alone, as usual, slowly tying his shoelaces when he heard Lloyd

Mangrum from the adjoining bay of lockers in a voice loud enough to be heard: 'That guy from South Africa is a good player, but he uses too much right hand.' As Locke was on his way to the first tee he saw Mangrum in the distance. He made sure his journey diverted in his direction and as he passed him he whispered, 'I save my left hand for the cheques!' Locke won that tournament, and fourteen others in his three seasons on the US tour and, 'those were in the days when Snead, Demaret, Mangrum and Hogan were in their prime,' says Thomson.

In late 1951, when the young Australian arrived in Johannesburg, he was immediately shown some generous South African hospitality. Locke provided a room in his own apartment building for the young man and invited him to join his family to celebrate the festive season. 'I spent a delightful Christmas Day with Locke's family,' says Thomson. 'His parents were people from the old world and it was easy to see where Locke had learned his impeccable manners and style. His father was an Ulsterman, a successful mercer, and a thorough gentleman. Locke was very much a lone wolf, but for some reason he took a shine to me and my golf, and took me in as a friend. He was at the height of his career then; certainly he was undisputed champion of the British world and it could have been strongly debated whether Hogan or Locke was the world master. It was a marvellous opportunity for a young professional like me to sit at the feet of such a man. Indeed, he was very, very kind to me and apart from getting an insight into the mind of a big winner, it was also possible to study his technique. Obviously I learnt a great deal from watching, but he also actively encouraged my play and suggested I try my luck again in America.'

On Boxing Day they set off in Locke's big Ford V8 for a series of tournaments and exhibitions around South Africa and Rhodesia (now Zimbabwe), taking in such places as Cape Town, Port Elizabeth, Durban, Pretoria and Salisbury (now Harare). 'We toured around by car, everywhere we went,' says Thomson. 'I did my share of the driving, and I managed to see a great deal of South Africa, which was a very spectacular and a very pleasant place.' Thomson was thrilled by the travelling and has since been back to the continent many times, journeying deep into the remote regions of Kenya, not on tourist routes but with friends and under their own steam.

Clocking up thousands of miles there were plenty of opportunities for talking. 'He talked a lot about the United States,' Thomson says, 'and recalled his experiences there and I listened. We stayed in the same hotels and dined together most of the time and then I stayed with him in his home. Despite the differences in age I got to know him very well. He never once took me aside to teach me anything, but logically it was there to watch. On the golf course I learned much from his attitude. He never allowed himself to be ruffled by anything when he was playing — if he did have an unlucky run he put it out of his mind and carried on as if nothing had happened.' Thomson heard the story from Troon in 1950, when Locke was leading the British Open when he came to the short 5th hole and took a disastrous triple-bogey six. Many thought his grip on the silver claret jug was slipping, but with four birdies over the next five holes he went on to become the first successful defender since Walter Hagen in 1929. 'I have always remembered that little lesson,' says Thomson.

And there was also the lesson on putting; Locke was the undisputed world expert on 'the game within a game'. He used only one putter all his life. When he was nine he was on the practice green at Germiston, putting with a sawn-off 2-iron and attracting sympathy from a few senior members sitting on the verandah. It so happened that one of them had recently purchased a new putter and decided to give his old one to the boy. It was a long, hickory-shafted putter with a small, rusty upright iron blade and it was gratefully accepted. They became firm friends. On his first trip to the USA, Locke was so fearful of losing it he slept with it in his bed!

When putting, Locke's primary aim was to impart top-spin, meaning accurate end-over-end rotation. He considered every hole to have four entrances; the front of the cup for a dying putt; the back if the putt was a little too fast but on line; and either side if it was the right strength but marginally off line. He believed most people missed putts because they were not mis-hit, but mis-read. This explained his meticulous survey of all greens. He would never putt until he'd inspected the 'shade' of the grass and the direction of its cut, especially around the cup, where the slow moving ball was most likely to be affected by terrain. 'He was probably the first person to really examine his putts from all angles and take so much care. Of course everybody does it now,' remarks Thomson, who was beginning to develop a definite game plan in South Africa. No longer did he turn up to the course and try for his best possible round every possible time; he became more cerebral, even street-wise and, as Locke had done, he was developing a golfing philosophy. 'The real secret of success in golf,' said Locke, 'lies in turning three shots into two. If you miss a third of the greens in every round, but turn three shots into two four times, you save four shots a round. If you do that in every round of a tournament you save 16 shots. Thus, once I had my long game in reasonable shape as a young man, I worked for many, many hours — many, many days and weeks and months — on my short game. And it paid off well by taking the pressure off my long game. I was always confident that I could make a few pars when I was playing poorly and that when I was playing well a few birdies might come my way.'

One aspect of the tour that surprised Thomson was Locke's penchant for providing entertainment off the course as well as on. Away from 'the office' he gave full rein to his companionable and fun-loving nature. 'He would still be at the golf club long after the sun went down and he'd settle down to a jolly time,' says Thomson, seeming to suppress a smile. 'This happened most nights at tournaments and certainly at exhibitions.' The huge man with all the appearance of an English squire liked to enjoy himself as much as anyone and, while his young friend could not and often did not want to keep pace with the South African, he tagged along on a few occasions to find Locke in a crowd around a piano bellowing out a song and not caring at all what anyone thought of him. If he was in a state of 'pleasant weariness' from the day's activity on the course, he would melt into a large, comfortable chair, chat to someone about anything other than his game and say: 'Well Mawstah, the truth is that I'm actually a singer. All this other business is just a sideline . . .'

'He didn't drink anything other than beer,' says the Australian, 'but he was fond of it. He could also play the ukulele and banjo in a primitive kind of way and he fancied himself as a singer; he had a small repertoire of what I would call rude, bawdy ditties!'

Locke was a character all right, but Thomson noticed that he was completely self-centred and lapped up the limelight as a kitten does a bowl of milk. Many have argued that, as a solitary child, Locke found he could express himself on the golf course — his ability attracted plenty of attention and eventually brought him out of his shell. From time to time the basic insecurities surfaced for all to witness, mainly in the clubhouse late at night, but this is offered as a reason why Locke was so keen to assist in the shaping of Peter Thomson's career. Perhaps it was intuition on Locke's part, but there is about Thomson, beneath the eloquency and the cosmopolitan sophistication and the detached manner, a very real shyness that was never far beneath the surface in his youth. Regardless of the many friendships and his renowned composure, nothing could compensate for the distance between him and his younger brothers. He was virtually an only child; subject to the diffidence of not having blood close by during his formative years. 'I was a bit of a loner,' he has said. 'One reason I played golf so much was to be by myself.'

When nine of the most memorable weeks of his life ended, Thomson departed Johannesburg with £1,100 in prizemoney and two tournament victories to his credit — the Mobilco and the Mills 1,000 guineas. Much more than the money though, there was the reward of knowledge and wisdom, and he couldn't put a price on that. His exhibitions with Locke were head-to-head contests under matchplay conditions and it is far from coincidence that after this tour Thomson became one of the most successful exponents of matchplay in the world. He came to relish it. 'Matches are entertaining from the first ball hit,' he has written. 'There is a great deal of monotony about four days of strokeplay. For one thing it doesn't get really tense and exciting until the last hour or two of the final round. Sadly, the increasing role of commercial television and player management groups into top professional golf these days means that we don't see many matchplay events at all on the tour. To my mind that is a great shame because a match is a much more personal clash between the two that are engaged. Assuming the form of both is somewhere near similar, the stronger personality will invariably come out on top. Of course there are variations and accidents, but in principle your opponent in a match has a big influence on the way you perform unless you can somehow exclude him from your attention. From 1951 to 1957 I played more than 200 matches against Locke in many parts of the world and he was a very hard man to beat. I will never forget some of the finishes we had. For a start I would strain so hard to win I would tie myself into a knot. Out of the first fourteen matches he won eleven of them and at that stage I had to take stock. With nothing more of my reputation to lose I began to sit back and watch what was happening, and suddenly it all became clear. I had known that golf was a psychological game, but up until then I had no idea just how much the mind came into play. I was trying to outdrive, out-approach and out-putt him, while he just stood back and watched me defeat myself. At that stage I took up a new attitude and relaxed and tried nothing except to keep out of the trees and stick to par. I struck oil. Normally he was completely unflappable, even in a crisis, but our matches took a new twist. I gave away no holes to him by impetuosity. I made him earn every one he chalked up to my deficit, and suddenly, an odd thing happened. When I refused to take the risks, Locke instinctively did so himself, and that was when I began to beat him. On one section through the Rhodesias in 1956 I beat him eleven times straight. This was unheard of in Africa at that stage of Locke's career. I learnt an enormous amount from him. Mainly to do with pressure and tactics and how to get the best out of my game.'

Thomson twice toured South Africa for nine weeks with Locke, in the summers of 1951–2 and 1955–6. By the time of the second tour he was twice British Open champion and there was enormous interest in their clashes, particularly the two major 108-hole matches, both of which were won by Thomson. The crowds flocked to watch the two giants of the game outside America, and the pair kept their part of the bargain with a battle royal over 63 competitive rounds in 63 days. At the conclusion of the marathon series Locke emerged the victor by the narrowest of margins, 22–21 from 47 matches played, with four draws.

One might have expected the local interest to wane during such a lengthy contest, but clearly the two were evenly matched and spectators knew they would be treated to excellent golf every time.

Although he lost the series, Thomson's performance was remarkable when put in its proper perspective. On his home soil, Locke was considered the next best thing to unbeatable. In fact for an astonishing twenty-one years, until Bruce Keyter defeated him in the Transvaal Open, Locke was not once beaten by any of his countrymen in any 72-hole strokeplay event in his native land — and he played in plenty of them! From the man who accumulated this unbelievable record, Thomson learnt well. Together he and Locke were recognised as firm friends wherever they travelled and they achieved global fame as the couple from the Commonwealth who dominated the British Open in the 1950s.

By 1957 Thomson was playing almost every available tournament in the United States to make the most of his successful 1956 there. He hadn't seen much of Locke all year by the time the British Open came around at St Andrews. Originally the Open was to be played at Muirfield, but due to petrol rationing brought about by the Suez crisis, the Royal and Ancient Golf Club decided on a change of venue and opted for St Andrews. Rationing ended some weeks before the Open, but the change was adhered to — St Andrews it would be — the cradle of golf where Peter Thomson felt very much at home. This fact, combined with truly stunning form leading up to the Open, gave many observers the view that Thomson was already home and hosed. 'I'd won the tournament before the Open, the Yorkshire Evening News, by a record margin of 15 strokes and with a score of 264,' he says. 'Everyone was saying that the Open was mine before I'd started it.' This was compounded by the widely held opinion that Bobby Locke was fading from the international scene. 'His golf had certainly slipped,' says Thomson. 'He'd become more heavy and portly. His long irons didn't fly the way they used to do and he substituted a 5-wood where formerly his 2-iron was one of his best clubs.' At St Andrews nobody gave the South African much of a chance and the bookmakers had him at 25-to-1. Thomson was the hot favourite at 5-to-2.

Once the tournament was under way it was clear that Thomson was far from comfortable on the St Andrews greens, which he later criticised for being too slow. He claimed that the local council, the controllers of the course, 'panicked in the dry months of May and June when the Old Course was slowly baked dry and poured water on all the greens with the local fire engine.' He believed this had made the surfaces extremely soft and the greens were not the ones that normally struck fear into the hearts of even the most experienced players. 'They were not easy, but rather bumpy,' he says. 'My play from tee to green was really very good, good enough to win easily if I'd putted like the previous year, but I couldn't hole anything. It was really miserable. I was even missing little short ones and I was in a bad mental state on those greens. It cost me any chance I had and in the end, to me, second place seemed like a terrible failure.' The greens certainly created no bother with Locke. To obliterate suggestions he was over the hill, he carded 69–72–68–70 (279), not a round over-par, to whittle two strokes off the record score for an Open at St Andrews, set two years earlier by Thomson. No one, least of all the defending champion, begrudged Locke his fourth title. He won by three shots and only 'the Great Triumvirate' of an era past, Harry Vardon (six), J. H. Taylor (five) and James Braid (five), had won more Open Championships. It should have been Locke's finest hour, and yet St Andrews in 1957 turned sour for not only him but also Thomson. A bizarre hostility developed from seemingly nothing and, sadly, the greatest casualty was their friendship.

In that final round Locke was paired with another Australian, Bruce Crampton, who was not faring well on the Old Course. Thomson was playing behind them and was in the hunt for his fourth successive Open, a feat achieved only by Tom Morris in 1872 when there were just eight players in the field and the Championship was played over 36 holes. Locke and Crampton came to the final hole of the Championship. Locke, as usual, appeared to be aiming his approach onto the roof of the St Andrews woollen mills, but with his characteristic swing, curved the ball around in a high arc and to thunderous applause plopped it less than a yard from the flagstick. Crampton was not so fortunate; on the vast green his ball was a long way from the hole and upon surveying his putt found that Locke's marker was on his line. He asked Locke if he wouldn't mind moving it to one side. The South African obliged by moving his marker a putterhead's width to the side clear of Crampton's line to the hole. The Australian missed his putt, holed out and then backed off to allow Locke to take the spotlight. Everyone was hoping he could cap off his fourth Open with a birdie finish, but what happened next seriously damaged a fine friendship and was the catalyst for a controversial debate that rages to this day. Incredibly it was not spotted by Crampton, the championship committee, or any one of the many thousands of spectators.

After Crampton had putted out, Locke stepped forward and placed his ball down exactly where his marker was. Whether it was a lapse of concentration or the excitement of the moment, or both, is something Locke never explained, but he completely forgot to return the marker to its original position using the width of his putterhead. The marker went into his pocket, he lined up the putt, and stroked it in. A burst of applause and cheering came forth; Locke was once again the Open champion ... or was he?

The infringement went unnoticed until later that evening when a BBC television film was shown. After viewing the record of the incident there were murmurs of an irregularity, which slowly built until everyone was convinced that Locke had failed to replace his ball on its original position before holing the winning putt. It may have been a matter of only four inches difference, but rules were rules and under the Rules of Golf such a mistake should have incurred a two-stroke penalty and, inevitably, disqualification for signing an incorrect card. The person who would have benefited most from Locke being disqualified was the man alone in second place — Peter Thomson.

The then chairman of the championship committee, Neville 'Bobbie' Selway takes up the story: 'Four days after the Open finished, Peter Thomson and a friend of his called on me in London and told me of the rumours that were circulating. I had not been aware of these rumours and naturally I was astounded and very concerned. I at once rang Brigadier Brickman, the secretary of the R & A, who confirmed the rumours, having received calls on the subject himself. I called a committee meeting immediately in London and we were in session, on and off, for the next few days. It was then unanimously decided that the situation would be dealt with under Rule 36 (5) and that Locke's winning score would stand. Locke, meanwhile, had remained in Scotland, and around ten days after the finish of the Championship was informed of the Committee's decision and then I confirmed it in writing. To put it mildly, he was greatly relieved.'

In the letter to Locke, Selway wrote: 'This Committee considers that when a competitor has three for the Open Championship from two feet, and then commits a technical error which brings him no possible advantage, exceptional circumstances then exist and the decision should be given, accordingly, in equity and the spirit of the game.' And that's where the matter should have come to an end. Yet at the time it was alleged from some quarters that Thomson, who was in London and who had stood to gain a fourth Open in succession from a disqualification, had deliberately alerted the R & A Championship Committee to Locke's mistake. These utterly unfounded claims hurt Thomson. 'Peter Thomson, who was a personal friend, came to see me in London,' says Selway. 'But he did not then, or at any time, suggest that Locke should be disqualified.'

Thomson maintains: 'I had no knowledge of Locke's mistake until days after the Championship had finished. I was not a witness to it and I heard about it as the rest of the world did. I had finished in second place, but I was three strokes behind so I really didn't have any claim and I didn't want to make any claim about the matter. It was really a silly, trivial thing that had nothing to do with the playing of the game and quite frankly, when I thought about what had happened and the mistake Locke had made, I thought, well it's just by the grace of God that I haven't done the same thing myself — it's a very easy thing to do, especially in a moment like that. Locke certainly spelt out his resentment of me and that I had caused the trouble he got into over that incident, but I was certainly not the cause of it. I was writing for the Melbourne *Herald* at the time and when the incident did come to light I had to write something about it, but I was not the person that alerted the world to what had happened — I was simply reflecting the news at the time.'

Under the heading 'It might have robbed Locke of his title', Thomson's Melbourne *Herald* article says, 'Any viewer of the BBC TV film of that final green must have been convinced that Locke had indeed forgotten to place his ball in the exact same spot from which he lifted it at the request of his playing partner ... It would have been a very "sticky situation" if the tournament committee had been forced to give a ruling. Fortunately the game of golf is free from those controversial disputes that mar many other ball games ... In Locke's case he would have been on his honour to have invoked the correct penalty ... This was explained to me by the Chairman of the Match Committee, Mr Bob Selway, who gave an answer to this effect when I posed this hypothetical question to him — What would have been the tournament committee's decision had the matter of Locke's infringement been brought to their attention immediately after the last dramatic moment? He said that Locke would have been asked officially if he had made such a breach. No match committee, however observant, could have argued with him if he had stated that he had complied explicitly with all the rules. His word would have been the end of the matter. If, however, he had admitted that he had not played the ball into the hole from its original position, he would have been obliged to have taken the penalty that any golfer should know. The putt he made into the hole would have been technically a practice putt for which the penalty is one stroke. But it would still have been necessary to have played the ball from the correct spot into the hole in order to finish the round. If he had signed his card and handed it in, then there would have been no alternative but for him to have disqualified himself. He would have been entirely on his honour to have done these things ... Certainly, Locke took no advantage from his unfortunate lapse of memory when he forgot his marker coin was four inches away from where the ball had been lifted. Such a mistake is easily made in the heat of the moment ... It makes no difference to the record — he won by a very comfortable margin of three strokes and thoroughly deserved his win.'

The article was published in the Melbourne *Herald* a fortnight after the Open finished. Locke was made aware of its contents. The South African is understood to have interpreted the article as an attack on his honour and considered it proof that Thomson was the person who'd approached the championship committee over the incident. For his part, Thomson says he was merely making an inquiry to Selway in his role as a journalist, just as any reporter worth his salt would be expected to do. Nothing contained in his article was not fact, but he believes the situation was made more combustible by the executives of a sporting goods company in Australia. Thomson says it was these men who sabotaged his friendship with Locke. 'The mischief was made by an organisation in Australia, which was rather frantic about my rise in the world of golf, as it was affecting their share of the marketplace in my home country. This attitude continued for most of may career. I was considered a thorn in their marketing side and I thought the executives [of this company] were most unlikeable people and one of the reasons I formed this opinion was through this business with Locke. I'm certain they were the people that wrecked the friendship I had with him. I'm sure they must have either written him a letter or sent him a cutting of what I'd written for the paper and they did it purely as a source of mischief. That's how they were.'

The big loser in this most unfortunate public spat was the friendship between the biggest names in British golf. Thomson and Locke never looked at each other in the same light again. 'Our paths didn't really cross after that,' says Thomson. 'I didn't go back to South Africa and he didn't come out to Australia. I saw him across the fairways in Britain, but we didn't have any reason to talk or join each other's company. I must say that it was never a bitter ending on my part, for I firmly believe the incident made no difference to the outcome of the Open, but Locke, who was so careful to do everything right on the golf course, never really got over it. I think it affected him tremendously. In his case it really destroyed him because he'd gone to every length to be the perfect gentleman on the course and to have a mistake like that happen, well, I was shocked by the change in the man after that.' Seven months after that Open, Thomson tried to entice Locke to go on a four-man exhibition tour of New Zealand, scheduled for October 1958, but Locke bluntly refused. The series went ahead with South Africa represented by Gary Player and Harold Henning. Thomson and British Open runner-up that year, Welshman Dave Thomas, made up the four. Locke did make a defence of his Open crown at Royal Lytham in 1958 and although he matched Thomson over the final three rounds he was never in contention after an opening 76. He came in tied for 16th and sadly it was to be his last challenge for the championship he cherished so dearly. Soon after, he was involved in a car accident that almost claimed his life.

'As I heard it,' recalls Thomson, 'he and a companion apparently stayed on late after a round of golf at a club in Capetown and they were returning home. At a railway crossing, Locke stopped and waited for a train to pass, but then drove across to be hit by a train coming from the other direction.' Travelling at 70 m.p.h. the train hit the driver's side of the car and dragged the crushed vehicle along the track. When emergency teams arrived on the scene Locke was given up for dead. It was a miracle he survived. He was rushed to hospital with serious head injuries and clinging feebly to life. Then, once his progress improved, there were fears he would lose the sight of at least one eye. Apart from a prolonged period of blurred vision though, Locke made a remarkable recovery. But his golf was never the same and he drifted away from the game, never winning another tournament. This was another reason why Thomson saw very little of him during the 1960s and 1970s. Locke did make a celebrity appearance here and there, including a trip to compete in the 1973 Australian Open at Royal Queensland. Thomson played in the same event, but still relations between the two remained strained and few words were exchanged.

With the passing of time their lives had changed completely; Thomson had remarried and fathered three children; Locke had put on even more weight, slipped well away from the public eye and spent most of his time living the life of an elder statesman with his wife in his homeland. And there was no truce. A once fruitful, memorable friendship had simply disintegrated.

Thomson's second wife, Mary, his intimate ally for more than thirty years and the closest observer of his moods and relationships, can fully understand how some people would interpret his manner as reserved, distant, even cold. Some say he can often be downright stubborn; refusing point blank to open up to anyone, even his wife. 'Peter copes with things very privately,' says Mary. 'He never gives the impression that anything is very difficult. He is the sort of person who doesn't show a lot of emotion and I must admit that at times I have found that difficult to deal with, but everybody has their way of dealing with things and Peter copes very well. I couldn't cope with things the way he does, but he can do it and that's great for him. He is a very controlled and strong-willed person.'

At no time was Thomson's mental control more evident to his wife than in December 1965 when doctors discovered that Arthur Thomson had a brain tumour and was given very little chance of surviving. Peter visited his father in hospital on Christmas Eve and knew that there was little hope, but he did not reveal his feelings to anyone. He drove down to Portsea where his wife and children were spending their holiday at their summer home and prepared himself for the arrival of a large group of close friends the next day for Christmas lunch.

The next morning, amidst the joyful sounds of the Thomson children unwrapping and enjoying their presents, the telephone rang. Their grandfather had passed away in the night. Peter took the call and his expression did not change. He told Mary the bad news and she immediately decided they should cancel the lunch and make the journey to Melbourne to be with Grace. Peter would have none of it. Mary was to go on preparing the lunch and they were to welcome their guests as if nothing had happened. That day none of the visitors realised, as he was enjoying their company and laughing at their jokes, that their host had lost his father only hours before. It was not until they had all departed that Peter, Mary and the children travelled to Melbourne to be with Peter's mother, and that Mary was able to reveal the bad news to those outside the family.

As a successful professional golfer, one who had left the family home at age 19 to travel the world, who had been twice married and had raised four children, and had rigorously pursued self-improvement and excellence throughout his life, it stood out that the one area of neglect was his own backyard. Thomson had nowhere near as much contact with his parents and brothers during the 1960s as he would have liked and it remains a source of much regret. And then, in the year that he was receiving the acclamation of the sporting world for his fifth British Open victory, his father had died. The irony was not lost on such a deep thinker as Peter Thomson. In the following weeks at home, when the public mask was removed, he was shattered by his father's death, intensely affected by the passing of a loved one that he did not know as well as he thought he should have. Throughout it all, the tragedy was never allowed to pervade his outward manner.

On 9 March 1987 Arthur D'Arcy Locke died of heart failure in Johannesburg. It would have been a truly tragic finale had two of the finest golfers the world had ever seen not been able to put aside their differences. Happily, just a few weeks before, Thomson had bumped into Locke at a Seniors tournament in Sun City, Bophuthatswana. He says Locke was 'very amiable'. The South African, then 69, had been playing in the pro-am section of the event and their paths crossed at a cocktail party that evening. Thomson took particular note that Locke was drinking orange juice that night, and he says they had 'a nice chat'. A quiet corner of the room was nigh impossible for the holders between them of nine British Open titles, but they managed to talk privately, openly and without dragging up too much of the past. Why Locke felt so strongly about Thomson and his ability during the 1950s is something that he never revealed in any depth, but many of those close to the pair believe that Locke came to consider the young man a perfect protégé: he could play stunning golf and, more importantly, was not American or European. Just as puzzling was why Thomson, of all people, managed to penetrate Locke's enigmatic personality. There is no question Locke and Thomson differed in many ways. Thomson is not an extrovert as Locke was; he is not a drinker or renowned fabulist as Locke was. They had different ideas on health, fitness and relationships, and on the mechanics of a golf swing. Yet they forged remarkable playing careers, inspired and stimulated by competing not against other golfers, but against each other. They lifted each other, improved each other, and ultimately locked horns over an issue that could only be resolved by some mutual concession of guilt. It was a classic case of opposites attracting; both men almost obsessed by their individuality.

That Sun City cocktail party was the last time Thomson saw Bobby Locke alive. Just a few weeks later, eight months short of his 70th birthday, the king of South African golf died of heart failure. Thomson was glad they'd been able to resolve their differences finally. He was also deeply saddened by the passing of one who had been an immense influence on his golf and his personality. Although he would never allow sentiment to shake his equilibrium, Thomson was the first to concede that as a man, Arthur D'Arcy Locke was something of a puzzle. As a player though, he made a vast contribution to the shaping of Peter Thomson.

CHAPTER 3

Good Ol' Uncle Sam

THE professional golf circuit in the United States has more than its share of paradoxes, reflected not simply in the variety of shapes and sizes to be found on the fairways. It's true that in the space of just half an hour it's possible to watch the style of the walking-thermometer that is Paul Azinger; the glamorous, Adonis-like power of Greg Norman; the clean-cut, no-frills manner of Curtis Strange; the blatant podginess of Craig Stadler; the clothes-horse that is Payne Stewart; and the wiry coiled-spring of Corey Pavin, who would not seem out of place waiting on tables at a Mexican restaurant. Their names could fill a zoo — there's a bear, a walrus and a shark. From the outside it seems the very pinnacle, one of the most envied, highly publicised and truly elite ways of earning a dollar; nothing more than a leisurely, luxurious romp to riches for the smart, sun-tanned player who doesn't need to win to be rewarded with sums other sporting people can only dream about; and it is all achieved on lush courses in the peak of condition and not in some cold, concrete stadium. The tour progresses at such a pace that players hardly seem to raise a sweat, let alone place their bodies in any form of personal danger. The tour has the image of a social gathering; a picnic; a stroll in the park.

For all its glamour, professional golf in the United States for the majority of those who play it is more like a soul-destroying struggle. For every household name that has surfaced over the years, there are countless people who have not. Few players come to terms with the endless travel and grind of tournament after tournament, city after city. If he is at odds with his swing, his putter or his private life, a player's head begins to spin from the itinerant lifestyle and every event begins to look depressingly alike. Players who boldly farewelled loved ones with the intention of returning home wealthy have ended up with nothing but familiarity with airline travel or hotel accommodation.

In January 1950 Peter Thomson made his first ambitious assault on the US tour, planning a three-month stint that would begin with the popular Bing Crosby pro-am on California's Monterey Peninsula and, all being well, finish with a strong performance in the US Masters at Augusta National. 'I am taking the same step that Jim Ferrier, Norman von Nida, Bobby Locke and Henry Cotton took when they reached the same stage in their careers,' said a confident youngster on the eve of his departure. 'My trip is purely for the experience, but after the big names have taken their share of the spoils, I will try to pick up what is left.'

There was not a lot left. Within three weeks Thomson had abandoned his trip and was making a beeline for home without a cent of prizemoney. Such a setback for a player barely 20 years old and technically still an assistant professional could have caused irreparable damage but Thomson had too much strength to be affected in the way other juniors had before him. He always looked for the positive side of things.

From the outset it seemed Thomson's debut in the US was doomed to failure. Even his close friends say one of his biggest foibles is his lack of detailed planning. On this occasion, alone and uncertain, he flew from Sydney with just a single golf club, a small amount of money and an important letter tucked safely in his coat pocket. The club was an aluminium putter given to him by Norman von Nida — a new set would be waiting in San Francisco courtesy of Jim Ferrier. The letter, written by George Naismith, was an open introduction to any of the numerous players Naismith had befriended on a tour of California in 1936 as a member of an Australian PGA team. Naismith wanted to do 'everything possible' to help the lad's career and was hoping his buddies in the States would take good care of Thomson.

First stop was the Bing Crosby pro-am, which attracted the cream of American pro golfers, the biggest celebrities from the entertainment world and, naturally, huge galleries. Three famous courses were used for each of the tournament's three rounds, all nestled in the foothills of the Santa Lucia mountains. The famous crooner himself put up the prizemoney of US$10,000 and the gatetakings were donated to charity. There was a carnival atmosphere and claiming much of the attention was none other than Ben Hogan, the man with the blocked-off main artery, making a ruthlessly determined comeback after a near-fatal road accident. There, rubbing shoulders with the stars, was the boy from Brunswick. At the end of the first day he was introduced to Harry Lillis Crosby, universally known as 'Bing', who said he was very pleased to meet the lad from down under. Later all the players were invited to Crosby's home for a lavish party where there were introductions to Bob Hope, Esther Williams,

Phil Harris, Randolph Scott and Johnny Weismuller, of whom he had previously only heard or seen on the big screen back at the Waratah Theatre in Ascot Vale. For the first time since he'd picked up a golf club, Thomson was finding it difficult to concentrate purely on his game.

'As far as the tournament was concerned,' he recalls, 'I landed far too near the event and I was very, very jet-lagged and in a daze for quite some time. It was my first experience at that sort of thing and nobody advised me to get there early enough to be able to recover from it in time. I was asleep when I should have been awake, and vice-versa. Also I was foolish enough to take off from home without any clubs, relying on the ones Jim Ferrier was arranging for me and I really had a bad time with them.'

Thomson's first round in the US was at Cypress Point (another Dr Mackenzie creation), teeing off at 7.20 a.m., on fairways so frosty 'they snapped under your feet as you walked'. He carded an 80. Typically, he did his best to make light of the poor start, especially when he plopped his ball into the surging waters of the Pacific Ocean from the 16th tee, set on one promontory of rock and the green on another. The famous par-3 of 210 metres can lay claim to being the most photographed hole in world golf and represents a supreme challenge; all carry across water, rocks and scores of wallowing seals. Thomson found the mammals 'most distracting and one trumpeted when I was halfway through my downswing. I was assured that he was not trained! Certainly I was disappointed with my 80, but when Hogan came in with a 75 I was happy.' He was also pleased with his closing rounds. He missed out on the prizemoney but carded 80–72–75 (227) to finish tied for 32nd, 13 strokes behind the winner, Sam Snead. The following week there was another US$10,000 event, this one 72-holes, at Long Beach, California. 'I expect to do better in this one,' he said on arrival. 'I'll have the chance to practise on the course and get used to my new clubs.' But his score was no better. It was off to Phoenix, Arizona, and another US$10,000 tournament, officially dedicated to Hogan's comeback, simply called 'The Ben Hogan Open'. Jimmy Demaret scorched around the layout with a course record 64 to start, while Thomson began with a 73, saying the narrow Phoenix fairways contributed to 'the toughest golf course I have seen'. When asked by a local reporter if it was the big crowds that were bothering him, he replied: 'No, because they don't follow me!' Demaret won with a score of 269 and Thomson's best American performance of 73–71–70–70 (284) was only good enough for equal 26th, still out of the money. That's when he decided to head for home.

'I realised the standard I would have to attain to survive and I was well aware I wasn't at that standard,' he says. 'Also, I wasn't equipped in the way I wanted to be, so I had really no alternative but to back off and give myself time to get organised. I knew that emotional security was absolutely necessary for any golfer who tackled a fiercely competitive circuit like the US one.'

For the next two years Thomson's visits to the United States were deliberately brief as he worked on that emotional security by improving his game on the British and Australasian tours, and by marrying his long-time girlfriend Lois. No one was surprised when they were engaged soon after Thomson's apprenticeship concluded, and in April 1952, well before the British Open triumphs and the millions, and years before any of Peter's friends chose to take such a step, he and Lois were wed at St John's Church in Warrnambool and afterwards celebrated at a large reception at the Brauer residence. They made the perfect couple: Peter, a level-headed professional bound for a glorious future, and Lois, a beautiful, charming daughter of a well-to-do doctor, prepared to sacrifice her nursing career to support her husband.

From the outset their marriage was under enormous strain. Peter's bride was very young; just as his mother had been when she married Arthur. The difference, though, was that Arthur was not required to travel the world to earn a living. Three days after their wedding the newlyweds flew to London for a brief honeymoon before Peter resumed his professional career, and for the remainder of the marriage their most familiar meeting ground seemed to be hotels, golf clubs or airport terminals. On their first trip to Britain, Lois became pregnant and returned home to Warrnambool while Peter flew on to America for two tournaments. Since ending his work at Riversdale he had been continuously on the move; to Britain via Egypt, Melbourne via the USA, to New Zealand, back home for his Australian Open win, to South Africa via the Philippines, back to Melbourne, to Britain, the USA and, finally, home once more. It was little wonder that when he arrived in Australia to be met by Lois after this whirlwind first eighteen months as a full professional, Thomson muttered to reporters that he was 'very tired' and would be taking things easy for a while. Two months later he began a fitness programme designed to increase his endurance for the plan that he'd mapped out for 1953. It would be his busiest year yet, and would hinge foremost around the British Open at Carnoustie, but would include his most strenuous assault on the US circuit, beginning with his first US Masters in April.

In February 1953, several weeks before the couple were due to leave for America, Lois gave birth to a son, Byron John Thomson, in Warrnambool. Thomson was over the moon at the prospect of raising a son to carry on his name and immediately plans were rescheduled to allow them to take the infant to the United States with them. To Peter, the family picture seemed complete – he knew it would be difficult for Lois and himself to cope with the responsibility of travelling a strange country with a baby at their side — but as far as he was concerned it would be a wonderful experience for them all. If he could be happy playing golf and successful golf, while at the same time making sure Lois and their son were content to be tagging along, it would go a long way to laying the groundwork for future tours. Memories of the United States would always seem that much sweeter if this trip would only work out smoothly.

Thomson was confident it would. Buoyed by bringing his first child into the world, and a boy at that, the future seemed all so exciting. Suddenly and cruelly, within two short weeks, Peter and Lois were dealt a devastating blow. Baby Byron died of sudden infant death syndrome, or cot death.

The shock was traumatic; it had to be put out of mind. Never was Thomson's self-control put through such a stringent test. He reacted as any normal father would and his immediate response was, 'why me — why us?' But calling on the control that was to become his most familiar trait, he kept his emotions barricaded within and saw absolutely no sense in dwelling on what might have been. With a singleminded determination, he comforted his wife, one who could never come up with the answers as readily as he, and Peter placed his son's death firmly behind him and pursued his goal of conquering America. That was the future. A shattered Lois clearly needed more time to recover, but she thought the US trip would at least take her mind away from the memory.

The tour was always going to be an extremely difficult and testing one, after such an experience, and it showed at the US Masters. Completely out of touch and lacking concentration on the notoriously slick Augusta greens, Thomson three-putted no less than five greens during his opening round and eventually completed a 'miserable' Masters, tied for 32nd place, 26 strokes behind Ben Hogan with rounds of 77–76–73–74. To make matters worse, the Thomsons thought they'd lost all their travellers' cheques and money. The word went out and the local pros showed their generosity by passing around the hat and starting a fund, but the young couple returned to their hotel room to find the missing dollars hidden in a suitcase. They were 'terribly embarrassed' over the whole affair. From the depression of Augusta they journeyed north-east to Virginia for the next tour event and despite squeezing into joint-12th placing with a score of 275, the prize of US$190 hardly covered expenses. When Peter and Lois returned to their hotel a tough decision had to be made. It had been a very difficult year for them. Thomson realised he'd grown away from his youthful Brunswick days and no longer kept in touch with his close friends; he'd lost his first child; for the first time since he'd chosen to turn professional he was feeling despair; and probably most significant, he was not playing the brand of golf he knew he could. Together, Lois and Peter discussed packing it all in and heading home once more to take stock and begin their married life anew. It seemed like an ideal time to make a move: there was a two-week break in the US circuit. The fighter surfaced in Thomson. He'd heard of a big money tournament to be staged the following week in Mexico City. It would require an outlay of at least a third of the Thomsons' remaining funds, but they decided to give it a try and hoped for a drastic change of luck. It all turned out wonderfully well.

'I played the first two rounds with Ben Hogan, finished fourth and earned $1,500 which paid the air fares and expenses and left quite a profit. I was getting the hang of winning money in America.'

It is quite conceivable Peter and Lois would not have remained in America had the local professionals not been so kind and helpful to them. Players like Jimmy Demaret, Johnny Bulla, 'Dutch' Harrison and Jackie Burke knew that Thomson and his young wife were taking tentative steps on their soil and did their utmost to make them feel at home. Thomson has never forgotten this, nor the influence of the great Ben Hogan.

Like most players on the tour Thomson had a deep respect for the seemingly aloof Hogan, but he came to know Hogan better than most players on the tour. He was able to observe closely the personality of the man once voted the greatest golfer ever. 'He wasn't very talkative on the golf course, which was quite understandable, but he wasn't even talkative afterwards in the locker room,' recalls Thomson. 'After a while though, I found him to be a very friendly and polite man and I got to know him well.' It was true that among his fellow players, 'Bantam Ben' had the reputation of a dour, humourless man who pursued golfing perfection relentlessly. He had an almost fanatical attitude to competition and success, but after they came to know each other, Thomson got to know Hogan's surprising sense of humour and, much to the Australian's delight, he discovered it was very similar to his own. There was the story from Claude Harmon, the 1948 US Masters champion. They were playing together in front of a large crowd at Augusta one day, when at the short 12th, Hogan played his ball to within 10 feet of the flag. Harmon stepped up and hit a superb shot over the creek guarding the front of the green and watched his ball bite hard, and skip neatly into the cup. The roar was heard back at the clubhouse and while Harmon and the crowd showed their glee, the expression on Hogan's face did not change. He didn't say a word. Harmon walked up and picked his ball out of the cup to more applause as Hogan diligently lined up his putt, then knocked it into the hole. The pair walked to the 13th tee and still there was no comment from Hogan. It was only after both had played their drives and were walking down the fairway that Harmon noticed out of the corner of his eye Hogan moving up beside him. 'Ah, at last,' he thought, 'he's going to congratulate me for my hole-in-one.' He was wrong. 'You know

Claude,' said Hogan with deadpan delivery, 'that was the first time I've ever birdied that hole.' And then he walked off!

Hogan was once the guest speaker at a golfing dinner when the subject of his much publicised quest for playing perfection was raised. 'The other night I went to bed and dreamt about a round where I had 17 ones and a two,' he said. 'And when I woke up — gee I was mad with myself!' Then there was the time the first pro tournament was played on Pinehurst's legendary No. 2 course and Hogan won. One of the world's finest golf course designers, Donald Ross, was responsible for creating the layout and on hearing of Hogan's triumph sent him a brief cable saying: 'Excellent, the greatest.' Hogan cabled back: 'Undeserving of such praise.' Ross sent another cable: 'I meant the course.' Hogan cabled back: 'So did I.'

It is no coincidence that Peter Thomson's name is engraved on the British Open trophy immediately below that of Ben Hogan's. As he vividly remembers, playing alongside the legend for those first two rounds in Mexico City in early 1953 was 'probably the best thing that ever happened to me'.

The trauma of his son's death and the depressing beginning to the tour had been put at the back of his mind. Hogan was in a class of his own in world golf that year, and in his only appearance in the British Open came up with the perfect answer to whether he could win on a totally different course to that on which he'd been weaned in the US. After memorable victories in the US Masters and US Open, he chiseled his name into the record books by conquering links golf and the small ball at his first attempt — and again, right there watching it all, this time from the group behind, was Peter Thomson. The tragedy of the previous months had well and truly melted into the British summer and, with Lois improving each day, his life was now back on track. 'By that stage I'd played quite a few events in the US so I felt comfortable with my game, but I'd also seen Hogan many times and seen how really good he was, and I had no thought that I would be able to beat him at Carnoustie,' he says. 'I was simply confident of doing well, so I tried my hardest and in the end, that was good enough for a second place tie. I saw a good deal of Hogan's finishing holes and was greatly impressed by the way he handled himself. I thought he played beautifully under what were, for him, strange circumstances.'

When his mighty career came to a close with nine majors and 62 tour wins in America, Hogan said: 'I had a mental blueprint for every hole of every tournament that took into account distance, lie, weather — even the grain of the grass. Hole by hole I would move my ball into a predetermined position. My score was a result of following the plan.' Thomson learnt that preparation was as vital in a round of golf as the play.

'Hogan's play set standards which I've found no other golfer has equalled,' says Thomson. 'Professional golfers don't rate a man's performance wholly by the number of putts he sinks or the long drives he makes. Firstly, consideration is given to how many bad shots he has played in any one round. Hogan could go a whole tournament of 72 holes and not play one shot that could be called in any way a bad one.'

As much as he was in awe of Hogan and believes him to be the finest player he has ever seen, Thomson rates another American a very close second and, as far as an influence off the golf course is concerned, even greater. In Thomson's mind, Samuel Jackson Snead, 'will forever remain my golfing idol'.

In 1952 when they first met, Snead, with one of the most envied swings in the history of the game, had already won six majors including that year's US Masters. It was expected that he would at least double that tally before his days were over, but with his seventh major, the 1954 US Masters, the well ran dry. Not that Snead was no longer a dominant player — quite the reverse. Dogged by bad luck and afflicted with the most pathetic attack of the shakes whenever he stood over a holeable putt, he found the major titles agonisingly out of his grasp. Yet he can still lay claim to being the most 'durable' of the greats and in terms of longevity, the greatest ever. Between 1936 and 1965 Snead won a staggering 84 tournaments on the American tour. No one, not even Jack Nicklaus, has won more. As late as 1979 'Slammin Sammy' became the first player to equal, then beat his age in a US tour event when he had 67–66 in the Quad Cities tournament, at the age of 67.

The mere mention of Snead's name and Thomson flashes a warm smile. It is clearly a subject he revels in discussing. You can almost sense his heartbeat increasing. 'Like the classic plays and symphonies he doesn't just belong to a generation,' he says. 'His mark will be left on golf into eternity. He loved to play golf with a passion and never got sick of it. Even when earning his fees I never saw him yawn or become bored. I have never believed that golf is just swinging, or vice-versa, but Snead brought a grace and artistry to golf that lifted it out of the tradesman's craft. Watching him win tournaments was not just watching a man at his work; to see him perform was to see poetry in motion.' In Thomson's mind 'Uncle Sam' was the consummate professional golfer. There was an enormous amount to be learned about golf; golf in America; professional golf in America, simply by chatting to Snead. And, as Thomson discovered, Snead loved to chat. 'With Hogan it was different because he kept things pretty much to himself, and the way to learn was to observe,' says Peter. 'With Snead you could listen as well as observe. In my days on the American circuit I used to room with Snead when accommodation was scarce. He would allow me in with him because I drank very little, I didn't smoke and I was happy to retire early, the same as him, so he reckoned I was a good room-mate. Sam was a particularly fit man. Waking in the morning he could sit up and touch his toes with his legs straight without any difficulty. He could also kick his foot up to touch the doorway above his head and show no strain at all. This fitness had a lot to do with the beautifully powered swing he had. Undoubtedly I learnt about his way of success from the many conversations we had. When he played in tournaments and he played them seriously, he seldom extended himself, planning to hit the fairway with his tee shot and rely on accuracy for his score.'

Sam Snead nearing his 80s still lives in the town in Virginia where he was born, and delights in relating the story of his doctor, who recently told him: 'You know you're a damn freak, don't you Sam?' He rarely plays golf these days, even senior tournaments, and in 1990 spent his first winter in his home town since 1935. His memory though, remains remarkably clear. Of Hogan's US Open win Snead said, 'Yup, that's right. He won one tournament in 1950 and I won eleven and he got golfer of the year. That year I played 96 straight rounds and averaged 69.2!' There's possibly no one on earth who loves golf more than Sam Snead, and vividly he remembers the young 'Ahssy' on the US tour in the 1950s.

'Peter was and is his own man, which is somethin' I think every man should be,' he said. 'On tour he was always a jolly fellow and always nice to the people and I know he liked the pros over here — I never saw him not get along with anybody. He was a nice guy to get along with and to play with. I thought he was one of the better foreign players that I met. He liked a good joke and a huge grin would break across his face and he'd just kind of walk off laughin' to himself. He was a regular guy. As a player, I would say Peter wasn't a real super-dooper type, but hell, he was the next best thing to it. I played a lot of golf with him and I never, ever saw one thing that he needed to brush up on. He was what I call a 'heady' player — he used his noggin a bit more than most of them. I was paired with him quite a bit. He didn't do anything that you'd call very spectacular but he was very straight and he thought his shots out. I really liked the way he handled himself on the course.'

The friendship between the two developed to such an extent that in May 1972 Thomson was 'overjoyed' when paired with Snead in the final round of the Chunichi Crowns tournament in Japan. 'I went into the final round five shots ahead and with a pack of hounds on my heels, eager to bring me down,' says Thomson. 'It's in circumstances like these that a man gets tinges of anxiety — what if I should make a mess of it? With the great man for a playing partner I could not have asked for better luck. I had never played a poor round with him in twenty years. How could I, with such a marvellous example beside me? I struck only two bad shots in that whole round, had a 66, and won by six shots. But he was the marvel. He was nearing 60 but there was the same spring in his step and twinkle in his eye. It was the majesty of his golf that set my young heart aflame twenty years before. Since then he has been my constant idol. Whenever I got into a tangle with my play I'd think of him and his superb rhythm, perfect stance and balance. Then, mentally restored, I would find myself too. It never failed to work.'

Eighteen months after the thrill at Osaka, Thomson and Snead were standing together on the 1st tee again, this time in Melbourne for an exhibition at the Yarra Yarra Golf Club arranged by Thomson. Ten thousand people turned up to watch Thomson glide around in 67 to Snead's 72. 'Yeah, I remember that,' says Snead. 'He kicked my ass!' As the hometown hero stated: 'If we forget his tribulations on the greens he gave us an astonishing performance.' Snead, at 61, played near faultless golf from tee to green and at the par-5 9th hole, a searching 528 yards, the veteran smoked two drivers to the edge of the green. 'I know of no other golfer, past or present, who could have done such a thing with such grace and power,' marvelled Thomson.

Of the things that made the biggest impact on Thomson, it was perhaps not Snead's play but his nature. In the mid-1950s when he was in his impressionable 20s, Thomson appreciated Snead's honesty and strength of character and, as someone who always spoke his mind, the youngster struck a chord with the American. 'I believe Snead to be a most misunderstood figure,' he says. 'One thing he has never been is an actor. He always calls a spade a spade, no matter whose corns were stood on. Naturally a lot of people were offended by Snead, but a lot of people openly admired the man for speaking his mind. Compared with the ever-smiling, ever-acting public-relations-conscious opposites, Snead's candid attitude was refreshingly honest.' Thomson could almost have been talking about himself.

Another parallel in their lives was that both men failed to win a US Open. While this was made more of an issue in Snead's career, the truth of it is that their influence on world golf extends far beyond arithmetical and statistical claims. Snead never won the biggest prize in American golf and the media never let him forget it: he is the finest golfer never to triumph. He was runner-up in 1937, 1947 (losing the play-off by a stroke), 1949 and 1953, and in 1939 took eight at the final hole when a five would have been enough to win. He was also third in 1955. It has been said countless times that Thomson never won a US Open because he disliked the American version of golf, with its lush, watered fairways, soft greens, manicured bunkers and massive prizemoney. When he questioned things like the introduction of rules officials, the big ball, yardage charts and events like the Masters and the defunct World Championship at Chicago's Tam O'Shanter, and then you look at the record books to discover he won only a single tournament in the US, it's easy to conclude that Thomson did not at all enjoy his time there. The truth is, however, that Thomson received great pleasure from his trips to America. As an international player he had every right to express his opinion; he was genuinely concerned about the welfare of the game in America and did not dislike the country or her people.

It wasn't only players of the calibre of Snead, Hogan, Burke, Harrison and Bulla who were impressed by Thomson's easy-going, pleasant disposition. American golf writers openly showed support and in August 1954 named him with Gene Littler and Bob Toski as the three 'hottest young tournament professionals in the United States'. Another scribe wrote: 'Nothing bothers him. A photographer not versed in the ways of golf, snapped his picture while he was putting on the 15th green, but Thomson was not at all upset. I believe he's one of the most interesting golfers playing at the moment.' Another publication praised him as 'a world traveller with a keen judgement of how a professional golfer with ambition to become a world-wide figure in the game should develop his career. He is not money mad. He has a fine sensitivity for respective values in golf. The golfing world is his universe and he plays where the titles and not the purses are the biggest.' One of Thomson's closest friends was Jimmy Demaret, winner of the US Masters in 1940, 1947 and 1950. The popular Demaret was instrumental in getting the Australian a start at Augusta and introduced him to some of the most influential people there. 'He was like a father to me and saw that I didn't want for anything,' states Thomson. 'It was an early lesson in just how kind those people could be.'

The Masters, which made the legend of Sam Snead, also made a big impression on Peter Thomson. When it started in 1934 it was no more than a gathering of a few old friends of Bobby Jones on a magnificent course he'd co-designed with the renowned Dr Mackenzie. Indeed, to create some local interest in the inaugural Masters, Jones himself came out of retirement to play, though the first champion was Horton Smith, who was promptly made an honorary member of a club with one of the smallest and most exclusive memberships in the world. 'When I first was there the club had no fewer than 85 members,' says Thomson, 'with the famous Bobby Jones as president. I was fascinated to meet him. He was most anxious to talk about British golf and the British courses where he had achieved a great deal of his fame. He still recalled quite vividly the various holes and courses he had played.' In 1935 Jones's exclusive tournament received massive publicity when Gene Sarazen holed a perfectly struck wooden approach for an albatross two at the par-5 15th on his way to a stunning victory. The event has never looked back. Soon after the second world war it gained the status of a 'major' even though it was played on the same course each year. 'There is no golf tournament in the world that carries more ballyhoo than the Masters,' Thomson has written. 'It's the greatest private sporting event in the world.'

These days admission is by advance ticket sales only, while such is the television coverage that even those who have never been to Augusta are familiar with the azaleas and dogwood that highlight the sheer beauty of a layout sculpted from land that was once a plant nursery. Aside from the ubiquitous logos on the players' shirts, visors and bags, no advertising is allowed on the course. Once a spectator has managed to buy a ticket (it has been said that it is easier to obtain dinner at the White House), he or she may like to purchase a drink in a forest green tumbler or sandwiches wrapped in forest green paper and a forest green napkin. If any rubbish should find its way to Augusta's hallowed turf, it will thus be less obtrusive until the ever-present garbologist can spike it into his forest green carry bag.

'I think Augusta National is magnificent,' says Thomson. 'It's a very fine golf course on an unusual piece of land, but as far as the tournament is concerned, well, when I was there I saw it as a very clever piece of promotion by a master planner, New York financier Clifford Roberts [co-founder of the Masters with Bobby Jones], who hit upon the trick of spoiling the journalists. Each golf writer would convince his editor that he had to attend this particular event as it was a very important tournament, when really it wasn't so big at all; at least not until Hogan and Snead started winning it. It became big because every golf writer said it was important. In the first years I went it was a very cosy sort of semi-private arrangement. An elite group went to play and an elite group went to watch and although the authorities of the game support the US Masters, it's not run by them. It's run by the club. The Masters certainly was innovative; they had the first leader board that I ever saw and they invented the concept of rules officials. Cliff Roberts made the decision to put his band of green jacketed members to some use, standing them at various points along Rae's Greek to watch that his invited friends obeyed the Rules of Golf. Now, we find that no championship passes without the deplorable spectacle of some player, famed or otherwise, stopping in the middle of play to call in someone with an armband to tell him how to proceed. Rules officials have become standard procedure for big tournaments everywhere and I disapprove of them strongly. We shouldn't have policemen. We don't need them. Golf is perhaps the only sport that doesn't and that's something precious. It has always been a game of honour and a player should be able to make up his own mind. I was brought up in golf to believe that the bad breaks in the course of a game were a test of character and honesty, and that in this game it was possible to meet men one could admire; men who could meet adversity with a smile while trying their utmost to overcome it. The only time a player should ever feel the need to consult an outside agency is when there is doubt about a position. For instance, whether a ball is in bounds or out; in a water hazard or out. In my view that's the only time you need an official to adjudicate. I must admit I got quite a surprise when I saw these men in green jackets holding up play by enforcing rules at Augusta, but that's where they came from.'

The Masters is certainly unique indeed, but another event Thomson found had a character all its own was May's 'World Championship'. The event no longer exists, but its creator George S. May was largely credited with transforming professional golf into the spectator sport that it now is in the US, and therefore it can be argued, he influenced the world over. It all began in 1937 when May, most likely inspired by the success of the Masters, bought the Tam O'Shanter club outside Chicago. 'George S. May had a firm involved in business efficiency,' says Thomson. 'And in those days I suppose there was a fair amount of bluff and showmanship involved in that sort of work, and that was May all right!' In 1940 May asked, 'What is the biggest prize in golf?' On discovering it was the US$10,000 offered in the Miami Open, he said: 'I will give $11,000.' Within a few years he'd built an annual ten-day carnival which drew the biggest crowds in the game's history and for which the total prizemoney reached a staggering US$212,000. There were three different tournaments over the ten days. On Thursday to Sunday there was 'The All-American Championship' for professional and amateur men and women and a minor share of the purse. Then on the following Tuesday and Wednesday eight American male pros would play eight foreigners in singles matchplay for the 'International Cup', each participant receiving a set fee of US$500. The 'real' event began on Thursday, through to Sunday, again featuring men and women, pro and amateur. The winner of the men's pro section would collect US$50,000 cash, plus a contract for a minimum of 55 exhibitions at US$1,000 each, plus transportation and expenses, plus an option of 50 additional exhibitions at US$1,000 each, plus expenses, plus US$1,000 for his caddy!

Thomson first competed at the Tam O'Shanter in 1951 when he and Norman von Nida, Kel Nagle and Eric Cremin stopped off on their way home from Britain. Thomson was amazed at the venue for the world's richest tournament. There were twenty-seven 'one-armed bandits' or poker-machines dotted about the course. There was a telephone on every tee. Members could be located on the course at any time, or could stop to put in a call to ascertain the state of the stockmarket, or to explain to their wives they would be delayed. 'Doctors, undertakers and other professional men,' boasted the club brochure, 'find this service to be very valuable.' Elevator music, or 'muzak' was piped into the dining-room, locker-rooms and all thirteen bars.

'The tournament was the epitome of American hype,' remembers Thomson. 'It was the first tournament of its kind to have blaring jazz music filling the air while play was in progress, and it was the first to have such huge prizes on offer. That was like a million dollars today. May insisted we wear numbers on our backsides because he thought that was a great innovation. And we wore them. I had a great big number pinned to my trousers!' The distinguished British golf writer and broadcaster, Henry Longhurst, who was later to receive 'The Walter Hagen Award' for the furtherance of golfing ties between Britain and the US, was shown around Tam O'Shanter by George S. May himself. He later wrote: 'It is in no harsh spirit that I say it represented everything in golf that I cannot stand!'

The World Championship was not everyone's cup of tea, but Thomson liked the course and, although amused by the circus atmosphere, was easily able to distance himself from it. Some of the finest golf he played in America was at Tam O'Shanter, and he almost always picked up a good prize.

Peter Thomson's Tam O'Shanter record				Prizemoney (US$)
1951	– T-33rd	World Championship	289	240
1952	– T-54th	All-American Open	293	–
	– T-65th	World Championship	305	–
1953	– T-31st	All-American Open	287	143
	– T-41st	World Championship	294	245
1954	– 3rd	All-American Open	279	2,000
	– T-6th	World Championship	280	1,900
1955	– 7th	All-American Open	284	1,120
	– T-3rd	World Championship	284	3,500
1956	– T-33rd	All-American Open	291	117
	– 4th	World Championship	278	3,000
1957	– T-16th	All-American Open	286	490
	– T-39th	World Championship	292	258

In fact Thomson came close to winning the world title. In the early stages of the final round in 1954 he found himself one shot off the lead, but could not match a blistering finish from New Jersey's Bob Toski, and faded to tie sixth. Toski finished eagle-par-par-birdie to snatch the event by a stroke from Earl Stewart and Jackie Burke. The following year came Thomson's best chance of taking out the 'world' when he took a stroke lead into the final round after scores of 71–65–70. In fact during the second round he was on target to smash Lloyd Mangrum's course record of 63. George S. May was offering an incredible US$10,000 for anyone who broke the course record and hearing Thomson was setting the course alight, immediately jumped in his red cadillac and dodged the spectators to drive out to the 15th green to remind Thomson of his chance at history. The Australian wasn't sure whether he was trying to encourage him, or that he was trying to make sure his prize stayed where it was! Thomson missed out on the record, and in the end, the title. Julius Boros claimed his second World Championship and Thomson tied for third with Gene Littler and Henry Ransom. 'I never quite pulled it off,' he says. 'But it was a course that suited me well for length and shots to the green, so I was always comfortable there.' In a way, Thomson was glad he never won first prize at Tam O'Shanter. He once wrote of the problems that plagued the 1956 winner, Ted Kroll. Not a household name, Kroll took the first prize of US$50,000 and signed a contract to play the minimum of fifty exhibitions at $1,000 each. Kroll completely disappeared from the tour for nine months until one rainy day at Fort Worth he wandered into the locker room and told a group of players, including Thomson, 'Man, have I had enough. I have played on sixty-three courses from Mexico City to Winnipeg, Canada, drunk more social whisky and given more speeches than Harry Truman ever thought of! Most places I play against the local champion. He is waiting on his home course, fit and ready for poor me, just flown in from a hundred miles away and given a 20-minute speech at a Rotary luncheon down town, and they say "go". They're murdering me. They make a fool of me every day. I'm no speechmaker,' said Kroll. 'I really don't have anything to tell 'em —just lie about how happy I am to be there and what a beautiful golf course they've got. Then I have to smile happily while they take pictures of me with the local champ who has just clobbered me. What I wouldn't give to get my wife and kids and travel this tour again!' Thomson and friends merely laughed, and knew that May's 'fabulous fortnight' of events had passed its zenith and was on the decline. The entrepreneur had tried everything except bringing elephants and clowns onto the course! The World Championship did fold soon after, but it was not through a shortage of money.

As Thomson discovered in Las Vegas, golf and money made a spectacular combination. One just had to ask 'mule-train' singer Frankie Laine, who despite a knowledge of golf that would struggle to fill the back of a postage stamp, won a phenomenal US$250,000 over three years gambling on his favourite player, Gene Littler. Players were bought in the big Calcutta pools at the Las Vegas tournament of champions and while the young Australian considered this to be a most distasteful element of the game in the US, typically, he saw the lighter side and went about his business. He was more flattered than anything when he discovered a prominent hotel owner had 'bought' him for US$13,000. 'I was his horse for the week,' he says. 'He followed me everywhere I went. He stood to win $95,000 from the pool if I came in first. He followed my footsteps hole by hole like a faithful watchdog, but his exclamations of dismay and wails of sorrow at each green were more than I could bear. I had to speak to him. "Your noises are a little disturbing. I prefer you watched from afar with a telescope." Thereafter he bit his lips until they bled and suffered in silence. Then a short, dark man with bulging cigar and stomach, slapped my back. "Come on kid, I got five on you against Middlecoff." I knew from the weight of his hand that it was $5,000 he had wagered! On the second day I was approached. The man said to me, "Are you going to try today?" "I usually do," I replied. He wasn't satisfied. "You feeling good? Can you beat Ford today?" "Depends a lot on what he does, don't you think?" said I. "Well, I'm going to go for you today. You're my boy. This is your kind of weather," referring no doubt to the 40-mile dust storm that had all but blacked out the sun. They cheered and cheered as each putt dropped or missed — either happening meant money in someone's pocket.'

Thomson was no stranger to betting on the golf course, but it was always a friendly wager in social matches; never in tournaments. As a golfer raised to believe that nothing, not even money, should be placed above the game itself he considered the high-rollers in the US diametrically opposed to the spirit of competition.

There was another aspect of golf he found distasteful — yardage cards. They were conceived in the US and Thomson found them a complete aberration. They encouraged players not to use their own judgement of the distance between their ball and the green. These days, at any tournament around the world, players are provided with a rundown of every hole and the precise distance from any spot of the fairway, to the cup. In effect, they tell the player which club he should be using. Nobody ever saw Peter Thomson deep in conference with his caddy over the shot that lay ahead, or flicking through notes to decide how far it was to the green. He fathomed the distance with his eyes and brain and then told his caddy which club he thought was appropriate. 'Jerry Barber invented them in the US in the 1950s and then Nicklaus developed them further,' he bristles. 'If it were up to me I would do away with distance markers and caddies who helpfully pace off everything. I'm amazed at the note-takers. They all take measurements from prominent landmarks and bunkers by marching it out. With this information documented it then fits a formula of club selection. I came up in an era of Locke and Hogan; Locke taught me by example much about "distance reading". He was very nearly infallible at picking the right club. He trained himself to be so. Yet I suppose that if you asked him how many yards it was to the flag he'd be hard pressed to answer. He never thought in yards — only clubs.'

One story, to Thomson's mind, sums up the sheer absurdity of studying a piece of paper in order to get a ball close to the hole. At Oak Hill in New York the Australian watched an amateur agonising over his third shot to the long 4th hole. To Thomson's amazement the youngster pulled out a sheath of foolscap paper from his bag and flicked through incredibly detailed notes on distances, pin positions and conditions. 'After he found the appropriate page he then stepped out another fifty paces forward to the green until he was opposite a large tree,' recalls Thomson. 'Now that the reckoning was made he then performed his 120-yard pitch with a 9-iron! It seemed to me that the young man growing up in golf in this modern computerised society, was making no attempt to train his eye even from pitching distance. What is it all coming to?'

Thomson was absolutely astonished by the attitude of some players on the tour; those who would let fly with an enormous drive then stride to their ball and question their caddy. A typical response would be, 'You've got 147 yards to the flag, which is eight yards from the front edge and 10 yards behind the front trap. The wind is right to left, not very strong, and the green slopes from left to right. Looks like a seven.' The player takes his 7-iron and makes his standard full swing, fading the shot against the wind and leaving an uphill putt (downhill is more difficult) for another birdie. For the experienced player this is as simple as falling off a log. There is no great challenge and golf becomes a non-thinking man's game.

It has often been argued that what prevented Thomson from more aggressively attacking the tournament scene in the US was simply an inability to drive the ball as far as the best Americans, and a lack of height in his shots. While it's true Thomson was never a big hitter, even in his prime, the fact is he never tried to be one. No matter how badly he was outdriven by his playing partners he used to take Locke's example and continue to drive for safety and position. 'Muscular strength is not particularly advantageous in golf,' he maintains. 'Control of direction pays off better than length. Unbridled power hitting from the tee courts disaster.' Thomson's tastes run to the way golf is played in Britain where the subtlety of shotmaking rather than brute force is emphasised. From the tee he prefers to drive the ball on a flat trajectory and watch it roll along fairways that are not heavily watered. 'By nature, I am a "feel" player,' he once said. 'I developed this approach out of necessity and never changed.' And then his convictions come through. 'Golf is a game of judgement, not strength. This is what its founders intended. One idea is that to sort out the better players you put them further from the target, and then the stronger men win. Is that the best test of golf?'

If anything sums up Thomson's objections to the automated robot-style of golfer produced in the US, it would be the sort of talk from

Above: Thomson tees off in his first exhibition series against Bobby Locke in South Africa, 1951.

Above: 'More fruit for the sideboard.' A happy, dapper Thomson accepts another winner's cheque.

Right: Few words were spoken when Thomson strode the fairways of America alongside the great Ben Hogan in the 1950s.

Above: Inspired by ghosts. History provides the backdrop at Thomson putts on the massive 18th green at St Andrews, 1955 Open Championship.

Opposite, top: Peter and first wife Lois outside the Royal Birkdale clubhouse after the 1954 Open Championship presentation.

Right: With his jacket returned, Thomson, and wife Mary celebrate with Kel Nagle after Nagle's win at the 1960 Open Championship at St Andrews. Nagle drank lemonade.

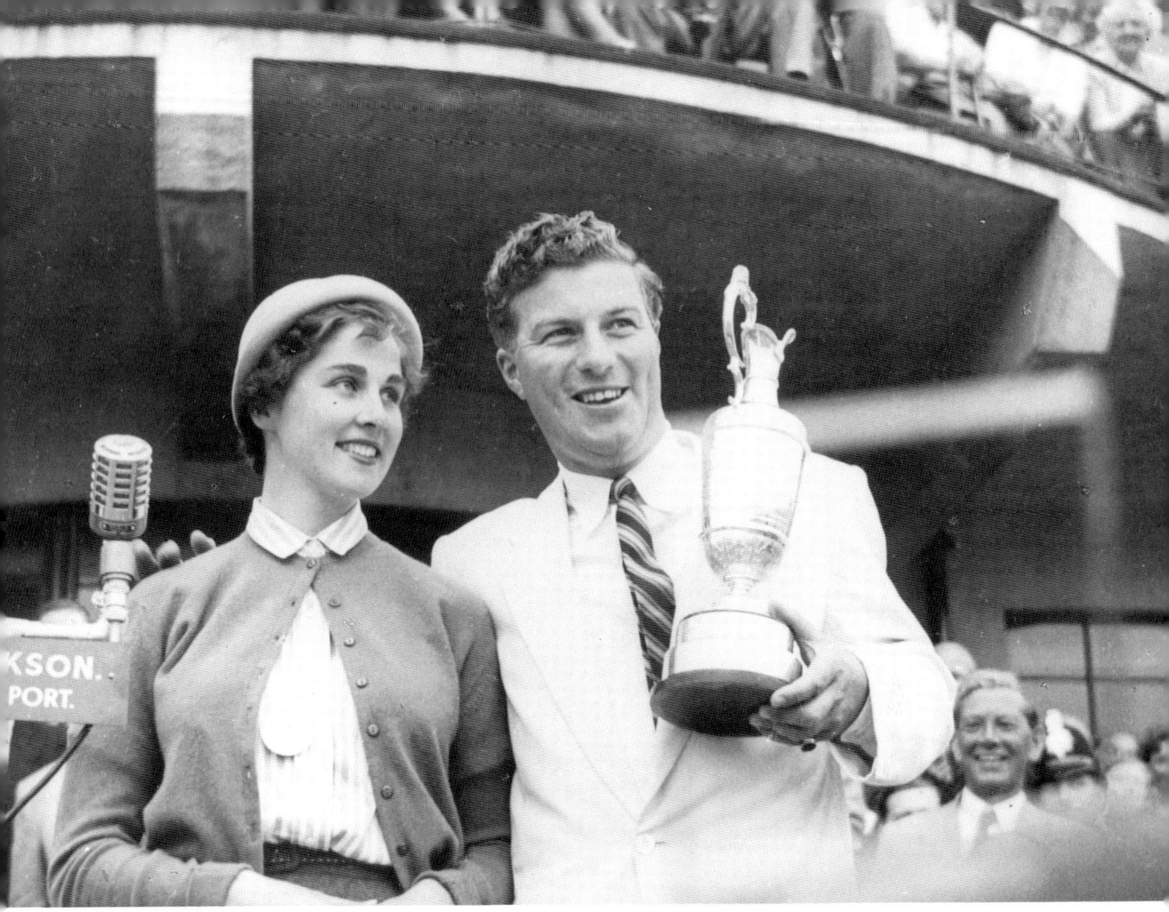
KSON.
PORT.

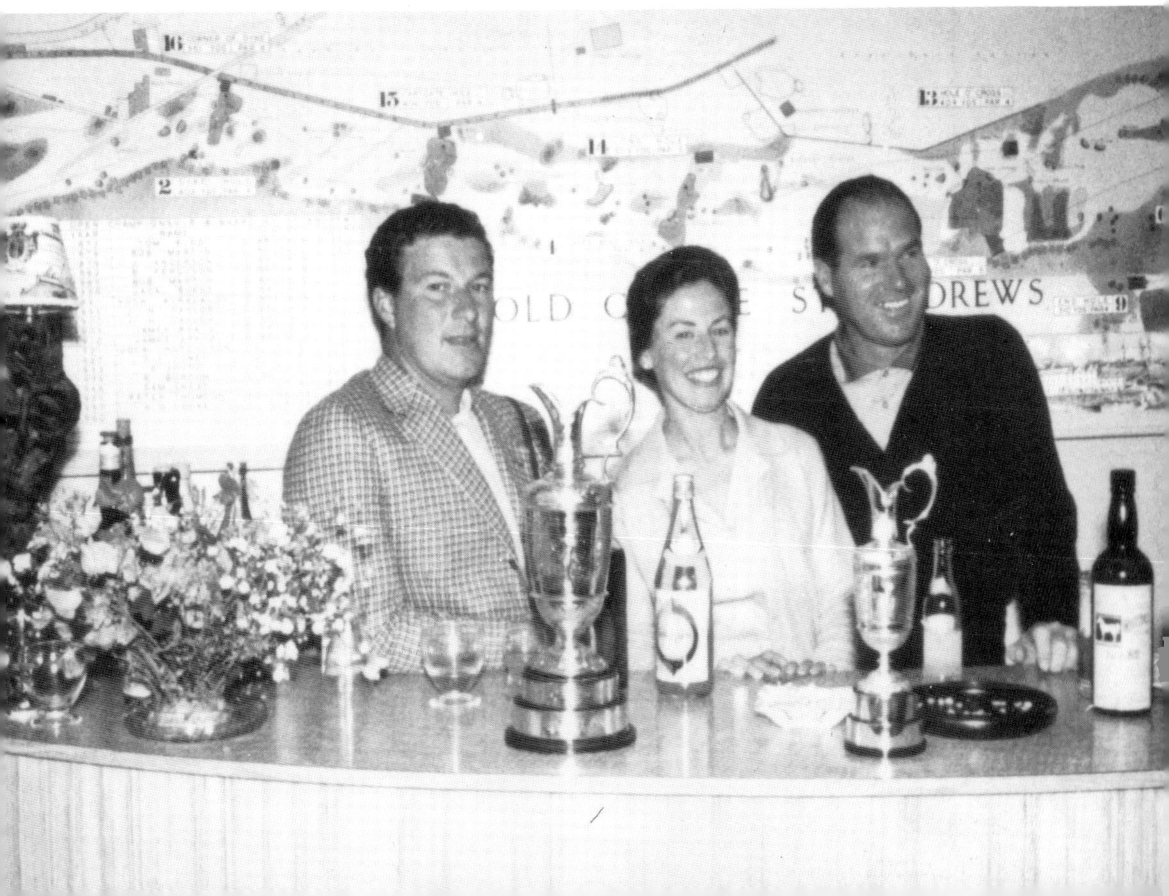
16
15
13
14
2
OLD
DREWS

Ready for another lesson around St Andrews under the watchful eye of local caddy Wallace Gillespie, PGA Matchplay championship, 1954.

On the way to victory in the final of the PGA Matchplay championship against Johnny Fallon at St Andrews, 1954.

Frank 'Fuzzy' Zoeller at the 1979 US Masters at Augusta. Zoeller, a rookie, won the title in a play-off and, while displaying admirable composure to win, calmly sat down afterwards to admit: 'I never had a thought the whole week. I figured my caddy knew the course a lot better than me, so I just put out my hand and played whatever club he put in it. I'd say, "how hard do I hit it?" He'd tell me and I'd swing.' And then there was the remarkable case of Johnny Miller. After years of misclubbing and subsequent failure, he turned up for a practice round at Augusta in the late 1970s and brought along a 100-foot tape measure. Astonishingly he proceeded laboriously to measure every inch of every hole until he was satisfied he had the course beaten. 'Man, is my right arm tired from winding and unwinding that steel tape,' he groaned. 'But I finally know the exact distance on every shot!'

To Peter Thomson American hype, and spin-offs like rules officials and yardage charts, weren't representative of traditional golf and, to make matters worse, his views further separated him from those Americans who could not come to terms with his beliefs. For many, many months he was the sole non-American on the tour. 'I can remember tournament after tournament when I was the only foreign player in the field,' he says. 'I was looked on as something of an oddity because I came from outside the United States. Bobby Locke was the first invader, but by 1953 they had seen the last of him and I was looked upon as his successor. I'm sure the players breathed a sigh of relief when they discovered I was not another Locke. The life in America was completely foreign to me and it wasn't always a happy experience, but I did get a great deal of pleasure out of it too. In those years even the top money winner like Cary Middlecoff would win no more than three times a year, even though he played over forty tournaments. The aim on that circuit was really to win money, not tournaments, and one got into the habit of playing safely for a good prize instead of taking the risks necessary to win. Most weeks I took my place in the first ten on the final list and quietly went on my way.'

While Thomson's playing record in the US says he won only a single 72-hole tournament, the truth is he never, at his peak, left American shores without an adequate share of the prizemoney. In tournament finishes between 1953–9, he was 42 times in the top-ten and in the top-five on no less than 19 occasions. He was runner-up in three tournaments in 1957: the Baton Rouge Open, the Pensacola Open and the Kentucky Derby Open. In 1956 he played only eight events, yet finished 9th on the US money list with more than US$20,000 — enough in those days to buy three average Melbourne homes! He once carded a scintillating 29 on the front nine of the arduous Quail Hollow course in Oklahoma City, a score made all the more remarkable by the fact that he did not break par on either of the par-5s. Along with his high placings at Tam O'Shanter, he was ahead for two rounds in the US Open once, but finished fourth, and was also in contention at Augusta for the Masters, again ending up with fourth prizemoney. 'I always won enough money in America to make it well worth my while,' he says. 'My friends were always fun and I used to make my headquarters for six months in Houston, Texas, where Jimmy Demaret lived. I was taken on to the staff of the McGregor Golf Company, the second biggest golf company in America. I took this to be a great honour because I was one of a group that included Demaret himself and the great Byron Nelson. These two, because of my association with the company, helped make a golfer out of me. In a way, looking back over my career I have a sense of frustration that I wasn't able to win one of the big US tournaments, but I have no regrets that I didn't win more in America. It was a pretty hard job trying to beat Snead, Hogan, Demaret, Middlecoff and all the rest of them. It was a totally different league and a different standard of play completely. Besides, winning there wouldn't have changed my life at all — my sights were always set on the British Open and I'm more than happy with my victories in that.'

The closest he came to winning a US major was in 1956. On one of the tour's toughest courses, the 6,902-yard Oak Hill Golf Club at Rochester, New York, Thomson carded brilliant rounds of 70–69 to lead the field at the halfway mark of the US Open. Again, the USGA had prepared a colossal test, particularly from the tee. Drives only had to be 10 yards off line to be gobbled up by a voracious, six-inch-deep rough. Thomson handled the conditions superbly, belting out a series of arrow-like drives, and after two rounds such names as Hogan (140), Furgol, Middlecoff, Ellis, Barber (141), Boros, Palmer and Kroll (142) were trailing in his wake. Even for a dual British Open champion there was plenty of tension at the start of the third round, but Thomson refused to be intimidated by the rarefied atmosphere. He gave promise of becoming the first Australian winner of the title by starting confidently, and through to the back nine had retained his lead with some wonderful play. Then he was harshly dealt with by Oak Hill's version of the brick wall. The notoriously brutal finishing sequence of long par-4s at 16, 17 and 18 contained a large portion of the 150 bunkers dotted around the layout. These holes leapt up to grab Thomson by the throat. With wayward driving and tentative putting there followed a rash of bogeys and he eventually signed for an ugly 75 and found himself three strokes behind the new leader, Cary Middlecoff. 'Those three holes found my weakness and eventually cost me the championship,' he says. During the last round he never gave up hope of winning, but then the USGA secretary Joe Dey entered the picture. Thomson played the final round alongside the eventual winner, Middlecoff, but with the power to inflict two-stroke penalties, Dey 'harassed' the pair for several holes. 'Dey used to run the US Open like Matt Dillon ran Dodge City,' says Thomson. 'He didn't need any deputies. If confrontations had to be made Joe walked out in the street alone, armed only with his authority.' On that final afternoon at Rochester, Dey approached Middlecoff and Thomson on the third tee and did not mince words. 'Gentlemen, you are two holes behind. Please close the gap.' Three hours later Middlecoff had won his second US Open and Thomson has often wondered whether he would have made it without the USGA secretary's imperative warning. 'There was no precedent in championship golf for a committeeman to follow players in such a way,' says Thomson. 'All that affected my bid for victory, but in golf there's no one to blame but yourself. I felt sad at having lost a great opportunity to win.' He finished with a solid round of 71 and a tie for fourth. With only Middlecoff, Boros and Hogan ahead of him, Thomson took consolation in the fact that he'd been beaten by three of the world's finest players.

1956 US Open Championship, Oak Hill, New York		
281 –	Cary Middlecoff	71–70–70–70
282	Julius Boros	71–71–71–69
	Ben Hogan	72–68–72–70
285	Peter Thomson	70–69–75–71
	Ed Furgol	71–70–73–71
	Ted Kroll	72–70–70–73
287 –	Arnold Palmer	72–70–72–73

Fourteen months later, Thomson gave an even better display at the US Masters. The experts were quick to write and broadcast that Augusta was not a course for Thomson. Yes, he'd been right up there with the game's greatest in the Open, but Augusta's 7,030-yard layout favoured the long-hitters who could draw their tee shots and manage high approaches that fell feather-like to earth and stuck beside the pins. Green jackets only went to 'thinking gorillas' and, as everyone realised, the Australian was not a thinking gorilla. Thomson was not at Augusta by accident. He'd earned his invitation, and nowhere was this spelt out more clearly than on the leader board after day one. There was Thomson with an even-par 72, and of the 117 players in the field, only Jackie Burke, the defending champion, did better with a 71. Over the next two rounds the perennial favourite Sam Snead made a move and, gunning for an unprecedented fourth Masters title to break Jimmy Demaret's record (before the days of Jack Nicklaus), was a stroke out in front with a round to go. Thomson slipped with a pair of 73s but was still handily placed four shots adrift of Snead.

In the end it made little difference. 34-year-old Doug Ford from New York, scorched home in 66 for a comfortable three-stroke win over a dejected Snead. Thomson finished with a strong 71 for his highest placing at Augusta. Fifth place turned out to be good enough for fourth prizemoney, however, since the man above him, Harvie Ward, was an amateur.

It has often been said that a player gets more recognition in America from a good performance in the Masters than he gets from a regular tour win. This was certainly the case in 1981 when Australia's Greg Norman, making his Masters debut, shot a first round 69 to share the lead, and followed with 70–72–72 for 4th place behind the winner, Tom Watson. The mass media at Augusta got the notion that Norman used to shoot sharks as a hobby in his native Queensland and he was dubbed the 'Great White Shark'. After his fourth prizemoney in 1957 Thomson didn't receive a nickname, but he also lapped up plenty of attention. Some writers went as far to suggest that it was only a matter of time before the Australian 'invader' waltzed away with one of their major titles. Indeed Thomson seemed poised on the threshold of a long and illustrious career in the US — he'd served his apprenticeship, was close friends with many of the tour's biggest names and was becoming more familiar with the American courses every day. But as he drove out of Magnolia Drive after that 1957 Masters his career on the pro circuit in the US had already reached its pinnacle.

1957 US Masters, Augusta National, Georgia			
283	–	Doug Ford	72–73–72–66
286	–	Sam Snead	72–68–74–72
287	–	Jimmy Demaret	72–70–75–70
288	–	Harvie Ward (a.)	73–71–71–73
289	–	Peter Thomson (Aus.)	72–73–73–71
290	–	Ed Furgol	73–71–72–74
291	{	Dow Finsterwald	74–74–73–70
		Jack Burke	71–72–74–74

Without question Thomson's finest achievement on the US tour came in 1956, his biggest year in America, when he broke through to the winner's circle at the Preston Hollow Golf Club, Dallas, Texas.

Back-to-back tournaments were scheduled for Dallas in late May-early June of 1956 — the Dallas Open and the event to celebrate the state's hundredth birthday, the Texas Centennial Open. The latter tournament attracted a mighty field and enormous interest with a first prize of US$14,000 up for grabs, the second largest purse ever offered in world golf. Along with the usual crowd of star names on the circuit there was Middlecoff,

Littler, the gifted Brazilian Mario Gonzalez, and the great Ben Hogan, making one of his few appearances. It was a virtual US Open field. The previous week Thomson had squeezed into a tie for 11th in the Dallas Open and admits he wasn't particularly thrilled about his chances at the Centennial. His hopes of performing well continued to plummet once the first round had started. He arrived at the course well before his 2 p.m. tee-time only to find black storm clouds hovering ominously overhead. Worse still, the leader board told him that a 65, a few 67s and numerous 69s had already been posted. When Thomson strode to the tee there was a fierce gale blowing. He tried to tee his ball, but the furious wind knocked it from its perch. Finally under way, there followed a series of disasters and his score ballooned to 39 on the front nine. There was virtually no chance of matching par, let alone catching those out in front. In a desperate bid to put some life into his round, Thomson at the 11th tee, pulled out his driver and simply had to post a birdie. Seconds later he watched as his ball scuttled from the heel of the club and bounced through an out-of-bounds fence. He dropped his head, grabbed his tee from the ground and marched from the tee. 'I told myself there would be no money coming in that week,' he recalls.

Up in the heavens the golfing gods must have felt a touch of sympathy as they looked down on Preston Hollow. As he walked down the 12th fairway, Thomson was alerted by the cries of a tournament official telling all players to mark their balls and run for cover. 'A tornado is coming through, quick!' he yelled. 'I didn't need to be asked twice,' says Thomson. 'I prayed the tornado would blow the course away!' The eye of the storm passed a few miles away and this meant that the course was lashed by a ferocious thunderstorm. As he peered out from the clubhouse window and through the torrential rain, Thomson remarked to a nearby player that he could not believe his luck. The first round was a washout and all scores were wiped.

The next day, extremely grateful for the reprieve, Thomson came out in fine conditions to score a sparkling 67 to be up with the leaders. He managed to follow that with solid efforts of 69–68, but such was the quality of the field that as he began his final round he was several shots from the lead, and given little chance by the experts of winning. Yet as he crunched his drive down the opening hole of that final round, the Australian felt 'right'. More importantly, he felt even better on the greens. Using an old hickory-shafted putter he'd exchanged with Bobby Locke for a 3-wood in South Africa a few months earlier, he out-putted everyone. He knew he was set for 'one of those days'. He grins at the recollection: 'I slipped into this delightful groove. Everything felt comfortable and I holed the majority of putts I stood over. It was an incredible feeling — as if I could do no wrong.' Less than four hours later the huge crowd surrounding Preston Hollow's 18th gave the Australian a tumultuous reception as he plucked his ball from the cup. He signed for a round of 63. It was a new course record and had catapulted him from a tie for eighth place to the very top of the leader board. As he took his position beside the 18th green, all eyes were on the British Open champion from down under. Would the local heroes ruin his memorable day?

'Anxiously I watched the leaders and saw them one by one make mistakes to finish behind me. Only Middlecoff and Littler came to the last green with a chance to beat me. And both of them missed! That made a three-way play-off necessary. There was no suggestion from Middlecoff and Littler that we split the prize. No doubt they felt they could take care of me. Like all play-offs on the American PGA circuit this was to be a sudden-death affair. The first to win a hole would take the cash. The first hole was a rather short par-5, but Littler and I missed the green and only Middlecoff was on in two. Littler made a marvellous recovery from some rough short of the green and I chipped up from the edge to within a yard. We all made four and marched to the next tee. The second hole was the worst hole that I remember seeing in America. It had a huge pecan tree slapbang in front of the green and the second shot had to be hit very high over the top of this tree to hit the green beyond it. The tree was meant to be the feature of the hole and the idea was to use your brain from the tee, so you wouldn't finish too close to it and have no hope of pitching over. Middlecoff's second shot didn't go quite high enough, rattled around in the tree and fell onto the bridge over a little creek nearby. That was the end of him.'

Now Thomson. With the crowd pressing close to the fairway and with the tension reaching fever pitch, he chose a 6-iron and merely concentrated on swinging smoothly. Placing the pressure firmly on Littler's shoulders, Thomson's approach cleared the tree and nestled safely at the back of the green — a long way from the hole, but he was on. It didn't seem as if Littler would be able to do any better from where his tee shot rested, but he was lucky. He should have ended up with Middlecoff. His ball passed through the top of the tree without touching a leaf. Littler arrived at the green to find his ball just 12 feet underneath the hole! 'My putt down the bare looking green had to be aimed at least a yard to the left,' says Thomson. 'I hit it carefully and walked off after it, hoping it would stop somewhere near the hole. As it trickled on I began to hope that it might even go in and then after what seemed like many seconds, it in fact dribbled in! There was a mighty roar from the spectators who were no doubt as surprised as I was. That roar, or the weight of the money, must have had some effect on Littler. He missed, and I was in full possession of the $14,000. The crowd was probably a bit stunned that I'd beaten the two Americans, but Middlecoff and Littler were most gracious and offered their congratulations immediately. I think they knew how importanl that win was for me.'

With birdies at both play-off holes to follow his brilliant 63, Australia's Peter Thomson, Texas Centennial winner, answered his critics. As he says modestly: 'I'll never forget how a tornado helped to win that $14,000 in Dallas.'

1956 Texas Centennial Open, Preston Hollow, Dallas		
267	Peter Thomson (Aus.)	67–69–68–63
	Cary Middlecoff	64–67–68–68
	Gene Littler	64–66–67–70

*Thomson won at second play-off hole

Those unimpressed with Thomson argue that he was an average player who defeated poor fields to win his British Opens and struggled to come to terms with golf in America's big league where it really mattered.

It is true that if you apply the crass standards of measuring a golfer's success by winnings, Thomson is not in the race. Yet the reason he was considered a lesser golfer, at least according to those in America, is because he wanted it that way. He did not play regularly in the events by which the world of golf measures the stature of players because the majority of them are American. He has always believed the 'grand-slam' of British Open, US Open, US Masters and US PGA Championship to be a media creation. He played in America because it was the richest, strongest circuit around and because it gave him an ideal build-up to his annual golfing assaults on Britain: 'I could never have won the British Open without the grounding I received in America and the toughness I developed in my time there. I saw the US tour as an ideal training ground and often tested out new clubs or aspects of my game there. Of course I would still be trying my hardest to win in America, but my main priority was the British Open. That to my mind was the pinnacle of golf, a true World Championship. While my opponent in Britain were competing in tournaments about once every three weeks in May and June, I was playing an event every week in America against the toughest competition in the world. May and June were key preparation months. After eight or ten weeks of play in the toughest of all fields, the Open seemed second-grade by comparison. The home players in Britain never realised that.'

As far as the three US majors were concerned, Thomson, back in the 1950s, simply didn't consider them majors. To start with he never once played in the US PGA Championship because he wasn't eligible. His journeys to Augusta were hardly regular because he wasn't always invited, and the US Open, admittedly a prestigious event, simply didn't figure as boldly in his mind as its British counterpart, and subsequently he played in it only half a dozen times. 'I was not a member of the United States Professional Golfers' Association,' he says, 'and back then, the US PGA Championship was strictly for members, so that was that. I never gave much credence to the Masters because it was an odd event run by the club and was played on the same course every year, so there were players suited to Augusta and they became specialists on that course. I'm not trying to say I wouldn't have gladly accepted any of these tournaments, but in those days it simply didn't occur to me that they were the big ones.' He has a distinguished ally in Sam Snead. 'By hell, we had four other tournaments that were considered majors at the time,' says Snead. 'There was the Los Angeles Open, the North and South, the Western Open, which I think should still be in there yet, and the Metropolitan. The US Open was the big one of course, but after that the rest of the tournaments were pretty much level.'

Perhaps more than anyone, Thomson was acutely aware that to succeed fully in America a foreigner had to devote himself totally to the tour. He would have had to relocate his wife and family and begin a totally different lifestyle, and it must be remembered that Thomson was the first Australian to play the entire US tour who did not move himself over there lock, stock and barrel, as Greg Norman has done in recent years. Other Australians have done it too, Bruce Crampton, Bruce Devlin, David Graham, but not Thomson. He is quick to point out that he has never been interested or tempted into living anywhere other than Australia. It has always been his home. He wasn't prepared to sacrifice that for anything — even if it meant not becoming the world's No. 1 golfer.

'I don't rank Peter as I would a Nicklaus or a Hogan or a Snead,' says Crampton. 'Simply because he didn't prove himself in the US. But I don't have any doubt in my mind at all that he could have, had he set his mind to it. If he had severed ties with Melbourne and gone over to America with a singlemindedness and purpose, I think there's no doubt we'd be mentioning him in the same breath as the others. From my standpoint there is no way I could have travelled back and forth the way he did and still been able to compete favourably with the guys in the US. I had no choice but to go over there and be one of them and stay there and compete that way.' This was one reason Thomson did not immerse himself in the mainstream of US golf. It suited Crampton's ambitions and temperament to accept the American way of golf in its entirety — become 'Americanised' if you like — and he has done very well from it, but that sort of thing was simply not up Thomson's alley. 'Peter is his own man,' says Snead. 'Nobody tells him what to do. From what I saw of him, a social life was just as important to Peter as his golf.' One of his friends said that when Thomson won the Texas Centennial, he won a trophy 'that would struggle to fit aboard the Queen Mary'. Most players would have rushed it home in cotton wool to take pride of place on the mantelpiece. Thomson gave it away soon after he was presented with it.

'People have said that Peter Thomson chose not to play in America because he wasn't good enough,' offers David Graham, the only Australian to win a US Open. 'I think that's absolute bullshit. He could have played anywhere he wanted to play and clobbered everyone. America in his time was not for everyone and it had nothing at all to do with skill. Peter was born and raised in Melbourne, was married and had a family, and to pull up all of his roots and move to the United States to play would have been an enormous commitment for someone who had already succeeded where so many others had failed. He simply did what he wanted to do.'

Thomson was a superstar in his own environment and of course he had every right to choose what that environment should be — exactly as some modern US heroes do; those who never leave the comfort and security of their own tour, even for the British Open. There was significant pressure placed upon Thomson to play in four places at once. The British naturally wanted him to play their circuit because he was a respected Open champion; Australians expected him to compete in every tournament at home because he was theirs; the Asians hoped he would continue his remarkable work setting up the Far-East tour; and the Americans expected him to compete on their tour because they thought it was the best. But Peter Thomson only did what Peter Thomson wanted to do.

Some American players and journalists openly labelled his decision to opt out of the big-time circuit as 'sour grapes' after he was disqualified from the 1959 US Masters for signing an incorrect card. Thomson sets the record straight: 'That was a bitter experience,' he says, 'but it had nothing to do with my desire to explore other places.' The Australian carded rounds of 72–74–72 in difficult conditions at Augusta and was in the top fifteen heading into the final round. Thomson never played that final round. He was back in his hotel room relaxing when the telephone rang. It was the Masters co-founder Clifford Roberts, saying that it was his unfortunate duty to disqualify him from the tournament. Thomson's astonishment quickly boiled to anger when Roberts explained what had happened. The Australian's playing partner that day was veteran Michigan pro Chick Harbert — the man beaten by Jim Ferrier in the 1947 US PGA final. He'd handed in the card at the end of the round, and Thomson, noticing the correct score of 72 had been pencilled in, gave it his authorisation by signing it. That was that. Or so he thought. 'But the scores on two holes had been interchanged,' he recalls. 'Harbert marked down a five at the 13th where I took four, and at the 17th where I had a five, he marked a four. The score added up all right, but I didn't detect the change and under the rules I was out. I completely understood Cliff's position, but I was very angry with Harbert — he'd done exactly the same thing with another foreign player before. He did not apologise to me about the matter. Once bitten, I wasn't caught again.'

Several weeks later Thomson informed the USGA he would not be competing in the US Open at Winged Foot in preference to a tournament in Britain and for some Americans this merely confirmed their suspicions. But they were wrong. The real reason Thomson chose to scale back his appearances in America drastically was because the US tour had instituted a player's ticket system.

'In the late 1950s and early 1960s the ticket system came into the US and that meant I would be restricted from playing elsewhere,' he says. 'As a foreigner it was tolerated that you could play in your own country, but you had to get permission and releases to play in other countries and that didn't suit me at all, so I made up my mind not to play in America as much as I had previously. I came back now and then, but only because I was invited to compete. It was all a rather nasty business. I think they were trying to keep out the riff-raff. Anyway, I'd reached the point where I wanted to see the rest of the world. I'd been a pro golfer for more than ten years, the British circuit was beginning to blossom and I thought that's where I should be, putting in my weight. Not long after that the Asian circuit took off and with the Australian events as well, I was wholly involved and had very little time left for the United States.'

Although Thomson did not completely cut ties with the US and for instance finished 19th in the 1961 Masters, and then sixth, seventh (twice) and ninth (twice) in following tournaments, the jibes and broadsides continued. Years later (1967), a writer for *Sports Illustrated* went as far as to pen: 'On the United States tournament tour, Thomson, a curly-haired, diffident, intelligent fellow from Melbourne, is about as popular as a shank or a 3-putt green. He is a masterful golfing technician who can hit the ball any way he wants to except far. He has won the British Open five times, but in the United States the only title he has for his efforts is the Texas Centennial Open. Somewhat bewildered by this lack of United States success he has left behind him a collection of unflattering remarks about the crude power game so popular in America and the long, heavily watered golf courses that nurture it.'

After Thomson triggered a wave of patriotism with his stunning fifth British Open win in 1965, American Mark McCormack, then manager of the so-called 'big-three' in Arnold Palmer, Jack Nicklaus and Gary Player, said that Thomson won the Open 'because Sanders left the tournament in a trap at the 10th, Nicklaus left it in the raspberries at the 37th, Palmer left it in the willow at the 59th, Devlin left it in the bunker at the 60th,

Lema left it in Chicago at the Western Open, and Gary Player (who had a stomach upset) left it in my bathtub.' He neglected to mention that Thomson also won the Open by playing outstanding golf. Actually many people believe McCormack dearly wanted Thomson to join his stable to become the fourth member of his stable of golfing thoroughbreds, and a promoter's dream for exhibition matches: Palmer-Nicklaus v. Player-Thomson; USA v. The World. There is no doubt Thomson would today be close to a billionaire in the Arnold Palmer mould if he'd accepted such an offer, but that kind of lifestyle simply did not appeal to Thomson. McCormack, a man who'd achieved just about everything he'd set his heart on in life and business, and an American, could never understand Thomson's attitude. After the Open *Sports Illustrated* said: 'To American golf enthusiasts the results of the 1965 British Open read like a list of tourist-class passengers on board the *Queen Mary*.' The article went on to describe Thomson as a 'hibernating, hay fevery Australian who says he has always been one to keep Americans at their distance'.

Golf in the US made much of this feud and it was in evidence at no lesser place than St Andrews when the inaugural 'Alcan Golfer of the Year' tournament was held in 1967. Thomson had failed to qualify for the highly select field, composed largely of Americans, and had to be content to play in a secondary event, 'The International Golf Championship', over the same course at the same time. A few days before the tournament, Thomson, for the Melbourne *Herald* wrote: 'There is every possibility that the low-scoring player will come from those of us in the lesser event. Sadly, he will not be entitled to a slice of the big cake, but obviously there will be some confusion as to who is the real Golfer of the Year.' This was not mischief-making. Thomson was highlighting the absurdity of running separate tournaments on the same course at the same time with such a discrepancy in prizemoney — £65,000 for one, £15,000 for the other. Call it his humble beginnings; a desire to see the worker rewarded; a chip on the shoulder; even frustration at not being a person able to let his emotions flow freely, but in such circumstances he found powerful inspiration and was close to unbeatable. As Peter Alliss said of him: 'As brutally tough and uncompromising as any Australian games player you could mention.'

In glittering form, Thomson rolled in a 15-foot birdie putt on St Andrews final green to finish with a final round of 68 and a total of 281 — two shots better than the men who tied for first in the Golfer of the Year, US Open champion Billy Casper and US Masters champion Gay Brewer. On receipt of his £3,000 cheque, Thomson could not let the moment pass without raising the subject. He adored such moments: 'I must say I find it a little embarrassing to have shot the low score with all these 'Golfers of the Year' here,' he fired. 'Maybe I should just be called the Golfer of the Week!' Moments later a US pro by the name of Mason Rudolph stepped up to remark that the Americans were happy to be at 'Saint Andrews' and were glad Peter Thomson had won something that week, 'since we so seldom get a chance to see him win a title on the US tour'.

The ghost of Old Tom Morris must have shuddered. It didn't end there. The following week at the Wentworth course in England, Thomson and three Americans, Casper, Brewer and Arnold Palmer, were included in the exclusive field of eight for the World Matchplay Championship. The media immediately focussed on the USA v. Thomson battle, but had to wait for the semi-finals for it to eventuate. The Australian advanced by toppling the reigning British Open champion Roberto de Vicenzo on the last hole, and then in the quarter-finals defeated Gary Player in a marvellous contest. Now he was pitted in the semi against the King of American golf, the man just a few weeks his junior, Arnold Palmer. It has been written that with a hitch and a heave and natural grace Palmer lifted the country club game of golf onto his square back, carried it to the people and made it a sport. People who weren't interested in golf were interested in Palmer. 'I like to beat anyone I'm playing, no matter who he is,' he said at Wentworth. 'But I guess you could say that all US players especially enjoy beating Peter.'

'The Americans? Oh, I imagine they like to beat me,' Thomson returned. 'But don't they like to beat everybody, even themselves?'

Thomson had already created a few sentences of golfing folklore in the World Matchplay of 1965. In the semis that year Thomson bravely withstood a spirited finish from Palmer to triumph 1-up and it grabbed the headlines. Arnie's famous finishing bursts were almost always rewarded with a glorious victory. It was as if Thomson had changed history. And delightfully, exactly two years later, they were in the same position again and the match, in atrocious conditions, was even better. If the two felt personally antagonistic it was not obvious. Any differences between the two were set aside as they attacked Wentworth, and Thomson, putting superbly despite the rain, held a 3-up lead at the 10th, but by lunchtime the match was all square and into the afternoon back nine the pair was still locked together. Then the volcano of Arnold Palmer erupted. He floated a 6-iron over trees guarding the 190-yard 10th hole and dropped the seven foot putt for birdie: 1-up. He clipped a magnificent 2-iron approach into a fierce wind at the 480-yard 12th that bounded in and slowed to a halt just four feet from the cup: 2-up. At the next, a 437-yard par-4, he punched in a 9-iron that kicked off an embankment and rolled to within inches of the cup: 3-up with five to play. It was the kind of play from Palmer that generally blew his opponents right off the course; the type of golf that made his name.

Through all this Thomson retained the look of someone who'd been told his dinner was ready. Completely unperturbed he birdied the 14th and walked from the 15th with a quite sensational eagle. Palmer's lead had been slashed to 1-up. At the 16th, the Australian hit his approach stiff to the flagstick. Palmer followed with an 8-iron to 15-feet below the hole and hit a birdie putt that ran right up to the hole, slowed down, perched on the edge, then dramatically fell in. The momentum needed for that ball to drop in was enough to halt Thomson's challenge. There was another half at the next and when he failed to reach the last in two the match was all over. Throughout a riveting contest Palmer made 12 birdies and an eagle over 36 holes, and Thomson, far from disgraced, 11 birdies and an eagle. The moment the match ended Thomson walked over to Palmer, looked him in the eye, shook his hand and said: 'Well played, Arnold.' Later, the media crowded around, waiting for some display of bitterness. They had the wrong man. 'Arnold isn't flogging at the ball the way he used to,' he said. 'I was beaten by a better man.' The better man was impressed too. 'It was one of the best matches I've been in,' said Palmer. 'Peter played such excellent golf I really enjoyed the whole thing.'

This is exactly what Thomson would have wished. As he had prepared himself for that semi-final in the morning, he hoped for nothing more than for golf to be the victor in the match ahead. Of course he wanted to win, but it was not the end of the world if he lost. So many people had manufactured the wrong impression.

When he departed the US tour full-time in the early 1960s Thomson had decided that pro golf, and the new style of golfing professional in the US, did not suit his tastes. This compounded his belief that life was much more than acquiring money and momentary glory by winning golf tournaments. It's not that he ever lacked dedication; it's just that so many other interests claimed his attention, and still do. In 1960 he'd remarried and immediately began raising a second family of a son and two daughters. He decided it was high time to put up the 'gone fishing' sign occasionally and he developed his education in other areas. He still likes to read deeply, write meaningful newspaper articles, attend the opera and classical concerts, and he remains profoundly interested in the political, economic and sociological sciences. He also likes to roam the world for the educational opportunities that travel offers, and enjoys total changes of scene and culture. On the American tour he found limited chances either to indulge in these interests or discuss them with those on his wavelength. Locker-room and dinner conversation rarely strayed beyond the game itself, the merits of a new putter, or the colour of a certain player's trousers. It was possible to travel for weeks, even months on the tour without hearing a word about Vietnam, human rights or the environment.

'He was simply more at home in Europe, and Britain in particular,' says Peter Alliss. 'He enjoyed the conversations, the food, the odd drop of wine, the theatres of London and Edinburgh, and the classical music. I believe he considered America a bit too wild and woolly. It's so vast and so big that many friendships were hard to cement then, and he much preferred his many, many friends in Britain. He was very much an Anglo-Briton-Australian; a Commonwealth man.'

When Thomson came to know America better, and for that matter the golfing world, he found that the vast majority of professionals were limited in outlook and conversation. 'I suppose 95 per cent of players were like that, but that's necessarily so. If you want to be good at golf you have to immerse yourself in it. The fellows would all join together in their little groups, all of them with similar attitudes. Some were drinkers and searched for their face in the bottom of a glass, some were womanisers, some would be with their wives, some wouldn't be interested in anything, and then there were the loners.'

And there was Peter Thomson. There is no question he was a largely misunderstood figure in American golf, and yet more than thirty years after his regular trips he returned to embrace the country like never before during a magical stint on the tour for the over-50s, the US PGA Seniors. Who could have predicted that the reunion would ignite in Thomson his fiercest competitive instincts and yield a staggering nine tournament victories in the one season of 1985?

The respected veteran writer, Jim Murray, co-founder of *Sports Illustrated*, *Los Angeles Times* columnist, and winner of America's best sportswriter award eleven years running from 1968, summed up the eventual about-face from the US when he wrote in the *Los Angeles Times* in May 1985:

> Not too many people with golf sticks in their hands can claim to have done something Jack Nicklaus never did. And wishes he had. One who did is down here at the Tournament of Champions this week — and hardly anybody even knows who he is. He may be the biggest secret since the Japanese naval code. His name is not Hogan, Hagen, Jones, Snead, Nelson or Sarazen. But he's done something none of them did, either …
>
> Even the fact that he's a foreign player doesn't entirely explain his mystery status. Gary Player, Seve Ballesteros and Bernhard Langer are rock stars by comparison. But they haven't done what he's done either.
>
> Peter Thomson has won the British Open five times.
>
> … Someone once estimated that winning the US Open is the equivalent of winning five or more regular tour events. If so, the

> British has to be worth at least as many. It is not too exaggerated then to evaluate Thomson's British wins as worth 25 tour wins ... So why isn't he a portrait in coast-to-coast clubrooms? Why isn't the big four Nicklaus, Palmer, Hogan and Thomson? Why does he need two references to cash a check? Why can't he leave home without his credit card? Why should a man who has won the granddaddy of all tournaments five times need the same introduction as someone who never made the field there? Why shouldn't he be the author of 'Winning it the British Way'? Why shouldn't he be Peter the Great instead of Peter the Who?

In a land where Peter Thomson was openly criticised for his atypical attitudes, he was eventually feted in 1988 as an inductee to the prestigious USGA Hall of Fame. To everyone connected with American golf he is no longer anonymous. Professional golf in the United States has its share of paradoxes all right.

C • H • A • P • T • E • R 4

Kel and the Canada Cup

NO one took much notice of the Australian wearing a cardigan and straw hat as he strode out across the rolling links. Most of the locals didn't even know his name. They were more interested in the man playing alongside him. It was this man who'd won their Open Championship four times; and one of them on this golfing holy of holies, St Andrews and, after all, this was the man awarded the Freedom of the Old Course. As everyone in the historic little town knew, the Royal and Ancient Golf Club did not bestow such honours lightly. But as Peter Thomson smiled warmly and doffed his cap to the small gathering of Scots that had turned up to watch on that quiet practice day, he knew something they didn't. He knew that the man he was playing with, the man in the cardigan and straw hat, was going to win the 1960 Centenary British Open. And he did.

It speaks volumes for the character and nature of Peter Thomson that his most pleasurable moment in the game of golf, the one he cherishes above all others, higher even than his own triumphs, was to stand amongst the crowd at St Andrews and watch his close friend Kelvin David George Nagle receive golf's glittering prize. In a delightful twist to the sentiment of the occasion, Nagle, unable and unwilling to wipe the smile from his face or loosen his grip on the silver claret jug, stood before the eyes of the world wearing Thomson's tweed jacket. His friend had lent it to him once he realised Nagle would never make it through the sea of back-slappers to his hotel room. 'This is the most wonderful moment of my life,' Nagle told the crowd.

How the pair arrived at this historic moment in golf is the tale of a remarkable friendship that has lasted for more than 40 years and, as both are quick to point out, without so much as a cross word. As a playing combination their crucial nexus gave the world of golf one of its most compatible, feared and respected teams; thoughtful, considerate and encouraging, blending rich skills with quiet composure. Thomson and Nagle were, and still are, more than staunch buddies. Many of their friends, colleagues and even opponents have suggested they were more like blood brothers. Nagle, an affable and unassuming person, was content to play second fiddle to the brilliant Thomson, who in turn gave his more senior partner every possible respect — this was the secret of their incomparable teamwork and loyalty. Any account of Peter Thomson's life cannot neglect to mention Nagle's influence.

They first met in 1949 at the Australian Golf Club for the inaugural McWilliams Wines event. Thomson was the young amateur with 'wraps' on him, Nagle a 28-year-old from Sydney, building a professional career after five years in the Army at Darwin where he 'dodged the odd bomb', and in the Pacific where he 'dodged the odd coconut!' At 16, Nagle had been an apprentice carpenter until he had an argument with his boss and took a job as assistant professional to Tom Popplewell at Pymble Golf Club. 'I couldn't get into the PGA as a youngster because I had an apprenticeship to serve,' he says. 'And then they decided to close the deal because there were too many members, so I had to wait around. Next thing I knew the war was on and by the time I'd finished with that I went back to Pymble, still as an assistant. The PGA then decided to let all the servicemen join, so I was a late starter, but I was in at last.' All this prevented Nagle from playing professional golf until he was 26. In his first tournament at Manly he had an opening round of 73, but faded right out of the picture. For twelve months he hardly won any prize-money, and did not give any indication of the golf that was to come. In those days he attracted attention as a long hitter, but the people soon turned their backs when they discovered few of these drives found their mark. Melbourne's top golf writer of the day, the Melbourne *Herald*'s Jack Dillon, wrote that Nagle would never ever have the consistency to win a four-round tournament. It is still the source of much pleasure to the man himself. 'After I'd won a few I saw him one day,' recalls Nagle with a chuckle. 'I said, "Jack, I still remember that article you wrote about me," and he said, "Oh well, we all make mistakes sometimes!"'

Despite the fact they met only in passing at the Australian, and both had their focus purely on the tournament in progress, Nagle remembers being struck by Thomson's manner and personality. 'He was obviously intelligent, had a good head and handled himself very well,' says Nagle. 'No matter what challenge he was given I'm sure he thought that he could do it. Another thing that stood out was his ability. He was such an excellent striker of the ball for such a young fellow.' Jealousy is not something alien to the world of professional golf and it manifests itself at an early age when the ruthlessness of winning at all costs is drilled into a young rookie.

Nagle was almost nine years older than Thomson, promoting a feeling of instant respect between them, and as both were seeking a stabilising friendship in the often unstable atmosphere of big-time golf, they were attracted to each other immediately. Of course golf was their common bond, but both had technical school backgrounds, both were health conscious and non-smokers. Thomson drinks very little, Nagle was and still is, completely teetotal — both were modest, shy types, both preferred a quiet room to the raucous clubhouse bar. Nagle was married; Thomson had his girlfriend. Both were scrupulously honest, both believed in traditional home-spun philosophies, both had calm, even temperaments and dry, clever senses of humour and, more importantly, there was not a jealous bone between the two of them. To Nagle, Thomson seemed completely unaffected by all the hype associated with his name. 'We hit it off pretty well from our first meeting,' says Nagle.

The Melburnian took the spotlight over Nagle, and most others, at the McWilliams event, but the latter was far from disgraced, finishing in a tie for 11th. A few months later, as Thomson was back behind the bench at the Riversdale pro shop, Nagle surprised the experts by trouncing Ted Naismith 7 & 5 in the final of the Australian PGA championship at Royal Perth. The next year he won the West Australian Open and when Norman von Nida came to organise a tour of Australian pros to Britain for a series of exhibitions and tournaments, Nagle, along with Eric Cremin, was pencilled in. Ossie Pickworth was to make up the four, but when he declared himself unavailable, the young Peter Thomson, fresh from finishing his apprenticeship, became the touring party's late inclusion. Pickworth had no idea of it at the time, but his decision to withdraw sparked a friendship that gave Australia two of its finest ambassadors and one of its greatest sporting combinations. Thomson and Nagle each on their first trip to Britain in that year 1951 became firm friends. 'The more I spoke to Kel on that trip,' says Thomson, 'and the more I came to know him better, the more he struck me as the nicest person I had ever met in golf. He came up the hard way too, with no sponsors or managers; and all that he has gained in glory has been by dint of his iron constitution and honest determination. What immediately struck me about him was that there was absolutely no malice in him, or vice of any kind, and he was always in good humour. You cannot ask for a better companion than that. Even though he was several years older than me we seemed to click. He and I thought the same thoughts and did the same things.' Nagle is just as sentimental: 'It didn't take long to get to know Pete. I respected his talents and his bright, enthusiastic personality and I guess he looked on me as a big brother.'

Thomson was not yet 22 on this tour, and Nagle was 30, and virtually living out of each other's pockets their fledgeling friendship was put to the most stringent test. Of all the Australians, Thomson, with his high finish in the Open Championship and record round of 62 en route to second place in the North British event (to be discussed in the next chapter), attracted the most attention from the British public and press, while Nagle languished at the other end of the scale — 'the only event in which I qualified was the British Open at Portrush.' This was largely because he would drive the ball vast distances instead of concentrating on keeping it in play. Yet Nagle remained in high spirits and not once did Thomson ever detect a hint of depression. If the experience of constantly outgunning his opponents and getting nowhere made Nagle an angry man to tour with, it didn't show. And just as Thomson was impressed by Nagle's personality, Nagle was affected by the youngster's sound, logical approach to how golf should be played, and this had more than a little influence in convincing him that he needed to change his swing dramatically if he was to have any hope of surviving on the pro tour. Thomson saw little of Eric Cremin and Norman von Nida on this tour compared with the time spent with Nagle. Cremin, the Australian Open champion that year and winner of twelve tournaments in 1949–50 was, at 37, the same age as von Nida, and also came from Sydney. It was only natural that the more senior pair stuck together, leaving the younger couple to their own devices.

After a memorable trip home via America, the Australian four arrived back after five months abroad keen to attack the major domestic tournaments. Nagle, with his mediocre tour behind him and a new friendship, immediately set to work on rebuilding his swing at Pymble Golf Club. The urge to hit the ball those extra few yards quickly disappeared. With a shorter, more compact swing, he began to develop reliability and accuracy to the green and this paved the way for what was to become his main offensive weapon — his putting. The season of 1952–3 was a turning point in Nagle's career. In three weeks he won the McWilliams Wines event and the Adelaide Advertiser tournament, and was runner-up to von Nida in the Canberra Open, collecting £1,500 in prizemoney. He also took out the NSW PGA championship with a remarkable 14-under-par total of 270, which included an 8-under 63 over the picturesque Pennant Hills layout.

It was at the Australian Club for the McWilliams Wines that Nagle proved he was a player of world class. Amongst a field that included Argentina's Roberto de Vicenzo, Englishmen Max Faulkner and Harry Weetman, Italy's Ugo Grappasonni and a barrage of Australian talent in

Thomson, Pickworth, von Nida and Cremin, the solid Sydney-sider started with a patchy 73, but then stormed home with rounds of 69–67–68, for an 11-under total of 277 and a seven shot victory over de Vicenzo. Playing alongside the winner, a despairing Argentinian watched as Nagle holed a succession of long putts from all angles. He constantly shook his head in disbelief and muttered, 'Oh Kel, what you do to me!' It was not the only time de Vicenzo would witness Nagle's magic with the blade. This performance, and several like it, elevated the name of Kel Nagle to one of star status in Australian golf.

In late 1952 the ugly topic of appearance money arrived in Australia when the Ampol company paid four Americans, Lloyd Mangrum, Ed 'Porky' Oliver, Jimmy Demaret and Jim Turnesa to come down under in a revival of the previously ill-fated Lakes Cup, an attempt to stage a bi-annual match between professionals from both countries. It began in 1934 when Sydney's Lakes Club donated a trophy, but the US team butchered the Australians nine matches to nil. Two years later the Americans defended the Cup against an Australian team (including George Naismith) at Lakewood in Los Angeles, winning seven and a half matches to one and a half, but there was little interest in the contest and the idea was scrapped until Ampol showed interest in 1952. An Australian team of von Nida, Thomson, Pickworth and Nagle was selected, and it was decided the Cup would be played over two legs in Sydney and Melbourne, with foursomes and singles at each venue.

No one is quite sure who was actually responsible for creating the fine partnership of Nagle and Thomson but at Melbourne's Huntingdale course for the opening foursomes, von Nida was partnered by Pickworth, and Thomson was told he'd be pairing Nagle. Neither thought much of it; it seemed a natural progression from their many rounds spent practising together. Now they were representing their country for the first time, and overjoyed to be given the chance.

Like many great partnerships though, their fusion did not at first bear fruit. They came up against a former US Open champion and US Masters champion in Mangrum and Demaret, and were beaten two up. Then in Sydney they lost to Oliver and Turnesa, 5 & 4. Australia lost the Cup, four matches to two, and the challenge was again shelved, this time permanently. By this time another golfing event had sprouted from nothing, but this one was to have a lasting effect on world golf, particularly in Australia, and unlike those tentative moments in the Lakes Cup, was to carry the Thomson-Nagle partnership to the corners of the globe and onto the front pages.

The Canada Cup, which in 1967 became the World Cup, began as a modest venture in 1953 when John Jay Hopkins, a high-profile Canadian industrialist and founder of the huge General Dynamics Corporation, dreamed a dream. Though no great golfer himself — his scores were usually in the 90s — the game gave him great pleasure and through it he was able to meet other prominent businessmen, statesmen and plain 'nice guys'. He believed that what golf had given him in a private sphere could and should be presented to the whole world. He organised a massive trophy weighing 97 pounds, and invited two players from each of the major golfing nations to 'foster the improvement of international relations and to further good fellowship and better understanding between the countries of the world'. It was a wonderful gesture from a confirmed golf addict, but behind it all was an ambition to see his tournament become the biggest golfing event in the world. Against the tradition of the British Open and the US Open, Hopkins knew he had a struggle ahead, but he cleverly dubbed his event the 'Olympic Games of Golf'.

In its inaugural year the Canada Cup was played during Coronation Week at the Beaconsfield Club near Montreal, with fourteen players representing seven countries over 36-holes of aggregate strokeplay. As the previous year's British Open champion and the leading player in the Commonwealth, Bobby Locke was approached by Hopkins as a tournament adviser and indeed had a large say in the selection of the teams. Locke recommended Thomson and Pickworth from Australia, whilst having the effrontery to name himself and Harry Weetman as the team to represent Great Britain. In the end it was the team from Argentina, Roberto de Vicenzo and Antonio Cerda, that outplayed everyone and won handsomely by ten strokes over Canada and by eleven over Australia. Those closely involved with the event naturally proclaimed it a roaring success, but the facts were that no player broke 70 for the two rounds and the competition drew little attention from beyond the boundaries of Montreal. US golf certainly turned its back on the event after its team of Julius Boros and Jim Turnesa both opened with 80s.

Despite obvious teething problems the slogan 'international goodwill through golf' became a catch-cry and changes were quickly made to transform the event into what had initially been planned. Officials conceded a monumental error by not giving the inaugural event the

1953 Canada Cup, Beaconsfield GC, Montreal			
287 — Argentina	A. Cerda	70–70	140
	R. de Vicenzo	75–72	147
297 — Canada	S. Leonard	74–70	144
	W. Kerr	79–74	153
298 — Australia	H. Pickworth	77–70	147
	P. Thomson	78–73	151

status and prestige of 72-holes, so that was immediately rubber-stamped for 1954. They also realised that team selection was best placed in the hands of each country's golfing administration. By August 1954 the word had spread and no fewer than twenty-five nations were represented.

'There was no such thing as an order of merit list in those days,' says Thomson. 'The PGA had to make its own selection for the Canada Cup and to my great delight they named Kel and myself.' In the eyes of international golf Nagle was largely an unknown at Montreal and, as such, the Australians weren't given much hope of winning in the company of the game's biggest names. Thomson was considered a threat for the individual title, the 'International Trophy', but in the teams event, observers thought it was the American pair of Sam Snead and Jimmy Demaret all the way.

'Pete had already won his first British Open and was an established player,' says Nagle. 'Even though I was older than him I was struggling a bit and still trying to get established. I'd won the Australian PGA and the McWilliams Wines, but Pete was the really big name — a much more recognised player than I was.' In Thomson's eyes though his friend had every right to be there at Montreal and, more than he would with any other of his countrymen, went out of his way to make sure Nagle enjoyed himself. 'I suppose it was the first proper Canada Cup of 72 holes and with such an international field it was something special to be representing Australia and a great thrill to be playing with Kel,' he says. 'We were very close at that stage and always felt we were a good combination.'

Thomson and Nagle were the ideal 'team' in the purest sense of the word. The wisdom behind selecting not simply two of the country's finest, in-form golfers, but two men who thoroughly enjoyed each other's company, was seen immediately. Thomson had not shown nearly as much outward enthusiasm with Pickworth the previous year, and in the later Canada Cups with other partners he never displayed the cheerful exuberance and loyalty he clearly reserved for Nagle. And it always showed where it mattered: on the scoreboard. 'The Canada Cups were extremely patriotic affairs for Peter and me,' explains Nagle. 'He'd say to me, "Righto Kel, this one is for Australia!" There wasn't any money in it in those days — we were in it for the pride of representing our country. Because of this, and the fact that we were great friends, we had a certain harmony on the golf course.' The Australian duo stayed in the same Montreal hotel that week and spent a great deal of time in each other's company off the course as well as on. Their enthusiasm and readiness to play were all the more remarkable when it is revealed that the venue for the 1954 Cup did little to inspire either player. Thomson vividly remembers the course as a far from thrilling piece of architecture. 'Laval-Sur-Le-Lac, meaning on the lake, was vastly different to the courses I had seen in the United States,' he says. 'It didn't seem to be very well prepared at all — the greens were slow and the fairways needed a good cut. Despite this, Kel and I just seemed to combine together very well from the start. We played about the same standard and were about the same length from the tee, so we could give each other ideas about club selection and all that. We were a great help to each other.'

On the first day the Australians jumped from the blocks superbly. Importantly, both secured confidence-boosting birdies early in their rounds and lifted each other with their play. By the time all scores were posted in the evening, Nagle's 68 and Thomson's 69 had pushed them into the lead by four shots over the home country and by five over defending champions de Vicenzo and Cerda. The following day Argentina drew level with Australia after 36 holes and, with Canada, Scotland and the USA all just three shots behind in second place, the competition was wide open. That evening a dejected Nagle felt he'd let the team down with his one-over 73. Thomson had managed 71 which matched de Vicenzo's score, but Antonio Cerda's 68 was the reason the Australians no longer held the outright lead. Still, Nagle believed he'd cost his country the lead and after discussions with his partner, vowed to give the final day everything he had. 'I didn't want to see Pete make any mistakes,' says Nagle, 'and he didn't want to see me make any. I wasn't about to throw it [the good start] all away.' Playing alongside their main rivals over the final 36-holes, Thomson and Nagle played excellent golf, but were powerless to stop the Argentinians from surging ahead. Again, Thomson matched de Vicenzo's 71, but Cerda was running hot. He compiled a wonderful 67 and under the circumstances Nagle did a superb job to stay in touch with 69. Incredibly, at lunchtime some experts had all but written off the 'faltering' Australians. With a round remaining, they believed the titleholders from Argentina, the fast-finishing Scottish team and the USA would fight it out. Barely a mention was made of Nagle's brave 69 and Thomson's rock-solid 71. But the scoreboard suggested Australia was far from dead and buried.

As the final round unfolded, Scotland, with Eric Brown fumbling his way to a 79, collapsed first. Then the US fell behind with Demaret and Snead unable to find the spark needed, and it became clear the winner would come from the Argentina-Australia group. And this was when Thomson, as reigning British Open champion, showed his class. His good friend was also duly inspired. The former was unusually inaccurate from the tee, but with some spectacular recoveries and some deadly putting, the Canada Cup began to swing back Australia's way. Thomson grabbed four birdies from the first eight holes after dropping massive putts from all angles, and after canning another monster at the 9th, the smiling de Vicenzo made an inquiry about the Australian's putter. Once he had it in his hands the Argentinian, half-jokingly, pretended to snap it in half over his knee, and probably later wished he had. The younger of the Australians turned in a remarkable 31 and it didn't stop there. He eagled the 515-yard 10th hole, then at the long 12th seemed headed for his first bogey when he hooked his drive deep into trouble behind a thick clump of trees. If anyone needed convincing that it was Australia's day it came when Thomson played a truly brilliant controlled hook that curved around the fairway and rolled up onto the green within several yards of the flag. Nagle let out a joyful yelp and although the eagle putt stayed out, the tap-in birdie took Thomson to eight-under and in sight of a new course record. This was no one-man show. While Thomson was calmly setting the Laval layout alight, Nagle turned the performance into a marvellous double act. Memories of the McWilliams Wines in Sydney came flooding back for de Vicenzo and suddenly he was worrying about a second Australian putter. A disappointing double-bogey at the short 17th put paid to any thoughts Thomson entertained of a new course record and if not for Nagle's timely surge things might have been different. At the final hole Nagle put the issue beyond doubt with another superb long putt for birdie. This time it was Thomson's turn to let out a joyous cheer and the teammates embraced warmly as four-stroke victors over Argentina. Thomson's blistering six-under 66 and Nagle's fine 69 proved the fighting qualities of this remarkable duo. De Vicenzo said as much when he walked from the final green into a handshake from John Jay Hopkins and said it was the first time he'd come close to feeling inadequate on a golf course. For Thomson's part, his 66 was three strokes better than anything else carded that afternoon and it elevated him to a tie for second in the International Trophy with Cerda, two strokes behind Canadian Stan Leonard.

1954 Canada Cup, Laval-Sur-Le-Lac, Montreal				
Australia	556	P. Thomson	277	69–71–71–66
		K. Nagle	279	68–73–69–69
Argentina	560	A. Cerda	277	73–68–67–69
		R. de Vicenzo	283	69–71–71–72
USA	565	J. Demaret	278	70–68–69–71
		S. Snead	287	74–72–70–71
Canada	570	S. Leonard	275	66–68–71–70
		J. Huot	295	75–75–72–73
Scotland	571	T. Haliburton	284	72–71–71–70
		E. Brown	287	72–69–67–79

In a way, it must have been fate that decreed Thomson and Nagle would win. It capped 1954 as the finest year in the history of Australian golf — a year etched deeply in the record books for the quantity and quality of Australian performances on the world stage. No year came close to it previously; none has since. It remains the country's most remarkable and successful twelve months and more than any other period trumpeted loud and clear Australia's name as a global golfing force.

The Canada Cup triumph — equivalent to the world professional teams championship — was the pinnacle, but underneath there were wonderful foundations. Australia won the inaugural Commonwealth Amateur series at St Andrews, to mark the bi-centenary of the Royal and Ancient. The Aussies toppled Canada, Britain, South Africa and New Zealand in foursomes and singles matchplay and the happy contingent of Doug Bachli (Vic.), Harry Berwick (NSW), Peter Heard (NSW), Jack Coogan (Qld), Bill Sheperd (SA), Bob Stevens (SA) and Ray Howarth (Vic.) proudly brought the trophy home. Berwick also returned with the prestigious amateur title, the St George's Vase. Watching it all was former prime minister Stanley Bruce (the man in charge of the country when Peter Thomson was born and who officially opened his beloved Victoria Golf Club), as the first and only Australian to receive the honour of captain of the Royal and Ancient Golf Club.

After the Commonwealth series Doug Bachli, Thomson's former pennant teammate from Victoria GC, travelled south to Muirfield for the British Amateur Championship. A rank outsider, Bachli notched seven stunning wins over the cream of amateur golfers in Britain before holding on to defeat America's famed Bill Campbell in the final, 2 & 1. The Australian lost the first two holes of the final to birdies, but fought back to square the match for the sixth time at the 32nd hole. He then won the next two holes with remarkable play to gain the decisive break. With each man facing four-foot putts at the 35th, Campbell said, 'Yours, Doug.' Bachli did not hesitate. Just as the Australian took his putter back, Campbell realised he had just given Bachli a psychological advantage and cut in: 'I think we should get a measure.' Bachli sensed the ploy. 'No Bill — I'll hit it and I'll sink it.' And he did. Campbell was then always going to miss. The affable Australian became the first from his country to win the prestigious title since it began in 1885 and at the time of printing, is the last. What made this superb triumph all the more remarkable was that just a few weeks later Thomson won Australia's first British Open. This meant that the two oldest and most esteemed trophies in the world of golf sat side by side on the mantle at Melbourne's Victoria Golf Club. Never before or since has any other club in the world been able to boast a similar achievement from two of its members.

Continuing the Australian glory, Norman von Nida led the qualifying rounds in that British Open at Royal Birkdale and Tasmanian Peter Toogood was leading amateur. Then, back at St Andrews, another victory for golf in the antipodes when Thomson won the British PGA matchplay championship on his first look at a course that would have a profound effect on the man and his character. 'Australia's emergence as a power in world golf was among the most interesting sporting news of 1954,' wrote *Washington Times-Herald* golf correspondent John Gonella. 'It is a truly remarkable about-face when you consider that a decade ago, Byron Nelson could have given any Aussie professional a 3-up start and still been accepting congratulations around the 16th green!'

'That year was a supreme one for Australian golf,' remembers Thomson. 'Doug Bachli's win in particular was quite magnificent. It was phenomenal how it all came together in the one year and I can offer no explanation as to why. It certainly took Australia's name to the forefront of world golf, particularly in Britain, and not so greatly in America, because the USPGA all thought their tour was where golf began and ended. It was wonderful to be a part of it all though.'

In 1955 Thomson continued his romance with the Old Course at St Andrews by winning his second British Open, and in the US was beaten in a sudden-death play-off for the Canada Cup individual title. Nagle fought gamely to stay with his more illustrious partner in that event at the Columbia Country Club in Maryland, but in the end no team could catch the US duo, Ed Furgol and Chick Harbert.

As the flags were being packed away and the scaffolding dismantled at Columbia, no one was more disappointed than Kel Nagle. His total was only two-over par, but nine strokes behind Harbert and that, of course, was Australia's losing margin. It would be three years before Nagle would play in the Canada Cup again. In 1956, and with the

1955 Canada Cup, Columbia CC, Maryland, USA

USA	560	E. Furgol	279	73–70–69–67
		C. Harbert	281	70–69–70–72
Australia	569	P. Thomson	279	67–74–67–71
		K. Nagle	290	72–72–72–74
Scotland	571	E. Brown	285	72–70–70–73
		J. Panton	286	73–71–71–71
Argentina	573	A. Cerda	286	74–70–72–70
		R. de Vicenzo	287	70–69–72–76
Belgium	573	F. van Donck	279	70–66–73–70
		A. de Vulder	294	74–73–70–77

event gaining more and more prestige, the Australian selectors ignored him for Norman von Nida at Wentworth in England, but the partnership was a nightmare: in the third round Thomson carded 82, von Nida an 80! They ended up tied for ninth, 17 strokes behind the legendary American pair of Hogan and Snead.

The following year the Canada Cup moved to the Kasumigaseki Club in Tokyo, and again there was a different Australian combination. Thomson retained his usual role of key man, but with him was the reigning Australian Open champion and winner of the Speedo event at Victoria GC, 22-year-old Bruce Crampton. For both men it was their first trip to Japan and they had difficulty putting on the extremely slow greens of korai grass which were ideally suited to the locals. They finished fourth behind the Japanese pair of 'Pete' Nakamura and Koichi Ono, who notched an unexpected yet convincing win. The host nation, awakening to the possibility of the greatest triumph in its sporting history, was gripped by excitement and anticipation and 14,000 spectators watched the play while the television audience ran into many millions. If it is possible to pinpoint the start of the incredible golfing boom which now grips the land of the rising sun, this would be it. Thomson witnessed all of this and it is no coincidence that he returned to Japan many, many times. Such was his influence on the development of the game there that many dignitaries referred to him as 'Sir Peter'.

In 1958 the event moved to Club de Golf, Mexico City, and in the mile-high atmosphere there was another unlikely triumph, this time by the Irish duo of Harry Bradshaw and Christy O'Connor. Thomson did not play in the Cup that year — Kel Nagle was joined by the new Australian Open champion Frank Phillips, for fifth place. Thomson withdrew on the grounds that he'd just won his fourth British Open at Royal Lytham and St Anne's, had been travelling for a large part of the year and needed a rest. He recommended that Nagle take his place. The critics pounced immediately, saying he was 'stabbing his country in the back', but what these people didn't know was that Thomson had been working tirelessly behind the scenes in an effort to bring the Canada Cup to Royal Melbourne. In late January 1959 the announcement came from the International Golf Association that the Canada Cup would be played from 18–21 November at Royal Melbourne. To secure the event for Australia considerable persuasion and perseverance was required, and alongside Thomson, one of the hardest workers was William G. Walkley, then managing director of Ampol, the tournament's major sponsor. Together they lobbied the sole organiser of the Cup, quietly spoken, thick-set Boston-born Irishman, Fred Corcoran.

'"Fix-it Fred" had a remarkable record in golf administration, which started from the caddy ranks at a top Boston club and jumped to official handicapper for the state of Massachusetts,' says Thomson. 'Eight years later he was executive-secretary for the state's golf association. From there he became tournament manager for the US PGA and in a lone-man effort he paved the way for a huge rise in the number of tournaments and amount of prizemoney. He also gave Sam Snead his big start in golf and became his manager.' John Jay Hopkins clearly liked his style and shortly before the tycoon's death in 1957, handed over the reins of the 'Olympic Games of Golf' to Corcoran, who immediately sensed the value of taking the event to Melbourne. Not only had the Canada Cup never ventured south of the equator, Melbourne had just three years earlier hosted one of the most successful Olympiads, and was considered one of the most 'sports-mad' cities in the world. All that was needed was somewhere to play, and that's where Thomson had a few ideas of his own. He was a prime mover behind what eventually became one of Australian golf's finest creations, the Royal Melbourne composite course. The secretary-manager of the club at the time, Bill Richardson, recalls the momentous day the composite layout was born. 'We sat around a table in the clubhouse over a map of Royal Melbourne's East and West courses,' he says. Joining him were Maxwell Shaw (Club captain), Hughie Hamilton (chairman of the match committee), George Burgess (chairman of the greens committee), and Peter Thomson. Their priority was crowd control: they anticipated huge galleries and with both courses crossing busy roads it was clearly necessary to contain play within 'the home paddock'. Thomson believed the most important hole would be the 18th, where the bulk of the crowd would need to be comfortably and safely accommodated. There were no such luxuries as grandstands available to course planners in those days so the group agreed that the 18th green on the East Course which had been built around one of the most beautiful natural amphitheatres in golf should be fully utilised. This was pencilled in as the final hole of the composite course. 'From there it was simply a case of working our way backwards. Everyone offered opinions as to what they thought were the best holes and Peter was particularly helpful from the playing point of view and raised problems that we would never have considered. In the end the whole thing fell into place beautifully with twelve holes from the West and six from the East and we were all convinced we'd come up with a superb test of golf.'

The year 1959 had been far from Thomson's best competitively but when it came time to nominate the home country's team, the selectors had no alternative but to go for the proven team of Thomson-Nagle; the latter was in brilliant form, and the former was really never going to miss out after his hard work. Indeed, it would have been the height of insult had the Australian selectors gone for someone else to partner Nagle.

Two months before the Canada Cup at Royal Melbourne the big Sydney-sider, at his twelfth attempt, won the Australian Open at Kensington and at the presentation made by Attorney-General Sir Garfield Barwick, Nagle said: 'It is wonderful to win the Open. I felt that I had been a bridesmaid for too long!' He could have been forgiven for thinking the title was destined never to be his. In 1955 at Gailes in Brisbane he tied for second, just a shot behind the winner Bobby Locke, and the following year seemingly had the Open 'in the bag' at Royal Sydney as he took a six-shot lead into the final round. The gallery stood silent and horrified as he failed to find a fairway over the last four holes and threw it all away. Bruce Crampton took the honours with a closing 68. In 1958 he was again runner-up, this time behind Gary Player at Kooyonga in Adelaide. The golfing gods had been particularly harsh on a man who was nearing his forties. The public loves a sportsman who can grin when he loses, one who has nothing but good words for the winner, and does not make excuses about his play or the conditions — that was Nagle. It made his triumph in the 1959 Australian Open all the more popular, but while Nagle was reaching peak form at Kensington, and was on the threshold of a truly glorious twelve months in golf, there was much concern shown for the game of his placid pal.

A few days before the Open Thomson was experiencing one of his lowest points since turning professional; with every stroke it seemed that he was just digging himself deeper and deeper into a hole. In July he had finished out of the top ten in the British Open for the first time and it was clear he needed a massive injection of confidence. And here again, he went about obtaining it in a most unique way. Slogging it out on the practice fairway was widely thought to be the best remedy, but Thomson headed indoors, to a sporting goods factory in Sydney, rolled up his sleeves, selected the best woods and irons from five complete sets of clubs, and then set to work on creating the perfect set. This was not a case of a poor tradesman blaming his tools. It was a journey back in time to his days over the workbench at Riversdale and provided inspiration from within; a typical Thomson solution. After assembling the irons, changing the length of the shafts to suit his height, adjusting the loft on each face to precisely where he wanted it and adding his tailor-made grips, he emerged to say he could not wait to put them to the test. The set of clubs catapulted him out of the doldrums. After a solid effort at Kensington he took off to New Zealand where he won their Open championship yet again, helped by the fact that he tied with his pal Nagle after 72-holes and lifted his game another notch to beat him in a play-off. The following week he took out the Caltex event at Paraparaumu. 'Those new clubs suited me so well, felt so good and gave me so much confidence that I set off on a moment's notice for the closest tournaments I could get to.' They happened to be the Italian Open and Spanish Open the following week, and his friends thought it was rather a long way to go for a lightning raid. 'Don't worry,' said Thomson. 'I've got a seat on the plane — I won't have to strap-hang!' He won both tournaments and by the time the Canada Cup came around, like Nagle, he was in peak form.

November 1959 was the month when Melbourne turned golf-mad. The crowds almost reached those of the big football and Test cricket matches, and were just as boisterous. Australians at home first gained an inkling of what big-time golf was and the effect upon the dignified Royal Melbourne Golf Club was devastating. Members, even such dignitaries as Victorian Governor Sir Dallas Brooks, had to clear out their lockers to make way for the international stars. The club was transformed into a canvas town, a carnival. In all, a record thirty nations sent representatives to the tournament, including for the first time Indonesia. Their players registered as simply Salim and Sjamsudin, two former caddies who had never previously strayed beyond the shores of their own country. They had never worn spiked golf shoes before, nor read a single book on golf, nor had a lesson, nor played with a full set of clubs. 'Who's Sam Snead?' said Salim through an interpreter when he was asked how it felt to be playing in the same event as the legendary American. He'd honestly never heard of him. Not surprisingly, the pair came home in last place, each with a best round of 87 and the remainder in the 90s. They were presented with trophies as 'the players who had tried the hardest'. This was precisely what John Jay Hopkins would have wished, the spirit of the Canada Cup, fostering international goodwill through golf.

Without hesitation Thomson claims the four days of the Canada Cup in Melbourne as the finest in his distinguished career and in all respects the event turned out to be *the* ideal tournament for him. 'It gave me such a great thrill because it was the first and only time I actually played for Australia in my home town. That's a tremendous thing to happen to anybody,' he says. He was also playing alongside 'a gentleman and a fine friend' in the heat of battle; many of the world's finest players were there to provide immaculate opposition; prizemoney meant little; a nationwide golfing boom was triggered as a result of the tournament; and Thomson was playing on a course he quite simply adored. 'I was also fit as a fiddle in that dreamy state of youth that imagines the whole world revolves around you,' he recalls. 'In respect to golf, it spelt that this tournament belonged to Kel and I before it even started. Everyone else thought the Americans were favoured to win though. They looked the best team on paper.' Certainly the US team of Sam Snead and Cary Middlecoff arrived with intimidating credentials — Snead was at his peak after notching his hundredth tournament win, and Middlecoff, a dual US Open champion, came with the reputation of an outstanding putter. Then there was the duo from Canada, Stan Leonard and Al Balding; the young South Africans, Gary Player and Harold Henning; the team from Wales, Dai Rees and Dave Thomas; and of course the defending champions from Ireland, Christy O'Connor and Harry Bradshaw. But reputations meant nothing on the sandbelt that week — in fact they were torn to shreds by the hot northerly winds that gusted around the treacherous composite course.

Responsible for Royal Melbourne's appearance was the man who'd arrived as head curator in 1935, Claude Crockford. He retired after more than forty years lovingly tending it seemed every blade of grass at Royal Melbourne, and his manner and ability left a deep impression on Thomson, who once wrote: 'I would dearly love to build a lot of Royal Melbournes all over the world, but even if we constructed exact replicas I doubt if they would be as good. For one thing, there are definitely not any Crockfords roaming abroad, and without his art and skill RM wouldn't be quite what it is today.'

For Crockford, presentation was the key at Royal Melbourne. He made apparently minor, but vital changes in the way of presenting the course — taking the greens in graduated fashion from the very low cut on the putting surfaces, out in stages to the fairway. It all came back to what Dr Mackenzie had taught him — everything had to be pleasant to look at when it was finished, and an emphasis was placed on a player's judgement in approaching the putting surfaces. No 'dartboard' golf here — with the greens so hard and fast there was no chance of landing a ball on the area like a butterfly with sore feet. Run-up shots were almost always in demand — shots that Thomson thought epitomised golf.

And it was exactly the same for the biggest test of many enormous challenges presented to Crockford in the time before his 1975 retirement, the 1959 Canada Cup.

'Whenever I prepared the course for a big event I always knew it was the course on show and nothing else,' he says. 'Not the clubhouse, not me, not the committee and not even the players. The course had to be perfect from the 1st tee to the 18th green. With the world watching, I didn't want any blemishes anywhere. The weather during the Canada Cup was very hot but it hadn't been prior, so the course couldn't have had a better preparation. The big problem was the hot northerly wind. It blew an absolute gale. The wind whipped across the course and blew plenty of sand from the bunkers and dumped it on the greens and the spectators!'

'Several things stand out in my memory about that week,' says Thomson. 'One thing was the speed of the greens. They were as fast as any I had seen before or since. Just the gentlest of taps would send the ball trickling down the glassy slopes by yards and yards. It was frightening. The professional player whose daily bread is won on lower class courses was unprepared for the searching examination of nerve and touch such as the Royal Melbourne greens provided, me included, even though I had grown up on them. Most of the visitors had never seen anything like it.' In truth though, Thomson was one man who could cope with the greens and he certainly proved it that week.

'Peter knew how to handle fast greens just as Ivo Whitton did,' says Crockford. 'Ivo was a truly marvellous player, a member and one time captain of the club, and if I ever prepared the greens with a bit of grass on them, by god he'd hit the roof! He was an absolute perfectionist and when people came up to me and said "why on earth do you have the greens so fast?" I'd think to myself, "I'm glad Ivo Whitton isn't standing behind you to hear that!" He loved to have the greens shaved bare and I thought, well here's a fellow who won the Australian Open five times, so he should know what he's talking about. That had a big effect on the way I thought. For big events, where the best golfers in the world were playing, the greens had to be fast, but true; a proper test and challenge.'

'I must say I relished it,' says Thomson, revealing at once his traditional side. 'I enjoy hard, fast courses. I find it infinitely more enthralling to tackle the approach that must inevitably bounce hard and roll thereafter, than mechanically pitch full strength to a green that accepts the ball like a dartboard does a dart. Another thing that stood out was the crowds. We never had crowds like that before at tournaments, whether they were in Melbourne or Sydney or anywhere else. Of course this caused a tremendous scene at the 18th green, with everyone crowded around, six, seven and sometimes eight deep. We didn't go in for grandstands then and those watching had to look over everyone watching at the front. 1959 was a different era. In those days international sporting events were musts — especially if the flags flew and the bands played. It wasn't so much Thomson and Nagle playing there that week as it was Australia. For that reason alone the Canada Cup had to be witnessed. People came from near and far, from city and from farm. Some came from interstate and a few from abroad. It added up to the biggest crowds we'd ever seen on fairways, some 20,000 people a day, and every one of them as keen as mustard. I definitely felt a great lift out of it. I was the sort of egotistical sportsman who liked that sort of thing — I felt wonderful in amongst it all.'

Again proving that he played his best golf when he was happy and that he was at his happiest in the big occasion events, Thomson seemed intent on wrapping up the contest on day one. With immaculate long-irons and some fine putting he went around in 67, and with Nagle contributing a flawless par round of 70, the Australians led Canada, Wales and South Africa by seven strokes and the US by eight. The rest of the world was nowhere. 'Kel and I calculated that the teams most likely to sneak in front of us would be either Canada or the United States, but Middlecoff soon showed he was completely out of touch with the Australian-size ball, and Snead, for all his great prowess, could not seem to handle the dog-legs at all,' says Thomson. 'He frequently drove miles too far into trouble, and we could see that he was far from happy with the firm, running fairways. Sam Snead is a fellow who loves to win — it is his sole purpose in life, and he got into a bit of a sour mood about the way things were going and he really became very cross with Middlecoff. When you find yourself getting angry with your partner the team is in a bit of trouble.' On Middlecoff's woes, Snead's response is unusually brief: 'That was easily the poorest I'd ever seen "Doc" play in a tournament,' he says. 'The guy just couldn't get the hang of it.' The dentist from Memphis who gave up pulling teeth to pull off the riches of the golf circuit, was back filling cavities again — only these cavities were Royal Melbourne's notorious bunkers. Although Snead fought back superbly with a magnificent course record of 65 on the second day, Middlecoff's score was ten strokes worse. Thomson and Nagle dismissed the Americans as a threat and turned to the Canadians, expecting pursuit. Playing alongside the Irishmen on the second day, the Australians began to hijack the front pages of the nation's newspapers with their blistering performance. Canada's Leonard came in with a superb 66, but his partner Al Balding could only manage a 73 and the importance of team play was again underlined. There was no better team striding around Royal Melbourne than the Australians, and Thomson with 69 and Nagle with 70 were still seven shots ahead at the halfway mark of the Cup.

Thomson takes up the story: 'It was on the third day that we met the Canadians head to head, and what with everything that happened, it proved an ordeal of five hours and more in a hot northerly wind that sapped our energy. Stan Leonard and Al Balding kept having conferences on every shot and the more complicated the shot, the longer the conference. I shall ever remember the 6th hole where Balding overshot the green with his second shot into enough rough grass to make his chances of getting down in two about 100-to-1. But the two discussed it all so long and carefully that in the end Balding committed the worst possible mistake under the circumstances. In his anxiety to keep his chip down that glassy slope from running all the way to the bunker, he left it halfway short. From there it is 2-to-1 that you three-putt, and that's what he did. The experience so shattered Balding that he slid steadily backwards from then on. That incident typified the whole week for me.

Royal Melbourne cruelly slew you if you were anything less than perfect. It reduced grown men, and successful ones at that, to drivelling fools by week's end.'

On the final day Thomson and Nagle were paired with the Americans and, with an Australian victory virtually assured, an enormous crowd turned up to watch. 'Unless we run hot and they blow up, we can't win,' said Snead, yet the excitement was far from over; there were many who remembered what had happened at Tokyo two years earlier, when Japan held a 10-stroke lead only to see a rampaging Wales knock off nine strokes in nine holes. In team strokeplay anything could happen. There was also plenty of interest in the International Trophy — naturally the whole of Melbourne, indeed Australia, wanted to see Thomson win it and there could not have been a spare piece of turf remaining around the 1st tee as the President of the IGA, Frank Pace jr, introduced the players. The gallery reserved its loudest cheer for the heroes from the home nation, but then came the imposing figure of Snead. 'Now, here is Sam Snead,' said Pace, 'the greatest money-maker golf has ever known.' Snead gave a slight grin, dipped his hand into his pocket, pulled out a few coins and a couple of golf tees, showed them to the crowd and shrugged his shoulders. A most entertaining day was in store.

It turned out to be another long day. With each player needing to hole out, with frequent consultations over each shot, and the strength-sapping northerly wind making its usual appearance, the going was indeed tough, but the Australians refused to yield under the pressure. 'I recall someone saying there were more than 20,000 people out there on the course,' remembers Nagle. 'I reckon most of them were following our group. It was very, very hot — Pete and I had our supporters bringing us cold drinks and wet towels from the clubhouse. It took us nearly six hours to play and it was a bit crazy with all those people walking up through the sand dunes creating a huge cloud of black dust. My wife was following us and her legs were jet black from the powdery dust and perspiration. As far as Pete was concerned, well, he just played magical golf. For me it was just a nice feeling to be walking along the fairway with him.'

After stumbling on the third day with a 76, Nagle, to his credit, fought back with a final round 72. Thomson, who set about the last day in typical businessman-like fashion, had a 71 and the door was firmly closed to all competitors. Again, his thoughts were primarily with his friend alongside him: 'Kel won the Canada Cup with me in 1954 and blazed a few times in his native Sydney when visiting internationals were around,' he says, 'but it wasn't until the Canada Cup came to Melbourne that he really shone. No greens could have suited him better. He was born with the perfect putting stroke for such a situation. The day we played with the Americans he produced some of the finest putting I have ever seen. It was terrifying putting downhill on those glassy surfaces, but with a short, solid tap he holed nearly every six-footer he looked at, either uphill or down. It was a putting touch that had Sam Snead agog.' The American is the first to agree: 'I couldn't believe that anyone could putt like that,' says Snead. 'Kel never hit one bad putt. Every single one of 'em gave the hole a scare. I said at the time that anyone who putted as good as that should be in the States. I've never seen puttin' like that in my life. They were never going to lose as long as he and Peter kept cannin' those putts all week.'

'Kel's putting at Royal Melbourne gave me great confidence that we would win,' says Thomson. 'We led from start to finish, although never by enough that we could coast home. Not, that is, until midway through the last round when the margin reached double figures. We had the home cheers ringing in our ears and a big feeling of pride and relief at the same time. At that stage, I began to think of myself, for the first time wondering about the individual low score prize. Stan Leonard, I was told, was in the clubhouse with 275. Pars were then all that was needed for me to win the honours.'

Meanwhile in the locker room, an exhausted Leonard was gingerly peeling off his spikes, certain the individual title had already been wrapped up by Thomson. After doing his utmost, concentrating for more than five hours in the hot, sticky, difficult conditions, he was ready to relax. Bill Richardson, the man responsible for making sure every Cup player was happy, was close by. 'Billy,' said Leonard to the secretary-manager, 'I'd like the biggest glass of beer you can find in the place. Thomson can't be beaten.'

The Australian was, however, on the crest of a wave. Australia seemed likely to cap off the week with the big double. 'All went perfectly well until the short 16th,' recalls Thomson. 'I put my tee shot well up the back of the green and had a frightening putt down the hill. From there I three-putted, missing the second one from about a yard. So I needed a birdie at one of the last two holes, quite a tall order.' Meantime Leonard was still in the clubhouse, gulping down his fifth beer, oblivious of all the action outside. Fred Corcoran stepped up. 'We might have a play-off, Stan. Peter has just dropped a shot at the 16th,' he said. The Canadian sat firm: 'There's no way I'm havin' a play-off Fred. I've just had all this beer and I ain't goin' nowhere!' Corcoran remained calm. 'You'll be having a play-off Stan,' he said. 'It's in your contract!' Leonard asked for an alka-seltzer and immediately headed for the practice fairway. But it still seemed in vain. Thomson had his chance and everyone expected him to do it. Such was the excitement and appeal of the afternoon that some familiar faces were seen striding the hot, dusty fairways, including the nation's leader, Robert Menzies. Despite proclaiming that his sporting interests were 'watching cricket and walking — without the distraction and emotional stress attached to the pursuit of an incorrigible small white ball', the big man was moved by the atmosphere and became part of the gallery. 'As we walked up the long 17th,' says Thomson, 'our prime minister gave me a friendly greeting and an encouraging pat on the back. He had a great smile, the great man. When he smiled at you it really conveyed something, an inspiration, a prod. But a birdie against the wind blowing that day just wasn't possible. My third shot, with a 7-iron, was straight at the flag, but about 20 feet short. Two putts from there was the best I could do. That left me needing a three on the last hole to win.'

And here, at the climactic moment of such a mammoth tournament, when the tension begins to gnaw at a competitor's stomach so severely that he experiences dizziness and nausea, at a time when we are led to believe that a player loses control of his mind and body and switches to auto-pilot as a last resort, Peter Thomson provided redoubtable proof of his remarkable personality. A close friend, former Victorian premier and self-confessed golf nut, Lindsay Thompson, was among the thousands trudging the fairways that day. 'Peter and Kel were leading the Americans by ten shots, but Peter was tied with Stan Leonard for the individual trophy,' recalls Thompson. 'Nearing the end he spotted me in the crowd and wandered over to tell me a joke! It was something that Bob Menzies had told him and he thought it was a real laugh. Well, if I was leading the D-Grade medal on a Saturday I wouldn't do that, let alone the critical stage of the individual title in the World Cup. He is such a relaxed person and this was clearly one of his features as a player.'

With his characteristic smile, Thomson cracked his driver down the 18th as a swarm of spectators bolted for the best positions. By the time Thomson arrived at his ball, they ringed the green. 'Again I had a 7-iron approach,' he says. 'The pin was tucked away in a difficult position, but as soon as I struck the ball I knew it was one of the best shots I'd ever hit. In the air it looked absolutely stone dead and just the perfect length, but it touched the green slightly left of the flag and bounced one or two small bounces, tending farther left.' The enormous cheer must have been heard by the fishing boats out on the bay! Thomson, close to exhaustion but still walking briskly arrived to a tumultuous reception at the green to find a putt of 18-feet facing him. A hush fell over the fans as he sized up the task. He conferred with Nagle and together decided he should aim for the left lip. 'Just hole the rotten thing so we can go and have a cup of tea,' whispered Nagle in his ear. Thomson's heart was beating fast, but he gave the putt a firm rap and decided that he'd hit it perfectly. It looked in all the way, but at the last moment died, touched the edge of the hole ever so slowly and sat defiantly three inches past. The gallery let out a huge groan. Nagle, who'd used more body language than Thomson in an effort to coax the ball into the cup, was incredulous. It was an awful anti-climax.

And so to the play-off, but while Leonard was finishing up on the practice fairway, hopeful he'd worked off the effects of Royal Melbourne's hospitality, Thomson was in the locker room, proving once again his unique attitude to such moments. Inside, to offer his congratulations to Thomson and Nagle on their marvellous win was the English team member, Peter Alliss. 'I vividly remember shaking hands with Peter,' he says, 'and saying to him, "I'm going out there now to watch this play-off." Well, he just gave one of those little laughs of his, turned and opened his locker and took out a brand new set of clubs, still in their box. He pulled all the paper off them, gave them a bit of a waggle and said, "Hmmm. I think I'll try these." I couldn't believe it. I thought, "You're mad!" Fancy doing a thing like that and having the arrogance or the confidence to try out a totally alien set of sticks in a play-off for the individual title of such a championship. He did some extraordinary things like that. His self-confidence was overwhelming. One of the things that stands out in my mind about Peter is this almost frightening belief in his own ability.'

Another reason Thomson tried new clubs in the play-off was because the grips on his usual set were soaking wet with perspiration, but it wasn't the reason he lost the play-off. 'It was really the King of anti-climaxes when Stan Leonard and I set off down the 1st again with seemingly the whole population lined up on either side of the fairway from tee to green,' he says. 'I just wanted to be back inside resting with Kel — after all, we'd won the main event. Anyway, after we both hit good drives, my second shot was pulled slightly to the north to allow for the wind, but it didn't drift back and I was stuck with a nasty chip down the slope. Sadly, I struck it too hard and it careered past Leonard, who from short of the green had run his third absolutely stone dead. Again I lipped out and that was that. I felt no great disappointment since it was a team thing. Kel and I were pleased beyond measure and so proud. To have won the contest before our own people was the greatest thrill of our lives. I will be eternally grateful for the help and support Kel gave me, and I suppose he feels the same for me. In such a situation I could not have asked for a better companion; so calm, so reassuring and rock-steady in the crisis. I cannot recall that either of us felt nervous. I didn't, I know, and if Kel felt something of the sort, he didn't show it. In retrospect this seems strange, because of all the ordeals a sportsman goes through in his career, carrying his nation's colours is by far the most serious. Instead, we seemed to find tremendous exhilaration.'

1959 Canada Cup, Royal Melbourne GC, Australia				
Australia	563	P. Thomson	275	67–69–68–71
		K. Nagle	288	70–70–76–72
USA	573	S. Snead	281	73–65–73–70
		C. Middlecoff	292	72–75–75–70
Canada	574	S. Leonard	275	70–66–69–70
		A. Balding	299	74–73–75–77
South Africa	580	G. Player	284	72–72–71–69
		H. Henning	296	72–75–71–78
England	588	P. Alliss	293	73–74–70–76
		B. Hunt	295	77–71–76–71

Wales 590, Scotland 595, China 597, Argentina, Spain 601, Belgium 602, Ireland 603, Japan 605, France 608, Italy 609, Brazil 619, New Zealand, Chile, Mexico 622, Colombia 625, Egypt 631, Sweden 637, Switzerland 651, Denmark, Germany 652, Portugal 654, Philippines 655, Holland 658, Korea 662, Indonesia 726.

The influence of that Canada Cup on golf in Australia, and for that matter the world, did not depart with the Royal Melbourne crowds that balmy November evening. There was no lavish celebration for the Australian duo — the very next day they flew to Sydney for a 36-hole challenge match against the Americans, Snead and Middlecoff. Their appetite whetted by the action on television the previous four days, thousands of Sydney-siders turned out to watch the Australians win it 'by miles'. It was the start of a nationwide golfing boom. Alongside the glamorous sports of rugby, football, cricket and tennis, young boys now wanted to grow up to be Kel Nagles and Peter Thomsons.

'Right after the Canada Cup concluded, manufacturers found that the interest in golf went through the roof,' says Thomson. 'In fact it went up by an incredible 400 per cent within two years. It was staggering really — all due to that event and the fact we'd won it.' It capped off a mighty year for Australia. Jack Brabham became the first Australian to win the World Driver's Championship, Neale Fraser was the catalyst behind a remarkable Davis Cup triumph over the USA in New York, and Richie Benaud's XI regained the Ashes with a four-nil series drubbing of the touring Englishmen.

A week after the triumph and with the cheers still ringing in their ears, the Australian pair teed up in the Pelaco tournament against a collection of top-class internationals staying over from the teams event. Again large crowds turned out and on his home course at Victoria, Thomson was as close as anyone could ever get to invincible. Quite simply, he says it was 'the best golf I have ever played', and who could possibly argue as the 30-year-old tore the course apart to become the

1959 Pelaco Tournament, Victoria GC, Melbourne	
339 — P. Thomson (Vic.)	68–68–67–67–69
346 — K. Nagle (NSW)	72–68–69–68–69
348 — D. Thomas (Wales)	74–66–70–68–70
— A. Miguel (Spain)	71–71–65–70–71
353 — F. Phillips (NSW)	71–72–73–68–69
— J. Harris (Vic.)	71–66–72–73–71
354 — D. Rees (Wales)	72–70–70–71–71

first player ever to break 70 in all five rounds of a 90-hole tournament in Australia. No one has done it since.

The following week Thomson completed a six-stroke victory, again over Nagle, in the £3,000 Coles tournament at Huntingdale, and then rounded off the greatest individual winning streak in the history of Australian golf by coasting home to a five-shot victory in the £1,500 Caltex tournament in Wellington, New Zealand. In the three months from late September he'd played nine tournaments and won seven of them. The New Zealand Open, the Italian Open, the Spanish Open, the Canada Cup, the Pelaco, the Coles and the Caltex. When one takes into account the fact that Thomson worked and lobbied tirelessly to bring the Canada Cup to Melbourne, was instrumental in personally attracting the greater portion of the quality and quantity of the field for the event, and at the same time played some of the most scintillating golf ever seen at home, it can be seen that he was already well on the way to earning the tag of 'King of Australian golf'. It was a strange time indeed for Thomson. Somehow he managed to block from his mind the divorce from Lois, which was in its final throes in the courts, while compiling the most vivid purple patch of his playing career. For him the 1950s and his first marriage had come to an end and were history. Soon he would be married for a second time, was planning to raise another family, and was optimistic about the new decade. As the uncertain, unstable, liberated, youth-propelled days of the 1960s approached, he was simply glad that his fine friend Kel had chosen to put his new-found form to the test overseas. Thomson's greatest thrill in the game was only a few months away.

'On the strength of our win in the Canada Cup,' says Thomson, 'and by virtue of the air ticket to Dublin the next year to defend, Kel decided to try his luck en route in the United States. I joined him to find him struggling more than somewhat. I persuaded Kel to invest in a new and different set of clubs and he took a fancy to a spare set Bob MacAllister was carrying around. Suddenly with these he looked a different player. They were a lot stronger and his shots started to fly better. Then, during a spare week in Fort Worth, we decided to drive over to Dallas to a warehouse to look at some new drivers. He found one he just had to have, but it was part of a set of four woods. The manager wouldn't let Kel take the driver and leave him with the rest so we looked at one another and he forked out the money for the set. It seemed an expensive buy, but it turned out trumps. Armed with his new purchase Kel teed off next week in the Colonial Invitational at Ben Hogan's club and came within a stroke of winning.'

In fact Nagle played alongside the mighty Hogan during the event and fired a brilliant 65 that included some remarkable putting and a sensational hole-in-one at the 13th, a 200-yard hole across a deep ravine. The ball landed heavily, took one big jump, skipped a little, then dived into the cup. It was such a wonderful stroke that it even brought praise from his playing partner. 'Good shot,' mumbled a poker-faced Hogan. In the end, only Julius Boros had the chance to beat Nagle, with a par at the last. 'Boros needed only a 9-iron to hit the green with his second,' recalls Thomson. 'But he pulled it and it headed for the edge of the green guarded by a deep lake. It pitched within a yard of the water heading straight at it, and stopped stone dead. From there he easily two-putted to nose out Kel. Don't tell me soft greens are any test of iron play!'

At least Nagle's effort at Fort Worth indicated his delight with his new driver. With Thomson by his side he headed to Ireland in June to defend the Canada Cup, but the American team of Snead and Arnold Palmer were able to parcel it up without too much argument. Snead, the wily veteran, and Palmer, the ascending star of world golf, made an almost perfect combination of grace and power and won by eight shots from England. The defending champions weren't disgraced with third placing just one behind the Englishmen, and upon leaving Portmarnock were far from deflated.

In fact Thomson was most excited about something he'd noticed during the event, Nagle's ability with his new driver. 'During that week at Portmarnock,' says Nagle, 'Pete said to me, "Gee, you're hitting the ball beautifully Kel — you're putting it on a sixpence with that driver. Keep this up and you might be able to win the Open." I had to laugh at that, but Pete certainly put the thought in my mind that I could win.' Nagle did not let that driver out of his sight — except for one occasion — and it proved the camaraderie and good humour that existed between a couple of good mates. 'When I bought that driver back in America, Pete picked himself a similar one too,' says Nagle. 'Well, I went like gangbusters with mine, but Pete couldn't hit his at all and I couldn't hit his either.' Thomson immediately realised that his pal could make his wood stand up and sing once it was in his hands, and a few weeks later when they were playing together again, thought he'd play a little practical joke. After several holes they arrived at the next tee and Nagle thought he'd quench his thirst at the water fountain and left his driver leaning on the park-bench. He came back, grabbed the club and hit a dreadful tee shot that duck-hooked into the trees like a frightened rabbit. Nagle glanced at his precious piece of timber with absolute contempt and turned to Thomson, expecting similar bewilderment. 'Peter was laughin' his head off,' says Nagle. 'He'd swapped our drivers over while I was having a drink! He was honest though — he gave me back my old club and of course I ended up winning the Open with it. It now lives in the golf museum at St Andrews.'

The Centenary British Open at St Andrews was held the week after the Canada Cup, and while Snead headed back home, there was enormous interest in the Open debut of Arnold Palmer. For the first time since the glory days of Ben Hogan, the term 'grand-slam' again surfaced after Palmer won the 1960 US Masters and US Open and came to St Andrews amidst a flood of publicity. At Augusta in April he won his second green jacket by a shot after birdies at the last two holes, and then in the final round of the Open at Cherry Hills, crunched a drive down the 346-yard opening hole that bounded onto the green. It lifted the curtain on a final round of 65 that secured him his one and only US Open by two strokes from promising youngster Jack Nicklaus.

It seemed all St Andrews turned out for the Open Championship,. hoping to see something equally historic, but while the spotlight hardly moved from Palmer's broad shoulders in the lead-up to the event, one of the greatest lessons in golf history was taking place only a matter of metres away. Thomson was once again battling the effects of asthma — a notorious asthma and hay fever sufferer from an early age, this problem was to plague him whenever he travelled in Britain and Australia, particularly on golf courses where the pollens and dusty winds were at their peak. On this occasion asthma had all but ruled out his hopes of a fifth title, while Nagle was as enthusiastic as a wide-eyed novice and couldn't wait to attack the course. Thomson took him around. 'He spent hours showing me how to play St Andrews,' says Nagle. 'There are things you simply have to do off each tee — you have to aim in a certain direction, and Pete, who'd played and won there many times, showed me where to go. We played four rounds together in practice and he said, "go left" or "go right", "do this" or "do that". The help I got from him that week was fantastic.' Thomson felt his good friend had an excellent chance. 'I showed him everything I knew personally about the Old Course,' he says. 'It was a wet summer. The Old Course was soft and defenceless. It, therefore, became a test of putting since it was certain that every one of the top starters would hit the greens near the holes. Now, who was the best putter around at the time? Kel Nagle. A New Zealand buddy of mine, who had seen most Opens since the war, stayed with us. I told him Kel would win and why — in the end he was most grateful!'

Heeding Thomson's advice to the letter and firing out a series of spectacularly straight drives, Nagle made a confident start and backed up by a velvet touch on the greens he opened with brilliant rounds of 69–67 to trail his old sparring partner Roberto de Vicenzo by two strokes. Playing alongside the Argentinian over the 36-holes of the final day, Nagle hit the front at lunchtime with what was, under the circumstances, a superb 71. But no sooner had he putted out for a two-shot lead over de Vicenzo and four over the lurking Palmer, than the heavens opened above the ghostly, grey town and a flood, such as never had been seen before in living memory, cascaded down the steps of the Royal and Ancient Golf Club and filled the Valley of Sin to its very brim. There was no further play that day. Thomson, nine shots behind his leading mate, climbed the stairs to his room in Rusacks Hotel in his socks, carrying his dripping wet shoes. Above him he heard voices discussing the next day's prospects and coughing loudly so he wouldn't stumble across anyone mentioning his name in vain, or saying something a touch embarrassing, saw Gary Player and a South African friend of his. 'Isn't it incredible,' said Player. 'Can you imagine Kel Nagle as the Open Champion?' Thomson thought that was a little rich, but remained poker-faced as he strode past. He was even more determined to help his friend succeed.

Arnold Palmer claims the idle hours sitting around waiting for that final round ruined his winning chances at St Andrews, but if anyone was going to be affected by the sudden halt in proceedings it was Thomson's pal. Nagle rose the next morning, peered out the hotel window, and saw the local fire brigade pumping water from the bunkers. He was suffering from a bad case of tendonitis in the little finger of his right hand and as he stared down at those red trucks the hand was clenched in a tight fist. It was the best kept secret of the Open. 'After giving it the usual cold water, then hot water treatment for a while it slowly opened up,' he says, 'but when I went out for that final round I was hoping like mad that it wouldn't play up.' Palmer was playing in the group directly in front of Nagle and started to produce an Augusta-Cherry Hills charge. It was a head-on 'Arnie' style, seemingly transforming the hitherto dry and crusty game. Most were hoping Nagle would be nudged aside gracefully, like those before him at Augusta and Cherry Hills, but that he wouldn't be hurt too much by Palmer's inevitable overtaking. Yet for all his admirable two-fisted aggressiveness, Palmer came up against something of equal force that grey day — Nagle's sheer courage, combined with an unshakeable never-say-die attitude. They were qualities the Australian public had seen many times before.

'Kel was as steady as a rock,' says Thomson. 'Placing one sure foot in front of the other. He followed the agreed instructions to the letter. At the 14th he got the better of de Vicenzo when the Argentinian pushed a huge drive over the wall and never recovered. Palmer was his only threat now. The American made his run towards the end, and at the 17th, the infamous Road Hole, Kel faced a crucial 10-footer for his par, but before he could putt a huge roar went up from the 18th green where Palmer holed a long birdie putt for a closing 68 and a 278 total. If ever Kel was going to be rocked, that was going to do it. He needed to hole his putt and par the last to win. He backed away from that putt, came in fresh, addressed the putter ahead of the ball, lifted it over and then drew back. From where I was watching, from the clubhouse balcony, my hands shook so much that I couldn't hold my binoculars straight so I put them down and listened.' Like a blind man, Thomson relied on the thousands of spectators to tell him who would become Open Champion. 'Then the roar of the crowd came floating back just as big as Palmer's but twice as sweet. He had holed it. He later told me it was the best putt he had ever made in his life, dead in the middle. Now, barring catastrophes, he had it. He then drove straight and crossed the road. But still the doubts entered my mind. What if he collapses under the strain? What if he hits it fat and comes up short? What agony it is watching someone you know go through that moment. Glory be though, with the huge crowd practically rubbing shoulders with him, Kel hit his 8-iron to the last green within a yard while Palmer ruefully went through his card sitting forlornly on the stone steps. From there Kel had two to win. He missed the first out of excitement and with only momentary hesitation stalked around the ball.'

This is without question the climax of a professional golfer's life. Hole this putt and the Open, the British Open, is yours. Nagle had wondered about it all many times before, especially during that week. Was he good enough? Did he have what it takes? How would he feel when it came time to hole that winning putt? Now he knew. Exactly a decade later, almost on the same square inch of turf, American Doug Sanders was in exactly the same position — he missed the putt, tied with Jack Nicklaus and lost the 18-hole play-off the next day. The sight of that ball sneaking past the hole is burned into Sanders's memory and he will carry it to his grave.

A sight is also burned into Nagle's memory. 'Kel hit it hard into the back of the cup so that it bounced up into the air before it fell downwards,' says Thomson. 'Then all the pride and joy and noise and relief broke loose and my cobber was the winner. He was Open Champion! I must say I went out to embrace him with tears of joy in my eyes … I couldn't have felt as overjoyed if I had won myself.' It was the most emotional display from Thomson seen on a golf course. The moment summed up the sheer quality and value of their friendship. 'Pete was first onto the green to congratulate me,' says Nagle. 'He rushed up and gave me a big hug and said, "Good on you mate, you beauty!" And then suddenly there were people everywhere. He said to me, "Kel, there's no way you can get back to the hotel for your jacket, so take mine!" It was absolutely fantastic. Pete had shown me around St Andrews all week and there I was receiving the Open trophy in his jacket. It was strange how it all worked out. I'll never forget the party we had that night. Spalding arranged a big dinner party for me at Rusack's Hotel, the main hotel right alongside the golf course, and there were around thirty people on our table, including Pete. This young girl came around with the tray of vegetables to serve them out, and she was pretty nervous about it all. She dropped all the peas into my lap! She could have tipped them all over my head and it wouldn't have worried me — I was on top of the world!'

Everyone tried to get Nagle to celebrate with a glass of champagne that night, but having never drunk anything stronger than tea, he was just happy enough to see the smiles on the faces of his friends. As the new Open Champion he was in demand but he stunned the world by flying home, because of his tendonitis. 'I didn't play for three months after I won the Open,' he says. 'I tried to practise, but the pain in my finger was just too great. I had to give it a rest.'

Kel went back to Sydney where he had opened a new sports shop in partnership with the only other Australian to win a British Open, the Thomson-Nagle Sports Store in George Street, an ambitious venture designed to capitalise on the surging popularity of golf in Australia. The location of the shop proved unsuitable and the project didn't catch on. It was one of the rare failures of their association and of Thomson's business career.

Before the Canada Cup at Royal Melbourne, Nagle would have been content to stay at home, building up the store and playing for the biggest prizes Australian golf had to offer. Once he was over his tendonitis he was again influenced by Thomson's thinking. The shop was best left in the hands of those equipped to deal with it and Nagle, knowing that as Open Champion he could match shots with any player in the world, changed his attitude and developed a Thomson approach to travelling. 'A golfer has to travel,' Thomson has written. 'You have to go where the tournaments are. They won't come to you. There is no argument that travel also broadens the mind. Whatever it adds in depth is largely up to the individual. For me at any rate it has been the most enthralling experience. What I have seen has stimulated my appetite for more. There is much more I want to explore. With luck golf will give me the opportunity. Ever since I can remember I have been fascinated with other places. Even today, standing in a market place or crossing a strange bridge bemuses me. It is thrilling. I know golfers who never want to leave home. I think they are missing a lot. It is all very well to say: "I will do these things when I retire, when I have the time." If you don't do it when you are young and impressionable, you might as well stay at home. I have been charmed by the customs of Japan, intrigued by the workings of the Chinese, stunned by the poverty of India, enraptured by the green hills of Kenya, revolted by the tourist traps of Southern Europe, surprised by the advancement of Sweden and astonished at the pace of the United States. All these experiences have been much to my benefit. I feel enriched by it all. But it is easy to miss these things. If you never think past the out of bounds of golf courses you might as well live in a glass booth ...'

When Thomson was establishing the Far-East circuit in the early 1960s he could think of no greater contributor than Kel Nagle. Thomson first went to the Philippines in 1949 and when he returned some years later he found that not much had improved in the way of tournaments and overall prizemoney. With typical enthusiasm he set about establishing events in places that had never before had them. Nagle was at his right hand and today the region boasts a circuit of up to fifty tournaments and phenomenal prizemoney.

The pair also became honorary New Zealanders, singlehandedly building the credibility of the Kiwi circuit to the point where it was included with Australian events to become the 'Australasian tour'. Between them they forged an almost incredible record in the NZ Open. In the twenty-two years between 1950–71 the name of Thomson or Nagle was engraved on the NZ Open trophy a staggering sixteen times: nine titles to Thomson, seven to Nagle. The latter also won seven NZ PGA championships. They had similar successes in Asia as they explored new worlds and customs that they could never have dreamed of in their youth. The travelling gave a new perspective to their friendship. They were good times. A lover of Chinese food, Thomson ate little else on the Far-East tour and a running gag with the more experienced Australian players was to invite the younger golfers out for an exotic dinner, something a little different from the usual steak and potatoes. If an inability to come to grips with chopsticks didn't have them struggling first up, dishes of steamed chicken arriving at the table with the head still attached, red comb and all, certainly had them wondering whether the experiment was worth the effort. Despite his seniority, Nagle wasn't protected from the good-natured humour. At an elegant dinner party in Hong Kong he was happily munching away on what he thought was a magnificent chicken dish when Thomson leant over and informed him he was eating a common snake. After that, Nagle says he was always suspicious whenever Thomson invited him out to dinner.

Importantly, they managed to enjoy themselves on the golf course as well. Like the occasion when Nagle won the Hong Kong Open in 1961 with a remarkable score of 261 and the following week carded an opening round of 68 to share the tournament lead in Manila. Even more remarkable was the behaviour of a notorious Philippines gambler who told anyone prepared to listen, including Thomson, that Nagle had no hope of winning the event. 'While I was wondering whether to pity him or take advantage of his stupidity, he added that he had 2,000 pesos to back it up,' says Thomson, not normally interested in making such a wager. 'But a fellow who talks like that should not be allowed to roam around unchallenged. If I wasn't going to win I thought such a bonus would make Manila well worthwhile, so I set him. Alas, Kel had problems with the putter the next day, never recovered, and in the end I beat him home. I broke about even that week!' Despite his tribulations on the greens, Nagle could not help but see the lighter side of Thomson's plight and while embarrassed over the incident, says: 'We both ended up having a good laugh about it later on.'

Their tours through Asia, New Zealand and Britain were approached more as sociable and enjoyable sojourns rather than ruthless business trips. Wherever Nagle and Thomson travelled they managed their share of victories sprinkled amidst the consistent high finishes and in every country they made hundreds of firm friends, ranging from ordinary folk right up to heads of state. 'In Singapore we became quite friendly with Prime Minister Lee Kuan Yew, and his Finance Minister, Dr Gho Keng Swee,' says Thomson. 'Both were keen golfers. Kel and I were often asked to join them for morning rounds and, like Tunku Abdul Rahman in Kuala Lumpur, these eminent men in the new Malaysia believed golf was necessary for recreation and relief. Dr Gho told me that the Malaysian Federation would never have worked out if not for their regular games of golf!'

The journeys to the corners of the earth not only broadened the minds of Thomson and Nagle. The latter clearly blossomed as a player and continued to confound the critics who considered the 1960 British Open his first and final pinnacle. In 1964 Nagle won the Canadian Open and the following year, at age 44, came agonisingly close to causing one of the most remarkable triumphs in the history of golf. At St Louis, Missouri, he tied for first place with Gary Player in the US Open. No Australian had performed so well in America's greatest championship and in the 18-hole play-off the next day the pair could not be separated coming to the closing holes, when Nagle pulled a drive and his ball hit a female spectator. By the time he arrived on the scene the woman was a bloodied mess. Although she recovered quickly, Nagle was badly shaken. Player triumphed by three strokes after a 71. Thomson was absent from St Louis, but his pal's heroic performance was to inspire him in the British Open at Royal Birkdale where he claimed his crowning golfing achievement with a stunning victory. This time Nagle was first on to the green to offer his congratulations.

On his arrival back home, Thomson discovered that many golf writers were responding to his greatest performance by having him out to pasture. With a much cherished fifth Open in his pocket, they said, he could now gracefully bow out of the game. Thomson had no intention of putting his feet up. 'Maybe I'll give competition golf away in five years or so,' he said, when questioned at the airport, 'but I've still got plenty of time left. Look at Kel — he's still doing very well and he's well over 40! Why just the other day he suggested we bring the old firm back into business for the Canada Cup.' The PGA was thinking along the same lines. They sent the British Open Champion and US Open runner-up to represent Australia in the 1965 Canada Cup in Spain and there were many who had a sneaking feeling that the sight of one another under their country's banner would once again be enough to carry them to victory. Unfortunately Madrid turned out to be a gigantic let-down. Thomson tore a rib muscle during the closing stages of the third round and the next day was forced to withdraw. Even in their moments of extreme disappointment though, the pair survived through constant good humour. As always, Nagle could see the funny side. 'I know it wasn't very humorous for Pete at the time, but I still get a laugh out of it every time I think about that day in Madrid,' he says. 'Pete saw the doctor on the morning of the last round and thought he'd be clear to play. The Doc was an enthusiastic fellow who said he'd tag along behind us just in case. We were walking down the first fairway and Pete was apparently okay, when all of a sudden an old beat-up ambulance arrived and the doctor and a couple of ladies with white coats on jumped out and told Pete to whip up his shirt. They pulled out this enormous needle and shoved it straight into his muscle! At the next tee, Pete said he felt awful and scuffed his drive along the ground and that was it — he couldn't play any more. Who needs help like that?' Thomson recalls his distinct lack of respect for the good doctor's knowledge of medicine. 'The pain became worse and my side tightened up and the injection just left me feeling dizzy, and then it turned out he'd given me the wrong syringe! It was a drug that makes you feel like you're drunk. He was absolutely hopeless!'

Sadly it was to be the last occasion a Thomson-Nagle combination would represent Australia, and a less than fitting farewell for a team with such a glorious Canada Cup record. Before the Spanish disaster the duo had competed six times, for victories in 1954 and 1959, second placings in 1955 and 1961, and third placings in 1960 and 1962. They were clearly Australia's most successful combination. Thomson played in Cup partnerships with Pickworth, von Nida, Crampton and Billy Dunk, but never with similar success. Dunk, who partnered Thomson in the 1969 World Cup in Singapore, recalls that his more senior partner was an extremely difficult person to play with. 'We got to the first tee on the opening day and representing my country for the first time I was raring to go,' says Dunk. 'We were just about to hit off and Peter turned to me and said, "Oh well, we can't win here this week. These locals are tremendous putters — too good for us." Now I don't know if he was trying to use reverse psychology or something, but I thought it was a very strange thing to say, and it had an effect on my game.' The Australian pair finished 9th, 22 strokes behind the winning US team of Orville Moody and Lee Trevino. While Nagle has nothing but kind words for his partnership with Thomson both on and off the course, Dunk has been left wondering. 'It's my opinion that Peter is a very hard bloke to get to know,' he says. 'I totally respect what he has done for golf right around the world — he and Kel have done wonders for the tours in New Zealand and Asia — but he's not the sort of bloke you can get close to. Just when you think you might have him sorted out, he'll do something that completely knocks you for six. He's different all right. I remember watching him come up the 17th at Victoria in the 1961 Australian Open and after two shots on the par-5 he had a little chip to the green. Well, I couldn't believe it, but he shanked it — shanked it right into the rough! He stood there and without a trace of shock or embarrassment or anger, said out loud, "Gee, that wind is strong!" I think it sums him up that he then walked quickly to his ball and without fuss knocked it to within a foot and tapped in for his par!'

Similar stories abound from most of the professionals of his era, and not just Australians. Nagle will have none of it. 'Peter calls a spade a spade and always has,' he says. 'In the business of golf it's very easy for someone to get upset over what someone says or does, but I think Pete is an extremely honest man. Of course he doesn't always get it right, but then again, tell me who does?'

When observing Thomson, or talking to him, one can easily gain the impression he is aloof, distant and remote. He has an extraordinary ability to control his emotions — those within his inner sanctum pinpoint it as one of his major characteristics while his critics say it is one of the most frustrating: no expression of joy; no expression of anger. In the modern sporting era, when the most glamorous, charismatic and attractive competitors are usually the most handsomely paid, it is hard to

Left: Thomson (far right) and the Canada Cup field, guests of US President Dwight 'Ike' Eisenhower at the White House, 1955.

Below left: Help from daughter Deidre as Thomson pilots his cart during practice at an American tournament, 1955.

Below right: A family snap of Peter with Bing Crosby on the Monterey Peninsula, California, 1956.

'I'll never forget how a tornado helped me win $14,000 in Dallas.' The honorary Texan clutches two massive trophies and his prizemoney cheque after a final round of 63 and his only PGA Tour win in America, the 1956 Texas Centennial Open. Thomson gave away his trophy.

Peter flanked by Pan and Mary following another triumph on the US Seniors tour, 1985.

Friends for more than 40 years without a cross word. A lighthearted moment between Nagle and Thomson during a round at Spring Valley GC, Melbourne, February 1969.

Open Champions past and future: Thomson guides St Andrews novice Ian Baker-Finch around the Old Course in practice for the 1984 Open Championship.

believe that Thomson ever made it to the big time. In his life he has done everything possible through the years to achieve total control, to remove as far as possible any chance of the unpredictable and unpleasant from happening. His circle of personal friends is select, many and varied, and not only extremely loyal, but they all know their place. Thomson is in control. If you play the game of life with him, you play it by his rules. Since they are very fair, honourable and gentlemanly rules, it is difficult to object.

In the final week of March 1980 the friendship between Peter Thomson and Kel Nagle transcended a milestone that could never have been experienced on a golf course. It remains one of life's greatest ironies that nothing brings two souls closer together than personal tragedy and when Jean Nagle passed away suddenly in the night, Kel needed a friend. Thomson was there. 'Pete and I were supposed to go to the States for the Seniors tour in early April,' says Nagle, 'but suddenly my wife was gone and I didn't feel like doing anything. Honestly, I was ready to sell out cheaply. Pete was a great support, and really put me back into gear — "Come on, you've got to get on with it, you can't let it bog you down," he told me — Pete was the one who got me back on the tracks.'

With the memory of his wife both to spur him on and to pull him to his moments of depression, Nagle, at the age of 60, chose to throw himself in to the one thing that he felt safe with, golf. Thomson and Nagle made that trip to the US, rekindled the old friendships and competitive spirit and once again found success on the golf course. Thomson knew that no amount of money or titles would free Nagle from personal torment but he was cunning enough to perceive that his friend's idle hours were best spent on the golf course and in the company of old friends rather than mulling over memories at home. Within a year Nagle had taken positive steps to overcoming his tragedy and partnered together once again in the US$410,000 Legends of Golf tournament in Texas, they came within a stroke of an incredible victory after trailing the leaders by five shots with eight holes to play. Gene Littler and Bob Rosburg were the winners that spring day at Onion Creek in Austin.

Some have had the audacity to claim that Thomson went back to the United States simply to line his pockets. They say he didn't win enough in his heyday to be anywhere near satisfied and the Seniors, the 'over the hill' tour, represented his big chance to make hay while the sun shone. He was there for the pure enjoyment, and when his countryman, the fellow who would place a photograph of his wife and children in his hotel room before unpacking his suitcase, needed companionship more than at any other time in his life, the vulgar aspects of prizemoney trailed dismally on his list of priorities. In later years, when Thomson was sweeping all before him and winning tournament after tournament on the US Seniors tour, he would shrug his shoulders at local reporters, suggesting his latest triumph was far from remarkable, then head off to join his wife Mary and daughter Pan (at that time travelling with her parents on the tour) for dinner. Kel would always be waiting at the table. Many times the women members of the small Australian côterie would try to match Nagle up with a date, but every time Nagle would politely refuse. In the end and in good humour, he took Pan as his partner to many of the dinners and cocktail parties that became an integral part of the USGA Seniors tour. Kel was happy, the Thomsons were happy, and the family philosophy so strong on both sides was preserved. Thomson observed it all with his famous wry smile; he patently loved it. He felt he was watching the big brother he never had.

'We've had a friendship that's very hard for me to put into words,' says Nagle. 'I've got nothing but admiration for him because he doesn't make a lot of fuss and quietly goes about achieving just about everything he wants to. He's a brilliant course designer, he can paint and draw — I've sat beside him on aeroplanes many, many times and he sits there doodling away and sketching, and he is very talented in that field — he can also write well, can comment on television, make a good speech, run a good meeting, and he has raised a wonderful family. He's done a tremendous job building up the Australian PGA. A lot of people don't realise how tough it was back in the dark old days when the PGA was trying to raise a bit of money and was constantly dealing with sponsors and television. It needed someone who was diplomatic and Pete is just the right sort of man for that. Through all this he has played great golf too. I've seen many of the world's greatest players, Nicklaus, Hogan, Locke, Snead, Palmer and Player, and I tell you, Pete's right up there with them. I'm very fortunate to have been his mate. Golf has been good to both of us. We've played golf together all over the world; we've had a lot of fun together; we've become great friends; and we have a very pleasant relationship that has lasted more than forty years without a cross word. What more could a man want?'

In September 1990, and after their paths had taken them in opposite directions for many months, Thomson and Nagle were reunited at the Daikyo Legends of Golf tournament at Paradise Palms near Cairns. Nearing 70, and a mere ten months after a delicate back operation, Nagle finished a creditable third behind New Zealander Bob Charles and the US-based Bruce Devlin. Thomson was not among the placings — he had long since eased back on the competitive throttle and was simply happy to be there. No doubt in the back of his mind he would have loved to have won the event, but with Charles's winning margin a healthy 14 strokes, Thomson, as always, was quick to accept reality. He was concerned more with the days immediately following the tournament, when Kel and he would travel the short distance north to Port Douglas for a private, proper reunion at the Thomsons' second home. Peter and Mary had been trying for years to tempt Kel into making the trip and now, finally, he could see what it was that made the place so attractive to them. It was a time for mirth and memories, relaxation and rapport. A local fishing expedition under the piercing northern Queensland sun was none too grandiose but before they set out, Nagle, his tongue firmly in cheek and his familiar old straw hat in place, asked if his friend was a good captain. Thomson replied that it was a team effort. If fishing relied on teamwork, they should have come home with a boatful. When Peter Thomson and Kel Nagle are together everything seems easy.

CHAPTER 5

'My Life's Ambition'

HISTORY tells us that to be a truly great golfer one must be as much craftsman as magician. A great golfer operates on technique as much as on inspiration to achieve consistently good performances every week. When age inevitably interferes, stealing distance from the great golfer's drives and replacing it with a devilishly twitchy putting stroke, it is craft which keeps him going. Craft is staying out of the sand, water or trees when he is in contention. Craft is keeping a cool head whilst those around him wonder if they should be there at all. Craft is using all manner of cunning to gain best advantage for his round, whether it means putting through a deep valley to within a foot of the pin rather than attempting a chip, or punching in a low shot under a blanket of strong wind to birdie range rather than allowing the gale to wreak its havoc by trying to attack it head-on. Craft is being able to get up and down from a bunker when he simply *has* to get up and down from a bunker and being able to write a par on his card when everyone else can only manage bogey or worse. Craft is doing these things week in, week out.

On the famous sea-side links of Britain, where golf as a game of judgement not strength was given birth, where vicious gales and biting rain frequently lashed the treeless courses, where the direction of the small British ball was at the mercy of the wind, and where a golfer was truly humbled by centuries of tradition, Peter Thomson became a craftsman.

In 1951, when Thomson made his first trip to Britain, the professional golf circuit there was far different from its counterpart in the US and a mere shadow of the rich, solid tour that currently thrives in

Europe. There were fewer tournaments then, much less prizemoney, a more relaxed atmosphere and, above all, a style and class that permeated the clubhouse, the players and the championships. Sometimes when the weather was suitable, the biggest names in British golf, resplendent in their collars-and-ties, plus-fours and two-tone spikes, could be seen at lunchtime on the final day of a tournament leaning on their Bentleys and Jaguars, basking in the sun and swapping chit-chat with family or friends as they sipped cups of tea and nibbled cut sandwiches, seemingly oblivious of the pressures of the final round ahead.

It was another world, and Peter Thomson loved it. There were some big names to be found on the fairways: Welshman David 'Dai' Rees, Irishman Fred Daly, Englishmen Henry Cotton, Charlie Ward, Max Faulkner, Harry Weetman and a fresh-faced youngster named Peter Alliss, son of the famous pro Percy and a player who went on to win twenty tournaments around Europe before becoming a distinguished BBC commentator.

'I had just completed my National Service in the RAF regiment and I was demobilised in June 1951,' says Peter Alliss. 'There was a golf tournament being played at Bournemouth where I lived called "The Festival of Britain", and it was the first time I ever set eyes on Peter Thomson. I remember it vividly. He had on white shoes, dark green trousers, white shirt and white tennis visor, and was putting out on the 18th green. Someone said to me, "that's the wonder boy from Australia". Bobby Locke and Norman von Nida and Ossie Pickworth were very big names in British golf at the time, and Thomson struck me as someone to have a look at because all these men were saying he was set for an enormous future. I took to him immediately. He just seemed different. He had a jauntiness about him and a real twinkle in the eye. He had a strange sort of calmness, a methodical business-like way of doing things, yet he also appeared to be having fun, which is something you don't often see in professional golfers these days. Certainly it stood out back then.' A great many greats trudged around the courses heavy of foot, painstakingly determined, their firm steps seemingly unshakeable. Of Thomson it was said that, if he played on a snow-covered layout in Britain, his footprints would resemble those of a bird.

Thomson's opinion of the tour then, is typically succinct: 'The British circuit just seemed to me to be more friendly and more intimate than America's. There wasn't the hype that went with the US scene and I enjoyed that.' And of course there was the 'Open Championship'. If he was not exactly wedded to the game, it was in this event that everyone could see that he and golf were going steady.

The British Open is the oldest championship of all, its origins going back to Prestwick in 1860 when eight professionals played three times over the then 12-hole course. The Open Championship (strictly speaking never the 'British Open') stands supreme. 'It has the most claim to being a world title, because it attracts more world-class players,' says Thomson. 'You find few foreign players in the US Open, largely because of the difficulties of qualifying.'

When Thomson first played in the Open in 1951, many Britons considered him 'an overnight sensation'. His debut had been some ten years in the making. He had first heard of the championship back in his boyhood days at Royal Park. He had listened to Jimmy Grace talk of the big event and later the professional sat him down and told him of the exploits of his friend, the great Joe Kirkwood, who was never worse than eighth in his eight attempts at the Open. In fact the Australian had come close to winning at St Andrews in 1921. He was out in front heading into the final nine holes when a disturbing shout from the gallery at the top of his backswing resulted in a bad slice, an unconscious spectator and a blown chance. He finished sixth.

Like all young boys of the time, Thomson had a keen ear and a vivid imagination, and was spellbound by these stories. He would use them later as a passport to his own world, pretending Royal Park was St Andrews, Hoylake or Muirfield at British Open time. There are no prizes for guessing who was in the lead. 'The senior men at Royal Park would talk about the British Open quite a lot and they held its champions in very high regard,' he recalls fondly. 'Names like Hagen, Sarazen and Cotton were the heroes and even back then the Open became number one in my mind. I thought to myself, well, one day it would be nice to have a go at that. Eventually the Open Championship meant everything to me — it became the focal point of my year and my life's ambition.'

An analysis of Thomson's breakthrough triumph in the Open of 1954 cannot begin without first exploring the three previous Championships. At Portrush in 1951, Lytham in 1952 and Carnoustie in 1953 he proved he was a worthy challenger to the great names of the past. With an ounce of luck he might have triumphed earlier than 1954 but, significantly, he was in no hurry. He was prepared to wait; to be patient; to serve an apprenticeship; to learn the lessons that would clear a path to that trophy. He felt it was his destiny.

The 1951 British Open holds a unique place in the record books as the only one ever played outside Scotland or England. Royal Portrush, Northern Ireland, presented an almighty challenge to the field and throughout the entire championship there were only two scores under 70. The Scottish veteran Jimmy Adams, runner-up in the 1936 and 1938 Opens, carded a superb 68 to lead the field after the first round, and right there in the thick of it was Thomson, running second with Dai

Rees after a dream debut round of 70. He admitted to quite a few nerves on the first tee, but once he'd carded a couple of pars he was swept up by the thrill and challenge. By day's end he was a stroke ahead of Bobby Locke (attempting a third consecutive victory), and the player considered something of an eccentric on the tour; Max Faulkner. An extremely colourful dresser, 'the Jimmy Demaret of Britain' Faulkner was reputed to have tried no less than 300 putters during his pro career, one of them with a shaft made from a sawn-off billiard cue and a head made from driftwood! Whatever caused him to experiment so must have been absent at Portrush, for it was largely Faulkner's outstanding putting that gave him a second round 70 and a two-stroke lead over the field. And the golfing cognoscenti were horrified at his reaction. So enthused was Faulkner about his fortunes on the greens that he boldly declared he would never again miss a short putt! Further tempting fate when besieged by schoolboys and young ladies after that second round, he proceeded to scribble his autograph, adding the words 'Open Champion 1951'. The superstitious at Portrush could scarcely believe that he went on to win!

After his excellent start, Thomson faded to finish in a tie for sixth, eight shots behind the winner, but it was the beginning of a long, long romance with links golf: 'I wasn't the best player at Portrush by any means, however I was pretty pleased with the way I handled things. I knew I had to be patient and not try to rush things too much. There was plenty of time ... I knew I'd be back.'

Some members of the British press weren't sure what to make of Thomson. Norman von Nida had made some outrageous statements about the youngster being a finer player than himself, and frankly they were sceptical. They expected a better finish from him than the one they saw at Portrush, but if equal sixth from a field of 180 in his first Open

1951 Open Championship, Royal Portrush, Ireland	
285 — M. Faulkner (Eng.)	71–70–70–74
287 — A. Cerda (Arg.)	74–72–71–70
290 — C. Ward (Eng.)	75–73–74–68
292 — F. Daly (Ire.)	74–70–75–73
— J. Adams (Scot.)	68–77–75–72
293 — W. Shankland (Eng.)	73–76–72–72
— A. Locke (S. Af.)	71–74–74–74
— H. Weetman (Eng.)	73–71–75–74
— P. Thomson (Aust.)	70–75–73–75
— N. Sutton (Eng.)	73–70–74–76

was not enough to convince those writers of his talent, within a fortnight there was irrefutable evidence. After rounds of 68–70 on the way to the runners-up prize of £200 in the 90-hole North British Tournament at Harrogate, Thomson completed his third round in a phenomenal 62. Out in 30, home in 32, it was the best single round ever played in a first-class British event and thrust the young Australian into the spotlight. The local committee immediately made him an honorary life-member and labelled him a future champion. 'Sometimes I used to get into a mood, or a touch, and I would do everything correctly,' Thomson says of that blistering round. 'I did a lot of good one-round scores around Melbourne when I was 19, so I knew I could do things like that. I would just slip into this delightful groove where everything would feel comfortable and I would hole the majority of putts that I stood over. That was the important thing. When you do scores like that it's mostly the putting. That round did a lot of good for me. It came at the end of my tour, but it set things up for me and at least a few people got to know about this bloke from Australia.'

The following year Thomson began his tour after a brief honeymoon around Britain with his new bride Lois, and soon settled down to several solid performances and, with his new-found toughness after his South African experiences at Locke's right hand, made an impact; not so much on the course, however, but in print. Thomson astonished golf writers at London's Wentworth Club for the £2,500 Daks tournament when he was asked his impressions of the famous West course. It has never been Thomson's style to seek publicity through controversy as might Norman von Nida, but he has always called a spade a spade, and as close as he could come to boiling point after a poor second round of 78 to follow his opening 70, the 22-year-old looked the reporter straight in the eye and said: 'It is an insult to ask an Australian to play on this course. It is like one of our bush courses back home!' The sharks immediately pounced on this piece of bloodied meat. Bush course, indeed! The locals bristled with cries of sour grapes and some writers decided the youngster's seven at the 4th and nine at the 11th were the real reasons behind his controlled outburst. Others pointed out that no one had actually asked him to play at all, or that he was right at home playing on a bush course. Thomson's first brush with controversy didn't exactly endear him to the British, but as he'd learned from Locke, such setbacks were best placed firmly behind him. He preferred to look ahead, and in this case that was particularly easy, for he was soon motoring up to Blackpool in north-west England, one of his favourite parts of Britain, for the Open Championship at Royal Lytham and St Anne's. He took one look at Lytham's stately clubhouse, and the old Dormie House beside the practice green and he felt at home. There was nothing 'bush' about Lytham. He glanced out across the lush fairways, punctuated with hundreds of bunkers, and saw a sea of red tiled rooftops and the railway line running along the southern border of the course. He loved the greens, the tight fairways and the sheer challenge of it all. And it showed. He was paired with Locke on the opening day and the large gallery that followed was treated to some outstanding play. Thomson carded a 68, Locke a 69, yet it was Irishman Fred Daly who took the day's honours with a 67. Daly, the winner in 1947, displayed such outstanding form by the halfway stage that most pundits couldn't see him losing. A second round 69 gave him a total of 136 and a four-shot lead over Locke (69–71) and five over Thomson (68–73).

The final day dawned as a most ferocious wind whipped across the links from the Irish Sea. It came from the north-west; it was the traditional wind and it meant that good scores could only be made going out. The big test was whether a player could hold on to that good score coming home. Locke wasn't all that concerned about the wind, at least not in the morning. With 36-holes to be played his tee-time was 8.50 a.m. 'After an early breakfast at my Blackpool hotel,' he later wrote in his *Bobby Locke on Golf* (Country Life Ltd, 1953) 'I walked the hundred yards to the garage where my car was parked with my clubs secure in a box in the back. The garage door was locked and there was no one about. This was 7.45 a.m. I looked around — everything was closed. I found a milk delivery man, enquired where the garage owner was, and was told that he would be arriving about 9 o'clock and that he lived 15 minutes away. I gave the man ten shillings, scrambled in amongst the milk bottles and after a bumpy ride got to the owner's house. He was still in bed. I dragged him out and we arrived at the garage at 8.20. I got my car, raced to the course, arrived at 8.40, and with no time even for a few loosening swings, walked straight up on to the first tee.' Locke's jittery journey among the dairy products had no ill-effects. He calmly ran his ball onto the green at the par-3 1st and holed a 30-footer for birdie, which 'cooled me off'.

Although the top three of Daly, Locke and Thomson did not change position after the third round, Locke, significantly, sat down to lunch having moved to within a stroke of Daly. While his opponents struggled to find the fairways and greens in the wild conditions, the South African punched in shot after shot and relied on his wonderful short game to preserve his score, particularly over the brutal closing holes. Locke's 74 was not the best score of the morning, but it was not far from it. Daly and Thomson could only manage 77s. As the crowds swarmed around the clubhouse at lunch, the scoreboard said it was Daly ahead on 213, Locke 214, Thomson 218, Bradshaw and King 219, and van Donck, Bullock, Scott and Goggin on 220. It was at this time, as Locke placed his serviette on the table upon completion of a rather substantial lunch, that he was approached by members of the championship committee and told in no uncertain terms that he must play faster in the afternoon or be penalised. 'It was the first year of the slow play rule,' recalls Thomson. 'I remember Norman von Nida claiming Locke should have been penalised two strokes for slow play — I guess that was typical coming from Norman — but in those days we practically played on the run. Amongst a lot of quick players around at the time Locke was the slow one, but not by modern standards — he was like a hare compared with someone like, say, Peter Fowler.' (In fairness to Fowler, West German Bernhard Langer was once officially timed by a golf magazine as the world's slowest player.)

So the stage was set for a fascinating afternoon. The prevailing gale abated, but only slightly, and after his morning troubles Fred Daly gave the distinct impression he wished he was elsewhere. After a rash of bogeys he drifted from contention and, sadly, Ireland's big hope was again destined to finish agonisingly close to that elusive second Open. Of the forty-six players who set out for the final round, only a few had any realistic hope of winning. With Daly's demise, Locke became the man to watch and the South African decided that without any silly risks he would simply coast home. Despite his mealtime rap over the knuckles his ecclesiastical gait never varied. He moved around the links at his customary pace, was far from aggressive, and eventually doffed his cap to the crowd after a scratchy, but safe 73 for a 287 total. Two strokes clear of Daly, who'd struggled in with a 76, Locke felt he'd shut the door on the 1952 Open.

Playing several groups behind Locke (before the days of leaders out last), Thomson, after his mediocre front nine of 37, was not attracting much interest, but on hearing Locke's total, he knew what was needed: 69 to tie, 68 to win. As far as he was concerned Locke had left the door ajar. With his ability to dismiss a series of bad holes as if they'd never happened, Thomson embarked on nine holes of golf that was to spark an unprecedented run of brilliance in the long and illustrious history of the Open. It started with a 30-foot putt that dived into the hole for birdie at the 11th, followed by a superb pitch to two-feet at 13. Locke by now had showered, changed and was quietly sipping his first scotch, oblivious of the drama outside the clubhouse. His calm was disturbed, however, when news came in of the amazing homeward surge by the young Australian who'd started four shots adrift of Locke. Word quickly spread that perhaps the Open wasn't over after all. Almost everyone on the course streamed across to watch Thomson make his bid, and with each successful putt the British crowd let out huge cheers that were lifted high by the wind and carried across the links back to the clubhouse.

At the 15th there was an unlucky miss when another birdie putt rolled around the cup and stayed out. He now needed birdies at each of the closing three holes to tie Locke and force a play-off. It was, given the wind, an impossible task, yet he nearly achieved it. At the 16th, an ice-cool display yielded a birdie, and at the next he seemed to have another only this time his putt died at the cup, and to the gallery's large groan, lipped out. He now needed an eagle two at the last to tie.

When the news was relayed to Locke a broad smile broke across his jowled face and he sat down and ordered another scotch. Twos at Lytham's last, particularly in such an event as the Open were rare indeed. When the tournament was last at Lytham in 1926, Walter Hagen had been set the same task to tie Bobby Jones, but had 'blown up' and taken a six. Thomson did not blow up. He was the calmest person on the course as he drilled a long, straight drive over the cross-bunkers to perfect position. Someone once said his determination was as inviolate as a detective's daughter. Such was his concentration, it was added, that if the third world war was taking place on the adjacent fairway, he would not have noticed. By now, an enormous gallery had crowded around the 18th green and in front of the clubhouse balcony. Several minutes had passed since Locke had been told of Thomson's final drive, and then suddenly came an almighty roar from outside that seemed to shake the stately building. Locke nearly choked on his drink. He later admitted it had given him the greatest fright of his life.

It was not because of a holed second shot. Thomson had floated in a glorious 6-iron to within a few metres and the huge roar was in recognition of his closing birdie and the end of his wonderful attempt at winning. Locke joined the game's greats by taking his third Open, but many standing around Lytham's clubhouse at the presentation knew it was only a matter of time before the young Australian was walking off with the auld silver claret jug. His final round of 70 was the best of any player over the awkward 36-holes of that memorable last day.

1952 Open Championship, Royal Lytham and St Anne's	
287 — Bobby Locke (S. Af.)	69–71–74–73
288 — Peter Thomson (Aust.)	68–73–77–70
289 — Fred Daly (Ire.)	67–69–77–76
294 — Henry Cotton (Eng.)	75–74–74–71
295 — Antonio Cerda (Arg.)	73–73–76–73
— Sam King (Eng.)	71–74–74–76
296 — Flory van Donck (Belg.)	74–75–71–76
— Fred Bullock (Scot.)	76–72–72–77

'As there is such a big chance factor in golf,' Thomson has said, 'you've got to realise that you can't win every time, even when you've made tremendous preparation to win. It does not happen automatically. You lose more than you win, and you've got to look at it that way and take your chances as they come.' Such an attitude made Thomson even more determined that the Open would one day be his. He knew he'd let things slip with that third round of 77, but in retrospect, the cold score did not do justice to his performance. With Thomson it was not only his ability that stood out; it was his self-control. When he woke on that final day, around the time Locke was snuggled in amongst the milk bottles, Thomson was battling hay fever, not just a mild dose, but a serious one, as the links-lashing wind brought with it dust, grit and pollen, assaulting his sinuses. As long as he was to play golf in Britain this would always haunt him, but the extent of the problem at Lytham was seen in the fact that immediately the tournament concluded he was taken to hospital. 'It was very bad,' he recalls. 'I even had a couple of teeth taken out because they [the doctors] thought they were linked to the hay fever and sinus trouble. All I know is I used to have big problems. My nasal passages would be completely blocked, I would have enormous difficulty breathing and there was a terrible feeling of lethargy.' It might also be added that not once did Thomson use this as an excuse for not winning.

Thankfully the problem stayed away the following year at Carnoustie, but trouble for Thomson manifested itself in the form of Ben Hogan, who had finally been persuaded by his friends to make the trip for the British Open. He agreed that one day his retirement papers would seem incomplete without proof that he could win on a links course in Britain, so he posted his entry for Carnoustie. Arriving well before the qualifying rounds and with an intensity rare at the time, Hogan set himself to learn the Scottish course: how to play the small 1.62-inch ball; whether the ball should be struck differently from links turf. After several experimental rounds he was excited by the extra distance using the small ball and he chose to alter his striking with irons so that he grazed the turf rather than take divots. The Scots swarmed around him. Such was the American's stature that Hollywood had portrayed his life story the previous year in the movie, *Follow the Sun*, starring Glenn Ford, but the producers were a year early. Hogan made his name in 1953. No other golfer came near him. Still affected by the injuries he had received in a near-fatal car accident, he entered only a handful of events and won them all.

'I was lucky enough to watch Hogan when he was at his peak,' says Thomson. 'His play set a standard which I've found few other players, if any, can equal. Sometimes, of course, he missed the green, but there was usually a reason for it. Often he would attempt to fire his ball into a back corner of the green that to ordinary players was not even accessible. These were the shots that sometimes failed to find their mark, yet the fact that Hogan attempted them and nine times out of ten pulled them off, indicated his greatness.'

While Hogan was undergoing his crash-course in the British way of golf, Thomson's introduction to the Open in Scotland was not progressing smoothly. He struggled in the punishing wind and largely due to some wayward approaches and less than impressive putting, carded qualifying rounds of 74–80 to scrape into the elite field by the skin of his teeth. On the strength of this and despite the fact he was runner-up the previous year, the bookmakers didn't give the young Australian much hope and placed him well down the list behind the outright favourite Hogan. On the eve of the tournament, the American made no bones about his distaste for Carnoustie, with its dry fairways scarred by divot marks and the deplorably slow greens. He even offered to send for a lawnmower to cut them to what he described championship length!

A rather disgruntled Hogan came in with a first round of 73 and his thunder was stolen by another American, the amateur Frank Stranahan, who mastered the wind with admirable skill to take the lead with a 70. The canny Scot Eric Brown was well placed on 71, one ahead of Locke, Rees, and a bright prospect from Argentina named de Vicenzo, and the substantially recovered Thomson. Over the next two days though, Hogan's face developed that steely look that suggested he was in 'championship mode'. Regardless of Hogan's criticism of their course, the Scots were so taken by his demeanour that they dubbed him the 'Wee Ice Mon'. Into the final round he was tied with de Vicenzo for the lead, one shot ahead of Thomson, Rees and a second Argentinian, Antonio Cerda. Like a finely tuned middle-distance athlete, Hogan timed his run to perfection. His final round of 68 was the best from any player for the entire tournament and at his one and only Open attempt won by four strokes. A feat unparalleled before or since, 40-year-old Hogan had won the first three majors of the year. He may well have completed what is known as the Grand Slam had his dislike of flying not interfered. He took an ocean liner back home and arrived too late for the US PGA in Michigan and Walter Burkemo triumphed.

Hogan accepted the silver claret jug graciously and his supporters felt he was now a complete man. He felt he had nothing left to achieve in Britain so it remained his only appearance in an Open, although he did play in the 1956 Canada Cup at Wentworth. For Thomson's part, he could only back off and applaud a marvellous performance by a magnificent golfer, but he was far from disillusioned. When he'd first set

1953 Open Championship, Carnoustie, Scotland	
282 — Ben Hogan (USA)	73–71–70–68
286 — Frank Stranahan (USA a.)	70–74–73–69
— Peter Thomson (Aust.)	72–72–71–71
— Antonio Cerda (Arg.)	75–71–69–71
— Dai Rees (Wales)	72–70–73–71
287 — Roberto de Vicenzo (Arg.)	72–71–71–73
290 — Sam King (Eng.)	74–73–72–71
291 — Bobby Locke (S. Af.)	72–73–74–72

foot in Britain Thomson set himself the goal of winning the Open Championship within five years. He estimated 1956 would be his year. After his seconds in 1952–3 though, his thinking was altered dramatically.

The 1954 Open was scheduled for the Royal Birkdale Golf Club, making its debut on the Open roster. In West Lancashire, near the resort town of Southport on England's north-west coast, Royal Birkdale presented a classic seaside links challenge and no one loved such a battle more than Peter Thomson. Several weeks before the Open, playing in America as his traditional build-up, he was in dreadful form. The need for him to keep his mind on the job was paramount and he hardly needed distractions. Then with the memory of losing his first child hanging heavily over his shoulders, Thomson was told that his wife, comforted by friends, had gone into labour in London. Separated by hundreds of miles it was a very anxious time for them both, but eventually Peter received the news that Lois had given birth to a healthy girl, Deidre. As one who'd grown up without sisters and particularly one who'd suffered so much agony with his first experience at parenthood, Thomson came to dote on his baby daughter. He wanted to pack up immediately and join them both in Britain. Before he could fly out, however, he was bound to compete in the US Open at Baltusrol at Springfield, New Jersey. Ed Furgol waltzed away with the title while Thomson, understandably, was never in contention. According to a local correspondent, he 'hooked, sliced, topped, duffed and foozled his way to 15 holes over par out of 36 to eliminate himself from the final rounds'. It was precisely what Thomson wanted. He hot-footed it to Southport where he held his daughter in his arms for the first time and settled down amidst the comfortable family atmosphere. It was some time before he was able to concentrate on his battle plans for Birkdale.

The press was expected to follow Thomson closely in practice, particularly since the arrival of his baby, and the fact that he'd been runner-up in their Open the previous two years but, as he was relieved to discover, the limelight was directed away from him. A wave of sporting fever was still sweeping Britain, weeks after medical student Roger Bannister became the first man to run a mile in under four minutes. He clocked 3.59:04 at Oxford University to conquer the Everest of athletics. At Birkdale, the Fleet Street scribes expected the home golfers to carry on this wave of patriotism into a memorable fight for the silver claret jug.

A few days before the championship began Thomson was relaxing with Lois and Deidre in his hotel room when the telephone rang. 'I'm the best caddy in all England,' said the caller, 'and I've chosen you!' Cecil Timms had caddied for Hogan the previous year and had brought him home the winner, so that was good enough for Thomson. 'I'll meet you for a practice round tomorrow morning,' he said.

Royal Birkdale that year was baked hard, dry and fast under an unusually fierce northern summer sun and it was almost impossible to play a running drive to an advantageous position. 'The fairways also had many bumps and hollows and often a good straight drive would hit one of those bumps and deflect into the rough,' Thomson recalls. There was a much bigger problem. It came from the man who'd made the telephone call the previous night. Before the pair had reached the turn during that practice round, Thomson was wondering whether he'd made a wise choice for bagman. Timms, he realised, was different. To Thomson caddies were supposed to behave like children and not speak unless they were spoken to, but not Timms. As the round wore on and Thomson's play showed no sign of improving, at least not to the standard required of an Open Champion, Timms let Thomson know in no uncertain terms what he was doing wrong. The Australian was flabbergasted to say the least.

A former guardsman and professional soccer player, Timms was a tall, rugged man in his early 30s and more often than not dressed in brighter colours than the golfers he was working for. Thomson dearly hoped his caddy's behaviour could be put down to pre-Open exuberance and he retreated to his hotel room and his family, his inspiration for the week ahead. It would be a hard week. There were six rounds to play: two of qualifying and four of championship play. Even former champions were not exempt from qualifying rounds. These days the elite players are not forced to suffer the indignity, some would say sheer embarrassment, of teeing up alongside unknown hackers to qualify for an event in which they may be a warm favourite, but it was never a bother to Thomson.

On the eve of his biggest golfing challenge to date, he sat quietly in his hotel room, staring at his daughter deep in peaceful slumber, and he wondered where on earth he would find the momentum to carry him to victory. 'In practice I showed no great form,' he recalls. 'In fact I was playing so badly with a set of American clubs that I didn't fancy my prospects at all. Some desperate measure was needed. I rang the club-maker John Letters and asked him if I could see some clubs.' On the night before the qualifying rounds, Thomson and Letters 'broke into' the Letters of Scotland display in the Open exhibition tent and took down a set of the Panton model. 'Once I felt them I thought they were okay, so I tried them out the next day and used them throughout the championship,' says Thomson. When the tournament was over he handed them back to Letters with his eternal thanks. For one who preached exclusively that the mind was behind every good golf shot, many thought the plea for new clubs at the eleventh hour was most peculiar, but the late-night sortie was not for mechanical reasons. Thomson simply knew that a change of clubs would trigger a change of attitude. He knew what he was doing.

Without setting the course alight he qualified easily; there was no struggle like the previous year, but he noted that more than a few drives were running off the fairway. He decided to favour the 3-wood from the tee and while this placed pressure on his long-irons, he thought it better than hacking his way through Birkdale's notorious rough: 'I didn't discard my driver completely, but logically I leant towards the 3-wood a lot. I had a feeling it might end up being my major weapon.'

The sun was shining and the breeze minimal when Thomson set out for his opening round soon after nine o'clock. He'd slept well, risen early, had a cooked breakfast, relaxed with Lois and Deidre and departed for the course with ample time to loosen up. At no stage during the round did he feel any pressure, but once it came to compiling his report for the *Argus* he sounded displeased: 'The weather was in a comforting mood when I went out and the experts say it is going to last. I played fairly well without getting any of the breaks we all hope for. My first round was not a good one. 72 on an easy, comparatively windless morning was two shots too many, but fortunately no one did much better. Later in the day, Bobby Locke, who I thought would be the man most likely to beat me, scored a poor 74, which enhanced my prospects further. But I couldn't help thinking about my 72 ... it was one of those rounds which could have been much better.' Out in front with an equal course record 69 was the English veteran Sam King, who was joined late in the day by Dartford's T. W. Spence. They led by two over Argentina's Antonio Cerda, and by three over a large group including the cosmopolitan bunch of Italy's Uno Grappasonni, Ireland's Harry Bradshaw, Dai Rees from Wales, England's Peter Alliss, Jim Turnesa from the USA, and the Australian Peters, Thomson and Toogood.

The next day also belonged to the locals. While Spence held sway with a 72, 40-year-old Englishman Syd Scott burst into contention with a superb 67, smashing the course record. Scott was now tied with King, Rees and Thomson on 143. Cerda duplicated his first round for 142, one behind the leader Spence. Like Thomson, Locke had also come in with a 71.

The final day of the 1954 Open dawned with the best weather for the week. The wind had dropped considerably and as early as nine o'clock the sun was shining brightly and a warm zephyr floated across the links. After another restful night with young Deidre keeping her part of the bargain, Thomson woke early and was immediately encouraged by Lois, who told him she'd dreamt that he had won the Open. His confidence was high. It didn't take long for the drama to unfold. The bold early challengers fell away: Cerda closed with rounds of 73–71, King 74–70 and Spence 74–75. The Open came down to a battle between the four men who arrived back at the clubhouse with the morning's best score of 69; Scott, Rees, Thomson and Locke. The first three were tied for the lead on 212, Locke was two shots behind.

Many players have thrived on the Championship's ancient verity — 'Nobody wins the Open: the Open wins you' — some have been overcome by an eerie premonition. For Thomson it was no different. After that third round the top contenders retired to the Birkdale clubhouse for lunch, but Thomson headed for the carpark. 'I didn't want to be amongst all that noise in the clubhouse so I left for my hotel a few miles away. On the way to the car I was encouraged by many people telling me it was my year, so I decided to have a fairly large lunch.' Not only did he have no intention of playing the final round on an empty stomach; plenty of food meant there was no room for butterflies!

With his wife at the table, he sat down to eat, silently, in a quiet corner of the hotel dining-room. Their daughter was with them, peacefully asleep in her crib, oblivious of the apprehension felt by so many around her. All except her father. Halfway through his roast beef, salad and fruit, Thomson thought he might dash upstairs to grab his jacket and tie. With the eyes of the world watching he couldn't possibly accept the auld silver claret jug in an open-necked golf shirt, could he? 'The Open wins you.' It had passed on its message.

His main rivals, Rees and Scott, hit off around 40 minutes ahead for the final round, with another, Locke, 20 minutes behind. Thomson was again alongside amateur Frank Stranahan, himself a top contender, and at the first hole the American holed a tricky birdie putt while Thomson struggled to save par. The opener was considered a 'must' birdie hole and he realised it hadn't been a good start. Nothing was coming easily and after parring the first four the temptation was there to force things along. He tried. He bogeyed the 5th.

'I began a little sloppily, but I still felt comfortable and fresh,' he remembers. 'As the round wore on I chose to relax, and felt myself become stronger and keener.' The dropped stroke sparked him into action. He made a great save at the 6th and then birdied the par-3 7th after running his tee shot up to within three feet of the hole. He was now committed. At the 9th he was about to putt when a loud burst of applause erupted from the nearby 13th green. He showed not the slightest interest and holed his six-footer. From there he parred his way to the 12th, where he let his guard down and took a blow. A momentary lapse in concentration and a 'miserable' three-putt gave his rivals some encouragement. At the 13th, another par-3, his tee shot was too strong and scooted over the back of the green. Remarkably composed, he chipped back to within a few feet for his three. Then at the 517-yard par-5 14th he drove off the fairway and hooked his second shot deep into the high grass 80-yards from the pin. His impressive challenge for the Open was delicately balanced on a razor's edge.

His caddy wasn't helping. 'He was no help at all, in fact he was a handicap,' says Thomson. 'He was a real pest because he imagined he was a bigger name than I was. I could hear his moans and groans as my shots went astray and even heard him tell somebody in the crowd: "If only he would listen to what I tell him".' Golf's version of the Odd Couple was intent on acting out a bizarre finale. Timms had upset members of the gallery with his habit of tossing the ball and catching it in his mouth to clean it! 'I have been in the game a while now,' Timms told one reporter, 'and have caddied for some good people, but this fellow doesn't work with you. I don't think he'll win — I prefer Dai Rees.' It might have been the only time in the history of the Open that a caddy had hoped someone other than his boss would triumph! 'That was the last time he ever caddied for me,' says Thomson. 'However, I noticed the following year at St Andrews he carried the bag of US Open champion Ed Furgol, and at the 14th Ed couldn't take any more and bombarded Cecil with his sand-iron! Cecil slipped the bag from his shoulder and hurried to the railway station. He ended up in America where his salesmanship was more appreciated!'

Back at Birkdale's 14th, Thomson blocked Timms from his mind and focussed on his ball nestling deep in the long grass. There was virtually no chance of getting any clubface on the ball and therefore stopping it on the green, so he simply tried to make sure the shot became airborne. Yet from such a precarious position, Thomson played a truly magnificent stroke. He hacked through the jungle with superb touch and watched his ball bounce short of the green and roll up to within 16 feet of the flag. He then calmly stepped up and canned the putt for birdie!

At that time Thomson's main danger, Dai Rees, was playing the final hole. He had a great chance to finish with 71 for a 283 total, but after playing his approach onto a downslope at the back of the green, no more than 20 feet from the flag, the diminutive Welshman made a mess of his chip and nervously jabbed the par putt. It slipped by. Thomson had no knowledge of this until he strode to the 15th tee. A few minutes earlier he'd noticed a figure in a cap and green jacket sprinting towards the tee. It was Norman von Nida, who'd finished his round and rushed back out to guide his countryman home. His voice shrill with excitement, he yelled: 'Keep calm and you've got it in the bag. Rees and Scott have finished on 284.' So the challenge had been issued. Thomson needed four pars to win the Open.

He found the rough at the 15th, but ended up with four. After a superb drive down the 510-yard par-5 16th, he pulled his second into a yawning bunker 30 yards short of the green. 'I was at crisis point,' he says. 'I knew I wasn't the world's best from a bunker but there was no use standing there shaking, I had to play the shot. I tried to block everything out of my mind and concentrated to the utmost.' Von Nida felt a knot tighten in his stomach. 'Peter was presented with one of the toughest shots in golf,' he recalls. 'I always joked about him not being one of the best bunker players around, but this was no joking matter. I wished I could have stepped in there and played the shot for him. I honestly thought he was either going to skull it over the green or leave it in the trap and be robbed of his chance to win. I couldn't watch. I had to turn away. Then I heard this deafening roar of applause and looked up to see the ball only a matter of inches from the hole. Peter smiled at the crowd, looked straight at me, and winked. I knew then, the Open was his.'

The shot had nearly gone in the hole. Thomson says it was the greatest he ever played. After picking up his ball from tap-in birdie range, he gave it a gentle kiss.

He parred the short 17th after floating a 4-iron to the heart of the green, and stood on the final tee with the luxury of knowing he could take a five and still win. With an enormous crowd lining both sides of the fairway he drilled his ball down the centre, but under the terrific strain left his approach short, and the ball lay on a grassy bank. He chipped up beautifully, and needing two to win from six feet, cheekily tapped the ball in with the back of his putter after the first putt slipped inches by. As a twice previous runner-up the crowd gave Thomson an overwhelming ovation and no one could doubt the popularity of his triumph. He walked off the green 'feeling like King of all the earth'. Much to the crowd's delight his wife ran onto the green and gave him a kiss. 'I wasn't really choked up by it all because I honestly felt it was my destiny,' he says. 'George Duncan, the grand old man of the area [and veteran pro], was also there to shake my hand, but he didn't seem impressed with my final putt. He said to me, "I'll boot you up the backside if I ever see you do that again." But I knew what I was doing. I certainly wasn't about to throw away my chance of winning the Open. Anyway, my wife and Norman and all the other Australians showed their joy, but I just wanted a quiet place to sit down. The members of the press assured me that no one could beat me, but Locke came to the last with a chance to tie.'

In a delightful twist to the scene at Lytham two years earlier, Thomson had a cool drink and took a seat on the verandah overlooking the last green. Locke, in the penultimate group, was standing on the 18th tee and shooting for a 69 to tie. He needed to finish with a birdie; something he'd achieved in the morning when he fired in an approach to less than two feet from the pin.

This time he cracked two glorious woods that had his ball on the green, but quite a distance from the hole. With Locke though, that mattered little. He'd holed from such distances and under such pressure plenty of times before. He took his time to survey the task — to Thomson an unconscionable time — but he eventually stepped up and gave his ball a hard, true rap. Right on line the putt suddenly lost momentum and pulled up a foot short of its target. Thomson felt as if the earth had been lifted from his shoulders.

On the other side of the planet, the crackly, distorted sounds of the commentary on a local ham radio floated into the gathering of friends and relatives in Brunswick. They let out an emotional three cheers. Grace and Arthur's eldest boy was the toast of the golfing world and it seemed as if all Melbourne wanted to share their joy. It was many, many hours before their telephone stopped ringing.

1954 Open Championship, Royal Birkdale, England	
283 — Peter Thomson (Aust.)	72–71–69–71
284 — Bobby Locke (S. Af.)	74–71–69–70
— Syd Scott (Eng.)	76–67–69–72
— Dai Rees (Wales)	72–71–69–72
286 — James Adams (Scot.)	73–75–69–69
— Antonio Cerda (Arg.)	71–71–73–71
— Jim Turnesa (USA)	72–72–71–71
287 — Peter Alliss (Eng.)	72–74–71–70
— Sam King (Eng.)	69–74–74–70
289 — Jimmy Demaret (USA)	73–71–70–71
— Flory van Donck (Belg.)	77–71–70–71

At 24, Thomson was the youngest Open Champion since Bobby Jones in 1926. He'd outgrown the image of a promising youngster; he could now be ranked alongside the world's greats. But there was no time to bask in the glory, not that he wanted to anyway. Amongst the chaos that follows an Open victory he managed to escape to a 'quiet corner somewhere' to write an article on his victory for the *Argus*. He then took his work and drove to the local post office in Southport to cable the article to Australia. His words were rushed into the late edition. Like his play, the piece was controlled and conservative in its sentiment. 'How good it feels to be the Open golf champion of Britain,' he wrote, 'a title I set my heart on a long time ago. Now I find it almost impossible to believe that at last it is mine. What was the chief factor in my win? I should say it was my experience in American tournaments, in which one plays every last round tough to earn one of those 25 prizes ... Since January I have played a tournament every week in America, and while I tried my hardest for those dollars I was always thinking ahead and practising for the first week in July at Royal Birkdale.' There was no mention of his brilliant shot at the 16th, or of Lois, Deidre or the support and influence of people like Harry Young, Dick Payne and George Naismith. The pre-tournament visit to John Letters's display was not revealed, nor was the peculiar behaviour of Cecil Timms. He was concerned only with his winning, and with himself.

In keeping with this philosophy there was no lavish celebration that evening. A simple dinner with no fuss. It was not the traditional behaviour of someone who had that day achieved their life's ambition. He decided to head straight back to America with Lois and Deidre, 'while news of my win in the Open is still hot'. He needn't have worried — Thomson was to remain 'hot news' in America for quite some time. There was much more to come.

In 1955 the Open returned to St Andrews, the home of golf, for the first time in nine years. The quaint little golfing shrine in Fife on Scotland's east coast has had such a profound influence on the personality and philosophy of Peter Thomson that his experiences there deserve a full chapter. In 1955, no one was more excited than the defending champion. He arrived at the Old Course four days before the qualifying rounds, but did not rush to join the players lining up to practise. It was true, Thomson had won at his first look over the links in the PGA matchplay the previous year, but this was after all the Open, and the locals began to question a player's sanity if he chose not to practise during Open week. Thomson though, just as he had done at Birkdale with the new set of clubs, chose the most remarkable build-up to a major event, a build-up that would make front page news at any modern major. He took what he describes as a 'calculated gamble' by staying away from the course to visit the historically significant parts of the old grey town. So, while the world's best golfers were seeing the sights of the mesmerising Old Course, the man they had to beat was sight-seeing! 'St Andrews that year was bone dry and hard as a rock,' he says. 'I chose not to practise as I figured the rain must come before the week was out and the course would change completely. I know it was a big gamble, but on the day before the qualifying rounds, rain fell all day.' Some suggested he must have had some sort of deal going with the golfing gods! Others interpreted Thomson's absence on practice days as arrogance. In fact, he had for some time developed strong views on practice, views that were certainly unorthodox. 'I know golfers who go out onto the practice ground and for hour after hour, day after day, slog away at their strokes; we are told that our only possible hope of perfection is to imitate their example,' Thomson has written. 'When I was young I was wont to do the same. But there is no such thing as perfection in golf — if there was, every shot would go straight into the hole. Before a round I would practise until I thought I was hitting them perfectly and sometimes it didn't take more than two holes to hit a thoroughly bad one. All that practice was for nothing.'

He detested hitting ball after ball into a field. He could practise a certain shot a thousand times and never bring it off in the tournament. This is not to say his lack of a build-up at St Andrews was standard procedure. He did spend time hitting balls before he played, but the only things he tried to achieve on the practice tee and in warm-up rounds were rhythm and feeling: 'You may have a pair of hands that can tear a telephone book in two, but that doesn't mean anything unless you can learn to utilise the effective muscles of golf in a rhythmical and harmonious way. It gets down to doing what comes easily and naturally. On top of this is the longer search for feeling, for a more acute sense of touch, for a sharper appreciation of distance and judgement. I would strive for rhythm and feeling in practice, and never try to waste energy. I thought concentrating too much on practice before a round was foolish as energy might well be in short supply by the end of the day.'

As he proved at St Andrews, Thomson firmly believed that punishing sessions on the practice tee did not necessarily mean automatic success in golf. He held the same view as the great American Bobby Jones, who believed that all good scoring came down to what was rattling around between a player's ears as he stood over the ball. 'Concentrating on the results of a shot to the absolute exclusion of all other thoughts, especially about its method, is the secret to every good shot I ever hit,' Jones once said. 'While making my address I never thought of anything other than hitting the ball. If I thought of anything else, I didn't hit it.'

Thomson was out early on the first day and wore his Open crown with distinction. As the defending champion there was obviously a great deal of interest in his fortunes, particularly after his attitude to practice, but again the spotlight shone elsewhere. English veteran Frank Jowle, at 43, had stunned everyone the previous day with a qualifying round of 63 to equal the lowest score ever recorded in an Open. Buoyed by that start he produced a 70 in the event proper, a round that didn't seem anything out of the ordinary until the capricious winds blew in from the bay with increasing velocity as the day progressed. Thomson came in before the worst of the wind with a 71, a score that placed him alongside, among others, Flory van Donck, Christy O'Connor and the previous year's US Open champion, Ed Furgol. Jowle's 70 was then equalled by Welshman D. F. Smalldon and young Englishman Bernard Hunt, but by day's end Scotland's Eric Brown and the previous year's joint runner-up, Englishman Syd Scott, crept into the joint lead with excellent rounds of 69. Thomson wasn't too concerned about those ahead of him and again had his eye on Locke. He noted with interest the South African's 74 and retired to his hotel room a calm, confident man.

Fortunes changed dramatically the next day when the tee-times were reversed. Johnny Fallon, Thomson's sparring partner from the previous year's PGA matchplay final, took the plaudits with the day's best round, a brilliant 67. Fallon now found himself just a shot off the lead, held by three players, Brown, Smalldon and Thomson, the last compiling a faultless 68. Hunt, Jowle and John Jacobs were a further stroke behind Fallon, while Locke improved with a 69 to be four behind the leaders. Notable casualties were O'Connor (75), Furgol (76) and the joint first round leader Syd Scott (77).

On the final day Thomson made another brisk start and was helped by rounds of 73 and 78 respectively from his co-leaders Brown and Smalldon. With Fallon contributing nothing better than a 73, the Australian notched a deliberate 70, good enough for the outright lead as he sat down to lunch a shot ahead of the solid Jowle, two ahead of Brown, Jacobs and Harry Weetman, and four clear of Locke and Fallon. The Australian felt wonderfully calm as he teed off on his final round, perhaps he was too calm. Out ahead, it seemed no one was in the mood to prevent Thomson from winning back-to-back titles, but then through the mist emerged the slender, craggy figure of 42-year-old Johnny Fallon to muster a challenge. The brave runner-up to Thomson in the matchplay was again inspired by the large gathering following his fortunes, and after a blistering front nine of 31, five-under, Fallon drew level.

No sooner had Scottish hopes rocketed than tragedy struck. Fallon pulled his tee shot into a bunker at the par-3 11th and his attempt crumbled with a double-bogey. The veteran ended with 283, and now

Thomson could afford to cruise home. Yet as the wise old men of St Andrews never tire of saying to those who will listen, no round of golf is safe on the Old Course until the final putt is holed. However serene the progress, disaster lurks at every step. For Thomson it came at the par-5 14th. From the tee he drove into the fearsome collection of bunkers known as 'the Beardies' and from there could advance his ball only a few yards further. Shaken, he tugged his third into the tiny, square pot bunker aptly named 'the Grave'. 'So treacherous was that little sandtrap that I had to play out backwards,' recalls Thomson, closing his eyes. 'I ended up with a double-bogey seven and I thought for a few moments the championship might slip from my grasp. I certainly wished I could play that 14th again. In previous rounds I had twice snatched birdies there. That gives you some idea what was going on inside me as I walked to the 15th tee!' Any hopes still entertained by Fallon supporters faded when Thomson drilled his drive down the 15th, pulled out a 5-iron, took a quick glance at the huge double-green and played a superb iron that pitched short, rolled on and then up and down a mound to within several feet of the flag. Down went the birdie putt and the Open Champion looked like an Open Champion once again. In the cauldron-like atmosphere he survived the infamous 17th and came to the last with a two-shot cushion over the field. A safe par and the second successive British Open was his. 'The right man won,' wrote the legendary Bernard Darwin in *The Times*. 'Thomson is not only very, very sound mechanically, with the power of doing the same thing over and over again, but it is impossible to imagine a better temperament, marked by unruffled composure, courage and common sense. He had his bad moments as everyone must, and accepted and overcame them.'

The following year was Thomson's finest in the United States — a breakthrough win in Texas, a solid effort in the US Open, many top-ten placings — and when he arrived in Britain in June for the Canada

1955 Open Championship, Old Course, St Andrews	
281 — Peter Thomson (Aust.)	71–68–70–72
283 — Johnny Fallon (Scot.)	73–67–73–70
284 — Frank Jowle (Eng.)	70–71–69–71
285 — Bobby Locke (S. Af.)	74–69–70–72
286 — Ken Bousfield (Eng.)	71–75–70–70
— Antonio Cerda (Arg.)	73–71–71–71
— Bernard Hunt (Eng.)	70–71–74–71
— Flory van Donck (Belg.)	71–72–71–72
— Harry Weetman (Eng.)	71–71–70–74

Cup and the Open he felt 'superbly confident'. A man needs more than sheer confidence to become the first in the history of the Open to win the 72-hole version of the championship three times in succession. Thomson is the first to admit he had help from Lady Luck and Mother Nature to take the hat-trick at Hoylake. 'It was in the Canada Cup at Wentworth that I was again hit by a severe case of hay fever and asthma,' he says. 'Norman von Nida was invited in Kel Nagle's place to join me for that event but we both played poorly and I was in a bad way with my breathing. Thankfully when I arrived for the Open the following week by the seaside at Hoylake, I felt somewhat better. Wet weather helped to keep the pollens down.'

The Open began in drizzly conditions over the Hoylake links near Liverpool on England's north-west coast, and a thick mist rolled in from the Irish Sea for most of the day. Thomson, after leading the qualifiers with 71–69, was again out early and made the most of the tough going with a par round of 70, despite bogeys at the last two holes. It was good enough for second place alongside young Welshman David Thomas and Canadian Al Balding, a stroke behind an unlikely leader in Argentinian Enrique Bertolino. When Thomson woke the next morning strong winds and heavy rains lashed against the windows of his hotel room. 'The weather in the morning was frightful; as I sat in my room waiting patiently for my 2.00 start the course was almost flooded and, as I later discovered, officials toyed with the idea of calling play off.' Two of the more notable victims were Peter Alliss and Bobby Locke, who were paired together. Both squelched into the locker room with golf bags full of water, their tails between their legs, and scores well into the 80s.

'Then, amazingly, the rain stopped at 1.30,' says Thomson, suppressing a laugh. 'The sun came out and the birds sang as I teed off. It was a big break for me.' Without the encumbrance of waterproofs, umbrellas and towels, Thomson scooted around for another 70 and the outright lead by a shot over the Argentinian pair of Bertolino and Robert de Vicenzo. The rest of the field was a further four shots behind. On the final day the Australian posted a morning 72 while the men from Argentina floundered with 76 and 79 respectively. Thomson was suddenly three ahead of Flory van Donck, five clear of Bertolino and seven ahead of English legend Henry Cotton. The outcome was never in doubt. A closing 74 gave Thomson the hat-trick by a comfortable margin of three strokes and the Merseyside gallery paid tribute. It was the first Open treble since Musselburgh's Bob Ferguson way back in 1882, ten years before the Open became a 72-hole affair. Cotton, himself a three-time Open champion (1934–37–48), summed it all up when he said, 'It is just beyond all the superlatives. It's incredible!'

1956 Open Championship, Hoylake, Royal Liverpool	
286 — Peter Thomson (Aust.)	70–70–72–74
289 — Flory van Donck (Belg.)	71–74–70–74
290 — Robert de Vicenzo (Arg.)	71–70–79–70
291 — Gary Player (S. Af.)	71–76–73–71
292 — John Panton (Scot.)	74–76–72–70
293 — Henry Cotton (Eng.)	72–76–71–74
— Enrique Bertolino (Arg.)	69–72–76–76

From here Thomson admits that he felt it would go on forever — he would continue winning the Open as long as he cared to compete. He felt super-confident with his game, was right at home on the seaside links courses and, importantly, the British galleries and golf writers were now welcoming him as one of their own. They'd watched him develop from a member of the humble antipodean working class to a British gent; they felt he'd been anglicised. Of course, not everyone felt this way and many were happy to see him finish runner-up to Locke in 1957. When he next won the Open in a 36-hole play-off against Welshman David Thomas at Royal Lytham in 1958, some gossip writers contributed to his 'extremely tough week'. He arrived at the course to find a dry, humid dustbowl under sunny skies and his immediate concern was hay fever, but some members of the press were not interested in his hay fever, his play, or Thomson himself; what concerned them most was his female companion.

It had been known for some time in Australia that Thomson's marriage was not a happy one. In their six years of marriage he and Lois had seen their relationship completely reshape itself. They came together when both were very young and the infatuation had disintegrated. Peter's desire to succeed at golf, with the travel and experiences that went with it, his total obsession with what he wanted to do, almost certainly cost him his first marriage. The lifestyle had taken its toll on Lois; it gave her responsibilities that she was hardly prepared for. If she wanted to be with her husband she had to travel, and take along their young child. The spouse of a touring professional has to be a very special person who must live the life of a lonely parent and tag along if the budget permits, who has to adapt to an itinerant lifestyle acting as guardian and nurse, careful not to upset a delicate golfing equilibrium or ego.

Thomson had first met Mary Kelly at a reception given by the Lord Mayor for the thrice Open Champion at the Melbourne Town Hall just before the 1956 Olympic Games. A friend of successful Victorian amateur golfer Tom Crow, Mary came from a middle-class Melbourne

Catholic family, thoroughly enjoyed the game and was a familiar face on the golfing scene, attending many tournaments and functions.

By late 1957 she had met Thomson on numerous social occasions and during her first overseas trip ran into him quite by chance at the home of mutual friends in London. His marriage had finally come to an end, bar the legalities, and Thomson found a sympathetic ear in Mary, who had lived through her own parents' unhappy marriage. Their relationship blossomed and they fell in love.

'Peter dealt with the failure of his first marriage in his own private way,' says Mary. 'Naturally we discussed it and his main concern was always Deidre's future. He adored that child and although he realised there was nothing left of his relationship with Lois, he agonised over his decision to separate, and then divorce.'

It may have harked back to the basic insecurities of his often lonesome youth, but there are many close to Thomson who firmly believe that his cold, distant attitude to certain people was and is directly linked to his desire to be completely and utterly his own man. While never one to beat his own drum, Thomson enjoys the stardom that a career in golf has provided. He has no time for those who attempt to become 'stars' alongside him; those who invade his 'space'. Mary has always preferred to stay in the background alongside Peter. He likes that.

As far as the popular press was concerned at Lytham in 1958, Thomson was still married and the presence of this 'mystery' woman merely gave the scandal writers a field day. 'It certainly wasn't easy with the press,' says Mary. 'They did not help Peter's preparation for the Open at all and at the time we knew that stress had a lot to do with asthma — they were directly linked. That made it all the more difficult for Peter.'

The ebullient Norman von Nida, one who had continuously persevered with Thomson's career despite the difficulty he found in understanding his personality, was furious when he read the newspapers. He believed the reports were printed with malicious intent, designed 'to upset the mental equilibrium of a near perfect golfer'. He added that he was glad Thomson gave such 'a devastating answer to one of the vilest press attacks to undermine a sportsman's confidence I have ever known'.

For his part, Thomson will only reveal that he was 'concerned about reporters chasing me for some delicate information on my domestic life', but says he was easily able to block the furore from his mind. After all, he had much more to worry about. 'Peter was so severely affected by hay fever and asthma that he had to have injections and then, in a reaction to that, he broke out in a terrible rash,' says Mary. 'He was really very sick and could hardly sleep a wink at night.'

Thomson struggled his way through the first qualifying round with a less than notable score of 75. After another sleepless night and a futile attempt to relieve the agony with drugs, he arrived for the second qualifying round at his lowest ebb. Feeling dreadfully weak he was unable to hit six practice shots without losing his breath completely. His caddy, Jack Leigh, took him back to the locker room where he stumbled to a bench, lay down and tried to remedy his breathing. He considered calling the tournament doctor. For his part, Thomson was more sad than anything; he knew his chances of playing in his eighth Open were extremely slim. 'I honestly felt terrible,' he says, his brow knitted with the memory. 'I knew that to withdraw was a drastic step, but that was how bad I felt. I was tired and listless, but I thought if I could just control my breathing I could give it a go. I didn't want to give up. The only way I could get through was by taking my time, by taking things very slowly.'

Those ten minutes lying on his back in the Lytham locker room gave him time to think. In the back of his mind he entertained the preposterous thought that if he could just get going he might even win the Open again. It was the inspiration of the auld silver claret jug that pulled him up from his prostrate position. He decided to play that second qualifying round, and he did. He had a 63.

As a result of slowing to a virtual crawl, his swing was smooth and deliberate and his concentration impeccable. The results were stunning indeed; he hit the flagstick three times on the way to a score that equalled the finest round in an Open. 'Although it was not part of the championship proper, that round virtually won the Open for me,' he says, eyes lighting up. 'It not only boosted my confidence but dismayed the opposition.'

Once the first round of the Open was under way Thomson felt much better, and though still very weak, enjoyed the sun shining on his back and began to unravel his best ever start in an Open with a 66, including six birdies and an eagle. He was already out in front by a shot. Locke, the defending champion, was still suffering from the putting scandal of the previous Open at St Andrews, and came in ten shots behind after a 76. Dai Rees, another fancy, could only manage 77. Only Christy O'Connor came in with a score to rival the Australian, a 67, and the following day the Irishman threw down the gauntlet with a sparkling 68 that was certainly good enough to lead. Thomson, after a sloppy start birdied the 15th and 17th to salvage a 72, which put him three behind. Another of the collection of top players from Argentina, Leopoldo Ruiz, was a shot behind O'Connor in second place after a magnificent 65, while young Welshman David Thomas had drawn level with Thomson after a 68.

Bright sunshine illuminated Lytham for the final day of the 1958 Open, and a light breeze, just enough to keep the eighteen yellow flags waving gently, floated in from the sea. The course was at its most benign and with the top dozen players separated by just six shots, a finish worthy of the Derby was expected. Despite having the lead snatched from under him and the fact he was feeling far from one hundred per cent, Thomson arrived at Lytham feeling more confident than anyone realised. Again he went through the ritual of departing his hotel alone, leaving Mary to make her move later, escorted by the couple's close ally Tom Crow. Successfully dodging reporters and photographers they arrived to find their man paired alongside the solid, beefy 22-year-old Thomas for the third round. Thomson's spirit picked up immediately when he discovered this, for the Welshman was considered something of a protégé, by virtue of his trip 'down under' the previous year and the fact that the Australian had not only chaperoned him around that circuit, but also a section of the US tour. On his trip to Australia Thomas had met and fallen in love with a young woman who was to become his wife in January 1958. At the Open Peter and David took centre stage, but not many realised and certainly not the press, that Mary Thomson and Robbie Thomas spent many hours in each other's company at Royal Lytham and also immersed themselves in friendly rivalry.

Indeed both men seemed inspired by each other's presence. Thomas clearly wanted to prove to Thomson he was the heir apparent, while Thomson wanted to show Thomas he was a long way from abdicating. By lunchtime the leader board told the story of their absorbing tussle: Thomson, 67 and outright leader; Thomas, 69 and joint second with Flory van Donck, two strokes behind. O'Connor and Ruiz had drifted from contention while Scotland's Eric Brown burst from the pack with a 65 to join them three off the pace.

If it hadn't dawned on Thomson by the time he'd finished lunch, it took only a few holes of the afternoon round for him to realise he was playing alongside the man to beat. Thomas birdied the par-3 1st, Thomson bogeyed the 3rd and they were on level terms. Whispers spread across the course that Eric Brown's hot streak hadn't ended when he sat down to lunch. His putting blade was alight and the gap between his name on the leader board and those ahead was closing rapidly. Thomson though, was unaffected by the murmurs and calmly rolled in birdie putts of his own at the 5th and 6th to lead Thomas by two again, and it remained this way for the next hour as the pair struggled into a deadlock and traded shot for shot, putt for putt. At the 14th they overheard a spectator by the tee: 'Brown has blown up — he's taken six at the last!' The tragic double-bogey finish gave the Scot a 279. Thomson wasn't concerned — after the 14th he still led Thomas by two and could par his way home for 276.

Then came the killer punch that should have, by all accounts, put Thomson down for the count. At the 463-yard par-4 15th, seemingly from nowhere, he played his worst shot for the day, pulling his tee shot through the dog-leg. The deep, wiry rough quickly gobbled his ball. With it lying so low there was every prospect of damaging his wrist and he could only gouge the shot out a short distance. From there he played a dreadful third into a greenside bunker and then took three to get his ball into the cup. With a sturdy par against Thomson's double-bogey, Thomas was back alongside the triple-champion.

At the 16th, another par-4 but in the opposite direction, Thomas, clearly pumped up and with the smell of silver in his nostrils, drilled his drive and followed with a glorious approach to eight feet. He holed the birdie putt, much to the gallery's delight. They thought it was only fair. Thomson had been there three times before; with the utmost respect, they wished for nothing more than to see the young Briton triumph. Thomas was their David all right; Thomson, Goliath. And yet through those two holes; two holes where he'd lost three strokes to the youngster and now trailed by one, Thomson's expression did not change. There were only two holes left to play. It must be remembered that Thomson was still only 28, but if his vast experience told him anything, as it did throughout his career, it bellowed out the message that there was no winner until the final putt hit the bottom of the cup.

At the 17th, one of the most difficult holes on the links, Thomas, now completely in control of his ship, opened his shoulders and let fly with a massive drive that split the middle of the fairway. Thomson, under incredible pressure, was equally accurate though not as far. He then proved once again his extraordinary ability to compose himself by playing a glorious approach that followed the pin all the way and pulled up 10 feet past. It was all about the placement of pressure; a game of the mind within a game of muscle and Thomson was a past master. His policy was never, ever give his opponent the slightest sign that anything was awry. More than most watching that afternoon, he knew that his approach to the 17th had turned the game around. If Thomas had what it took to be an Open Champion, he would need to throw the pressure back on Thomson with contempt. He could not. He never looked comfortable. He fossicked for the right club, fidgeted, and then fell into the trap of taking far too much time. A fat shot caught a huge divot and dumped his approach in the rough well short of the green. An indecisive chip, two putts, and two from Thomson and they were all square coming to the last.

Both hit good drives that finished safely between the traps. They were both in prime position on the 412-yard par-4. Thomson, first away, could make out the yellow flag in the distance, flapping gently in front of the huge ring of spectators. There was no thought of knocking it stiff. He just wanted Thomas to watch his opponent's ball find the heart of the green. This was part of the reason he never felt the need to boom out monstrous drives. By playing first on the fairway he could always dictate terms. He chose a 5-iron and cleverly floated his ball high over the front bunkers and just three yards past the hole. To Thomas, the green had immediately shrunk. It looked as small as a bedsheet. He just managed to trickle his ball onto the front edge. The Open Championship came down to a battle of the blades. To his credit, Thomas rolled his enormous putt to within two feet and bravely holed what was left. Thomson desperately wanted to win another Open, but he remembered the feeling in his gut from St Andrews the year before. More importantly, he did not want to lose. If he missed, he wanted to make sure he could live to fight another day. He missed by an inch, tapped in, shook hands with Thomas and strode off to prepare himself for the 36-hole play-off the following day to decide the wearer of the crown.

It was difficult to predict a winner — both men bettered by one stroke the Open record set by Bobby Locke at Troon in 1950 and were playing the inspired brand of golf needed to triumph. If there was a decisive edge it was Thomson's experience over a 22-year-old, who, if he'd won, would have become the youngest name ever to hold aloft the trophy. Balancing the ledger though was Thomson's fitness. Even his loyal supporters thought that two rounds of qualifying, four of the tournament, and another two in the play-off would prove too much. A gruelling eight rounds or 144 holes to win his fourth Open: a daunting prospect for a man who only a few days earlier had been just a couple of deep breaths away from withdrawing.

Thomson says he would have much preferred an 18-hole play-off at Lytham; a distance he describes as 'sensible', far more so than the curious and controversial 4-hole format that concluded the 1989 Open at Troon won by Mark Calcavecchia over Wayne Grady and Greg Norman. Thomson agrees with the sudden-death format to separate players tied on the same winning score after 72 holes in tour events world-wide to accommodate the ever-increasing demands of television and sponsorship, but when it comes to 'the big open championships', he believes the interests of tradition and fairness on the course should outweigh any possible influence off it.

'The 36-hole play-off in 1958 was far too long,' he says, and contributed to 'the most nerve-tightening day's golf I have ever played'. It may well have been lengthy, but the play-off presented an absorbing contest and attracted a gallery of 10,000. Thomson, 'well fed and rested', and with Mary providing the emotional stability and inspiration that every golfer needs, covered the first 13 holes in a brilliant score of 46; enough to rattle any opponent, and yet at lunch he found himself only a shot ahead, 68 to 69. They remained locked together after the break and the pressure slowly built to such a force that something or someone had to give. The way Thomson was playing, stubborn as a mule and tantalisingly close to a fourth title, it simply had to be Thomas who buckled. 'The turning point came at the 11th hole in the afternoon,' says Peter. 'I birdied the hole and Thomas hit the ball twice in playing a chip shot. I was suddenly four shots ahead and I knew I had him then.' He finished with 71 to Thomas's 74 for a comfortable win. The Australian was 'ecstatic' with his fourth Open in five years and, after the events in the press during the week and the asthma episode, it seemed the whole of Lytham wanted to slap him on the back. There was no celebration. He and Mary immediately packed up, drove to London that evening and flew to Belgium next morning for yet another tournament. There the champion took time to reflect on the past week, and under the circumstances, he felt the 1958 Open was one of his finest performances.

1958 Open Championship, Royal Lytham & St Anne's, England

278	Peter Thomson (Aust.)	66–72–67–72
	David Thomas (Wales)	70–68–69–71
	*Thomson won play-off 68–71 to 69–74	
279	Eric Brown (Scot.)	73–70–65–71
	Christy O'Connor (Ire.)	67–68–73–71
281	Flory van Donck (Belg.)	70–70–67–74
	Leopoldo Ruiz (Arg.)	71–65–73–73
283	— Gary Player (S. Af.)	68–74–70–71

With Thomson back to his best form and Bobby Locke no longer considered a force, it was widely expected that the Australian's dominance of the event would continue, but strangely enough that win seemed to be the end for Thomson. In 1959 at Muirfield, east of Edinburgh, he slumped to joint 23rd, ten strokes behind a triumphant Gary Player. In 1960 he was eight shots adrift of his pal Kel Nagle at St Andrews, and six behind the phenomenon of Arnold Palmer at Birkdale in 1961. The following year he was never in the race and trailed the rampaging Palmer by a distant 16 strokes.

When the Open returned to Lytham in 1963, Thomson had seemingly shaken himself loose from the doldrums, starting the event with a truly remarkable front nine of just 29, which remains a British Open record. Coming home into a brutal wind he held on to card a glorious 67 for the first round lead. He followed with scores of 69–71 to be just a stroke off the pace heading toward the finale, but from there things went horribly wrong. He was paired with Frenchman Jean Garaialde in the final round, in the group behind Jack Nicklaus and Scotland's Tom Haliburton. And he still sounds bitter about it. 'Nicklaus was then a painfully slow player,' says Thomson. 'He was irritatingly painstaking over all shots. Haliburton was also a snail and Garaialde and myself had a really tortuous day. In the afternoon we reached the 11th hole, a par-5, and again, just as we had done on every previous hole, we had to wait to play our shots to the green. I'd had enough by this stage so I walked up and actually stood with the crowd beside the green watching Nicklaus and Haliburton putt — that's how long they took! I did ask the R & A committee to allow us to play through them, but that request was denied, which made me very irate actually and I really got fed up with playing. I was told to get lost. Had I not been the kind of person I am, I probably would have picked up my ball and stormed off the course. It was that frustrating.'

Then Thomson heads up a controversial path: 'I believe that R & A committee really wanted Nicklaus to be the Open Champion. It's different now, but at the time there were certain people involved in administration that were very pro the players who'd played Walker Cup [the amateur competition between Britain and the US]. There was the kind of attitude that it was right and proper that a distinguished former amateur should become the Open Champion.' These thoughts did nothing to aid Thomson and he buckled with a closing 78 to finish fifth, eight shots behind the eventual winner, New Zealand left-hander Bob Charles.

With his 1963 collapse, and his inexplicable performance at no less a place that St Andrews the following year, where he trudged in with his worst ever Open placing — a tie for 29th after an opening 79 — Thomson was rapidly becoming the forgotten man. The press decided that, with the advent of the 'Big Three', Palmer, Nicklaus and Player, Peter Thomson's reign was over. He had won four Opens and finished second three times in his eight Open appearances to 1959, but since then had played in another six Opens and had never come close. He was still winning dozens of tournaments around the world, as many as fifteen in 1959–60, but if one is seeking the cause of this 'dry' spell in the championship he cherished above all others it would be lodged in his private life.

This was his most unsettled time since he had ventured from Brunswick to begin a career that was initially considered to be an enormous gamble. Not only had he turned his back on the American tour which had previously provided the finest possible build-up or 'match fitness', he was exploring other worlds and cultures and developing definite political views and opinions on the world. He joined the

Liberal Party and became president of the Victorian PGA, then chairman of the Australian PGA. In his capacity as a world famous golfer touring the globe he met frequently with heads-of-state and observed the cogs of political machinery in such places as South America, Asia and the Pacific. More importantly, he'd had a change of wives. His life had reached the crossroads and he'd chosen to turn down a completely different path.

Soon after his divorce from Lois, Peter and his fiancée went through the anguish of Mary's excommunication from the Catholic church and they married at Marylebone Registry Office in London in May 1960.

Years later an American reporter asked Thomson his definition of maturity. He responded: 'It's partly the business of marrying, bringing up children, engaging in business, developing your capacities as fully as possible. Some people never mature. I'm not well enough acquainted with a lot of things. Each of us knows whether they are in control of their mind and emotions, free of fears and worries. I get touches and peaks and insights into this state, but it would be hard for me to say that I'm wise. I feel that I can attain wisdom.' In the early 1960s he was busy raising children to his second wife, and it was hoped they could tour the world as a family unit, but Mary's health began to suffer and she miscarried on more than one occasion. 'If we were to have a family I had to stay at home,' says Mary. 'So I wasn't able to travel and after two children, it became a pattern.'

A son, Andrew, was born in January 1961, a daughter, Peta-Ann born in December 1962, and another girl, Fiona, born in October 1964. 'The eldest had to go to kindergarten and although some families on the golf tour were able to cope with that, we felt that the family was the most important thing and it just became necessary to stay at home,' says Mary. 'Peter is a very family-oriented person and he always wanted a home to come back to after spending months away playing golf. I think it was a security thing too. We tried to exist without Peter for the months that he would be away, and operate as a family as best we could, and we certainly succeeded, but it was not without its problems.'

The worries for Peter didn't end there. Caught in the middle of the divorce early in the new decade was his first child, Deidre. One of the hardest decisions he was ever forced to make was to abandon his intention of contesting the custody battle for the 5-year-old, and to many this simply proved the heartlessness and sheer selfishness of the man. These barbs wounded Thomson deeply for they came from people who were not in possession of the facts. Those days during the late 1950s and early 1960s were traumatic times not merely for Peter and Lois, but the families and friends on either side and especially for young Deidre. Now happily married herself, living in Melbourne with her husband

Chris Alexander, and four healthy children, Marina, Jane, Nelson and Calum, and enjoying close relations with both parents, Deidre vividly recalls her confused early childhood, experiencing the torment of the dramatic change in her life. Understandably unable to fathom the reasons behind the split in her parents' relationship, she remained in the care of her mother and whenever her father visited, the confusion and frustration would immediately surface.

'Whenever Peter came around I used to throw these terrible tantrums,' says Deidre. 'I can remember misbehaving terribly when I went out with him, basically because I thought those things that children think, like if I was really bad he wouldn't come back. Or, that I'd tried being good and that didn't work, so I'd be really bad. My parents had lots of mutual friends so people made comments all the time about Peter and that I looked like him. It was difficult not being able to have any touch with him — it was all this pressure that started with my father, and I didn't have him about me.' Such was Peter's concern for his daughter that he consulted a child psychiatrist. The doctor decided that Deidre should be left to her own devices and if all went according to plan, she would eventually make up her own mind to see her father when she was old enough to comprehend what had happened. 'The psychiatrist advised Peter not to contest the custody case in the interests of my health,' says Deidre, 'because of my behaviour when I did see him, he was forced to keep away and he did, which must have been a very traumatic experience for him. I didn't see him again until I was 16. I received just the odd birthday card from him through the years, but I later wondered if some hadn't been intercepted on the way and deliberately filtered out.'

The tantrums stopped but it wasn't until she was a teenager that Deidre developed a deep curiosity about her father. Previously she had ignored several letters from Peter, but as the mail persisted, Deidre felt compelled to reply. The correspondence between the two became more and more frequent and eventually, delighted that his daughter had reached the adolescent stage where she could understand his side of the story, Peter telephoned and invited her to dinner. None of the patrons at the steak restaurant in South Melbourne that night realised the importance of that quiet, intimate meal. To them it was simply Peter Thomson, world-famous golfer, dining with his daughter. To the couple seated at the small corner table, it was the opening of sentimental floodgates. 'It was an emotional time for both of us, getting to know each other,' recalls Deidre. 'The first thing I realised was that he was completely different to the man that had been portrayed to me. He's terribly conservative and extremely family-oriented now, and I couldn't believe that he was anything like the man people had kept telling me he was. I was told he was a womaniser, a terribly bad tempered person and a real rogue. That is certainly not the case at all. He told me his reasons for not contesting the custody case and that he certainly had not ignored me all those years and that it had weighed on his mind a lot. We did get very close, although there was still a bit of a wall there for a little while. He's not very good at telling people how he feels at any point. I got to know Mary very well, and Pan, Andrew and Fiona, because I moved in with them for a couple of years before I got married. Now of course, I think Peter is a wonderful man, highly intelligent and very much a family person. He was very, very excited about becoming a grandfather for the first time and is very much into my family and my children. Before our last one was born [in June 1990] he was ringing me at least every day, saying, 'any news, any news?' He tries to visit us whenever he possibly can and always puts himself out to entertain my four, reading them books, chatting to them, changing nappies even! We are very close now.'

So the millstone that had hung heavily around Peter Thomson's neck during the 1960s was finally and gratefully removed, but it had doubtless left its mark. Combined with his new family, his desire to immerse himself in other places, his hard work with the Australian PGA, and his continued look at life through a deep focus, all meant that his golf, for the first time in his professional career, no longer held the attraction it had once commanded. Thomson has written that almost everything in golf conspires to defeat a player, particularly in the game's upper echelon, the pro ranks. His memories of playing poorly are as lucid as those of winning. 'It takes about two holes, or three at the most, to have you mouthing curses,' he wrote in the 1960s. 'Your second shot is flying straight at it. It might stick in close if it gets its grip. You might hole the putt and be under, right away … but you watch and see it bounce and bounce and run like a rat until it disappears over the back. So you swallow your pride and your rage and chip it back up and watch it run again like a drunken sailor. And then, as steady as the Rock of Gibraltar, you putt again with not so much as a flick of an eyelid — and in a flash it has missed. Damnation! Curse this grass. Why can't it behave like ordinary grass? Why does it have to do the opposite to what you think? Why does it look so slow when it's so fast? And why do you allow so much when there's no slope there to allow for? So you're one over already and more determined than ever to belt it, whip it, tread on it, rush it, kill it. And more things happen. You stick on the front at the third and putt up boldly. In your mind's eye you can see it crashing in. As you watch you see it slide by. Now, on your hands and knees you beg the next one to please drop in … Now it's two over. Worse to come. Bolder still and bolder. Get them back. How can you be two over when you've set your mind on being under? You strain harder on the putts. Hold on too tight. Begin to move when you should be staying still. Unfathomable, inscrutable greens. Why do I ever play in this town? Somewhere you remember. It's all happened before. There is something familiar about the situation. It has an awful, sickening taste about it. It's like an 80 coming up which you can do nothing about. It is the game of golf.'

Many players make the mistake of overcoming their worry and apprehension by assuming indifference — 'What the hell — it's only a game of golf for God's sake, not a firing squad!', but in trying to keep loose and calm by telling themselves it's only a game and there's nothing to worry about, they get slack, even lazy, which is much worse than being nervous. The man who keeps himself on edge is going to be a hard man to beat. Nerves, and the control of them, are what differentiates a thoroughbred from a plough-horse and nowhere are nerves more likely to surface than in the final round of a British Open. By 1965, after his earlier struggles, many people had forgotten that it was in the British Open where Peter Thomson proved beyond question he was one of the finest thoroughbreds ever to don a pair of spikes.

Most consider his triumph that year at Royal Birkdale to be his finest achievement in golf, not only because he became the first modern player to win the Championship five times, but because his performance shattered the myth that he could not win against Americans. It rebutted the frivolous, yet persistent question of just how many of his four previous Open titles would he have won had there been the strongest of American talent against him. For his part, Thomson says he never played in a British Open that didn't have strong American representation. Names like Middlecoff, Hogan, Demaret, Furgol, Souchak and Turnesa were there in the 1950s, 'and in addition there was one very big hurdle and that was Bobby Locke. I often said that at the time he ranked with Hogan and Snead as the best three golfers in the world.' So Thomson does not rank his fifth Open as categorically the greatest: 'It was equal with the others. It's like being asked to choose between your children as to which is your favourite. Each of my wins means something to me. I wouldn't like to pick one in front of another.' He does concede his fifth Open was 'very special' — and those close to him believe that although he would never say so publicly, the 1965 Open is treasured in his heart because it earned him the distinction of joining the 'Great Triumvirate' by defeating the modern version of golf's immortal trio.

Harry Vardon, J. H. Taylor and James Braid were masters of a bygone age and with sixteen Open Championships between them became known as the 'Great Triumvirate' for their domination of the event before the first world war. In 1965 Arnold Palmer, Gary Player and Jack

Nicklaus were known as the 'Big Three' for their domination of the world's majors — they'd earned fifteen big ones between them, all in spectacular fashion. Thomson was still only 35, but his triumphs of the 1950s had already receded into history. He had not won a single tournament in Britain in the previous two years. When talk centred on who would claim the biggest tournament of them all, the names of Nicklaus, Palmer and Player, who had placed 1st, 2nd and 3rd in the US Masters only two months earlier, were on everybody"s lips. As the current Masters champion, Nicklaus, 25, was the favourite; Palmer, 35, had already won two British Opens and was considered to be in his prime; while the South African Player, 29, was a past champion and had, only a fortnight earlier, joined Gene Sarazen and Ben Hogan as the only players ever to win a 'career grand slam' when he added the US Open to his British Open, US Masters and US PGA triumphs. The defending champion at Birkdale was another American, Tony Lema, who had won his first big American tournament in 1962 on the third hole of a sudden-death play-off. Such was his delight at finally breaking through to the winner's circle that he generously gave the press a case of champagne and immediately earned the nickname 'Champagne Tony'. Lema had played and won his first Open, at St Andrews, with a stunning display. The leading Australian fancies were Kel Nagle, who was in sparkling form after tying with Player in the US Open, and the American-based Bruce Devlin, 27, who had won on the tours in the US, Europe and Australia. Thomson's name was not mentioned. Nobody expected him to win, except, that is, Thomson himself.

When he arrived in Britain in mid-May, seven weeks before the Open, he told a reporter: 'A lot of people think I've lost the old killer instinct. Maybe a lot of people will get a surprise this season. I haven't come 12,000 miles to fool around. I am here to win the Open and I think I can win it at Birkdale or I would not be here.' He could not resist adding: 'I've won it before.'

Apart from spending time with close friends Guy Wolstenholme, Kel Nagle and Mike Wolveridge, all of whom were playing in the Open, Thomson had little contact with the outside world. He made a few calls back home to wife Mary and his young children, but largely divided his time between the golf course and his hotel room.

Thomson was well aware of the talk about town that the four-time champion had lost his spark. Many of his contemporaries speak of the single-mindedness he displayed during that fortnight at Birkdale. It was as if he arrived with only one purpose in mind; to concentrate fully on his '50 per cent' and hope the others slip up with theirs.

As soon as he met up with long-time caddy Jackie Leigh there was something in the air: a feeling, a hope, a determination. After Cecil

Timms in 1954 and Wallace Gillespie in 1955–6, Leigh guided Thomson home in that 1958 marathon at Lytham. He had met him at the Daks tournament of that year, when as 'a fat little boy sitting on the step outside his office', the caddymaster pointed him in the Australian's direction, knowing he was in need of a bagman. In the off-season, 18-stone Jackie Leigh worked in the haulage business. He had two wagons that he ran with another driver for the National Coal Board. He lived right next door to Royal Birkdale, adored the game of golf, and played to a handicap of four. 'Tournaments are a two man effort,' says Thomson. 'I first took Jack out of a pool waiting for mid-week jobs at Wentworth. Burly Jack took my bag and said nothing all the way around. For this reason he appealed to me especially. When we finished I asked him what the caddy fee was. I was accustomed to caddies asking exorbitant fees from professionals a long way from home. But he said 'Fifteen shillings', and I knew he was honest as well. So I handed him the fifteen shillings exactly, waiting for the look which never came. He said 'thanks' and turned away. 'Just a minute. Would you caddy for me in the tournament here next week?' He stopped and nodded a stiff 'yes'. He was clearly not a man to show his emotions. After that, I did not play four rounds of golf in Britain without him. I felt strange without him there beside me, mute and determined. I didn't know much about his personal life because he was not a man to tell everyone his troubles and this I liked too. Once on the golf course I wanted to hear no one's problems but my own. Jack absorbed himself in mine. He spared me the burden of his. Also, I never knew him to be unpunctual or the worse for the night before. One Sunday morning in Dublin, however, he arrived somewhat shamefacedly. Kel Nagle's caddy, "Blondie", did the honours for him and told the story. It seemed that the local Dublin caddies resented the invasion of itinerant ones from across the sea who cut them out of expected big assignments. In the flush of Saturday night revelries, Jack had to go in to bat for "Little Mac" [Dai Rees's caddy], who was set upon by some belligerent toughs. According to the story circulating that morning there was a broken jaw or two and ambulances and police vans taking people to the lock-up for the night. When Jack came next morning he was something of a hero with the other visiting caddies but he never said a word about it and I never asked him. He is not a man that needs helping. He never showed emotion of any kind during the play, even at the tensest of moments. He was a tremendous help to me and he loved his golf with a passion.'

So with his staunchest supporter once again at his side Thomson set off on his mission. The pre-championship headlines were devoted to the ubiquitous names of Palmer and Player, the hopeful challenges of Welshman Brian Huggett, Englishman Neil Coles and Irishman Christy

O'Connor, but above all, whether Nicklaus could turn the tables on Lema. The news that Thomson had gone out in 33 in practice hardly rated a mention. Yet at no stage did Thomson worry that his quest for a fifth Open crown was not being accorded its rightful attention in the press. He slipped back to his hotel room, dined quietly and bedded down for a good read on the eve of the championship.

When Thomson returned to his hotel room later the next day, his card had been placed even further at the back of the deck when he could only manage a one-over 74; even those who had given him any hope at all were now silent. Thomson did not share their view. Again, he kept his feelings to himself. In that opening round only two scores came in under 70. A five-under 68 from none other than defending champion Lema, and a 69 from Christy O'Connor, the perennial bridesmaid — 1958–3rd, 1959–5th, 1961–3rd, 1963–6th, 1964–6th — would Irish eyes finally smile in 1965? There was Palmer on 70, Devlin 71, Wolstenholme 72, and Coles, Huggett and Nicklaus on 73. Thomson though, stuck to his plan. Another quiet dinner with his friends and an evening of solitude locked in his hotel room reading. No one seemed to take much notice. Other pros with no affection for the Australian thought he was just being his usual cranky and anti-social self. Thomson, though, knew what he was doing. 'I knew my first round didn't sound good, and I was immediately six strokes behind [he had never won an Open from such a first round deficit], but I had everything under control and was doing everything well. I thought everyone would have at least one 74 that week and I still felt very confident about my chances.'

The next morning the breeze picked up noticeably, and Lema, out early, struggled. He birdied the 1st, but gave the stroke back at the 9th. He then bogeyed 10 and 12 before a finishing burst gave him birdies at 13, 15 and 17 to put him back on track with a 72 and the clear clubhouse leader on six under. For some time no player looked like finishing close to this — O'Connor stumbled in with a 73, and Nicklaus a 71. But then Palmer, Huggett and Devlin all sprinted to the line with a flurry of birdies. Palmer's 71 left him a stroke behind Lema, and Huggett, after arriving at the 13th square with the card, played the last six holes in a superlative five-under-par to finish with 68 and a share of second with Palmer. Devlin made his move with an eagle at the 13th and birdies at 17 and 18 for a 69 and the joint leadership alongside Lema. These four players took the spotlight, but out on the course in one of the last groups sent out, Peter Thomson was laying the foundation that would win him the Open.

Only a small gallery tagged along as the twilight descended over Birkdale and the air developed its notorious chill. Earlier, Thomson had destroyed any interest there might have been in his golf by scoring back-to-back bogeys at the 5th and 6th. He did manage to birdie the 1st to move back to even-par, but those bogeys put him two-over and at that stage, eight strokes behind Lema. He seemed to be fighting a losing battle. Through it all he retained the abounding impression he was enjoying himself. With a casual efficiency camouflaging his ruthless determination he clawed his way back spectacularly with birdies at the 7th, 9th, 10th, 13th, 15th, and at the last, for a magnificent 68. Suddenly, almost in defiance of his critics, there was the name of a four-time Champion lurking only two shots from the lead. After a quick shower Thomson managed to slip away into the darkness leaving those ahead of him to carry the burden. The breeze began to whistle in the night sky as he sat down, once again to read: he tried not to think about what lay ahead.

The skies were fine when Friday 9 July 1965 dawned over Royal Birkdale, but not too many of the world's top golfers were overjoyed. The strength of the accompanying wind bothered them. Not Thomson. If anyone in the field was comfortable playing in a wind, it was the Australian. When he found out he was drawn alongside Lema for the day's 36-holes, he was tempted to rub his hands together in glee. Play began at 8.00 a.m. and with only four strokes dividing the top fourteen players a mammoth crowd swarmed across the course. The wind was fickle and would play a vital, but disturbing part, for it moved slowly from strong south-west to north-west. The scoreboard showed that the game was several strokes more difficult than it had been at any stage of the championship. None of the leaders made any sort of progress over the opening six holes, and in fact the first significant thrust came from Thomson. Throughout his career he made no secret of the fact that of all days, the final day of an Open Championship was his favourite in golf. The playing conditions, whatever they were; the great courses; the tradition and the spectators. They all brought out the best in his game.

With Lema, and playing at the end of the procession, Thomson produced a flash of brilliance: 2, 3, 4 to turn in 35 against 3, 4, 5 from Lema for 38. Thomson was now leading the Open. A brilliant tee shot to five feet at the 158-yard 7th, a magnificent 30-foot putt at the 459-yard 8th and then three-putts from Lema at the 9th, were the turning points of the championship. The American managed to square the ledger with a birdie four at the long 13th, then at the short par-4 16th boldly regained the lead when he rolled in a long birdie putt. Again, there was the feeling Thomson had been put back in his place, but the last two holes underlined his composure and drive. They were both par fives, the 17th a fearsome test of 510-yards, the 18th, with its new tee in the sandhills a similar brute of 513-yards. Thomson went all the way down the middle for two magnificent birdies to finish, while Lema was lucky to escape with par at 17 after cutting his drive into the rough and hooking his second into the crowd. A bunkered second shot at 18 came out too strongly, and another wasted chance for a birdie gave Thomson the honours in a thrilling duel. Lema, Devlin and Palmer all posted 75s, and Huggett a 76, and with the afternoon round to come Thomson, after a 72, led the Open by a stroke. With just four shots separating the first eleven players, however, a fifth Open title was no foregone conclusion. The big topic at lunch was whether the Australian still had what was needed to hang on and win in what was certain to be a cut-throat final round.

With a birdie at the 493-yard par-5 1st, Thomson made the ideal post-lunch start and over the next few holes retained his distinguished gait and seemed in complete control. The greatest test of his composure and skill came in the closing nine holes. As he stood on the 10th tee he found himself in the comfortable position of leading Lema by three strokes and anyone else by at least four, and yet four holes later his lead over Lema had been whittled to a solitary shot. Many top-level golfers, especially those of world class, admit to feeling like imposters once they are thrust into contention in a big tournament; they fear they'll be exposed as frauds and mistakes creep into their play. They're almost relieved, even grateful to slip down the leader board and out of sight. The greats don't, however, worry about making mistakes. The adrenalin may be churning away inside, but there is no fear. It was in moments like these that Peter Thomson took some sort of morbid delight. When the pressure reached its climax, he relished the chance to put himself to the test. 'I used to get a great thrill out of that,' he says. 'I've seen a lot of people find themselves in that situation and I suspect that very few of them like it, but I really enjoyed it. That was the real thrill of it for me. That is what the professional game is all about; to be under that sort of tension is a thrill in itself, and it has nothing to do with character, because I know a lot of desperados who are very good at it.' There are golfers who are actually afraid of winning. Their feelings work completely against the grain of why they are there in the first place. 'It's certainly very stomach churning, but it can be much worse than that and very unpleasant,' says Thomson. 'It's more psychologically frightening. A player comes face to face with himself and it's not a nice thing for him to have to acknowledge he has a cowardly streak. The regular winners, of course, know what it is like to pass through all that, but the vast majority, even the technically brilliant ones, fail because they can't cope with the pressure. When I was playing well I wouldn't have any doubts at all. My thoughts would always be positive, and never, "Oh dear, can I reach the green with this, or do I need that?" I was in control and knew exactly what I was doing and what I needed to do.'

Thomson and Lema came to the 17th tee at Birkdale and the margin between them was still the same; Thomson by one. One slip, one false move, one moment of doubt and the grand finale of the Open's 'Thomson era' would have been snatched from his grasp. Watching it all was Peter Alliss. 'I have those last two holes at Birkdale engrained in my memory,' he says. 'The ground was running and both holes were reachable in two. The 17th drive at Birkdale when the wind is a touch against can be quite frightening indeed, but Thomson got his drive away and then hit a beautiful second shot which pitched some 20 yards short of the green and ran right up to the heart of the target. Two putts and a safe four and another birdie. A beautifully placed drive down the 18th, a second shot with a 2-iron which again pitched some 25–30 yards short of the green and threaded its way between the bunkers and rolled up some eight or ten yards from the hole. Two putts and he was the winner by two in a truly international field with all the big boys there. I can remember thinking to myself as he waved to the crowd, "Well, there you are, you've answered the critics in the best possible manner and you've done wonderfully well." The Old Lion had risen and been victorious!'

'I never once saw Peter Thomson lose his temper or be affected by the pressure of the big events in all the time I worked for him,' said his caddy, Jackie Leigh. 'He just got on with the game and never said anything to anybody. When we were on the course that year at Birkdale he never said one word to me until we came to the last hole on the last day and he turned to me and said, "How do we stand?" I said, "We need five to win from anyone else and if this fella Lema gets a three, we have to get a four to tie him." He nodded to me and made the best four I ever saw anyone finish with on my course.' Lema did not get his three. Outdriven and out of necessity going for everything, he finished five-six.

Now, the press were falling over themselves in order to toss bouquets. 'Monarch of the fairways', 'Master of the mighty', 'Ice-cold cobber', they headlined their reports. News of Thomson's win shared top billing with the escape of Great Train Robbery architect Ronald Biggs on the British front pages. Later, Thomson was to cherish one particular article, that from the incomparable Henry Longhurst, who wrote: 'One might say of Peter Thomson, in the old war-time adage, "it's being so cheerful that keeps him going". To watch him play the last two holes was pure delight. One would have thought that at the end of the long grind, with the prospect of winning a fifth Open if he did not now make a mistake, the strain would at least be visible in his features. Instead, he strode cheerfully along in the familiar white shoes at the head of the little procession inside the fencing, while thousands milled along the side. It might have been a summer evening's fourball. Both his drives flew as straight as a rifle shot down the middle and, when he reached his ball, he simply picked the appropriate club and without hesitation hit it straight to the green. I think the secret of Thomson's method is partly its simplicity and the absence of mannerisms or frills and partly the clarity of his own mind as to what he is doing.'

Once the euphoria from those around him had died down, Thomson was able to find a telephone in a quiet corner of the Birkdale clubhouse, and called Melbourne. It was 5 a.m. back home and Mary hadn't slept a wink. She had stayed by the telephone, as Don Lawrence, the doyen of Melbourne golf writers, had called her every time the telex churned out the score of Peter's final round — hole by hole. 'I've won it,' said the voice nonchalantly at the other end, 'and I'll be home next Saturday.'

1965 Open Championship, Royal Birkdale, England		
285	Peter Thomson (Aust.)	74–68–72–71
287	Brian Huggett (Wales)	73–68–76–70
	Christy O'Connor (Ire.)	69–73–74–71
288	Roberto de Vicenzo (Arg.)	74–69–73–72
289	Bernard Hunt (Eng.)	74–74–70–71
	Kel Nagle (Aust.)	74–70–75–72
	Tony Lema (USA)	68–72–75–74
290	Sebastian Miguel (Spain)	72–73–72–73
	Bruce Devlin (Aust.)	71–69–75–75
294	Jack Nicklaus (USA)	73–71–77–73
295	Arnold Palmer (USA)	70–71–75–79

By now one of the more familiar sights in British golf was the Mona Lisa smile of Peter Thomson as he sprightly stepped out the fairways of the world's most famous links in rain, hail or shine, seemingly immune to the pressure of an Open. As distinguished British writer Pat Ward-Thomas wrote: 'I never saw a golfer who seemed so assured of his destiny. There is about him an unmistakable air of success ... Thomson took success as though it was his due, not as something exceptional, but as part of the natural order of things.'

Peter Alliss takes a different tack: 'People thought Arnold Palmer invented this technique of "looking" at the crowd and staring into the sea of faces as he was playing — this is how he developed "Arnie's Army" of course, along with the fact that he was a new breed of animal — but Thomson did it first. He'd walk along maybe waggling a club, looking at the crowd in a relaxed, pleasant way, and patently enjoying it. It was just like a Sunday afternoon stroll. This was all part of Thomson's game plan and had an enormous influence on his winning, particularly when the weather was bad, as it often was in Britain.'

'When it was blowing a gale or bucketing down,' says Thomson's business partner, Mike Wolveridge, former British touring pro, 'Peter would think it was a fantastic opportunity. Every other player would be out there swearing or cursing, and Peter's belief was that if he stayed calm, didn't get cross, and actually welcomed the weather, he would have a head start on them already. With his remarkable humour he would say, "Oh dear, we've got a bit of a storm, hey? Well, it's only rain and I can allow for it." He actually taught himself to love the bad weather and the wind, and he'd walk along with a smile on his face, which of course infuriated many of the other players. A great many of them hated him for it. When this was the case he'd have them off their games and make it look like a walk in the park.'

Peter Thomson carried with him an aura of dignity and self-esteem that simply refused to buckle. Outwardly the world could only see the genial, practised smile, the club slung over a shoulder, and the brisk, unhurried step. In fact this was a fierce, trance-like concentration. It has been said that to be in a position to strike over the final few holes of an event such as the Open, a player needs a certain arrogance. He has to rise above, or in some cases, drop below the anxiety level. He has to spin himself into some kind of trance, some kind of self-hypnosis. Mistakes, things that go wrong — all crash against this trance and never penetrate. Thomson believed this, and his 'look' proved it. 'I always saw players going about their games with a solemn and serious look,' he says. 'Their brows were knitted, they were silent, they gave the appearance of being very deeply worried. People said to me, "these are the keen boys, the ones who take their golf seriously, the ones who get on". What rubbish! The knitted brow is not a sign of special concentration; it's an indication of anxiety. The players to fear were the ones with cheerful eyes and a calm smile. They were the ones with assurance and confidence; they were the hard ones to beat.'

There is a school of thought that says Thomson desperately wanted to finish his playing days with seven British Opens to topple the record of the legendary Harry Vardon: it has been said that chasing Vardon's ghost was Thomson's magnificent obsession. He did come close to a sixth, in 1969 at Lytham, but it was as if Vardon himself, long since laid to rest, had sent down a poltergeist to make sure Thomson remained stuck on five titles. In the ensuing years he made the top-ten a couple of times but, with the introduction of the larger-size American ball in 1974, his days seemed numbered. Yet there he was at Turnberry in 1977, the year of the famous Watson-Nicklaus 'shoot-out', carding a superb 67 on the way to a tie for 13th. Two years later at Lytham he walked from the 18th for the last time, or at least said it was, and the ghost of Harry Vardon may well have doffed his cap. But then, five years later he was enticed by Kel Nagle to play at St Andrews in the 1984 Open, purely because it was Nagle doing the enticing and St Andrews the hosting. The thought of winning never entered his head, but it was a chance for an emotional farewell and after rounds of 72–73–76 he missed the cut for the final day and thus ended a truly wonderful era. He might have missed out on his seven Opens, but he is not the type to lose any sleep over it all and remains more than content with his five. As for claims that Open Championships of the 1950s were not a patch on the modern extravaganza in quality of fields, prizemoney or prestige, Thomson, typically, answers with ruthless logic: 'Well, it was even less so in the days of Harry Vardon.'

The facts are that, when talk centres on the British Open, few men other than Peter Thomson have done better. For twenty-one consecutive years, from 1951–71, he finished out of the top-ten on only three occasions, 1959, 1964 and 1968 when he was 23rd, 24th and 24th respectively. Between the ages of 22 and 29, in the seven years from 1952 to 1958, he notched an Open record of never being worse than second. Four victories and three second placings. It took the mighty names of Hogan and Locke to beat him, and in seven years not a single British or European professional finished ahead of him.

The more you look at all that — the more you analyse the scores, the statistics and the weather conditions — the more astonishing his achievement seems. Against some of golf's most ruthless competitors and in such a competitive event, the man almost stood on his own.

A short while after that 1965 Birkdale victory he invited a very small côterie back to his room at the Prince of Wales Hotel in Southport. One of his friends grabbed a bottle of champagne on the way and on arrival in Thomson's room quickly popped the cork. The only glasses to be found were two dusty tumblers beside the sink. It was hardly a grandiose celebration for someone who had just joined the illustrious company of Braid and Taylor. It was the clearest indication that Thomson wasn't about to make a song and dance about it. He has never found the need to adorn his home with golfing trophies. If one was to look closely one might find an old Australian Open cup somewhere in his home, but only masquerading as a vase for flowers, and with the engraving side pointing to the wall. It is impossible to imagine the number of cups, urns, plates, medals, statues, vases and goblets he has tucked away over the years. Of them all, he cared for only one trophy, the auld silver claret jug. The replicas and medals associated with his British Open triumphs are stored modestly in a bank safety deposit box.

Thomson always thought he had a sixth Open inside him somewhere and quite possibly a seventh. Up until he ended his serious assaults on the Championship in 1979, people would stop him in the street, at functions, at tournaments, or wherever, and the topic of conversation would inevitably turn to Royal Birkdale in 1965, and his 'last' British Open. Thomson would immediately correct them with the words, 'you mean most recent'.

The Open was indeed his life's ambition.

C • H • A • P • T • E • R 6

Inspired by Ghosts

'NO one should ever venture North of the Tay to Pitlochry without climbing up to those glorious heights beyond Blairgowrie and Coupar Angus. I have never yet been less than warmed by those wild, old untamed mounts. You can see in the Scots themselves something of those raw and craggy peaks. All year they fight the elements of rain and snow and roaring winds and emerge unscathed in every spring and autumn a glorious blush of palette colours. Up there, where our ancestral tribes dared the Romans, and then the English to challenge for their eyrie. Now it's peace, and farm, and shaggy faceless beasts, and yet defies the modern columns still. Proud Scotland. Ignored and shunned by mighty industries' smoke and sprawl, her sons driven to the far corners of our earth to find their families' bread, it keeps its stony dignity for itself. The strangers come and stare and pass and with them goes a sprig o' heather or a heart-stopping sight. The highlands sleep forever dreaming on.'

P. W. Thomson

Several months after the hostilities of the second world war happily came to an end, the legendary Samuel Jackson Snead was among the many passengers rattling from side to side aboard the train from London as it completed its overnight journey to the Leuchars railway station at St Andrews. An excited golfing world was eager to witness the first Open Championship for six years. Snead, though he'd never before played on the Old Course, was one of the players expected to win. American Johnny Bulla had been runner-up in the last Open, in 1939, also at St Andrews, and as a close friend of Snead, argued that his countryman ought to put aside his memories of Carnoustie in 1937 (where he finished 11th) and aim for a place in golfing history by succeeding on the world's most famous course. Snead happily acquiesced.

As that train pulled into Leuchars in July 1946 and Snead looked eagerly out across the rolling linksland and down to St Andrews Bay, he could not see a golf course. Only after he made out flags flapping atop their sticks and men swinging their clubs did he realise there was a place for golf there at all. 'I looked out from that train and saw a course which looked like its fairways hadn't been mowed for months and the traps looked like they'd never been raked,' says Snead. 'The grass was up about everybody's knees and the wind was howlin' across the place. 'What kind of abandoned golf course is this?' I said out loud to myself. "Back home they wouldn't plant cow beet on that land!" This old Scottish guy next to me (who just happened to be a Royal and Ancient member) jumped up off his seat and said, "I'll have you know that's the Old Course, the most famous course on this earth!" I said to him, "You mean *that's* where they're playin' the British Open?" "It's not the British Open," he said angrily. "It's *The Championship*!" I quickly found out that you were considered some kind of nutcase if you didn't like St Andrews.'

Snead wanted to go back home and withdraw without playing but he could hardly do that. He stayed, and played, and won, by four shots over Bobby Locke and Johnny Bulla. He shot 71–70–74–75 (290), the same winning total as Dick Burton in 1939. It was to be the second of only three appearances by Snead in the British Open (Troon in 1962 was his last). He considered the playing of Britain's links courses to be the golfing equivalent of 'camping out' and made no secret of his particular dislike for St Andrews. A few days after his Open triumph he said his goodbyes. Snead never returned and no one missed him. No course has suffered as much from premature abuse as the Old Course. Bobby Jones, Gary Player, Lee Trevino, Tom Watson, Seve Ballesteros, Greg Norman, even the great Harry Vardon all thought, on first inspection at least, that there was nothing hallowed about the Old Course. Jones admitted to feeling 'puzzled and bewildered' and wrote: 'I could not play the course and I did not think anyone else could.' St Andrews was the scene of the most regrettable incident in the American's brief but wonderful career, when at the age of 19, and after notching a 10-over-par 46 to the turn in the 1921 Open, he started back with a six, picked up his ball and tore up his scorecard.

It has been said on numerous occasions that if a modern golf architect were to design a layout resembling the Old Course, he would never get another job. It has also been said, just as often, that Mother Nature and Father Time created the Old Course and man hardly seems fit to criticise it. It has been this way since Mary, Queen of Scots, played there just three days after the death of her husband, who'd been locked in nearby Loch Leven Castle.

The St Andrews Society of Golfers (which became the Royal and Ancient Golf Club in 1834) was founded on 14 May 1754 when twenty-two members contributed five shillings each for a silver cup to be presented in an annual competition. The Society had no particular authority and followed the rules devised in 1744 by the Company of Gentlemen Golfers in Leith. From the 1830s there was a gradual growth in the Royal and Ancient's influence, along with a decline in the Company of Gentlemen Golfers. Today, of all the world's golfing nations, only the United States does not take its lead from the R & A in matters of Rules of Golf and Amateur Status, and the Club's Championship Committee is responsible for the organisation of the Open Championship. Back in 1766 it was decided to reduce the number of holes on the Old Course from 22 to 18 so St Andrews was also responsible for establishing the length of the game.

Spreading away from the town, bordered by grey shops, hotels and houses, the tract comprises merely 93½ acres of forbidding linksland which was centuries old when it was protected by law in the city charter of 1552 and measures over 6,900 yards (6,300 metres) from the back tees and plays to a par of 72. The key to the mystery of the Old Course is its curious site. It stretches out majestically between the gorse in the shape of a huge shepherd's crook, on a thumb of linksland which sticks out into the North Sea and was formed by sand washed up by the retreating ocean. The narrowness of this thumb dictated the course's bizarre routing (by modern standards): holes 1–6 march in a straight line away from the town; holes 7 and 8 perform a tight clockwise loop; and then holes 12–18 move back towards the town in, as it were, single file. The expansive greens, seven of them doubles, many indistinguishable from the fairways (just as there is no clear definition as to where fairway ends and rough begins), are a supreme test in themselves and do not need bunkers for protection. The American Mark Calcavecchia once brought down the wrath of the R & A on his head in the Dunhill Cup by twice playing with a sand wedge from the green. He further displayed his irreverence for the cathedral aura of St Andrews when he returned as defending Open Champion in 1990. Not only did he not bother to show up for the traditional photograph with all the other former Open Champions in front of the famous clubhouse before the dinner held for them by the captain but said, 'It's really not too interesting to me what happened way back then. St Andrews is the place where it all started, and that's where it stops for me.' It must be stated that Calcavecchia's 1990 defence crumbled pitifully; he suffered the indignity of missing the halfway cut.

In the days when the course was allowed to bake under the sun, running approach shots were the rule. These days conditions are more lush (for reasons revealed later in this chapter) and the greens more holding of approach shots. As a result low scoring is easier, although wind and weather remain at the heart of the Old Course's defence.

Such are the conditions, it is not uncommon to play against the wind to the turn, and face it all the way back as well. It's all to do with the tide turning out on the Eden estuary and has dictated many a match or round. Also central to the strength of St Andrews is the multitude of bunkers, some 140 of them: most are merely potholes; some are as deep as mines from which shells of a former sea have been dug; others are deep pits with high, steep walls reminding a player that they were first carved out by sheep huddling behind the dunes to keep out of the biting wind. All are traps, especially for the player who tries to overwhelm the Old Course with power rather than reason with it. It is up to the golfer to chart his course for each hole rather like a sailor, tacking his way to the green by a route that steers him clear of the key bunkers — most with quaint, even romantic names like Cheape's, Scholar's, Principal's Nose, Ginger Beer, Coffin, The Beardies, Lion's Mouth, Wig, Strath, Hell, Mrs Kruger, Deacon Sims, and the favourite, a side-by-side pair at the 15th called Miss Grainger's Bosoms. There are other points of interest such as Granny Clark's Wynd, the Swilcan Burn, the Elysian Fields, the notorious Road Hole and the Valley of Sin. Players admit to feeling as if they've been out for a lesson in history more than a round of golf.

'The Old Course remains a monument to the origins of golf as a game played on links by the sea,' said distinguished British writer Pat Ward-Thomas. 'In the beginning it knew no architect but nature; it came into being by evolution rather than design; and on no other course is the hand of man less evident.' And this is why it gets them in. As it did Bobby Jones. His pieces of scorecard might have blown away in the wind, but his perseverance did not. Eventually he became known as the man who won the 'Impregnable Quadrilateral' — the British and US Amateur and the British and US Open titles, all of them in 1930, conclusively settling arguments that he was the greatest player of his era and perhaps ever. Jones also became the only man to win both the British Open and Amateur titles at St Andrews. 'The Old Course is the most fascinating course I have played,' he wrote, changing his earlier opinion. He eloquently expressed this change of heart in 1958 when he was made a Freeman of St Andrews and gave moving thanks, not to his fellow burghers of the town, but to the Old Course itself. '[That] wise old lady — whimsically tolerant of my impatience, but ready to reveal the secrets of her complex being if I would only take the time to study and learn. The more I studied the Old Course the more I loved it and the more I loved it, the more I studied it ... There is always a way at St Andrews, although it is not always the obvious way, and in trying to find it, there is more to be learned on the British course than in playing a hundred ordinary American golf courses.' Towards the end of his speech Jones said: 'I could take out of my life everything except my experiences at St Andrews and I would still have a rich, full life.' After many years suffering a crippling spinal disease, Jones died in December 1971 and as a final tribute a memorial service was held at St Andrews and the 10th hole of the Old Course, previously unnamed, was given his name.

Clearly though, not everyone has adopted the Jones approach; the transformation from an angry, tense relationship to a meaningful, reciprocated romance. There are golf professionals who never discover the secrets of the Old Course. It can be said that at St Andrews no unintelligent golfer has ever carried the day and that, after more than 500 years of salutary and sullen swinging, no two golfers have ever agreed on exactly how it should be played. 'It is odd,' says American Ben Crenshaw, a keen student of golfing history and a runner-up to Jack Nicklaus in the 1978 Open at St Andrews. 'All I want to thank,' he said then, misty-eyed on receipt of his cheque, 'is Nature, just for making this golf course.' His affection for the Old Course has increased each year. 'I've never seen a course that grows on you so much,' he says. 'It places a much greater emphasis on strategy than any other course I've played. There's an A, B and C way to play every shot, depending on your ability or how the wind is blowing, or if you feel like taking a gamble. Its ability to accommodate every class of golfer from the champion on down and to present him or her with every choice and challenge, is unique.'

It is these idiosyncrasies — some of them bordering on eccentricities — that make St Andrews the nonpareil that it is. Some modernists can see it only as a memorial to an old-fashioned and almost extinct style of golf, but most of the truly great players see it as a paragon of golf art.

There is one golfer who arrived at the home of golf, looked out and saw the play of the light on the burn, the sight and smell of the heather, broom, gorse and whins, and the striking edifice that formed the most majestic clubhouse in the world, and he was completely spellbound.

'It was September 1954 and when I first looked out it seemed like heaven,' says Peter Thomson. 'All my imaginings were proved true. There before me on the soft, damp ground of autumn lay the holy ground. There and then we became firm friends. The weather was glorious and the course was just soft enough to be a real delight. I remember my first visit vividly and St Andrews immediately struck me as a classic place with such an enjoyable and rewarding atmosphere. The tradition and history behind it all is quite clear and unavoidable. The first time I walked through the clubhouse and saw the things that had been achieved in golf at this place well before my own country had even been discovered, well, I was completely overwhelmed.'

Although he'd been playing the British tour since 1951, Thomson had to wait three years before a professional tournament was scheduled for St Andrews — the 1954 British PGA matchplay championship. 'Normally at that time of year [September] I would be back playing in Australia, but the lure of visiting St Andrews for the first time was just too great,' says Thomson. 'I chose to stay on in Britain for the matchplay championship and for the British Masters at Prince's Sandwich at Dover.' He clearly recalls his first round over the Old Course — a practice round for the matchplay event. 'It's a marvellous feeling to stand on the 1st tee for the first time on the Old Course, or any time actually, and tee-off on the same piece of turf where people have teed-off for hundreds of years. You feel as if all these eyes are watching you — the ghosts of the past, perhaps. That first hole is classic simplicity. Called "The Burn", it stretches away in full view for 374-yards between tee and flagstick. Nothing intrudes until the green edge, where lurks that horrid "sewer", the Swilcan, just four paces wide, flush with the green. The green itself is of enormous proportion, flat in the forecourt by the burn, but rising up into Himalayas at the rear, 30 yards on. In this age of target golf, the dimensions involved at this hole would seem to be ludicrous. The fairway, virtually unmissable; the green a target like a football field; nothing it would seem to bring a moment's fear to a top player. Except the burn.'

Before teeing off, Thomson was introduced to the man who would become his staunch and loyal ally over the links. Wallace Gillespie, a stocky, swarthy-skinned little Scot, was born and bred in St Andrews, knew the Old Course like his own backyard, and adored the ancient profession, even art, of caddying. Thomson wasn't sure how Gillespie came to be at his side or who had arranged the meeting, but by the end of the week he was more than grateful. With his extremely keen student in tow, Gillespie set off to again unlock a few mysteries. 'It was very much an exploratory round,' says Thomson. 'If you have never played at St Andrews before, you quickly realise you have no idea where to go. This is one of the beauties of the course. There are no signs or guides saying go this way or that way. I needed Gillespie to show me the lines and after that I was able to come up with my own ideas. He pointed the way and was very instructive.'

Their round was progressing smoothly until the 14th. Thomson asked for the line and Gillespie pointed to a church spire far in the distance. Thomson nodded, cracked a sweetly-timed driver straight down the line and immediately set off after his ball. He was most surprised to find it lying between two deep pot bunkers only a few yards apart. 'You didn't give me much margin for error that time,' he said to the man with the bag over his shoulder. 'Well, you are the Open Champion,' said a straight-faced Gillespie.

Thomson was soon the matchplay champion as well. In a stunning debut over the Old Course he became the first foreigner to win the event in its 51-year history. 'In all the long years of its history the Old Course at St Andrews can rarely have known a more absorbing week than that of the matchplay championship which was played there for the first time and which brought to Peter Thomson the great distinction of equalling the record of James Braid and Fred Daly, who won the Open and Matchplay titles in the same year,' wrote Pat Ward-Thomas. The locals were astonished that Thomson appeared so comfortable on a course that was notoriously brutal to first-timers, but with victories over W. Hancock (4 & 2) and W. Dixon (3 & 1) on day one, Thomson then eliminated J. Ballingall (2 & 1) on the second morning and found himself pitted against local hero John Panton in the afternoon. 'It seemed half of Scotland came along to watch,' remembers Thomson. 'Panton was the Scottish champion, a St Andrews specialist and a very clever player in those days — not very long off the tee but a skilful iron player. And he had a wonderful matchplay temperament. In the last nine holes of that match nothing seemed to go my way and then there I was, standing on the 17th tee, two down with two to play. There were a lot of Scots following us who were pretty pleased about that.'

Panton simply had to produce a single par over one of those closing holes and surely one of them would have been enough to halve and give him the finest victory of his career. Panton got his fours all right, but Thomson displayed his talents in no uncertain fashion. He birdied both the 17th and 18th to send the match into extra holes! It was an incredible finish.

If there is one symbol of St Andrews, one slice of the entire Old Course that provides a taste of its rich composite of golf lore, strategy and stubborn eccentricity, it is the 17th — the Road Hole. The trials and tribulations at this par-4 measuring 466-yards are enough to fill a book themselves. Way back in 1885, an innocent, respectable chap by the name of David Ayton came to the penultimate hole of the British Open with a five-shot cushion over everyone else. After an excellent drive and stylish brassie shot to easy chip-and-run position in front of the green, one could have been excused for popping a cork in his honour; his first Open seemed a mere formality. But then Ayton chose to putt up the hill. His ball failed to stay on line, rolled across the slope and then back down towards him. It continued to trickle down the hill and finally pulled up in the grass in front of the bunker. Ayton gave a wry smile, shrugged his shoulders and settled over his ball again. This time he had to chip over a bunker. Not a bunker; *the* bunker. Being asked to pitch to the flag over the Road Bunker is like being asked to play a famous tune on a piano whilst wearing boxing gloves. You can make yourself look very foolish. Too weak and you're in the bunker and almost certainly have to play out sideways; too strong and you're over the green, down a sharp hill and onto the road itself. Ayton, fearing the bunker, went over the green and onto the road. Then he duffed the ball up the bank and watched it trickle back down to his feet. By now he was not smiling. Next, he pitched across the green, past the flag, and straight into the bunker. Too weak, too strong; too weak, too strong. Ayton took three to remove himself from the Road Bunker. In the light of what had gone before he did superbly well to two-putt into the cup for an eleven. That was nine strokes from less than 75 feet without penalty. He lost the British Open by two strokes.

Over the years the road has decided many a match. In the 1978 Open, Japan's Tommy Nakajima, well up among the leaders, reached the 17th green in two shots. He stroked his first putt too gently, and watched it make a left-hand turn into the Road Bunker. He became another famous victim, taking five shots to extricate himself from the sand, and ended up with a nine. It's not only the green where trouble starts. The opening shot on the 17th could well be the most bizarre in golf. For a century, railway coal sheds extended across the fairway 75 yards in front of the tee. The 'drying sheds' were eventually torn down when the Old Course Hotel was built but purists demanded their return. Now, a peculiar looking half-modern, half-antique duplicate of a green shed makes the Road Hole tee shot entirely blind again. In the 1988 Dunhill Nations Cup final, Australian Rodger Davis was leading Irishman Des Smyth by a shot as they came to the 17th, but he carved his drive away into the hotel lobby and ended up carding a seven. Smyth won the crucial match by two strokes and Ireland won the Cup 2-to-1. The Road Hole's approach shot is also extremely difficult. It you're coming out of the rough and into a breeze, you may end up well short of the green in Scholar's Bunker or the sarcastic Progressing Bunker. If you go at the pin the Road Bunker awaits. Enough said.

In 1954, with his match against Panton lying dormie and against all possible odds, Thomson decided to take a gamble. He shaved a further few yards off the corner and drove over the railway sheds and down the side of the road. 'Then from a perfect upslope on the fairway I hit a 7-iron as hard as I could,' he says. 'The ball touched down on the front of the green and pulled up within 12 feet of the hole. My putt went in for a three to Panton's four!' At the last, both men put their approaches on the green, but a long way from the hole. Panton putted first and laid it stone dead, which meant a now-or-never putt from 20-feet for Thomson; but don't ask him to talk you through it. 'In it went to the great roar of the crowd and we set off again.' Simple. They halved the 19th, 20th and 21st holes and by now it was growing dark. They could barely see the green from the tee at the 4th. 'Going into the gloom it was decided by our PGA referee that if we didn't get a decision on the fourth extra hole we would have to come back in the morning. Panton tugged his shot left and his approach barely reached the green. I fired in a 4-wood and in truth I never saw it finish, but I knew from the way I struck it that it would end up somewhere near the green. On that 4th green, the flag at championship time is set between two ridges, so that if your second shot doesn't finish between those ridges you are faced with a very difficult putt. We were practically striking matches it was so dark, but when I got to the edge of the green I saw my ball in the valley near the flag.' Panton missed his long putt, marked, and backed away. Thomson casually stepped up and holed his four-footer for a quite astonishing birdie and the match. It was a remarkable turnaround from the position he held after the 16th and as the Scottish sun finally set on another fantastic day of golf, Thomson had a special feeling as he walked towards the clubhouse, Gillespie walking obediently alongside, muttering something about a fellow called Houdini. 'That, I think, was the most memorable match I ever had,' says Thomson with a grin. 'And after that match I knew that everything was in my favour and that something, or someone, was shining on me.'

The next morning he was to meet none other than Bobby Locke in the quarter-finals. That sounded a daunting prospect but more good fortune was on the way, again at the notorious 17th. The resulting clash, despite being played in heavy rain for most of the way, was described by Leonard Crawley, golf writer for London's *Daily Telegraph*, as the greatest match he had ever watched. 'Locke and I had played more than a hundred times head to head, and I knew his game well,' says Thomson. 'He knew mine just as well. We were both in good form and I believe that until the 16th hole neither of us played anything like a bad stroke. Locke birdied the 3rd and 5th, but I won the 6th and 7th to get back square and I took the lead at the 10th which is a short drive and pitch hole. We went along like that for the next few holes, each of us missing birdie putts one after the other after some grand second shots into the wind. At the 16th, with the pressure really on and Locke running out of holes to get back and catch me, he played a bad second shot and fell into a bunker some 40-yards short of the green. I thought then I had him because it didn't seem possible for him to get down in two from that bunker. But he took a long time about that shot and played one of the most remarkable strokes I have ever seen. He pitched it clean from the sand, making it rise quite high, and he got it onto the green within 20 feet of the flag and then holed the putt. Instead of being 2-up with two to play and seemingly assured of victory I was still only 1-up and that shook me a bit.'

So to the Road Hole and Thomson stuck to his policy of giving it both barrels. Again his gamble paid off and he shaved the corner by driving beautifully over the railway sheds, and was left with nothing more than a 4-iron to the green. Locke took the more conventional route wide of the corner, and a cruel kick meant he was now pulling a 3-wood from his bag for his approach. Now it was a battle of wits. 'Anyone going to the Road Hole with a wooden club needs a lot of nerve and usually a lot of luck,' says Thomson. 'Locke knew well not to try and pitch it on the green and stop it, particularly with a wood, so he played short to the front. I had to decide whether to take my chances and pitch on with a 4-iron or lay my ball beside his and match him from there into the hole. I knew of no one in the world who could actually beat Locke into the hole from 25 yards and I certainly wasn't the one to do it, so I took another gamble and played for the green. The shot came off perfectly; touched down on the very front of the green, like a jet would on an aircraft-carrier, and by the time it had finished bouncing and biting, stopped some 20 feet past the hole. That was the stroke that really won me the match.' Another match decided at the Road. 'Locke, in a desperate effort to hole his pitch, ran it by some 12 feet. After I putted up dead, he missed, and we shook hands.' Had Thomson parred the last he would have carded a 67. A par for Locke would have been a 69. 'Man, that Peter Thomson is just unbeatable like that,' said the South African. Given the dreadful conditions and over such a test as the Old Course, veteran scribes had to pinch themselves to make sure they'd witnessed a match of such quality. 'I can pay it no higher tribute,' wrote Tom Scott for *Golf Illustrated*, 'than to say I watched every stroke of it in a pitiless, drenching rain.'

Thomson had no time to relax. He changed his soaking clothes, grabbed a quick bite and immediately headed out for his semi-final against Exeter's Norman Sutton. They matched each other shot for shot over the first five holes, until Sutton began to pull away. Maybe the mental strain of playing such consistently outstanding golf was beginning to tell on the Australian, some thought. Others hoped. Then Thomson rammed home birdie putts at the 10th and 11th to grab the lead and was never headed. The match was another to finish at the 17th, rapidly becoming a glorious stretch of turf for Thomson. With yet another rock-solid par he notched a 2 & 1 win and was looking forward to a good night's sleep before the 36-hole final against the 41-year-old Scottish professional at the Huddersfield club, Johnny Fallon.

Thomson was relieved to awake to fine, bright skies, but there was a distinct chill in the air, so he wore tweed cap, woollen pullover and cardigan and set out early for a little practice. Wallace Gillespie was immediately at his heel, reporting on the weather and when and where the wind might come into play. By tee-time a huge crowd had turned out to watch the fortunes of their 'local boy' Fallon.

Continuing the form Thomson had shown all week, the Australian sprang from the blocks with a hot start. He won the first two holes with birdies and by the ninth was suddenly 4-up. 'We all felt rather sad,' said one press correspondent. 'For no player, we told ourselves, could give Thomson a four hole start and survive.' Fallon managed to win the 10th, but Thomson took the 14th and was headed for a comfortable luncheon lead. From this seemingly unbackable position, however, Fallon dug deep into his reserves and drew on his wealth of cunning to claw his way back. He holed a wonderful putt of more than 20 yards to win the 15th and much to the crowd's liking, struck another blow at the 16th. He sat down to lunch in a much better frame of mind than he might have, at only two-down.

The afternoon round produced a long series of halved holes in par figures. The turning point came at the 13th where Fallon, after a series of near misses, holed another huge putt for the win. He scrambled halves at the next two holes and then at the 16th rolled home an impossible-looking 10-footer across a vicious slope and observers say there must have been at least a hundred tweed caps thrown in the air. Incredibly, the match was back on level terms. It is these situations that gnaw away at the confidence and if ever there was a hole to exploit that dwindling confidence, it was the Road Hole. Surely now it might put an end to the Australian's precociousness? Thomson matched Fallon's glorious drive and iron shot to the green. The crowd did not stop cheering until Thomson huddled over his putt. With the eerie, distant squawk of a sea bird the only sound, both men gallantly putted dead for the half. Spectators were now lining both sides of the last hole, and the townsfolk were vacating the nearby shops to see the dramatic finish. There were more cheers when both made the green in two. Fallon's putt was an uphill one of eight yards. Up and up it came towards the hole and on reaching the cup, half disappeared, but alas for the local crowd, spun around to come fully into view again, Fallon spinning away in agony. Now Thomson had a putt of six yards to win, but he too lipped out, so down the first they went for the third time in the match.

At the 37th Thomson had to play a delicate chip from the back of the green after falling into the trap of over-playing the burn, but he brought off the shot with brilliance to halve in four. Finally, at the 38th, came the lapse in concentration that was necessary to decide the title. Fallon pulled his approach into a greenside bunker and Thomson, grasping the opportunity with both hands, threaded his ball through all the danger and to the sanctity of the green. Although Fallon made a good recovery he missed his five-foot putt and Thomson's lag was good enough to triumph. A great match was over. 'The greatest final ever,' wrote the *News of the World*. 'In years to come, when some of us who saw this great match are very old, we will talk about it, for we may never see its like again.' The esteemed Pat Ward-Thomas penned: 'Although the margin of many of Thomson's victories, including the magnificent final, was desperately close, I felt all along that it was his tournament. The assurance, self-possession and coolness of this remarkably mature young man suggested that his opponents always had much more to beat than his actual golf, and thus it proved.' *Golf Monthly* said: 'At the presentation ceremony Thomson said he felt that his draw was the toughest and that organisers had hand-picked his opponents, all of whom seemed to be inspired. However, Thomson endeared himself to all who saw his play and everyone is looking forward to see him return to St Andrews to defend his Open title.'

'There was a time through the 1950s when a significant move was afoot to make the Old Course the Open Championship's permanent venue in the same way that Augusta annually hosts the Masters,' says Thomson. 'Democracy had its way and the championship rotates through a list of superb and eminent clubs. None of them, however, has the status and seniority, eminence or authority of St Andrews Old. The Royal and Ancient, in a way, lets the Open have its head to run about like a nervous hound and then with a sharp pull on the leash, returns it to its kennel yard.' In 1955 the top dog was Peter Thomson. With rounds of 71–68–70–72 for a total of 281, he won by two strokes; again the disappointed Johnny Fallon was the man in second place. To master St Andrews in such a manner requires not mechanical precision but the perfect combination of skill, nerve and intelligence not demanded by any other course in the world. Few people see it this way until they have played it twenty, thirty or even forty times. Some never see it at all. It speaks volumes for Peter Thomson's skill, nerve and intelligence that he not only won the first two tournaments he competed in on the Old Course, but that those events happened to be the Open, and the PGA matchplay. And there he was in 1962 for the Martini tournament, carding 66–69–72–68 for a 275 total, a record over the Old Course.

One could be forgiven for thinking that to discover the mysteries of the Old Course as Thomson has, a person needs just to keep on going out and back until you've conquered it, until you know every square foot of it like the back of your hand. Thomson was quick to discover that the key to the Old Course lies not so much in its 93½ acres as in fully immersing oneself in the township of St Andrews. Those who think of the Royal Burgh in terms of golf alone are heir to only part of the town's fascination. It is a treasure chest of of tradition and lore. A self-confessed history buff, Thomson fell deeply in love with it all. 'The whole of Britain is a museum of history,' he says. 'You can find places that were of great importance hundreds, and even thousands of years ago — that intrigues me, and St Andrews was a goldmine in that regard. It is not just a course. It is a Royal Borough with an ancient history, a ruined cathedral and castle, an old university, five clubs and a passion for the game of golf unique. The whole town seems to give itself up to golf; the butcher, the baker and the candlestick maker, their day's work done, can be seen scurrying down to the first tee to get their round in before dark.'

The first written evidence of golf at St Andrews is a covenant on parchment dated 25 January 1552, giving the public the right to play on the linksland and the city the right to breed rabbits at the top end — so began the right of all pilgrims to St Andrews, a right that has gone on almost unchallenged over nearly 450 years. That earliest document setting out the community's right 'to play at golf, futball, schuting, at all gamis with all uther, as ever they pleis and in ony time,' was drawn up by the archbishop of St Andrews, John Hamilton. At the time, St Andrews was a prosperous city, a seat of learning since the founding of its university in 1410, and one of the five most important ports in the British Isles. Its archbishop was the most powerful Catholic figure north of the Border. Through the ages the game of golf continued to grow with the times, to the extent where the game and St Andrews became synonymous. The famous land changed hands many times before coming into the safe-keeping of the Links Trust in 1974 and the right of the public to play over it has been jealously preserved ever since. These days a green fee is required and in the crowded summer months a starting time has mostly to be balloted for, but the spirit remains the same.

Thomson went out of his way to explore the history of the place. When he stood on the 1st tee of the Old Course, he was totally enveloped by its atmosphere. 'No one who enjoys a game of golf should tee off at St Andrews on that 1st tee at the foot of the steps from the house without a racing of the heart,' he has said. They say that if one ventures onto the last fairway and walks up towards the Valley of Sin late of an evening when the last spectator on the railings has departed to supper, when the tide is quiet in the Bay except for the occasional mewing of gulls one can almost feel the presence all around of the figures of the past.

Thomson's respect for St Andrews and its Old Course follows him today. His partner in the firm of 'Thomson Wolveridge & Associates' is the diminutive, eloquent Englishman Michael Wolveridge, a moderately successful touring professional on the US circuit in the early 1960s. The Old Course is one of his favourite topics. 'I've had long, long discussions with Peter about the Old Course,' says Wolveridge. 'We share a similar sense of humour and we both like the challenge of St Andrews, which is, that there is always a sporting chance. Golf is meant to be challenging, fun and enjoyable — on a lot of courses these days, it's a serious examination. At St Andrews there are no hazards where you've simply got to reload and play again. The only water hazard is the Swilcan Burn, which is now the town's stormwater drain, but it used to be the town's sewer so you didn't want to put your ball in there!

'On other holes I found it wonderfully clever to have a fairway hugely wide and inviting, but because the green is angled in a certain way the only hope you have of hitting that green and staying near the flag is by being in a certain position from the tee. You're given a great big, wide fairway to hit, but you can reach the green only from a 10-metre square section of it. I find that enchanting and I know that is the original golf. I love the size of the greens, because that allows all people, everybody, to play the golf course and enjoy it. It breeds a camaraderie that sees a hot golfer mix it with his grandmother. There is no uphill walking, and it's springy, firm turf.'

'I would like to think that Peter and I have come to understand the principles of the Old Course and thus principles of golf, which these very ingenious people devised over centuries. All those bunkers, for example, come in for criticism at some stage because there are many that face the other way and you don't know you're in them until you see that you're in them. For hundreds of years, the Old Course was played in reverse. They'd play the 1st and the 18th the normal way, but reverse it on the holes with the double greens. How clever of the Scots to be able to play over those parts of the course most worn to give them a rest. The Old Course has had a colossal influence on us both at work and play. There is nothing out there in the world of golf course design that is new. It's all over 400 years old and comes from the Old Course. That has given us a lovely insight into design and has allowed us to have our feet very firmly on the ground. We haven't found anything better.'

Nurturing Thomson's deep respect for and understanding of everything that St Andrews stands for in golf were conversations with two men whose memories of the Old Course were extremely vivid. Willie Auchterlonie was born in St Andrews in 1872 and at the age of 21 won the Open Championship at Prestwick with a set of seven clubs, all of which he made himself. He never played with more than his seven clubs and was a great believer that to be considered a true champion, a golfer had to be master of the half, three-quarter and full shots with each club. Soon after winning the Open he founded the famous club-making firm in St Andrews and in 1935 was appointed professional to the Royal and Ancient Golf Club, a position he held until his death in 1963. The honourable tradition of fashioning wooden clubs by hand was passed to his son, Laurie, who diligently maintained the family's reputation as master clubmakers and took over the reins as professional at the R & A until he died in 1987. Both men lived into their nineties. When it came to knowledge of the Old Course and its halcyon days there were none wiser.

These informal chats first led Thomson, in the late 1950s, to the conclusion that the standard of the Old Course was declining at an alarming rate. Fighting a spirited battle he set forth to raise awareness of the plight of the home of golf, beginning with a 1957 newspaper article. He labelled the Old Course: 'A changed personality, docile, soft, easy to meet and no terror at all. Older players hardly recognised it. It was like a slain dragon. What has happened to the famous Old Course?'

Then through the 1960s: 'I have read and heard Player and Palmer express their contempt of the approach shot that must be dropped short and allowed to run its course to the hole. Personally I find this one of the hardest shots in golf, albeit an "old granny" one, [but] course preparation these days makes no provision for it. Fairways are fertilised right up to the putting surface and the excess water from greens usually finds its way into a lake at the apron. Careless preparation creates an area where there is a razor edge dividing two entirely different turfs. How excellent it must have been before World War II, before automatic water systems and the insane cry to pour it on until the green, not the player, stops the ball. Those of us who love the Old Course as a cricket lover cherishes Lord's saw with horror the ravages that artificial fertilisers brought about at St Andrews. Old bunkers that struck terror into the most steel-hearted golfer have been filled with beach sand to reduce the depth; and finally the most grotesque horror of all, an automatic watering system! In Scotland! What cunning salesman talked the Town Council into that! Will ignorant abuse destroy the Old Course? Will modern science slowly but inexorably change it into just another meadow course tempting the tourists to spend their miserable dollar on its hallowed sward, until it is despised and forgotten? All courses everywhere are compromise copies of the original. Where turf is not available naturally it has to be artificially created. It is now the case of the original being destroyed to match its copies! Will we awake in time?'

Then in the Melbourne *Age* in July 1973 came the most caustic attack of all, following Thomson's appearance in the Scottish Open, played over the Old Course. Until this time the R & A had remained silent over his remarks, but this stinging rebuke could not pass unanswered.

Thomson began his article: 'It would make you weep to see the state of the Old Course. This famed links is no longer fit to be shown off to the world as the epitome of the game. Its turf is either moth-eaten by years of callous divot taking and neglect or else fertilised and overgrown with long-stemmed grasses that have turned it into meadowland. Although it looks green in patches, close up it horrifies. Its sand traps are no longer the terrors they were, having been half-filled with fresh sand. This makes them shallower and quicker from which to escape. The road behind the 17th, the famous Road Hole, has been paved so it's a relatively simple matter to putt back on to the green. And the greens, no longer getting the tender, personal care they have for ages, are watered, ye gods, with an automatic system, and strengthened chemically so that one is no longer putting on soft and delicate blades of seaside bent, but stiff and wiry blades that have cut the speed in half.' He continued: 'In my view these hallowed links are doomed because the thinking to restore them to their glory is dead in this town ... Last week during the Scottish Open we found the Old Course like an aged beauty in rags and tatters — rouged and painted on the face, proudly trying to play her role but, alas, wide open to approach. You no longer have to go about wooing it with all the subtlest wiles. Any crude blade can take her straight on like any other old layout. Nobody holds her in awe any more. It's enough to make old Tom Morris turn in his grave.'

Several weeks after this article was published, the *Age* received a letter from Gordon P. Adam, chairman of the joint links committee of the R & A. It stated that Thomson 'should confine his remarks to subjects upon which he is reliably informed'. Mr Adam pointed out that St Andrews was subject to gale force winds that not only emptied bunkers of their sand but blew the sand against the face of the bunkers. He said the road behind the 17th had had a tarmac surface for many years and as for the greens, Mr Adam said that a three-year drought in Scotland had reduced the level of water in local reservoirs to 19 per cent of capacity and were it not for automatic watering, neither the greens nor the fairways would be playable in mid-summer. He went on: 'I would also like to know that if the Old Course was playing so easily during the Scottish Open, why was it that the winning score of 286 was not a good deal lower?' Mr Adam concluded his letter by saying, 'Nobody does more damage to a golf course than professional golfers and evidence of this can be seen on any course on which a championship has been played and for this reason alone, Thomson should realise that golf courses are there for the multitudes and not for the circuit professionals.'

Thomson was not content to let things lie. He called for the resignation of the joint links committee and its chairman: 'If the Old Course, as I described it, is indeed their best effort, they should hide their heads in shame ... My gloomy point, if it can be recalled, was that few people at St Andrews really *care* ... The Old Course is being slowly destroyed, not by Mr Adam and his committee in particular, or by his efforts or non-efforts, but by the 40,000 rounds that are callously played over it each year by all and anybody, including professional golfers. And the turf, preciously thin and necessarily delicate, cannot take it ... Funnily enough the world at large cares more about the Old Course than the citizens. Even as long ago as 1894 the rest of Scotland was concerned enough to pass laws protecting the Old Course from the townsfolk. The St Andrews Links Act said that "any person who shall contravene any of the fore-going by-laws shall be liable, on conviction, in a penalty not exceeding one pound for each offence, and failing payments, to imprisonment for any period not exceeding fourteen days". The regulation laid down that "no person shall play cricket, football, or any game other than golf upon the golf courses". And more: "to prevent destruction of the turf of the golf courses, play or practice with iron clubs is prohibited". And doubtless for those of tender age who might be disposed to sailing toy boats: "no one shall wade in the Swilcan Burn, so far as it flows through the Old Course, nor shall anyone, except caddies in search of their ball, do anything to cause its waters to become discoloured or 'muddy'." Somewhere along the line, that noble concern for the links preservation went down the Swilcan Burn and out into the Firth.'

Thomson's views, which naturally became widely publicised, hardly endeared him to the citizens of the old, grey town, and there was a strong belief among many of his friends and colleagues that this vehement campaign upset the applecart to such an extent that Thomson's consideration for honorary membership of the R & A was now in jeopardy. Typically, his campaign was not concocted from half-thoughts or an attempt to stir a hornets' nest. Thomson had the interests of golf at heart. He wanted change. And he got it. The following year the joint links committee was replaced by a St Andrews links trust and this body was bound to keep the links as they had been kept in times past. Currently there are plans under way to upgrade all golfing facilities at St Andrews under the auspices of the trust. The Old Course itself will not be touched. Activities are being concentrated on the other courses in the town — the New, Jubilee, Eden and Balgove (9-holes) — in an attempt to create a permanent infrastructure of services and facilities that will one day provide the best in the British Isles. As one committeeman said in March 1989, 'The current situation is totally unacceptable. The Old Course is arguably the most famous course in the world and yet the people who use it don't even have a toilet. We have a moral obligation to our visitors. Our plans will ensure that such a problem doesn't arise without disrupting the unique atmosphere which the town possesses.'

And this is exactly what Thomson was getting at in the late 1960s and the early 1970s. He was anticipating the golfing boom, and the pressure that St Andrews as the shrine of golf would subsequently be placed under. He saw the need to preserve that shrine, and it may not be too exaggerating to say that Thomson's enquiring mind, and conversations with Laurie Auchterlonie, at least laid part of the foundation for the establishment of a links trust and the preservation of the Old Course as the heavenly, historic tract of linksland that so proudly and successfully hosted the 1990 Open Championship.

'Those conversations with Laurie Auchterlonie were revelations because he had a very keen memory that went back to last century. After that piece in the *Age*, the one that was very critical of the management of the whole course and created quite a furore, Laurie fully agreed with me and in fact, said he'd give me further ammunition if I wanted to fire it, but I didn't. I rested my case and things changed quite dramatically after that. The people involved in the management of the course suddenly stood up and took notice. The course is managed by a joint committee of the R & A and the townspeople, who of course will not abide by it ever being closed because they lose business in the town. The club I'm sure would like to see it closed for at least a couple of months each year, but that would never be tolerated. Anyway Laurie thought there was a real neglect in the preservation of the course and explained to me in detail how much the course had changed in his lifetime. The greens should really be part of the fairways, and long ago they were cut square, not shaped as they are now. The bunkers have definitely become more shallow over the years and another disaster that came about was watering of the fairways. The Old Course should never have been allowed to change. It's such a treasure for the game of golf that it should have been kept as it was. It's such a link with the origins of the game and so very precious. If we didn't have that link to refer to, goodness only knows where golf would evolve to. Look at the implements and the balls we use now. If courses went along the same track and we lost the original reference — God knows what would happen ...'

Honest, logical, from the heart and, above all, with the future of St Andrews and the Old Course in mind. This was the traditionalist coming out in him; the man of vision; the man who wanted golf's heritage retained for the education and adulation of future generations: 'No other course on the British Open roster quite measures up to it,' he says, eyes twinkling at the prospect. 'It provides difficulty second to none, combined with variation of wind from all directions. Temperature comes in all degrees, even during an Open week in the middle of high-summer in July. The course, almost entirely nature made, has a subtlety no man can ever completely fathom. There is a razor edge between success and failure at every turn. My own experience has taught me the utmost respect for it as a championship test. If I was asked to define the word "golf", I would simply say the Old Course.'

There can be no underestimating the pleasure Thomson received in May 1982, when he opened a letter from St Andrews stating that he and Kel Nagle had been elected honorary members of the Royal and Ancient Golf Club. It is no easy matter to try to alert the world to the perceived problems of such a place as the Old Course whilst retaining so obvious a love for St Andrews and its people. Disapproval of their course is like questioning one's parentage; constructive criticism can so often be taken the wrong way. It is a tribute to Peter Thomson that there was no doubt in the Royal and Ancient Golf Club committee room or locker-room that his character never flinched and that ultimately, he fully deserved their greatest honour.

In a letter to club secretary, Keith Mackenzie, Thomson wrote: 'I would like to ask you to pass onto your Committee my heartfelt gratitude for the honour you have paid me in making me an honorary member of the Club. I must say it never occurred to me that I would one day be proudly adding the R & A to my list of clubs. It must now go to the top of the list! I would now like nothing more than to visit the Club and pay my respects. It will be a great thrill to change shoes and tee off as a member.'

Then fifteen months later, Thomson was invited to respond to the official toast for new members at the Royal and Ancient Golf Club's annual dinner. He was the first professional golfer to be asked to speak at this occasion and the first Australian. 'That was a very high honour,' he says. 'I was genuinely thrilled about that and it was a tremendous occasion for me to stand before the new members and speak on their behalf at the home of golf.' On that romantic trip back 'home' to the Old Course, Thomson carded a 77 in the Royal and Ancient's autumn meeting, playing alongside the new captain, John Salvesen, despite an eight at the Road Hole when he fluffed a chip and went into the road bunker, taking three to get out. It all meant that the following July, when the Open returned to St Andrews for the first time since 1978, Peter Thomson was 'talked into' breaking his five-year retirement to compete in his 30th Open Championship. He'd been playing well on the circus train that was the United States Seniors tour, which had pulled into Boston. That night Thomson was chatting with his tour companion and close friend, Kel Nagle, when their honorary memberships of the R & A became a talking point and the fact that their invitations to the Open lay unanswered. The 1960 Open Champion at St Andrews said to his counterpart from 1955 that he thought it was almost their golfing duty to attend the 1984 Open. Thomson knew they'd have to play in the event.

The Australian veterans were soon flying to Scotland. There was not a thought of winning the jug again; they were in it purely for the fun and the memories.

'Truthfully, I thought that logically we'd be paired together and have a chance of playing at our own pace and with each other,' says Thomson. 'But I was astonished to discover that I had to play with Andy Bean, who hit the ball about a hundred yards further than I did, and Kel had to play with Seve Ballesteros! It was a very foolish thing the championship committee did. I very much enjoyed playing with Bean [both men started with 72s], but I couldn't help feeling sorry for Kel.' First and last played in that grouping that day. Ballesteros went on to win a thoroughly exciting and absorbing event, but Nagle, after rounds of 84–75, finished in a tie for last placing. Thomson managed to make the halfway cut, only to bow out after the third round with scores of 72–73–76 for a 221 total. It wasn't such a bad effort for a man just a few weeks short of his 55th birthday — on the same scoreline were such names as David Graham, Ray Floyd, Larry Mize and Christy O'Connor jr.

Thomson and Nagle were about to set out on a practice round a few days before the championship started. On their way down the clubhouse steps towards the first tee, Thomson noticed the tall, slender figure of young Queenslander Ian Baker-Finch. He seemed lost. Thomson knew the 23-year-old well. He'd first approached him in late 1981 and suggested he take his game to the New Zealand circuit rather than heading back home to Queensland for the local pro-am tour. This was after Baker-Finch started the final round of the 1981 Australian PGA championship at Royal Melbourne with a front nine of 30, stringing together six consecutive birdies as part of a collection of thirteen he made over the last two rounds. Seve Ballesteros won the tournament; Baker-Finch, his playing partner, finished ninth. 'Peter thought I showed potential and introduced himself to me around that time,' says Baker-Finch. 'I think he saw me as a fresh, young guy coming through who didn't have anybody helping him, or any major tutor, and he helped me with the odd comment here and there. Then it got to the stage where I would ask for advice and he would freely give it. He wasn't like an adviser whom I would rush to every time I had a problem, but he was always there when I needed him, like a father-figure. A lot of guys think that Peter gave me full-scale coaching lessons, but that was never the case. He is always very, very simple in the way he explains things; it is always just a little thought or gesture; something that would stick in my mind. At the end of 1982 I was having a lot of trouble because I'd always tried to play like Nicklaus by hitting the ball high with a fade, but I was never really strong enough. I was in New Zealand at the time for the Airlines tournament and we had to practise down at a park not far from Titirangi. I was over to one side, hitting these pathetic, weak fades. Peter just happened to be walking past and he watched me hit some dreadful ones onto the road, well out to the right. He stepped forward and said, "Okay, now's the time. I think you should do this." That was the first time he changed my swing around and had me turning my left foot back into square and my right foot out a bit. I was suddenly hitting low hooks out into the middle of the park. That day in New Zealand was the start of it for me. I can still visualise everything he did to me at that time.'

Thomson insisted that Baker-Finch flatten his swing in an effort to produce more length from the tee, and his patience in showing him different ways of hitting the same kinds of shot made the youngster a much more complete player. By this time the young Queenslander had shown more than a passing interest in Thomson's daughter Pan. The relationship between the two developed to the point where they became good friends, and then came the invitation from Thomson for Baker-Finch to join him at his holiday home at Portsea on Victoria's Mornington Peninsula for three weeks at Christmas. In early January 1983 master and student played golf together nearly every day at the Sorrento or Portsea clubs. Previously Baker-Finch had trouble sliding, tilting and swaying during his swing — Thomson spotted this quickly and soon had him rotating his body and shoulders. 'I was honoured by the fact that he was so keen to help me,' says Baker-Finch. 'I used to get a hard time from the fellows around me — they thought the only reason Peter was helping me was because I was taking out his daughter, but that has since proved rubbish because to this day he still has time for me.'

In November 1983 Baker-Finch holed a four-metre putt on the final green in the Australian Open at Kingston Heath to be placed second ahead of David Graham, and the following week with the same set of clubs he'd borrowed from Thomson produced a score of 280 at Middlemore in Auckland to win the New Zealand Open by three strokes. He was entered in the 1984 British Open by virtue of finishing in the first six on Australia's Order of Merit, and only several weeks before the event had won the West Australian Open. On arrival in Britain his form plummeted. He missed the cut in the Lawrence Batley tournament at the Belfry the week before the Open and, arriving at St Andrews for his first look at the Old Course, was clearly in for a tough week. Thomson stepped in. He invited Baker-Finch to join him and Nagle on their journey around the mysterious linksland. The young Queenslander jumped at the chance. On the dry Old Course, alleviated only by some judicious watering of the greens before the tournament, there was no one better equipped to show the youngster around than Thomson. What he'd done for Nagle in 1960 he was about to do for his young countryman.

'At St Andrews a player doesn't need particular power or length and Ian doesn't possess them anyway,' says Thomson. 'But I could see that he had the game to win there. He was a beautiful putter then, and I reckoned that if he followed the lines that I showed him he would get to the green all right, and then it was up to him with the putter.' For the few people that noticed, it was a stirring sight. Baker-Finch, eager, excited and wide-eyed as a child on Christmas morning, hung on every word from the wise old lion. Thomson pointed to various church spires in the distance or other landmarks or to prominent bunkers, and in a quiet, soft but very dry manner, would say, 'I'll be aiming at that,' or 'I normally go this way.' Baker-Finch remained silent for most of the journey, listening, observing, learning. 'Of course there are many things to look out for at St Andrews,' says Thomson. 'To describe the course to those who have not yet felt its magic underfoot can be summed up as an adventure in risk-taking and, on first tackle, an odyssey through a golfing minefield. It is a tough proposition for the best professionals and a holy terror for lesser mortals. Each of us in our golfing life goes about the training that gets us to the target in the direct line, doing so by learning the "aiming" of the stance. The "last peek" at the flagstick before the swing is always by habit. It is against our natural instincts to hit away from the ultimate targets even though we know in our senses we have to do so to get close. It is this weakness, or lack of iron discipline, that gets us into trouble at St Andrews. Ian is a very friendly fellow. I was only passing on to him what I'd learned from Wallace Gillespie. For example, at the 16th, which runs along the old railway line, the temptation is to drive for a position between the Principal's Nose bunker, at driving range just right of centre, and the railway. This is the direct line to the green. Really though, it is a very foolish shot to try. Instead you've got to try what seems a stupid thing; drive way, way to the left and then you get a much longer shot into the green, but actually a much easier shot. I followed that faithfully every time I played there and I told Ian to do the same, which he did.'

Baker-Finch's dream of one day playing in the British Open came true at 12.40 p.m. on 19 July 1984. He was thrown into the deep end of the pool and told to swim; alongside twice US open champion Hale Irwin and the Japanese legend of Isao Aoki, but as he stood there waiting to poke his tee into the hallowed soil, he was calmer than many expected. 'Both Peter and Kel Nagle were tremendous before that day, but Peter had shown me how to steer it down the left side and keep out of trouble,' he says. 'I didn't hit off on the Thursday thinking I could win, but his help allowed me to play my own game. There I was playing the course the way Thommo and Kel had shown me and I was able to concentrate on just playing.' The results were remarkable indeed.

He birdied the 4th, but gave the shot back at the 6th. Then at the 372-yard 7th his round sprang to life. He hit a mammoth drive of almost 300 yards, calmly pulled out his wedge for his second shot and watched it roll into the cup for an eagle two that put him two under. A birdie at the ninth and he turned in 33. If there was any doubt that this was to be a special day it was dispelled at the 10th, when he drove into the rough and received a vital break when a spectator saw a schoolboy scoot off with his ball. It's difficult to pinpoint a certain moment that could be responsible for a player's overall performance in a 72-hole golf tournament, but if you could, this was it for Baker-Finch. The spectator heard the culprit say that it was a DDH-1 and, on the basis of that information, Baker-Finch was able to claim the ball where it had originally lain. He could drop without penalty as near as possible to the original position, which was, in fact, against television cables. He was subsequently allowed another free drop, one club length away, an incident Irwin later described as 'a bad decision'. Irwin insisted that Baker-Finch would probably have had to hack his ball out had it been dropped in the original spot. 'In the States we would have removed the cables,' he commented. 'He was very lucky.' Baker-Finch made the most of his good fortune by retaining his momentum superbly with a series of par figures, then after a 4-iron to ten feet at the tough 14th, holed the birdie putt. He showed remarkable composure at the 17th, with a good drive and a superb 4-wood to 20-feet and two safe putts for his par. A regulation four at the last and he completed his first Open round, and first at St Andrews, in 68.

It was a bright start, but on day two Baker-Finch was absolutely iridescent. He had the benefit of glorious conditions with an early morning time. Driving flawlessly he kept the ball left off the tee, birdied two of the first three holes, birdied the long 5th and, beginning with a birdie two at the 8th, played the next six holes in level threes. The only blemish was a bogey at the 4th, where he failed to get down in two from 20 yards. When he walked off the 13th green 6-under-par for the round, the course record of 65 seemed in danger. The Old Course has a way of bringing brashness to a halt and from there the youngster had to fight hard to hold on. He did so admirably, parring the 17th from the terror of the Road Bunker, and secured another four at the last. His seven birdies prompted Irwin to comment that it was one of the two best putting rounds he'd ever seen. By the time a cool wind sprang up from the sea in the afternoon, making the finishing stretch very demanding, Baker-Finch was in the clubhouse, having notched a glorious 66 for a 10-under total of 134. Over 36-holes he'd beaten Irwin by 9 shots and Aoki by 11, spread-eagling the field with one of the boldest performances ever in a British Open, let alone from a rookie. At the end of the day there were such names as Trevino, Ballesteros, Faldo and Watson behind him, but the good-looking youngster with the nickname of 'Sparrow', was three strokes clear. The hum around St Andrews was, 'Ian Who?'

The third round was always going to be a gigantic examination of Baker-Finch's composure and maturity. Only two years before at Royal Troon a youthful American with Harpo Marx looks, Bobby Clampett, had made an unbelievable start of 67–66, only to begin a dramatic and pathetic free fall down the leader board with rounds of 78–77. As Baker-Finch was teeing off in the last group on the Saturday, Thomson forced his way through the throng, grabbing Baker-Finch's attention, and said: 'Good luck today. We all hope you play well, but just remember one thing: championships are never won on Saturday.' With that, Thomson shook the youngster's hand and quickly melted into the sea of colour around the opening tee. 'That piece of advice is something I always remember when I'm leading a tournament or I'm in contention,' says Baker-Finch. 'It's so simple: you're not going to win it today, just go out there and play. It made me feel so good that I went out and birdied three of the first five holes. I felt like there was no pressure at all. It got to me a little towards the end of the day and I made a couple of bogeys, but I still shot 71 and was tied with Watson into the final day.' That was one of the most courageous rounds of 1984.

Some weeks before his decision to play in the Open, Thomson was asked to write a preview of the championship for the American magazine *Golf Digest*, and within the article revealed some of the special skills needed to have any hope of slaying the Old Course. One, which he passed on to Baker-Finch during that practice day, was astonishingly prophetic. He wrote: 'On championship days the hole at the 1st is invariably cut near the Swilcan Burn. To get at it one must hit the green within a few yards of the water otherwise the ball will bounce way to the back. It is very difficult for modern professionals to come to terms with the fact that on days when the wind is behind and the green firm, it is just physically impossible to get anywhere near the flag with the approach shot. One has to be prepared to hit the second shot somewhere past the cup and be content with that. Yet that inner weakness we all have will make us think again, near the start of the downswing, giving us a mental picture of the ball biting into the green, just over the burn, and miraculously braking right next to the flag. The next thing you know you are in the burn! It is this requirement of mental discipline to hit the shots away from the flags that makes the Old Course unique, so special and so searchingly fascinating. From the first hole through to the last there is a constant nagging temptation to attempt the impossible, to hit your approaches too near the gauntlet of straight-walled sand traps, to pull off shots that are commonplace elsewhere. If you don't discover and face this fact, you will surely join the ranks of those who detest the place.'

It would have been a fairytale finish had the 23-year-old gone on to win golf's most glittering prize at his first attempt. There can be no question of the courage, calmness and shotmaking abilities of Ian Baker-Finch, but it takes more than those qualities to win an Open, and something else to win over the Old Course. For three days the arrow on the Baker-Finch graph was in an almost unbelievable ascent — it was inevitable that it had to come down at some stage, and after a fine opening drive, his second shot pitched on the front of the green, screwed back and ended up in the Swilcan Burn, just as Thomson had eerily described in his magazine preview. It was the start of a 79 and while some American writers were glad 'the Australian kid with the funny name got out of the way' to allow the anticipated Watson-Ballesteros duel, that finale was to leave lasting scars. Baker-Finch slumped to a tie for 9th place and was devastated. 'Maybe if I'd been able to speak to Peter on the Sunday morning it might have been a different story,' he says. 'I completely lost my way after the 1st, and started to swing too quickly. I could feel it happening. Certainly it was a great chance to win it, but it showed me that I can get to that position and I was sure that chance would come again.'

Baker-Finch had to wait six years for another chance. The Open returned to St Andrews in 1990. With a superlative third round of 64 he again played in the final group on the final day but, amongst the heady atmosphere surrounding the eventual record-breaking champion Nick Faldo, his final round of 73 and a tie for fifth was again considered a failure. He had not blossomed into one of Australia's finest and most complete golfers, with victories in his homeland, Europe, Japan and the United States, by fluke. The youthful desire and determination detected by Thomson hadn't disappeared and, when the Open returned to England the next year — fittingly to the Lancashire links of Royal Birkdale, home of two of Thomson's triumphs — Baker-Finch swept aside doubts and insecurities with an emotional two-stroke victory ahead of friend and countryman Mike Harwood. 'I'm not a mean person and I never will be,' he said to the media afterwards. 'What I wanted was to become tougher, able to focus more on what I'm doing out there and see my way through all the distractions. Back in 1983 I was in the top three in Australia and that was the path that led me to St Andrews and that fateful day. It gave me the start to my career. The pain of losing that day has always been there but it remained something special because it was the start of it all.' One of the first of many telephone calls he made to Australia after his 1991 win was to the Thomson home in Toorak but unfortunately Peter, enormously thrilled at having the name of another friend engraved below his on the auld claret jug, was already on his way to Tokyo for business.

Baker-Finch one day may conquer the ghosts of St Andrews but, back in 1984 when he was the pupil, attracting so much attention in his debut performance, his teacher Peter Thomson was closing a chapter of British Open history that sunny Saturday when he completed his seventh and final Open Championship at St Andrews, and his thirtieth and final Open. A small crowd of Scots sprinkled above in the grandstand, the fans lining the fence outside the old shops, and the gentlemen watching from the clubhouse balcony cheered him home. Nobody really cared about his scores — there was simply warm admiration for what he'd achieved personally, sincere thanks for what he'd given the game, and sheer pleasure that at the age of 55, he clearly still relished the fight, challenge and excitement of the Old Course at St Andrews.

The influence of the Old Course lives on in his designing: 'There's not a course that I build that I don't try to use some tiny feature that I've seen at St Andrews.' He believes that the continuously undulating fairways found on the Old Course are a model to golf course architects around the world who would give us freeway fairways and contrive obstacles only at the greens.

Thomson and the Old Course are comrades in arms. When he visits or plays there, often in delightfully traditional events such as the Autumn medal, it is a merging of man and nature. They are both emotionless, yet full of emotion. There is nothing especially pretty about them, yet they are both extremely effective in their respective pursuits. Both are eminently fair and equitable. Both appear hard of heart, but they have a sense of humour. Both are unique in their 'design'. Both are liable to suffer an awful beating if the conditions are not in their favour, and yet both have the potential to exact an inspired, calculated revenge. Look into the eyes of both and you don't see the fire. It's hidden, but ever-ready to surface. Thomson learnt much from the Old Course. It taught him to be patient with things; never to rush; never to force it. It taught him to be balanced.

'St Andrews,' he says, pausing noticeably. 'It is the course, the original course. I'm a lover of classical things — music, paintings. And there's the classic golf course ... I can't remember exactly where and when, but the logic hit me one day. The only reason we have 18 holes at say, Victoria Golf Club in Melbourne is because there are 18 at St Andrews. And the only reason I'm building sand bunkers way up in the mountains of Japan is because there are sand bunkers at St Andrews, by the sea. Those two examples alone, prove that St Andrews is the original prototype, and everything else is a copy of it. The Old Course is, and must remain forever, the true golf.'

CHAPTER 7

A Cat Amongst the Pigeons

WORD quickly travelled around the press tent. The reigning Australian Open champion, just finished his final practice round on the eve of his defence of the title, was angry. And it had nothing to do with the way he was playing. It was about something he'd seen in the morning paper. He made his way to the press tent to let off a little steam. As soon as he was seated before the tape recorders, microphones, poised pens and expectant looks, he let fly. It soon became the story of the day. 'It seems incredible that a man who knows what it is all about out there in the championship world should be greatly lacking in understanding,' said Greg Norman. 'I find his remarks disgraceful and very offensive, and from my observations he seems to take every opportunity to have a go at Australians, whether it is in his newspaper articles or on television. You're out there doing your best, but he seems to be telling the public that you are not. He must forget that we travel all around the world and beat fields of much higher calibre than are here in Australia. I've never found a more critical commentator or writer in all my travels.'

The man on the receiving end of his pungent outburst was none other than the president of the Australian PGA, the five-time British Open champion, Melbourne *Age* columnist and ABC television commentator, Peter Thomson. The year was 1981 and the venue, Thomson's 'home' club of Victoria. The Australian professional circuit had been in full swing for several weeks, but it had been a less than profitable time for the local boys. The big names from overseas had taken most of the major prizes on offer, and Thomson made this quite clear in his *Age* column that morning: 'Australia groans under the yoke of foreign domination. Patriots cry out in anguish as multi-nationals plunder our resources unopposed. How much longer can we suffer? If an invader wins the Australian Open at Victoria Golf Club next weekend, it will be the sixth time in as many weeks that our forces have surrendered in the heat of battle. To list these catastrophes causes me pain. Suffice to say that in the past few weeks a New Zealander, an Irishman, an American, a Spaniard and a South African have in turn and in sequence, run off with the wealth of the Australian golf tour. Unless some hero rises up among us to stop the rot, we will have to give up golf and turn to boomerang throwing or some other special game at which we might fancy ourselves. It is some time since we copped such a devastating blow to our golf pride. Of recent times we have been more or less proud, the Victorian Open, for example, is still in our hands despite a concerted foreign effort to capture it. Guy Wolstenholme has done us proud more than once, and last February Bill Dunk saved us from ignominy. It has become a matter of smugness for us to say our Vic. Open is a difficult event for intruders to run away with. Suddenly, in the spring of 1981, things have turned bad. Our big guns have been unable to fire; someone has spiked the barrels, wet the powder, or pinched the ammo. We look like a primitive tribe fighting armour plate with bows and arrows. Why is it that our fortunes have slipped so far? Why is it that we could hardly wager a penny on our home-grown chances this week at Victoria? What, if anything, has gone wrong?

'We might explain it by saying our front-line troops are less than fighting fit. Jack Newton has a chronic tennis elbow, Bob Shearer has not recovered from his bout of trouble with his pancreas; Stewart Ginn is a walking hospital case; Kel Nagle suffers from old age, and Greg Norman, our best hope, is a shadow of his former robust self. Only Graham Marsh can parade in full battle dress and even he carries some sort of mysterious malady that makes him unable within Australia to repeat the deeds he performs overseas. David Graham, in his benefit year (carrying the US title turns out to be a 24-hour-a-day duty to a multitude of commitments), has his mind elsewhere. He wasn't much use at Royal Melbourne recently in the Australian PGA. None of it can explain though, why, when the chips are down, we have no-one who can keep from hooking into trouble or three-putting at the crucial moment. Errors that come more from the mind than the feet and hands. The trouble is that our professional squad loses the psychological fight before a shot is ever fired in anger. A fifth column weakens our moral fibre, softens us up before battle commences.

'Newspaper headlines, billboards and posters announce in bold type the imminent arrival of the invaders, each a much decorated hero of other wars of recent times. It is no wonder our troops condition themselves to losing. What we need is somebody who doesn't read newspapers while he is playing, who refuses to concede that the visitors are in any way his equal, who has the cheek and temerity to demonstrate a slow contempt for whoever opposes him. I have never known any international golf champion who wasn't human, who didn't suffer from the same weaknesses of character as anyone else, whose ego wasn't expanded and lifted by some indulgent spoiling while he is at the top. It is only when that ego is deflated back to size that he becomes ordinary and beatable.'

On hearing of Norman's vehement response to his piece, Thomson said: 'I'm pleased Greg's hackles are up. I hope it needles him into winning. There is nothing I would like more than to see him prove me wrong. I think it should be left at that.' Norman did not win his second Australian Open. Texan Bill Rogers, the reigning British Open champion, triumphed over the Queenslander by a stroke. Rogers birdied the 507-yards par-5 72nd hole to do so; Norman, after smashing his final drive an incredible 360 yards down the 18th fairway, selected a pitching wedge for his second shot, but dumped the ball in the front left bunker, from where he failed to get up and down for the vital birdie. He retreated to watch Rogers float in his 4-iron and safely two-putt. Norman immediately admitted his error of judgement and said he would have been better off going with a 9-iron, but amidst the back-slapping and speeches, the clamoring for photographs of Rogers with the Open trophy, and the lengthy press interviews, most people had forgotten that Peter Thomson's article the previous Wednesday had been proved correct. 'I thought the article was appropriate at the time,' says Thomson. 'I didn't write anything that wasn't fact and what I said was that I wouldn't bet a penny on any of them — and it was proved in the end because Bill Rogers won the tournament. I wasn't so surprised by his [Norman's] reaction to the article. If I write such a thing I know there's going to be a reaction. Anyway, everyone's entitled to their point of view, but I do think he missed the point of the article.'

Out of it all, the public was given the impression there was a rift between the man widely regarded as Australia's greatest golfer and his heir apparent. It was the beginning of a downward spiral in relations between them and their paths have rarely crossed since. This feud (if it can be called that) between the two men who represent probably the most powerful figures in Australian golf, is the most publicised aspect of Thomson's controversial nature. Despite Thomson's stature, no matter how much he says he loves the game and wants to see it preserved for all time, regardless of his remarkable contribution to all aspects of professional golf, there is a side of him that people love to hate.

Few in the world of golf are entitled to speak with greater authority than Thomson. He has a wonderful international playing record, and has watched the game grow and prosper world-wide through the careers of Ferrier, Pickworth, von Nida; Hogan, Snead, Locke, Cotton; Crampton, Devlin, Graham; Palmer, Nicklaus, Player, Jacklin; Marsh, Davis, Norman, Grady; Trevino, Watson, Ballesteros, Faldo. He has seen the golf professional grow from hard-working maker of clubs to multi-millionaire participant in gala extravaganzas. He received £750 for winning his first British Open; Nick Faldo collected £85,000 at St Andrews in 1990. All along the journey he has expressed heartfelt opinions. He feels it is his duty to express those feelings: if something needs to be said, someone needs to be stirred, the battler needs to be supported, then Thomson says, stirs and supports.

Anyone who is obstinate and dogmatic comes in for a share of abuse. 'Peter has never held any fear at saying, or writing something when he thinks it needs to be said or written,' says Mary Thomson. 'I suppose he's very opinionated, but he's absolutely sure of his views be they right or wrong.' One of Thomson's closest friends and someone who has seen at close quarters his idiosyncratic approach to life, is the Australian cricket identity Richie Benaud. The former Test captain and cricket and golf correspondent believes the clearest insight into Thomson's behaviour is a recognition that he is able to think clearly and immediately. 'Peter is one of the quickest men to sum up a situation I've ever come across in any sport,' he says. 'He has lightning reflexes and I would say this is why he was such a good golfer. He was able to sum up almost instantly the type of shot in front of him, and at the same time gauge what the penalties and advantages would be. He's a very quick thinker and he keeps things simple. I've found this to be the key to almost everything he says and does. The ultimate test of a writer is that whatever you are writing, you believe it. If you completely believe in what you are writing you shouldn't have to worry about upsetting people. The time to worry is when you believe something and then write something entirely different. Peter doesn't do that. If it's a question of treading on someone's toes, that someone might prefer he write something syrupy, that is highly complimentary. He's never likely to do that because he's a very straightforward guy who calls it as he sees it.'

Thomson's detractors believe the controversial, stirring side of his character, the one that people read in the newspaper and hear on the television, is merely an extension of the intelligent man who was out there playing great golf with the best of them. As someone who considered the game to be 'a rather silly way of making a living', they say he tried to liven it up for himself wherever possible, just as he does in his media work, through a little gamesmanship.

Many claim Thomson learnt a great deal about gamesmanship from crafty touring pros like Sam Snead and Bobby Locke. When Snead was a youngster he played against the cagey pro Willie MacFarlane. On a par-3, MacFarlane selected a 7-iron, which he hit lightly. Snead took out his 7-iron and flew the ball over the back of the green. 'Me boy,' said MacFarlane, 'never go to school on another man's club or ye'll not make a penny in this game.' These stories, some tall, some true, were part of golfing legend in the USA, and Thomson heard them all. Gene Sarazen told the one when Walter Hagen once took out a 3-wood from his bag on the tee of a 210-yard par-3 hole. It was Sarazen's honour. He trusted the great Haig's judgement, took out his own 3-wood and slammed it over the green. Hagen put his wood back and used a 2-iron to nestle the ball by the pin! 'The Haig' would also concede putts of all lengths early in a match, provided they were not for a win. Later, when the match became tight, he would make his opponent putt out all putts no matter what length. The competitor, suddenly burdened with unexpected pressure, would often miss easy putts. The oldest trick in the book is trying for sympathy by complaining of a bad cold, backache, fever or lack of sleep. 'I have lost to more players who had a fever and cold,' said one pro, 'than I care to remember.' Other golfers would try to 'out-psych' their playing partners with a timely turn of phrase. Walter Burkemo used to drive his opponents mad with the simple query: 'Say, how come when you address the ball you only take four waggles instead of five?' Frank Stranahan, the veteran amateur, once asked Australia's Joe Kirkwood on the 1st tee of a tournament, 'Joe, do you breathe in or out on your backswing?' Kirkwood couldn't get the thought out of his head and blew the match over the first nine holes. Then there was Cary Middlecoff, who would get rookies completely flustered by remarking within earshot to a fellow pro, 'Just watch this kid hit them out of sight.' Such mind games would invariably see the stronger personality win out. Players have made the same claim with Thomson. They have said loose change would miraculously jangle in his pocket just as someone was about to putt; mysterious shadows would be strategically cast within a player's eye-line; and of course there was the famous 'white shoes' incident.

In 1957 Thomson's name first hit the headlines for reasons other than his play. In Britain for the Dunlop Masters, the 28-year-old arrived at his Nottinghamshire hotel room to find several malicious, anonymous letters accusing him of unfair tactics in the the previous week's tournament, the British matchplay championship at Turnberry in Scotland. Irishman Christy O'Connor, who defeated the Australian 2-up in a quarter-final and went on to defeat Tom Haliburton in the final, repeatedly complained to Thomson that he was deliberately trying to distract him on the tee by catching his eye with his trademark white shoes. The next morning one newspaper alleged that Thomson had used tactics calculated to upset his opponents in the matchplay event, by shuffling his white shoes on the tees and greens. Thomson responded: 'If anybody believes I can't win without putting my opponents off, I would rather not play at all. All this gossiping behind my back around the tournaments is embarrassing and upsetting. I can't get it off my mind to concentrate on playing this tournament. Nobody seems to have bothered analysing just who was put off, me or my opponent. Who won anyway? At the 14th I wanted some chocolate, so I stopped below the tee, behind the crowd, waiting. But after a few minutes he [O'Connor] called me up on the tee where he could see me. I don't know what rule that was under. What was going on? He claimed my white shoes distracted him. It seemed unbelievable. I have played with hundreds of the world's best golfers, and always worn white shoes and this is the first complaint.'

Those close to Thomson recall his genuine hurt at O'Connor's accusations and the 'poison pen' letters that followed. While the Irishman has remained silent over the issue, the British Golf Writers' Association launched an inquiry into the conduct of the journalist involved, eventually writing a terse letter of complaint to his newspaper. Thomson also received the support of many of his fellow professionals, and within a few weeks the controversy had blown over. But it meant that whenever Thomson and O'Connor were drawn to play together, there was always a chill in the air. And Thomson continued to wear his white shoes. To this day he refuses to discuss the conflict. When asked about O'Connor's specific accusations during that match at Turnberry, his reply, accompanied by a cold blue look and a raised eyebrow, is: 'Christy was wrong. Next question.'

Well then, how about that famous Australian Open of 1972, at Kooyonga in South Australia? Forty-three-year-old Thomson fired in a brilliant 7-iron approach to the 72nd hole of the championship, which pitched several yards short of the cup, bit hard, and finished just a mere 10 inches away. The tap-in birdie tied him for the championship lead with the promising 26-year-old, David Graham.

1972 Australian Open Championship, Kooyonga, Adelaide

281	Peter Thomson (Vic.)	74-69-68-70
	David Graham (Vic.)	71-69-70-71
283	Maurice Bembridge (GB)	73-71-68-71
284	Peter Oosterhuis (GB)	71-71-74-68
286	Bruce Crampton (NSW)	73-73-70-70
	Graham Marsh (WA)	71-74-70-71
288	Billy Dunk (NSW)	71-71-70-76

In the 18-hole play-off the next day Thomson stepped up onto the 1st tee and drilled a superb drive straight down the middle. Graham, clearly unsettled, hooked his opening tee shot over the out-of-bounds fence and was penalised two shots. The Open was won there and then. Thomson birdied the hole while Graham notched a seven and the veteran went on to win the play-off with a brilliant course record equalling 68 to Graham's 74. Seconds after his shot went crashing through the trees and over the fence, a livid Graham turned to the tournament director and hissed: 'This is Rafferty's Rules. Why didn't we spin a coin for the honour?' He was still fuming after the sun had gone down and even now, it is clear Graham has maintained his rage. 'That was very unfortunate,' he says. 'I always have been under the impression that you toss a coin to start a play-off, but he just bowled right up there, teed it up and hit off. At the time I thought it was very poor sportsmanship, and I didn't talk to him about it afterwards and to this day I never have. I don't blame Peter and I certainly don't carry any grudge against him but I think the tournament committee had a lot to answer for that day.'

Thomson says he was confident he had the honour because the count-back system was in use and his final round of 70 to Graham's 71 meant he was first away. Graham simply was not aware of this, and to categorise his opponent's move as 'gamesmanship', as some Graham supporters openly did, is absurd. At the time, Thomson would only repeat that he was certain he had the honour and considered the entire matter a storm in a teacup. The next morning in his newspaper column, it did not even rate a mention: 'I cannot say I'm not delighted at being Australian Open champion in this particular year. It has been a year of great turmoil and strife. The PGA had other plans, and this championship might have been bigger than it was this week, but it was not to be. Even so, I feel proud to be the winner. I would have been equally proud had David Graham won. I rate him as a British Open winner of the future, and now that he has lost this year I'm sure he will be next Australian Open champion. Nobody among our young players has such promise. He started off in the play-off yesterday as tight as a drum. He had more at stake than I did. Much more. Had he won this title it would have been very valuable to him around the world. It's not quite the same for me as it is for him. Everybody knows my capabilities. He is still full of promise. Even so, if he would like to change places with me, I would happily do so. Yesterday, however, he made a tactical mistake. He assumed the role of underdog before he started, whereas, in truth, he was the logical winner. But he made such a mistake on the first hole that it destroyed his whole day. He drove out of bounds with his first shot, and this upset his equilibrium for the rest of the day ...'

Thomson once said: 'Golf doesn't select the people who play it. Most of us are misfits who have drifted into it at an early age when our narrow view of the world showed nothing else. Competition with other people for certain goals may even be a little show of insecurity, like young monkeys scrambling for peanuts. We are a circus of performers. Why should some of us be blamed for not coming out on top?'

Billy Dunk is one professional who admits he could never understand Thomson at all. 'I used to watch him play at the Lakes in Sydney when I was just a boy and I thought he was fantastic,' says Dunk. 'Then in the Australian PGA at Royal Sydney in 1967, I found myself ten shots ahead with two rounds to go on the last day. I was thrilled to be paired with Peter for those final two rounds, but at the first hole in the morning, I missed a tiddler of a putt which lipped out and as Peter came over to put his marker down, he said: "Don't worry about that young fellow, I did that once!" Anyway, I thought it was a strange thing for him to say and it played on my mind a bit, to the point where at lunch-time my lead had been whittled back to just one shot! Then, you wouldn't believe it, at the first green in the afternoon I again lipped out from a short distance, and again Peter said, "Never mind Bill, that happened to me once." I thought to myself, "You old bugger, I'm not falling for it this time," so from there on I walked on the opposite side of the fairway from him and we never said another word to each other! I just managed to hang on and win and I learnt an awful lot that day.'

Then there was the day in Japan in late 1988 when Dunk was competing in his first Senior tournament and Thomson was the only other Australian in the field. Dunk bumped into his countryman during practice and said to him, 'Peter, I'm glad you're here. Can you tell me where I can get some balata balls for the tournament? I'm not sure where to go.' Thomson replied: 'Don't worry, Bill. Leave it to me, I'll bring you some tomorrow.' Dunk thought it was a very kind gesture and the next day was eagerly awaiting his load of balls. He saw Thomson in the distance and waved to him. Over he came and tossed Dunk just three balls. 'There you go Bill, one for each round so don't lose any,' said Thomson. 'I lost them all on the first day,' says Dunk.

Jack Newton is another player who says he found it difficult to concentrate on his own golf when Thomson was around. 'I'll always remember playing with him in the Australian PGA at Surfer's Paradise, of all places, in 1971. It was my first year as a pro and I actually led the tournament going into the final round,' says Newton, a smile breaking across his face. 'I was paired with Peter in that final round, and there I was with someone that everybody knew was a tremendous golfer, but that not many knew possessed this amazing tongue, for a lot of what he said had double meaning. That particular day I wasn't swinging the club well, and I knew I wasn't swinging the club well and after not too many holes, he let me know that. I admit I was a hot-head at the time, but basically, he talked me out of the tournament. The next time we played together was at Manly in the 1971 Dunlop tournament, and I was ready for him. We reached the 3rd hole which was a short par-3 down over the hill and Peter found the right bunker beside the green. Now one shot that I thought he had trouble playing was the one where you had to open the blade of a sand-iron and throw the ball up high and bring it down softly. Sure enough, he hit it thick, and put the ball over the back of the green. As he came up I made my move, saying "That wasn't such a good shot for a five-times British Open champion, Peter!" He looked me straight in the eye and didn't say a word. It was only when we were walking to the 4th tee that he said, "You know, I think it's about time we called a truce." From that moment on we respected each other and later, at the 1975 British Open, I vividly remember him being out there in the play-off [with Tom Watson] and being very encouraging. But he's a hard guy to get to the bottom of, that's for sure. As a youngster I also had an awful problem coming over the top of the ball and hitting it out to the right and when I asked Peter what he thought I should do about it, he replied: "Aim more to the left"! I invited him to my wedding and he said, "I won't come to this one, I'll come to the next," and you can imagine how much that pleased Jackie!'

Thomson drily pokes fun at his fellow professionals who doggedly analyse the golf swing beyond its fundamentals. On the practice tee one day, an Australian pro asked Thomson if he could look at his swing and tell him whether it was open or shut at the top. Thomson told him it was 'slightly ajar'. He enjoys this succinct, straight-faced humour that clearly leaves many people unsure whether he is joking or not. 'He had an "air" about him when he was playing,' says Peter Alliss. 'Whether he did it on purpose or not, I don't know, but I remember the Open Championship at Royal Lytham in 1952 and I'd just bought a driver that I thought was the bee's knees. Peter came along and picked it up and gave it a couple of waggles, tut-tutted, rolled his eyes back a bit, handed it back and just walked away! Suddenly this club that I thought was magic was back in my hands and I was looking at it upside down and back-to-front and thinking, "Christ, what's the matter with this?" Lee Trevino used to do a similar sort of thing when he was on the scene much later on, but it was a way of putting just the slightest doubt in your head, and if you let it get to you, well then you'd be in trouble.'

Dual Australian Open winner, Frank Phillips firmly believes an opponent had to give Thomson just as much as he dished out, and that didn't have anything to do with gamesmanship. 'Peter would never do anything in a nasty or deliberate attempt to put another player off,' says

Phillips. 'He just wasn't like that. Sometimes he would make a little comment like, "Well, Frank — you've got a two-footer there," simply to remind you you had a two-footer in case you didn't know! I remember one time we were touring through Asia on the Far East circuit and he said to me that my clubs were illegal because the bottom groove on the clubface was too close to the bottom of the club head. Well, I became a bit stroppy over that and I immediately marched down to check my clubs in the locker room, and I noticed his were alongside mine. Well, his bottom groove was even lower than mine! I went straight back and abused him, but he just giggled and walked away! We were good friends after that, because if you came back at him I think he gave you a little more respect. You've got to remember, he was brought up in an era where he had to fend for himself on the golf course, what with the Sneads, Lockes, Pickworths and the like, and naturally he learnt a lot by his own observations. I think he considers that is the best way to learn and all these blokes who reckoned he used gamesmanship were simply getting it mixed up with Peter's way of testing the spirit or mettle of a few players every now and then, just as he had been tested in his early days.'

Arguments for and against. Who is right? Did Thomson employ tactics not in the spirit of the game? The question was put to the man himself: 'In your career, how much was gamesmanship a part of your play?' Thomson's eyes narrowed, both eyebrows shot upwards this time, and he gave an expression normally reserved for duck-hooks and double-bogeys. 'None at all,' he replied in a clipped manner. 'I just minded my own business ... I particularly tried to ignore the people I played with.' Some people just don't realise that gamesmanship is another word for cheat. Peter Thomson is not, and never has been, a cheat.

A most unlikely ally, and a rather angry one at that, steps forward; 'I've often heard people talk about this gamesmanship thing,' says Gary Player. 'They say Locke used it, Snead used it, Nicklaus used it, and they say Peter Thomson was a user of it. I don't believe that. We were all professional sportsmen and if I was playing with someone and he said to me, "Gee, my putt was fast," and then I stepped up and left my ball three feet short, then I was a bloody idiot. If I listened to that hogwash and let it affect me then I was an idiot. We were all experienced sports athletes travelling the world with a main aim of winning golf tournaments, yet we had these ridiculous people making stupid claims that players like Thomson deliberately tried to influence another player's game. It was all bloody hogwash.'

Peter Alliss agrees: 'Of course Peter had his little run-ins with people. Christy O'Connor will go to his grave saying that Peter used to put him off at the tee. Whether that was a figment of O'Connor's imagination I don't know, but Thomson never seemed to care about his partner or opponent, in the same way that Seve Ballesteros does today. If you see someone playing with Seve, and they're on the green, crouched over a big putt, you might notice Seve off to one side practising his putting stroke. Now sometimes, depending on whom he's playing with, this could be in just the right position to catch the corner of that player's eye. Sam Snead used to do that and so did Ben Hogan. Now of course nobody can prove that they're not completely wrapped up in their own world and simply don't care, or that it's a totally premeditated act. I don't think Peter ever deliberately tried to put people off and claims that he did are just nit-picking. Peter was an honourable opponent and one of the best ever to play the game in Europe. I'd have to put him in the top ten of all the players I've ever seen in my life.'

Why not leave it to Thomson's business partner, Mike Wolveridge, to put the whole thing into some sort of perspective? 'If you notice, these supposed comments and actions from Peter, the ones considered to be not in keeping with the spirit of the game,' says Wolveridge, 'could also be interpreted as humorous and friendly, because above all, Peter did think it was a game that should not be taken too seriously. Notice he never resorted to nastiness? A player might have just hooked his driver out of bounds and Thomson might say, "Crikey, you almost hooked it that time!" Or if they came to a tee with a lake on the left, he would say, "Well, you won't want to hook it again at this hole!" and invariably the other fellow would. Players would immediately think he was trying to put them off. But Thomson interpreted golf as fun and it was meant to be fun. It's a game, for goodness sake. If the other fellow came back with something witty or smart himself, then Peter was overjoyed. You've got to go with him and laugh with him or you're a total goner. There were some big prizes at stake for these golfers and there wouldn't be too much humour around. It was all too serious, but Peter never thought about the money at all — he wanted to have fun and enjoy it, while the others wanted to win the money and really needed to concentrate at all costs. To them Peter Thomson was a pest.'

Thomson can never completely forget that even at the highest level of championship play, it is still a game. Yes, he was disliked because of his apparently casual self-sufficiency, and also because he played the game so simply and won so easily. In depth of intellectual interest and achievement he stands apart. No one could accuse Thomson of not playing in the spirit of the game, when the spirit of the game provided the strongest reason for him playing professional golf. Of course he wanted to be the best he possibly could, and of course he wanted to succeed and build a comfortable life with all the trappings, but more than anything, this self-educated historian and deep thinker wanted to play golf in the way it was intended to be played, in the spirit of the game. Why, in the 1957 Australian Open at Kingston Heath, did he call a two-stroke penalty on himself when he, and he alone, realised on the first hole of the event that he was carrying fifteen clubs in his bag, not the regulation fourteen? Why, immediately upon completion of a tournament round in the Airlines Classic in New Zealand, did he march directly to the PGA secretary and pay a £20 fine for mistakenly flicking his ball out of the 15th hole with a sand-iron following a holed bunker shot? And why, did Thomson declare a one-stroke penalty on himself in the 1966 Dunlop Masters in Britain when he, and he alone, noticed his ball move slightly as he was about to putt on the 8th green? And why would he do such a thing when he might otherwise have tied for first in the tournament instead of ending up second, one stroke behind the winner, Neil Coles? 'It is satisfying to record Thomson's self-imposed act of respect for the rules in the full heat of competition, and at a time when the offering of large prizes encourages people to find a way around the rules,' said *The Times*. 'Of course, thorough knowledge of the rules and strict observance of them adds to the stature of a golfer, just as attempts to score off them, by applying them rigidly against the spirit of the game, has the reverse effect.'

So much for gamesmanship; the so-called controversial side of Peter Thomson *on* the golf course. As for the controversial side of the man *off* the course, well, that was a different matter. Peter Thomson, wearing his public face as president of the Australian PGA, columnist with Melbourne newspapers and television commentator with the ABC, was a responsible, powerful oracle. There can be no question he deliberately tried to stimulate vigorous argument and the world of golf quickly discovered that he held back no punches when he felt he was right. For this he was attacked.

With two issues in particular, it is possible to examine Thomson's attitudes. It must be remembered that he remains diametrically opposed to both. One was his long and heated campaign against the bigger-size American-style golf ball; and the other the issue of appearance money.

To many people observing the major issues of world golf in the 1960s, there must have seemed an awful fuss over a mere 0.06 inches in difference between the diameter of two golf balls, and yet here was Peter Thomson, apparently playing a lone hand, clearly angered, sometimes positively fuming.

Thomson had done his research and knew enough of golf ball manufacture to realise that aerodynamically there was a world of difference between a golf ball of 1.62 inches and another of 1.68 inches. In 1932 the United States Golf Association, concerned that golf was becoming too much a game of length and that the ball was being hit too far, departed from world-wide uniformity to adopt a larger, 1.68-inch ball for all tournaments, in an attempt to cut down the distance the ball would travel. The Royal and Ancient Golf Club, golf's ruling body, was powerless to stop their comrades across the Atlantic: here was the remarkable situation of the rest of the world playing with the normal 1.62-inch ball while the US played with a 1.68-inch ball. Thomson firmly believed that the attempt by the USGA to cut down the distance the ball travelled ultimately failed, but the bigger ball remained in use on the tour because it was popular, and it was popular because it was easier to use. Thomson used both sizes all his career and is convinced it is possible to score lower with worse golf by using a large ball than it is with a small one. 'The large ball is easier by far to manipulate around the green,' he claims. 'In plain language, you can get away with murder. It is just the same as enlarging the ball in any other sport, cricket, hockey, tennis; it slows down the speed of the game. It is no different in golf. You can spin the larger ball better. The ease with which one can "get down in two" after an outrageously bad second shot makes it possible to cover up a particularly poor performance.'

So from the early 1930s, the USA had the large ball and the rest of the world had the small ball and that's the way it stayed through to the 1960s. The Americans wanted to be a law unto themselves — foreigners playing in the US were forced to use the large ball and Americans journeying overseas were forced to play with the small ball. Then, in August 1961, in a locker room in England, Thomson was alarmed to hear of a concerted push by senior British administrators for the big ball to be introduced on their tour. The Australian was astonished to learn that apparently the only reason for this was to combat the dominance of the Americans. Thomson claims the professional players in Britain were told by their elite that if they adopted the 1.68-inch ball on their tour, they could expect to reverse the shame of their bi-annual drubbings in the Ryder Cup. 'I pointed out that they couldn't have expected to beat Australia at the time, let alone the US, and we didn't use a 1.68-inch ball,' he says. 'I said to the British that if they went ahead with an adoption of the larger ball they would one day realise, to their detriment, that the high standard of golf in the United States was due to the tremendous competition there, and what was in the minds and guts of their players. It had nothing to do with the size of the ball they used.'

The British elite did not adopt the big ball, but chose to take the rather watered-down approach of giving players the option of trying it in several tournaments. So at some events in the 1960s some players used the big ball alongside those using the small, and some were given blatant financial incentives to do so. There were tournaments like the 1964

Gevacolour event at Stoke Poges in Buckinghamshire, where Thomson had a profitable day even though he didn't win the title. He won £1,000 for a hole-in-one at the 16th in the final round and £400 for finishing runner-up to Spaniard Angel Miguel by a shot. He could have pocketed an extra £100 as the leading competitor to use the big ball, but before the championship had mischievously written 'maybe' on the declaration signed by players who intended to use the large ball. The secretary of the PGA, Colonel Harry Reed, well aware of Thomson's attitude to the big ball, said that the prize would be awarded to Britain's Peter Butler because the response from the four-time Open champion 'means absolutely nothing to me'. The British push was on. The wave of support behind the big ball gathered momentum and into the 1970s it seemed inevitable that it would find its way into European golf on a permanent basis. Then the R & A championship committee made the historic, far-reaching decision to deem the ball compulsory for the 1974 Open Championship at Royal Lytham. Gary Player triumphed on that occasion (and became the only man to win the Open in three decades), but significantly, it was the first Open in twenty-three years to see the name of Peter Thomson fail to make the halfway cut. Before Lytham, Thomson refused to accept that the R & A decision was final, and using his column in the *Age* as his public release valve, attacked the game's administrators: 'The saga of the large ball unfolds daily like a golfing Watergate,' he wrote. 'There are distant signs of a cover-up by the Championship Committee. At a press conference earlier in the year a persistent questioner dragged from the spokesman an admission that the US Ryder Cup team had sent a letter to the R & A either suggesting, advising or implying that some or all of them wouldn't be at the Open this year unless the large ball was made mandatory. The Championship Committee has on its hands an enormous financial undertaking in the Open ... It is put in a roundabout way that the financial responsibilities over-ride all else, including the rules of the game itself. This implies that the decision to enforce the use of the larger ball has more to do with money than sport ... It is unlikely that there will ever be an adequate inquiry into this piece of "dark grey-looking mail", but doubtless, like Watergate, the matter will keep dripping like a leaking tap.' Thomson finished the article with the paragraph: 'If it is finally shown that there has been a yielding to American pressure, somebody will have to answer for it.'

A few days later he followed up with an even stronger assault: 'Few people in the world will have feelings one way or the other about the decision to insist on the large US-size ball. The decision must now call into question the R&A's role as custodian of the rules of the game as we follow them. Australia for one should make its feelings known in no uncertain terms ... The truth is, as one member of the R & A Championship Committee put it to me earlier this year, the British Open is now hooked on the appeasement of the US professionals because the outsize prizemoney depends largely on the US television fee. "We have no choice. No top US players, no TV fee. I don't know where we would be without that," he told me. The British Open sadly is now an appendage to the US programme. The pity of it is that in the process the R & A has forfeited all credibility, together with the right to tell us what is good for the golf world. As in so many other fields at this point of history, I honestly believe the tired British elite would be pleased to be rid of the responsibility.'

Thomson, with a fair head of steam up by now, continued to criticise the British elite, but was soon forced to aim his sights towards his own country's golfing administration. In April 1977 the Australian Golf Union released a brief statement saying the Australian Open 'was now being brought into line with all other major championships throughout the world' and the big ball was now compulsory for the event. Thomson was playing in Japan when he was told the news. Rather than leap up and down or thump his fist on a table he calmly sat down behind his portable typewriter and from his hotel room in Nagoya began another two-fingered tirade, this one under the heading, "Death of the truly Australian Open":

'The Australian Golf Union's decision to make the large ball obligatory for this year's Australian Open is the final stage in the conversion of our championship to an annex of the US programme. Sadly, the switch from the smaller ball is bound to achieve the opposite to what the Open's sponsors hope to bring about. Far from bringing the event prestige in the world of golf, the move will only prompt the reaction "ho-hum there's another one gone the same way". Until now we had at least a championship that was unique in the world in that it was Australian in every respect. Played on a variety of Australian courses in rotation under Australian weather conditions to Australia's rules of the game, it was distinctive ... Now we have an event which will look no different to the world's top players than a dozen or more other largely professional events the world over that have arranged for the US ball to be rammed down the throat of the locals ... In Australia's case we have followed the lead of the British, although Australia at the time raised strong objections to the British departure. I have already written that the British caved in to a piece of "dark-grey mail" and that the British Open took to the 1.68 inch ball for the basest of reasons — the money. In our case, it took even less persuasion.'

In March 1978 the Australian PGA National Council voted to make the big ball compulsory in all professional tournaments in Australia. It was the final, bitter blow to Thomson's personal campaign and yet he refused to throw in the towel. 'The voting was 9/6, or 9/7 if the chairman's vote is included, which means there was by no means unanimity,' he wrote. 'Where there is a choice on a matter as esoteric as the size of a golf ball, it is a dangerously undemocratic thing for a slim majority to inflict its weight of numbers on the rest.'

Thomson was severely criticised by some readers and many fellow professionals for refusing to accept defeat, and some still claim that history has proven them to be correct and that the big ball has not had a single detrimental effect on golf. Not simply for the sake of taking a contrary stance, Thomson says: 'Or has it?' To this day he will not accept that the big ball has been good for the game and he still proffers quite cogent reasons why it hasn't. He is the first to admit that the large ball-small ball debate was greatly exaggerated, and he predicated his entire offensive around the fact that the whole golfing world was once upon a time quite happily playing with the small ball. Suddenly, for a seemingly inexplicable reason, the Americans chose to be different. Forty years later the rest of the world followed them. Thomson simply wanted to know why.

'I knew at the time my argument against the big ball was a fruitless one,' he says, leaning forward in his easy chair and clasping his hands together tightly, 'but the point I was trying to make was that the discarding of the small ball wasn't done with any sensible purpose. Of course, I was very, very disappointed when the R & A adopted the big ball under circumstances that I thought were pretty miserable. And then of course Australia just adopted it holus-bolus. I was very public with my views at the time because I wanted an opportunity to debate the matter. That was clearly what was lacking in the whole business. Nobody was willing to really examine whether it was of value to us as professional golfers to change the size of the ball we played with in our country. I constantly told our fellows that we shouldn't have simply followed like sheep. We have at least as many brains as any other people in the golf world and a whole lot more experience of our own conditions, and we should have debated the matter sensibly and made up our own minds purely on the merits of the big ball.

'Looking back now, I don't think the large ball has had the slightest effect on the popularity of the game — I'm certain it would be in its current healthy state regardless of what ball was endorsed, and I still believe we might be better off in championship play using a smaller ball, because the other one has become so easy to play with. The bigger the ball in any sport, the easier it is to hit precisely. Even in a strong wind the modern large ball is aerodynamically so good that it is much better than the small ball ever was in a wind. It's my opinion that the changes to the size of the ball, along with the improvements in ball and club technology, have dramatically distorted golf, making it easier to play and therefore the scores have dropped. The ramifications of this are that a "large ball player" has developed and the design of golf courses has been affected. Making the ball slower and therefore harder to impel has only stretched the gap between the "gorillas" and the ordinary player, bringing more brawn and less brain into our game. There are actually two games now — a championship game and a club game.

'The history of it is easy to follow; around 1900 the British Open was won by Harry Vardon with a score of 300. By the 1930s it was down to 285 with Bobby Jones, and then it made the 270s and the low-270s. The authorities said, "Wait on. This is wrong. It should be up at 288." To keep the score up they started to distort the dimensions. a prime example is Muirfield in Edinburgh. The normal course has a beautiful swarth of wall-to-wall open, turf grass. That's club golf. Every time the British Open comes around they cut a very narrow ribbon of fairway that would add ten strokes onto a club golfer's handicap. That's distortion.

'A solution to this lies in architecture and course preparation, so that the arena becomes so fast and slippery that there is ever a worry about hitting so far that you run off the edge, and of course you could make the ball smaller so we could see shots that miss the target by a wide margin get their just desserts.' Once upon a time this solution would have been right up Thomson's alley; tailor-made for his type of game. But not any more. Just as time says he cannot hit the golf ball the way he used to, it has proved that his argument against the big ball was not for personal reasons. His feelings, as always, are for the game.

Whoever it was who first coined the phrase, 'money is the root of all evil', did not have the Australian professional golf circuit in mind, but to many of those who follow the tour each summer it certainly seems that way. Just as it is possible to predict that the winner of the Australian Open will have a lower score than the runner-up, one can safely expect the issue of appearance money to grab a fair slice of the publicity. The name of Peter Thomson is usually found leading the charge against it.

As with the large ball issue, those on the opposite side of the fence to Thomson say: 'Just accept it. It's here to stay. Appearance money is a fact of life.' With this issue the anti-appearance-money lobby has strong support and Thomson is not pushing a lone barrow. In Thomson's mind appearance money is not here to stay, and he believes there is certainly something he can do about it. 'Yes, it's a fact of life in Australia,' he says. 'But it's not a fact of life anywhere else. That's the whole point. I'm not alone in this view. There are plenty of us working very hard to see that the integrity of golf, including professional golf, is eventually protected against this blatant exploitation. I can't say when, but it will be done.'

Appearance money has been a regular part of the professional scene in Australia ever since 1952. Four Americans turned up that year to play in the revived Lakes Cup at the Lakes course in Sydney. The visitors were the formidable foursome of Ed 'Porky' Oliver, Jim Turnesa, Lloyd Mangrum and Jimmy Demaret and huge crowds flocked to see them play in both Sydney and Melbourne, most of the spectators under the impression the men from the US had gladly flown the Pacific to lock horns with their Australian colleagues. In fact, Ampol had paid sizeable fees simply for the Americans to turn up and play. None of the Australian participants — Thomson, Ossie Pickworth, Kel Nagle or Norman von Nida — received a penny for their efforts. Virtually every year since, someone in Australia has opened a chequebook to 'welcome' an overseas golfing great to play in a tournament. A pile of money, the best accommodation, the finest transport, even food, clothes, entertainment, possessions, interesting company and a suitable challenge is showered upon the player. The game's greatest have visited Australian shores to tee it up in Australia's biggest and most publicised events; among them Arnold Palmer, Jack Nicklaus, Gary Player, Lee Trevino, Tom Watson, Tony Jacklin, Gene Littler, Don January, Raymond Floyd, Hubert Green, Johnny Miller, Ben Crenshaw, Hale Irwin, Seve Ballesteros, Larry Nelson, Craig Stadler, Curtis Strange, Bill Rogers, Sandy Lyle, Bernhard Langer, Nick Faldo and Mark Calcavecchia. Many of this imposing list of players have given breathtaking performances and left Australia with an indelible impression of their abilities. Many have made the trip more than once, giving an impression they enjoy the place, its people and the tournaments. As far as Peter Thomson is concerned, the very crux of the matter is, 'Who's to know?' His argument is simple: 'If someone has a full wallet before he starts, how are we to know he's not just here for financial gain? How do we know his hunger to win is not affected? I am against appearance money because there is no justification for it. Money generated by sponsors and promoters should be placed in the overall prize pool, so the man who wins the tournament finishes the week with the most money. The runner-up becomes the next richest, and so on, down the field. We should be able to attract the world's best players to compete in our events because of the prizemoney we offer, the state of our courses, the smooth running and organisation of our tournaments, and because they like the place and its people. Paying appearance money is demeaning to the other players in the field, and it destroys the whole credibility of a championship.'

His public outbursts about appearance fees have earnt him the admiration of many players and observers, and the derision of many administrators, promoters and media, who claim that he is living in the past and out of touch. The man himself merely smiles at these accusations, and maintains his belief that the payment of appearance money will be stopped before it brings the professional game in Australia to its knees. This is the quintessential Peter Thomson looking at life with a deep focus. He takes a visionary's view of the dispute and, far from living in the past, he looks a decade, or maybe two, into the future. If Australian golf is to thrive and be successful it has to be squeaky clean. But the men promoting the tournaments for the immediate season have to solve the problems of the moment. It is the promoter who has to tell the television networks, sponsors and patrons exactly who is going to be playing in the tournament he wants them to invest in. And the only way he can guarantee that a certain name plays in his tournament and not another on the other side of the globe, is by paying him.

Thomson's view is that Australia is seen as the golfing 'soft touch' of the world and that the circuit is a laughing stock overseas. To regain the prestige lost through paying players to tee-up in Australian events will take many years. It began in the 1950s with the Lakes Cup, remained alive during the post-Canada Cup winning boom of the 1960s, and reached new heights in the mid-1970s when Kerry Packer tried to make his mark in professional golf just as he later did with professional cricket. Packer, the media tycoon, wanted to 'buy' the Australian Open and have it played permanently at the club at which he was a member, the Australian, at Kensington in Sydney. As the underwriter of a project costing more than $1 million, Packer arranged for membership approval and then obtained the services of his good friend Jack Nicklaus to re-design the club's 18-holes. Nicklaus reversed both nines, introduced three new holes, dug three lakes and planted hundreds of trees, and then set about doing his part for the Australian Open. Just as he was totally flabbergasted by Packer's later intrusion into cricket, Thomson was astonished by the moves afoot at the Australian as such commercial plans went totally against his grain. Nicklaus said many times he considered the Australian Open to be the 'fifth major'. (It remains of little coincidence that Nicklaus, generally regarded as the greatest the game has ever produced, has not once played away from the Australian Golf Club in this so-called 'fifth major' since Packer withdrew his financial support of the Open in 1978.) At the time Thomson wrote: 'Everyone, it is said, finds his own preferred level in this frantic, competitive society of ours. Few relish the rarefied atmosphere at the top. All of which indicates that not many people among our list are capable of winning such a thing as the Open Championship this week at the Australian Golf Club. It would be undeniable that this particular one revolves around the American president of golf, Jack Nicklaus. Nicklaus has selected the dates, re-designed the course, brought with him the field, and insisted on his size of ball. It will be a curious thing if he doesn't win. Yet stranger things have happened. What might just stop him is the weight of things on his mind, one of which is his effort to make our Australian Open be seen and recognised as the fifth most important golf event in the world calendar. I assume the British Open, and US Open, Masters and PGA Championship, come first, then us. If we ignore the French and Canadian Opens, it is possible we are next in line. However, it is embarrassing that the Japanese are holding their Open on the same day as ours — or is it vice versa? — with prizemoney of 65 million yen which today is A$200,000 plus, with the added nobility of paying no one to play on principle.'

In a later article, Thomson also slammed the Nicklaus-designed changes to the course as 'a curious piece of architecture to say the least. For a start, the whole theme is wrong. Deep water in which a ball is irretrievably lost, set right next to putting greens so that it cannot be avoided, is an American fashion like Bermuda shorts and fins on cadillacs ... Water like that is, in the architectural sense, obvious, cruel and expensive, destroying the harmony and continuity of the play, driving the high-handicap player from the game ... He [Nicklaus] will get no thanks from the membership who must eventually carry the burden. The pity of it is that the club and the rest of Australian golf will never know what was possible had they called for designs from the world's leading architects.'

In a magazine interview, Thomson claimed that the only reason the organisers of the Australian Open succumbed to Packer in the first place was through greed. The Australian Broadcasting Commission together with the Open's previous sponsor, Qantas, provided the Australian Golf Union with a substantial sum of money, which it desperately needed to finance its own administration costs, and costs of tours abroad by amateur teams, he claimed. 'Then Packer offered a fee far multiplied with strong stipulations attached. One of these stipulations was that the Open be played at the Australian every year. This arrangement was accepted for a monetary reason, not because it was desirable. The Open Championship of Australia belongs in many places around Australia where in turn it gives each city and State a sense of belonging to something national, just as the Amateur Championship does. The Open is a difficult thing to finance although not impossible, as we shall see in the near future, by other means than at present.'

When Kerry Packer was asked his thoughts on Peter Thomson's claims that the Australian Open was being sold down the drain in the interests of commercialism, the ebullient media boss only gave the gruff response: 'He is pre-historic!' and with that, kept walking. The journalist involved might well have expected a terse response on approaching Thomson for the sequel, but the Melburnian, calm as ever, said: 'Pre-historic? I will be in golf long after Mr Packer has left it. That is all I wish to say about that remark.'

Money is an extremely thorny issue for many people and there are more than a few who claim Thomson's rigid opposition to appearance money is based on sheer bitterness and jealousy because he wasn't able to earn such sums in his day. His detractors say he looks at golfers who wouldn't qualify to carry his bag and sees they have made three-fold the prizemoney he ever did and in half the time. 'I've never had that thought in my head, ever,' he sternly replies. 'Good luck to them, I say. I've got no objection to any player earning big prizemoney. I received £750 for winning my first British Open — you could buy a house with that back then.

'As far as these skins games and other exhibitions and promotions are concerned — fine. If there are people out there who want to watch them then let's have them. I approve of matches purely for television. They can all go for their lives as long as they make it clear it's a TV show and not an Open Championship. I don't give skins matches any credibility and I don't think anyone else does. It's all stunt stuff. Perhaps they end up dividing the money equally — they all seem to have a laugh on their faces while they're doing it. I suppose I would if I was playing for someone else's money — I mean the real skins golf is when you play for your own money. Now that would be interesting. Anyway, I don't mind how much professional golfers earn away from the tour, but it has to be clear that the tour itself is honest and fair to everybody involved — a real sporting contest. I want the playing of professional golf not only to be fair but be seen to be fair. I've been vocal about this appearance money thing for many, many years since it first started here with that Lakes Cup. I was purely reciting my experiences in the United States. I was present on the US tour when it was outlawed, not by the PGA tour but by the sponsors themselves. In the early 1950s appearance money was being paid to Ben Hogan and Sam Snead, but the sponsors all got together and said it was breaking them, so they agreed collectively not to pay it any more. I clearly remember one of the leading journalists from Fort Worth writing that this would bring about the end of the tour. He wondered how it could possibly survive without Hogan and Snead. Well, Snead continued to play and Hogan was coming to the end of his career, so he wound down his involvement, but within a year the American tour had a new star, Arnold Palmer. Now, had they gone on paying Snead and Hogan the appearance fees, we quite possibly may never have heard of Palmer. Since then of course, the US tour has stuck to its policy of not paying players to turn up and play, and it has grown to become the very powerful and equitable organisation that it is today. Professional golf there is scrupulously above board and never poses to be what it is not. When the public there sees someone playing they know he is not just putting on an exhibition walk with his wallet full before he starts. If anyone enters, you can bet he is trying to win if he can. This is completely the reason for my stance on the matter. I would like things to be like that all the time in Australia, not just some of the time.'

And the battle rages on. The Australian Golf Union and the promoters and the sponsors continue to fork out huge sums to attract the world's best players, and Thomson continues aggressively to make his point: 'Appearance money, like bribery, corrupts those who give it as well as those who take it. Like tax evasion, it is not just cheating the government, it is robbing your neighbour.' And, as reported in the Melbourne *Herald*, the executive-director of the AGU Colin Phillips hits back with: 'I think it's sad that we don't get support from Australia's great golfer. Whether Peter understands it or not, the public of Australia wants to see the top champions and the only way they will come out here is if we pay them to come. The other disadvantage is that we are at the end of the season and every player has played thirty or more events and they're tired. All they want to do at this time of year is go home and have a holiday. So, in some respects, it is a sacrifice for them to come all the way down here. Peter's ideals are sound, but he is not facing the realities.'

It was this very public airing of dirty linen over money and conscience which ultimately led to a fierce and open clash between Thomson and Greg Norman. Peter Thomson is the unashamed traditionalist; Greg Norman is the trend-setter in modern day commercialism on and off the fairway — the man nicknamed the 'Great White Shark', the man whose career earnings are over eight figures and who generates half as much again annually from business deals with such corporate giants as Toyota, Reebok, McDonald's and Daikyo. Thomson raised Norman's ire when he wrote in the *Age* on the opening day of the 1989 Australian Open: 'Today at Kingston Heath there begins a golf contest that has all the hallmarks of a big championship. Several of the world's leading players will tee off in the Australian Open in a head-to-head battle with the best we can pit against them. It should be an exciting contest, since at least twenty names on the list are possible winners, for the reason that the Kingston Heath course gives everyone equal chance. This is where Peter Fowler bobbed up in 1983 against all odds, and more telling still, would be the fact that the course has, on each occasion, frustrated Greg Norman at his mightiest. Viewed from the armchair in the comfort of one's lounge room, the event might appear as something powerful in the world of sport. A broad sector of sports fans might even compare it to watching the British Open or the Masters. After all, the same people are there on the screen wearing the same advertising on the same visors.

Sadly, the truth is that it does not bear comparison. It does not rank with those major championships for the simple reason that players here are paid to participate. They are not, of course, induced in any way to play in the big events in the world. No one has ever been paid to start in the British or US Opens. This golf contest has been 'put together' or 'packaged' for television, principally, in the same way that next week's event at Royal Melbourne, the Classic, has been staked. Indeed, the two are hardly distinguishable, but for the name and the fact that one is 80 years old and the other two. Considering the amount of money paid out just to get players to the tee (rumoured in Norman's case to be $200,000), the two events seem more like rorts than championships. The leading British billing, Nick Faldo (whom many astute judges rank as the world's No. 1 rather than Greg Norman), yesterday put in a plea for the status quo, reminding us that our championship had to be 'international' to be credible, and it also had to be won by an international. I wonder if he will ever have to suggest the same thing to the R&A should the British Open ever fall upon hard times. Indeed, I wonder whether he would play at St Andrews next year if he found out that some people were being paid to play. I call attention to this state of affairs for the self-satisfying reason that I want our Open to be a real championship and credible worldwide. I have never subscribed to the notion that we are too far away from anywhere and have to beg people to visit us otherwise they will not come. Where is that great Australian pride? Do we really want people who won't come if they are not bribed? Also, I have a strong view, contrary to Faldo's, that our championship (if it can indeed be called an Australian championship) has to be won by one of us to give it status. It has to have a reputation of being 'hard to win' to give it standing. If it is easy for paid performers to waltz in here, sing their lines, and race off with the prize, then it will be no more or less than the opens of Brazil or Zaire. I am convinced that we now have enough talent in depth to keep this title in Australia. I suggest that Fowler, Senior, Davis, Grady, Parry, O'Malley, Evans, Tinkler, Baker-Finch, and ten others have the ability to resist the world. This might be a historic first time that the Australian Golf Union has joined with two other oganisations to present the event, but it also might be the historic occasion when we "come of age". I'll go for the man with the southern cross on his visor.'

On the Sunday after Thomson's article was published, the appearance-money wrangle made headlines, not through anything Thomson had said, but through comments made by Norman in an interview immediately after his final round. It had been pointed out by most media that week, Thomson included, that the International Management Group, Norman's agents, had been appointed co-promoter of the event with the

AGU, and had brought not only Norman to Kingston Heath, but also reigning US Masters champion Nick Faldo, US Open winner Curtis Strange, and British Open champion Mark Calcavecchia. All were paid handsome fees to turn up and play, and Norman, Faldo and Strange, as IMG clients, gave a percentage of their fee back to their agents. The statement that landed Norman in hot water was his admission that he had gone out with Strange and Calcavecchia and let his hair down on the night before the final round. The British Open champion carded 67-69-69 but finished with a 75; the US Open champion carded 65-71-73 but finished with a 75; Norman carded 72-70-71 but finished with a 77. The average score from the field that final day was 74.1. When questioned on national television about his round, Norman joked: 'I'm just glad it's all over. The three of us went out to a restaurant last night and we just seemed to sit around and talk like three old women for a couple of hours, and that's reflecting in the way we played today. It's getting toward the end of the year and basically we probably let our hair down a little too soon.' Interviewer: 'Mark, you, and Curtis Strange?' Norman: 'Yeah. And you can see how we played today (laugh)!'

The next day Calcavecchia contacted the organisers of the Johnnie Walker Classic and withdrew. The British Open champion had been given star billing and a hefty appearance fee to tee-up in the Classic, but his walk-out for 'family reasons' did absolutely nothing for those arguing that appearance money was the only way to get top players to play. Then an obviously distressed Norman, after finishing 19 shots behind Open winner Peter Senior, was upset by an offering from Thomson, who wrote that during the opening round of the Johnnie Walker Classic at Royal Melbourne the following week, the world's No. 1 ranked player shot a 73 and gave 'the performance of a star actor just going through the motions'. Just as he felt at Victoria in 1981, the blond Queenslander was fuming. 'I've never gone through the motions in my life and I never will,' he said. 'I have always given a hundred per cent and I believe that most people realise that. I don't read what Peter Thomson writes any more. The way he criticises his fellow athletes is disgraceful. One minute he's nice to you and the next minute he stabs you in the back.'

Norman continued his attack on Thomson in a later interview when the subject of Thomson's opposition to appearance fees was raised, in particular, his opposition to Norman's. 'It's none of his damn business,' said Norman. 'If I do a deal with a company or a tournament, then that deal is between them, my agent and me. It has nothing to do with anyone else. In any case, it shouldn't stop young Australian players from making the grade. When I won the Westlakes Classic in Adelaide, all those guys like David Graham were paid to turn up. It didn't stop me. I was 21.' Norman receives support in this argument from many quarters.

Of course his management can be expected to stand by their man: 'Anyone who runs a tournament, in this country or anywhere else, without the chance of getting Greg Norman to play in it needs to go see a doctor,' says James Erskine from IMG. 'The overall effect of having Norman play your tournament is an increased turnover in gate takings, world TV, sponsorship and the like, of $1.2 million. In some quarters, they complain about Greg receiving appearance money. Surely he is entitled to some of all that money he and he alone generates. They are getting him cheaply. In world golf, there are only two men who can generate sums like that on their own: Greg Norman and Seve Ballesteros. Call it charisma, if you like, and these men are the men who have it.'

Once prominent tournament organiser, David Inglis, the man who steered the Australian Masters for a decade before jumping ship to the Bicentennial and Johnnie Walker Classics, said the same thing. 'I'd say Seve is worth almost as much, if not as much, as Greg Norman to an Australian tournament. Get Seve and you wouldn't add more by getting Calcavecchia, Watson or Crenshaw. Get Seve and Greg together and you can lock the gates,' says Inglis. Yet Ballesteros has not played a 72-hole event in Australia since 1983, simply because it is a long way to come and he just doesn't need the money. Some players, like the great Ben Hogan, refused point blank to come to Australia. But still the mammoth cheques are handed over for overseas golfers simply to turn up and tee up in Australian tournaments and, if their performance is good or bad, no questions are asked. Still people like Peter Thomson fight against it, and still sections of the media fight against Peter Thomson. They say however strongly and rationally he disputes it, European and American attitudes are that the Australian professional golfing tour remains unattractive from both a calendar and geographic point of view. They maintain that the clock can never be turned back; golf tournaments are no longer run by the ladies and gentlemen of the hosting clubs but by ruthless, powerful and shrewd individuals who expect to make money.

Thomson has always been a forthright, even stubborn individual. This part of his character no doubt played a significant role in his success on the world's fairways. Now it is a cornerstone of his campaign against appearance money; he simply will not cave in: 'I am old enough to remember people telling us that Hitler was a fact of life and that we should learn to live with it,' he has written. 'Living with it is an option we all have in this free land, but it's not one that I care to use … Golf, including professional golf, has a basic integrity that is worthwhile defending against rapacious exploitation. To the general sports fan I'm sure it doesn't matter two hoots whether the players in the "United Hot Cross Bun Classic" are all paid in the Bahamas before they start or not, but when it comes to a long established national championship it should be another concern. Golf tournaments may be entertainment to most people, but to those entrusted with their management it is first and foremost a game which should be conducted under rules of fairness and equality ... Appearance fees in sporting events are a fraud on the public, in as much as it is made to appear that those who take it are here in Australia because they like us. Nothing could be further from the truth.'

Thomson believes the tradition and appeal of professional golf, put in the wrong hands, could easily choke the game. He says that if some management companies and promoters were banned from the tour they would soon find another sport to exploit. 'What they're doing is not through a love of golf. They are only in it for what they can get out of it,' he claims and then his convictions come through. 'Someone like Greg Norman is in the grip of his management. I think he and a lot of other players waste their talents on extraneous money-making events instead of concentrating on the important tournaments. Norman is sold under the premise that he is the potential winner of everything in sight, but the expectations haven't been reached. He has been very cleverly marketed, but it's mostly on his potential and I think this in turn places a tremendous burden on him and if he's being held back, I think it is because of this burden that he's under. He's obliged to win these big championships now. He doesn't go there in the hope that he's going to win — I'm sure he's going there fearful that he's not going to do it. Just about everything he says is indicative of this; that he's under enormous pressure. And that of course is the penalty for the amount of money he's earning.'

Thomson says Norman is the best Australian player he has seen in his time and, like the rest of the country, hopes that one day he might fulfil his quite phenomenal ability. 'I would like to point out that I have never written anything detrimental about his game,' he says. 'I would like to see him become the best player of all time because I think he has the potential to do it. I think he has been very unlucky — in fact I can't think of a player who has been as unlucky in his career and if he doesn't become one of the all-time winners it would be a great shame. As a person, I can't comment — I don't know him. I don't talk to him much. We are from different generations and are involved in different activities, so I don't see him much face to face. As far as the amount of money he earns *off* the course is concerned, I say good luck to him — it's not my money! But appearance money is a different matter. The sums he receives for playing in Australia are, I believe, deplorable, and contrary to what quite a few people believe, Australian golf does not revolve around Greg Norman. He's one of the big figures in the total scene all right, but if he was run over by a bus tomorrow, or if he chose not to come to Australia ever again because he had to buy his own ticket, the golf would carry on beautifully. Norman doesn't need to be in the field for an event to run successfully. I believe it is about time we started to recognise the depth of talent we have in Australia now — players that can be promoted alongside, even independent from, Norman. Look at Wayne Grady's effort at Troon [in the 1989 British Open]. All the publicity centred on Norman losing it, but Grady's effort was quite remarkable (as it was in the US PGA championship the following year). And he's not the only one — we could hinge our tournaments around at least twenty other Australians.'

Many people believe it is conceit talking when Peter Thomson agrees that he is the elder statesman, or father figure of professional golf in Australia. The facts are that nobody yet comes anywhere near him in depth of experience and contribution and this should qualify him to voice his opinion wherever and whenever he thinks it needs to be voiced. There are those who believe he simply likes to be contrary but they are far outnumbered by those who say the game needs people like Thomson. He may be a voice calling in the wilderness; he might hammer the point but more often than not he hits the nail right on the head. He has criticised courses around the world, some as famous as Muirfield, Carnoustie, Royal Birkdale, Wentworth and those of the Melbourne sandbelt. During the 1969 Australian Open at Royal Sydney he was practising over the course when he felt the cups looked smaller than normal — he measured them with his putter head, discovered they were indeed smaller than usual and they were restored to the proper size before the tournament began. He has called Seve Ballesteros 'a prima donna' for taking Jack Newton's side when the Australian was disqualified from the 1981 Australian PGA championship for attending the Melbourne Cup when he should have been registering for the event. He laments the passing of the ancient sand bunker and considers modern bunkers ridiculously easy from which to escape, more like 'a Japanese courtyard'. He lambasted the match committee for contributing to 'Australian golf's day of shame' during the 1987 Australian Open at Royal Melbourne when play had to be postponed after a vile north wind trumpeted to all that the positioning of the cup on a slope at the 3rd hole was far beyond the realm of fair play. Even Scotland's Sandy Lyle flatly refused to hole out. Aside from the much publicised large ball-small ball debate, and the on-going appearance-money saga, there have been criticisms of high profile players flocking to their coaching gurus once they realise their game is in tatters, or blatant attacks on the strategy used for the marketing of golf clubs and golf balls. Thomson has been vocal about the lack of matchplay in professional golf, the repaired spike mark on greens, and the preferred lie. Despite all these vehement paragraphs, written sometimes he admits in the interests of a good story, Thomson's foremost priority has been to steer his fellow Australian professionals to a better deal. One prominent colleague claims he was the equivalent of a trade union leader, eager to see his members treated fairly. Thomson's son Andrew clearly recalls sitting down to the dinner table alongside his father, who had arrived home from a tough day at the office. 'He wouldn't speak about the brilliant shot he'd played to lead the Victorian Open or some other tournament; it would be something to do with appearance money or some player getting a rough deal somewhere.'

Peter Thomson's multiple role off the golf course as administrator, observer, broadcaster and critic is one he takes extremely seriously. If he comes across as a crusader; if his work has been labelled offensive, deliberately provocative, controversial, mischievous and blatantly political, Thomson smiles, squirms in his chair, but calmly dodges the flak: 'I wouldn't be worth printing if I wasn't something like that. I enjoy an essayistic style in preference to a terse recitation of facts. I write responsibly, I hope, on things I see and sometimes on things I wish for. I don't write nonsense — I write things as I see them; things that the other journalists might not be happy to write. I don't have to interview people. I only write about things that I observe.'

It is the same with his commentary work on television during the Australian summer. Thomson has been criticised by many for not bringing more of his own personality into the telecasts; for not colouring his commentary with stories from his playing experiences around the world. He is quick to cut that one down: 'I would never be able to bring myself to talk about myself,' he says. 'People want to know about what is happening on their screens and not what happened 40 years ago. We simply don't have time for such stories and truthfully, I believe there's too much talking on TV. Most commentators these days talk over the action non-stop, even while a fellow is putting. I'm a big one for letting the atmosphere of an event do its own talking.'

Thomson is an individual all right; a quick-thinking, yet deep-thinking individual. As his former playing colleague Frank Phillips says, noticeably raising his voice, 'People have always been keen to knock him down, knock him off his pedestal, but they simply don't know the man. I've played alongside him, I've travelled overseas with him, I've stayed in hotels with him and I've talked with him many, many times. These people who knock him, just don't know him and have never bothered themselves to try and get to know him. I'm very, very proud to say that I've been a fellow Australian professional golfer.'

When Peter Thomson looks in the shaving mirror every morning, he sees an Australian. His entire professional life has been fiercely patriotic; geared towards promoting and helping his fellow pros in

Australia. He resents the way his former colleagues like Crampton, Devlin, Graham and Norman have been forced to leave their country to stamp their success on world golf. What's more when they return, they sound like aliens; it seems like they are no longer locals. 'We are a very friendly bunch, we Australians,' says Thomson. 'We seem to like foreign visitors to do well. I don't know quite why. Why do Australians feel so strongly that golfers from overseas must always succeed? Why don't they want local golfers to win? I remember taking Rod Laver, surely one of the world's best tennis players of all time, out to play golf after he'd lost at Wimbledon and he was saying, without being bitter: "If I'd won, they'd want to know how come I didn't win by more." We accept the visitors, but our fellows are taken for granted. We have an exaggerated regard for overseas players and we build up their reputations far beyond their normal ability.'

In 1981, after finishing runner-up in that Australian Open at the Victoria Golf Club, Greg Norman survived fierce questioning over his choice of club for his final approach. He said, prophetically, that it probably wouldn't be the only time the closing moments of an event would come back to haunt him. At the same time, Thomson, having seen his prediction come true, but not his wish, tapped out his newspaper summary of the final day's events and packed up his belongings before heading home for dinner. Significantly, Norman never had the chance to read Thomson's follow-up article to the initial piece that caused so much ill-feeling. It stands as one of the most important columns written by Thomson, and remains the closest he has ever come to delving into the autobiographical. Although he is a very private man, he is occasionally very public — exposing the workings of his mind for all to see and read. Under the title 'Whimsy ruled out of bounds', on 26 November 1981, he wrote: 'A few years ago when I wrote regularly for *The Age*, often from afar, I tried whenever possible to inject a little whimsy into my pieces — something that might just entertain a little as well as inform. Mostly it worked, although doubtless some of the humour fell flat. It is difficult indeed to tickle all of the people all of the time. This is especially so with people involved in one's story. Sportsmen whose standard of living depends on their reputation in the marketplace are as sensitive as any. Last week I offered a piece about foreign golfers raiding our tournaments, carrying off the prizes. It touched a few exposed nerves, was quoted interstate without the essential whimsy, and ended up back on my desk in the form of a couple of rude letters. I don't mind that. If people don't write, you know that you are not being read, which means that before long you are not being published. Jack Fingleton taught me that a long time ago. Before he fell ill five years ago, he wrote regularly for South African newspapers which meant that when Gary

Player was in town, Jack had to find out what he was doing. I saw a lot of Jack at golf events. Jack Fingleton wrote when he could in the manner I have described. If you read his words carefully, there was always a line or two of whimsy. He found this easy because it was his nature, even though he showed stern demeanour as often as not ...

'Reverting to last week's piece, the reaction from our golfers surprised me, because I really set out to defend them, to drum up some public sympathy for their efforts, since we had what any football coach would call, "a long injured list". If they are not injured physically it might be psychologically. And that is *the* most vital factor in sports competition. I am firmly of the view that Australian performers, whether sportsmen or artists, suffer from the undue extolment and exaggeration which accompany visiting opponents. Whether the visitors are more proficient or gifted has nothing to do with it. It is the fact that they are made out to be more *important* that tells. A lot of it has to do with the amount of money they and their managers hold out for, enticing them here in the first place. Having paid out a fortune, it is only to be expected that the promotion machine will see that it gets its money's worth. In the end, it makes for a distortion of their real contribution. Our own players can hardly ignore it. It pervades. Deep down it probably hurts. The reverse doesn't happen when our players go overseas. I suppose it means that getting to the top in Australia is tough. If you make it, you can more or less claim to have done it on your own. We have a national tendency to denigrate. Tall poppies are something we don't want in our field ...

'Our suffering pros have my deepest sympathy and support. I would dearly love to see them win, and win by more. What would help considerably is a change of emphasis. If we exaggerated for a change the importance of our own players, I am sure it would work wonders. Performance lifts with the ego, but it has to have a little prodding, a little booster rocket.'

Thomson concluded the column with the footnote: 'I have read this to see if anyone could be offended or touched on a raw nerve. I think I am safe, but then I cannot be sure. Someone's manager might ring the Sports Editor in the dead of night and complain, but I hope not. I only want to help.'

It seems that all his life Peter William Thomson has been marching along successfully and happily, oblivious of the fact that he is often out of step with those around him. Or is it they who are out of step? Thomson sometimes thinks so and will continue whenever and wherever he can to try to persuade them to follow his lead.

C • H • A • P • T • E • R 8

When One Door Closes ...

THE Windsor Hotel of the early 1950s epitomised class. With its stylish façade overlooking Victoria's Parliament House, it might have been lifted directly from the streets of old London. With its warm service, old-fashioned decor and immaculately dressed doormen, it was Melbourne's answer to the Savoy or the Ritz. Many famous visitors from interstate and overseas came to stay in the Windsor's plush suites and eat in its Grand Dining Room. During the summer of 1953 the hotel boasted a couple of popular locals on the guest list. One was the man whose usual residence was the Lodge in Canberra, but when federal parliament was in recess he would immediately retreat south for his beloved Melbourne. Fifty-nine-year-old Robert Menzies was in between the sale and purchase of homes in the southern capital and could think of nowhere better to stay than the Windsor. Coincidentally, Peter Thomson and his first wife Lois were also using the Windsor as home base for the same reason.

One balmy evening after a practice round on the sandbelt, Thomson was making his way through the hotel's grand entrance when a stranger grabbed his attention. Menzies made no secret of his passion for sport. He knew that a famous golfer was staying in the hotel and had sent his press secretary, Hughie Dash, to collar the youngster as soon as he came in the door. During Thomson's lengthy stay at the Windsor this became a regular occurrence.

'I first met Sir Robert then, and Hughie Dash used to stand guard over him in the lobby and bar and would give me a wink when he knew the Prime Minister was free and wanted to have a chat. Most evenings when I'd come in after playing golf Hughie would say, "The

PRIME MINISTER,
CANBERRA.

-6 SEP 1965

My dear Peter

I am writing to tell you how grateful I am for your help and assistance in arranging the manufacture of the set of golf clubs for the President of Pakistan.

They were delivered to our Ambassador at Karachi and he presented them to the President on Australia Day this year. The President subsequently wrote to me expressing his utmost delight at having a set made to his own specifications.

It was a kindness on your part to have agreed to give this your close attention and I warmly appreciate your co-operation. I have asked my Department to let you have a cheque for their cost within the next few days.

Your victory in the British Open gave me great joy. I am, as always, proud of you.

Warm regards
Yours sincerely

Mr. P. Thomson, M.B.E.

Robert Menzies

Another example of Thomson the diplomat, and friend of his Prime Minister.

boss wants to see you," and the boss, as I found out, just wanted somebody to have a drink with.' The significance of these informal meetings would be felt in Melbourne more than twenty-five years later, but at the time they had a deep personal effect on Thomson. Chatting and drinking and staring at those famous black and bushy eyebrows, Thomson was made to feel quite at home. 'Sir Robert was a giant of a man and thoroughly Australian,' he says. 'He was a very warm man and it was so simple to adopt him as a role model because he was dignified and eloquent; a very wholesome man in every way. He was a great listener and got a great deal of pleasure out of listening to other people and had a way of drawing them out. I used to talk to him about my theories and ideas. It wasn't as if I was a party to cabinet secrets, but we would talk about the affairs of the day and he used to laugh about some of my thoughts. I was never impertinent enough to ask him outright for advice on a political career, but as a young man I certainly became interested in politics.'

Over the next few years Thomson and Menzies met many times in private and in public, both in Australia and Britain, and they became close friends. When Sir Robert was recuperating from an operation on his tonsils in a London hospital, Thomson paid him a visit immediately he had completed his round in a local tournament. There he found the PM, being plied with custard and ice-cream, but extremely keen to chat about Test cricket. It was another topic they both knew plenty about. Thomson enjoyed Menzies's sense of humour and sharp wit. At the presentation of prizes for the 1959 Canada Cup at Royal Melbourne Menzies, after trudging the final few fairways to urge Thomson and Nagle to victory, commiserated with his friend when called upon to present the individual title, won by Canada's Stan Leonard over Thomson in a sudden-death play-off. 'I would say to you, Peter, what I have often said to my political opponents after an election,' said the prime minister. 'You shouldn't feel too badly about this, for you were beaten by a very good man!' Later, only half-joking, Menzies said he would like to have Thomson in his cabinet.

Sir Robert openly fostered Thomson's interest in politics and in the early 1960s was delighted when he discovered that his friend had joined the organisation he founded, the Liberal Party. There were many who saw Thomson's move as hypocritical for one whose background was firmly rooted in the working class but Thomson has never been interested in socialist ideas, preferring from an early age notions of individual initiative and enterprise. There is also no doubt the influence of Robert Menzies helped his decision. The prime minister was fully aware of the advantage to the Liberal Party when high-profile sportspeople joined it: he had been an enthusiastic supporter of the former cycling champion, Sir Hubert Opperman, who had won the federal seat of Corio in 1949.

Thomson had no intention of quitting the game while he was in his prime to pursue a seat in parliament. Instead he opted to use his political skills by standing for presidency of his state's PGA. In December 1963 he defeated two candidates to win the vote. Less than a year later he became president of the Australian PGA when his nomination came in a surprise move at the association's annual meeting in Sydney. Australian golf in the early 1960s had a wealth of talent; what it needed was someone who knew how to manage it.

'I was approached by quite a number of people to stand for the national job and I was willing and eager to play my part,' say Thomson. 'All my time in pro golf had been as a player and it was always my hope that the players would one day be able to run their own show. I saw our main task as pulling the entire PGA together and to lift its prestige. The PGA was in bad shape at the time; it was in debt and it took a long time to get the finances into good shape. Initially an enormous amount of my spare time was occupied by the PGA and of course a lot of it was to do with tournament golf. I thought it was about time the players started getting a better deal.' Confident that he was the right man for the job Thomson relished the prospect of becoming deeply involved with the inner-most workings of the sport, and of course, the political interaction of it all. He developed a reputation as an analytical, unforgiving chairman who refused to tolerate illogicality and stupidity. He always kept control of his meetings. 'He was a very, very hard man in a meeting,' says former Australian Open champion, Frank Phillips. 'He always had his facts and figures ready and if the people on the other side of the table weren't prepared themselves, he used to bring them down in flames.'

Thomson loves a good argument, and is a skilled debater who can often swing the feeling of a meeting around to his way of thinking. This is partly why he has remained chairman of the Australian PGA for more than a quarter of a century. He agrees that his time with the PGA has progressed from his early days as players' representative through to modern times and his position of figurehead, a leader, an elder statesman who is there for advice.

Thomson considered the PGA job ideal training for a career in politics and always had the thought in the back of his mind that some day, when all his golfing business was eventually at an end, he might make a run for public office.

An avid reader of the leading thinkers of major political and religious systems, Thomson often felt he was frittering his life away on an irrelevant and useless occupation. Journalists recall approaching him in locker rooms and hotel lobbies for comments after his rounds and, no matter how spectacular the golf might have been, he would invite them to compare his score with the day's casualty figures in the Vietnam war, or some other conflict. There were times when he considered his golf score a totally meaningless statistic in the larger field of life. He felt that Australia was indeed a lucky country, a nation with untapped resources and unlimited potential. 'Our country is second to none and it is worth preserving,' he said on his retirement from golf. 'The things that I always believed in as a young man were honesty and hard work. Of course I wasn't always honest, but I tried to be, and I tried to work very hard, if you can call golf hard work. It is these things that will preserve Australia the way we'd like it preserved.' Thomson simply felt he wanted to be remembered as more than a champion golfer. The golf course architecture, the writings, the commentaries, the directorships of several companies, the life of 'semi-luxury' were all fine, but not quite enough. Throughout his career he made generous donations of time and money to underprivileged and disabled children through the Variety Club and to other charities, but he always wanted to make a much greater contribution to society.

In the 1960s and 1970s he refused several invitations to stand for parliament. 'I have a lot of contempt for career politicians,' he once said. 'They act out of self-interest. The best politician is a man who has been successful in other fields. A blacksmith might make a better politician than a professional politician.' It was clear that, if Thomson was going to do it, it was going to be done his way.

In the 1960s he was content to observe political life through the eyes of people like Sir Robert Menzies and Victorian premier Sir Henry Bolte. After Menzies retired from public office in 1966, Thomson remained in close contact with him and later invited him to become patron of the Australian PGA. 'I pointed out to him that Her Majesty Queen Elizabeth was the patron of the PGA in Britain and he said, "Well that's good enough for me!" At the time though we were having a real to-do with the Australian Golf Union and I decided it would be very unfair to involve him at that point. I tended to delay it until we had the dispute sorted out.' One way or another the PGA seemed to be perpetually locking horns with the AGU and the former PM was never approached again. When in May 1978 at the age of 84 Sir Robert died at his home in Melbourne, Thomson was invited to be a pallbearer at his state funeral, but was contractually obliged to be at a tournament in the United States and was unable to return hom in time. He was deeply affected by Sir Robert's passing. Within twelve months he was to quit golf and embark on a political career. He did not harbour thoughts of becoming prime minister, even premier, or of changing the face or the course of Australian politics. His approach would be just like a round of golf — a lot of little things, achieved with clear thinking and commonsense. They would eventually add up to a good score.

'I felt I could have achieved a lot of things,' he says. 'Just before I turned 50 I thought it would be an appropriate time — that's a good age I think — although I'm sure many people think it would be better to start earlier than that, but as I've said, that's for a career politician and I didn't want to become one of them. Anyway, I just wanted to make a contribution in areas that I thought needed fixing. For example, things like digging up the street in Malvern. They've dug up the footpath in High Street twenty-seven times. When I was in England I found out that there is only one authority allowed to dig up the street — you don't have the Gas Board having a go and the Electricity Commission and the local Council and everybody else who thinks they've got a reason. That's just one of the little things I wanted to do in Victoria.'

There was no shortage of opinion in the Liberal Party about where a clear-cut political acquisition like Peter Thomson would be best placed. The Federal Liberals wanted him in Canberra where they could take advantage of his national profile; others said he should start with a blue-ribbon state seat in Victoria and earn a few stripes before tackling the national capital. Thomson had his own views. 'I did not think about a federal seat,' he says. 'It was Henry Bolte who told me, "You don't want to have anything to do with those bludgers up there. The real power of politics is right here in the state!" I was prepared to accept that and I wanted to stay in Melbourne and help the Victorian government work its way out of its electoral trouble. Anyway, I was thinking one step at a time; let's get Prahran first.'

The seat of Prahran, the smallest in the State Legislative Assembly, comprised 7.68 square kilometres and included parts of leafy middle-to-upper-class Toorak, South Yarra and Armadale and the bulk of middle-to-lower-class Prahran and Windsor. It had been held for the Liberals since 1955 by former Test cricketer, government whip and friend of Thomson, Sam Loxton. When Loxton announced his intention not to stand in the 1979 state election, the Liberals took a punt on little-known candidate Tony De Domenico, banking on votes from the increasingly migrant population of Prahran. 'He was a somewhat controversial candidate,' says former Liberal premier, Lindsay Thompson, 'who didn't have the full support of the branches, and Bob Miller, the former Melbourne footballer and lawyer, won the seat handsomely and in the next three years became one of the best Labor members in the House and entrenched himself into Prahran.'

After De Domenico's defeat in May 1979, the senior members of the Liberal Party turned to Thomson. After thirty years in professional golf he earmarked the 1979 Open Championship at Royal Lytham as his last event in Britain, and four months later the curtain would officially come down after the Australian Open at Metropolitan, fittingly the scene of his first triumph in the championship. 'It seemed like the ideal time,' he says. 'I'd turned 50 and also the Liberal Party, to which I'd belonged for the previous fifteen years, was in a lot of trouble electorally.' The 1979 state election had been one of the closest in Victoria's history — the Liberals won by only one seat, and that by a mere 86 votes on the second re-count. Thomson and his advisers thought that if they could win back Prahran at the next election it just might tip the scales in the Liberals' favour in what was expected to be another extremely tight poll.

So now Thomson had Prahran in his sights. He cut his golfing commitments back to the bone and began lobbying for the Liberal pre-selection ballot in August of 1980. At the heart of his approach was management. He didn't have any old-style fire in the belly: he was a technocrat. He was safe, moderate, and at the time thought that Victoria wanted solutions without great upheaval. He thought the Liberals could remain in power by going back to basics; gaining the confidence of the electorate.

He involved himself with many community issues, but the one that consumed most of his time was the establishment of the drug rehabilitation centre, Odyssey House. Obsessed with his new challenge, Thomson went into the streets of St Kilda to observe the problem first hand. 'I was horrified by what I saw,' he said after the journey. 'The advent of drugs in our community is absolutely shocking. I am enraged at the continuous spread of this evil and the way it is sapping the younger members of our society. I've got four kids of my own and luckily they've all escaped the drug threat so far. But I got a call the other day from a woman in Frankston who said her son, who's 26, had asked her for help. He was distraught, haunting discos, railway stations, looking for vulnerable, lost children to get his ten new customers so he could get his own supply. They're sitting ducks these kids — the bloke knew it and that's why he was in a mess. He's the sort of person Odyssey was founded to help.'

Odyssey was established in New York in the late 1970s to give aid, advice and sustenance to drug addicts, particularly those whose lives had decayed under the ravages of heroin. Thomson was stung into action after 18-year-old James McGrath from Sydney was found dead on a bathroom floor from a heroin overdose in 1977. 'I had previously come to know his father, Walter McGrath. I had no idea what he was going to do after that tragedy, but I watched him get Odyssey House going in Sydney. I had the highest admiration for him. When he suggested such a thing for Melbourne I was only too pleased to throw my weight behind it,' he said at the time. 'The people in it are very dedicated, but they haven't either the time, or in some cases, the energy, to be the chairman. I have both. I've made money out of sport and I've had a lucky life. The best thing I can do is put something back into society.'

It was a long, drawn-out battle. When a million-dollar property at Lower Plenty north-east of Melbourne, formerly the site of a monastery, was finally earmarked after an exhaustive six-month search for prospective homes, local residents strongly opposed the project and prepared to slug it out in court. After countless meetings and public rallies, protests and debates, the Supreme Court found that the Planning Appeals Tribunal's approval of a permit for the centre would stand. The Lower Plenty Residents' Group refused to concede defeat and appealed three times for the ruling to be quashed, fearing that up to 200 'drug-crazed hippies would be wandering the grounds, endangering our lifestyle and dramatically lowering the tone of this attractive, semi-rural neighbourhood'. There were also personal attacks on the designer and head of the Odyssey programme, American Dr Judianne Densen-Gerber. This provoked much emotion from both sides of the fence and a personal plea from Thomson in the pages of the *Age*: 'It is a matter of dismay that those of us who have taken on the task of establishing Odyssey House here in Victoria find ourselves under such attack,' he wrote. 'We are convinced of the desperate need of Odyssey as a treatment programme that supplements other treatment agencies in Victoria. We believe strongly that the Odyssey concept, of being in residence, drug-free and under constant supervision by psychiatrically qualified people over a long period, is capable of saving the lives of hundreds of young Victorians, and more, of turning them into healthy tax contributing citizens with every hope in life ... The drug scene of horror is a perfect reflection of our society and what is wrong with it, deep down and hidden away. As we learn more about it we learn more about ourselves. Eventually, by learning from those who have been to the brink and reeled back, we might be able to do something about it.'

The third appeal from the Lower Plenty residents ended in the High Court, which backed the Supreme Court decision and cleared the way for the centre to operate. Time has proved the verdict a just one, for Odyssey House continues to return hundreds of rehabilitated drug addicts back into the community, and into responsible and successful positions at that. It was a time of great satisfaction for Thomson. The High Court decision came only four days after he defeated four other candidates to win preselection for the seat of Prahran.

For the first time since he was a young boy, Peter Thomson was distancing himself from the game of golf. During the early stages of his election campaign he still played the occasional tournament and he remained chairman of the Australian PGA, but he was fully prepared to sever ties with the game to concentrate all his attentions on politics should he become a member of parliament. It became his life's ambition. 'It would have been a far different life,' he says, 'but it might have been a better thing for me to do. It might have been more satisfying. It might have been anything.'

In early 1981 it was clear the Liberal government stood a very good chance of being defeated at the next election. After a vitriolic attack from one of his former ministers in a Warrnambool newspaper and editorials in the Melbourne media slamming party disloyalty and in-fighting, Premier Dick Hamer resigned amidst a blaze of publicity. Desperate for someone to plug the holes in their sinking ship the Liberals turned to Hamer's deputy, Lindsay Thompson, a man with twenty-six years experience in office, and an old-style politician who preferred tackling issues head-on rather than playing personality politics. He knew there was a gigantic task ahead to restore the confidence of the electorate in his party before the next election, but he was satisfied that he had the team to win. He expected part of that team to be Peter Thomson. 'I first met Peter in the late 1950s,' says Thompson. 'Sam Loxton and I would play a few rounds with him and his mentor Harry Young, and Guy Wolstenholme. I could see that Peter was far more than just a good golfer. He was a person who basically educated himself through wide reading from a fine personal library. He struck me as being a very calm, well balanced character, and I did say to Sam at the time that it's a pity we can't get Peter involved in politics because he would do a tremendous job. When he finally decided to make a run I was very pleased, because I felt he would have made a first-class politician. He had a constructive approach to the solution of problems, had a progressive outlook and was very interested in developing Victoria, from the tourist point of view and the area of general economic development.'

Thomson is the first to admit that the election campaign was the hardest he has ever worked in his life. He and Mary walked almost the entire electorate, door-knocking every dwelling from the large, opulent mansions to the small, decrepit housing commission flats. Working closely alongside Peter and Mary was Andrew Hay, a former private secretary to one-time deputy prime minister Sir Phillip Lynch and the chairman of the Prahran Electorate Committee. 'I suppose we always tend to think of sportsmen and women as having some limitations when it comes to an understanding of the political world and public policy issues,' says Hay, 'but Peter made a great impression on me as someone who was immensely well informed, very intelligent and extremely articulate. He wanted to make sure he gave himself the best possible chance of being elected. We raised a great deal of money locally for the campaign — it didn't all come from the Liberal Party — I'm not quite sure how much we spent, but it would have been a great deal more than average. One thing that came through for me during that campaign was his immense degree of determination. He and Mary were very heavily involved and were very, very good with the door-knocks, street walks and getting around to the voters.'

Thomson's campaign increased in intensity when the premier announced in early February 1982 that the state election would take

Right: British Open Champions playing on the US Seniors tour in the late 1980s.
Left to right: Bob Charles, Gary Player, Arnold Palmer, Peter Thomson and Kel Nagle.

Below right: 31 Open Championships between them. Past Champions gather before their traditional dinner at St Andrews, 1990. *Back row, left to right*: Tom Weiskopf (1973), Seve Ballesteros (1979–84–88), Greg Norman (1986), Jack Nicklaus (1966–70–78), Nick Faldo (1987–90), Tony Jacklin (1969), Bob Charles (1963), Sandy Lyle (1985).
Front row: Lee Trevino (1971–72), Tom Watson (1975–77–80–82–83), Arnold Palmer (1961–62), Fred Daly (1947), Peter Thomson (1954–55–56–58–65), Gary Player (1959–68–74). Mark Calcavecchia (1989) attended the Open, but not the dinner.

Left: Congratulations from the country's leader. Sir Robert Menzies at the 1959 Canada Cup, watched by Victorian Governor Sir Dallas Brooks and IGA President Frank Pace.

Below: Destined for defeat. The political candidate stands before an election hoarding on the old South Yarra Post Office, March 1982.

Above: A toast to Peter on the lawn of Government House, Melbourne, after the awarding of his CBE in 1980. *Left to right*: son Andrew, mother Grace, wife Mary and daughters Pan and Fiona.

Right: Immersed in the life of a political hero. Relaxing at the Thomson residence in Walsh Street, South Yarra, 1968.

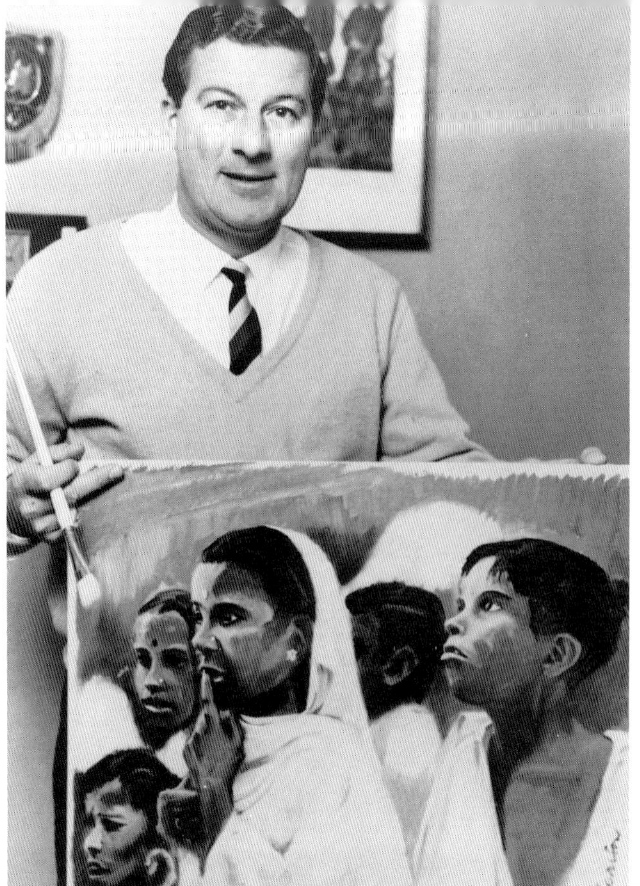

A public showing of his skills as an artist. Thomson's painting of Hindu children was auctioned for charity, June 1963.

Building an empire. A career in golf course architecture takes shape in the late 1960s.

place on Saturday, 3 April 1982. Everything went into top gear. 'I've never worked as hard at anything as I did trying to win that seat,' Thomson says. 'Playing golf was never hard work and I'd never done anything else. Of course I made a number of mistakes, as anybody would, but I was very proud of my campaign. Everybody who opens their mouth makes mistakes and they can't be avoided, but the trick is to keep that percentage of mistakes down to a bare minimum. I was completely satisfied that I'd given it my best efforts.'

'Peter worked assiduously for that seat and ran a very high profile campaign with a lot of effort and energy,' says his Labor opponent, Bob Miller. 'I thought the Liberals had chosen extremely well with him. While he didn't live in the electorate, he was a very well-known figure and a highly respected golfer. The Libs had obviously targeted Prahran because Sam Loxton had held it for them from 1955 to 1979 and they regarded it as their natural fiefdom. Peter was clearly one of their big guns and they wanted Prahran back. In 1979 the seat was extremely marginal and I only won by 433 votes, so I knew the 1982 battle was going to be remarkably close.'

On the lighter side Miller was not the only one at Parliament House who was worried. The members of the press gallery golf team were deeply concerned that their opponents in the annual Press v. Pollies match would swing the new chum directly into the post-election team and some members of the press team went so far as to seek an assurance from the premier that they would not. The official response came that the new member for Prahran would have every right to play, so the press immediately began working on a change of rules that would allow the five-time British Open champion to play only on condition that he give them free tuition.

During a hectic campaign Thomson was attacked by Labor supporters for placing two giant election hoardings on prominent walls of the old South Yarra post office. They complained to the Prahran City Council that the signs, in the party's blue colours and trumpeting, 'Peter Thomson — Liberal for Prahran', contravened the Melbourne Metropolitan Planning Scheme, which stated that signs erected without a permit were limited to eight square metres. The hoardings put up by Thomson's electorate committee, without a permit, measured 45 square metres. A week later and little more than a fortnight before election day, vandals broke into the disused National Trust classified building and leant out of windows to slash large strips in the controversial billboards.

'On the morning of the election Peter was very excited and he felt he was going to win,' says Mary. 'I didn't share his confidence, but we went off expecting that it would be a big day.' He headed for the campaign office near the Prahran market to plan the strategy for election day with his advisers, and spent the remainder of the afternoon visiting as many local booths as possible, handing out how-to-vote cards and making himself known to those who had somehow previously slipped through his net. Once the polling booths closed, he was back at the upper-level campaign office with Mary, Andrew Hay, and a large gathering of local Liberals and supporters who had already opened the champagne. Exhausted, Peter slumped into a chair to watch the election coverage on television. Judging from the mood of voters during the day there was an obvious disenchantment with the government, and a strong wave of support behind the opposition, led by the son of a former Labor premier, John Cain Jr. Thomson had originally planned a political knock-out, but once counting was under way he knew he'd settle for a points decision.

From the early voting it was clear the Liberal government was in trouble. Thomson didn't feel at all comfortable. If there was a mighty swing building against the government, then he had virtually no chance of taking a seat already held by Labor. He closely monitored the results from local booths posted on a large board in the office and each set of new figures spelt out in brutal terms that his quest had ended in stinging defeat. 'It was an awful blow,' he recalls. 'I think anyone that loses an election feels a terrible disappointment because it's not only yourself involved, it's hundreds of other loyal people that you feel with. It's terrible. But then of course, you've got to expect that if you choose to put your head in there in the first place.'

When it was clear the sitting member, Bob Miller, had been returned, Thomson immediately decided to head for his opponent's electoral

1982 State Election — District of Prahran
(percentage of voters — 89.1%)

	Hoobin (Dem.)	*McCandless (Ind.)*	*Miller (ALP)*	*Thomson (Lib.)*	*Inf.*
Armadale	254	37	2,501	2,100	107
Prahran	189	43	3,626	1,252	156
S. Yarra	267	57	2,953	2,644	157
Toorak	138	13	787	2,263	40
Postal	21	3	461	637	7
Unenrolled	5	—	63	22	2
Absentee	164	42	850	828	77
Total	1,038	195	11,241	9,746	546
	4.5%	0.8%	49.3%	42.8%	2.4%

office in a small hall in Prahran. Words were scarce in the car on the way over. It was purely an instinctive reaction. He knew it was something he simply had to do. A hush fell in the hall as Thomson made his way over to Miller. 'Peter came in once it was clear I'd been returned and walked directly over to me,' recalls Miller with affection. 'He shook my hand, offered his congratulations, wished me well for the future and departed. It must have been extremely difficult for him to have to do that, but he was a gracious loser.'

From a total of 22,766 votes polled Thomson received 42.8 per cent of the vote and lost by 1,495 votes. His advisers and supporters tried to console him with the fact that the overall swing to Labor was around 5.5 per cent and that with John Cain's party comprehensively swept to power, he would have been in opposition anyway. Thomson knew that a loss was a loss and he wouldn't have sulked on the opposition backbench if he'd been elected. 'I was prepared to spend years in opposition,' he says. 'I feel any opposition can do an excellent job if the media would only be prepared to listen. There's a lot of people working very hard in opposition politics who never get their opinions aired. I felt I could have achieved at least that.'

Over the next several weeks there much soul searching in the Thomson household. Senior members of the Liberal Party felt that at any other election Thomson would have been elected; his defeat was entirely the result of the overall swing to Labor. They wanted him to try again. Lindsay Thompson had considered resigning from politics immediately after the election, but he was persuaded to stay on as leader of the opposition. Seven months later, satisfied in his replacement in Jeff Kennett, Thompson went through with his resignation and his seat of Malvern became vacant. Thomson was widely tipped as the most likely replacement, but he was also being touted as a strong candidate for the Federal seat of Flinders on the Mornington Peninsula, which became vacant upon the resignation of Sir Phillip Lynch. Thomson never considered running for Flinders and, less than a month before the Malvern by-election, he announced officially that he had withdrawn from the preselection battle. 'I am really thinking about Prahran,' he said at the time, and indicated he would seek preselection for the seat at the next state election. He never did. In the months since his distasteful defeat Thomson had given a great deal of thought to politics. He felt he had given his utmost at the 1982 election; he'd given it his best shot and it hadn't come off. Ironically, a redistribution of boundaries since 1982 has moved east, taking in almost all of Toorak and making it an impossible seat for Labor but, for reasons never explained fully, Thomson backed away from the political spotlight. 'Myself and others spoke to Peter on a number of occasions to try and persuade him to run again,' says Andrew

Hay. 'His response was that he'd thought about it in considerable depth and he'd decided not to. It was as simple as that.'

Those close to Thomson say he accepted the election failure just as he would a defeat on the golf course, but this had meant more to him than any tournament. It took a long time for him to come to terms with the fact that he hadn't achieved what he'd set out to do. If anything, he was disillusioned. In a way, his friends were glad he wasn't successful for they believe he may have been a little too statesman-like as a politician and would quite possibly have been hurt by the political processes. Although he would have made an excellent people's representative, he may not have found satisfaction. Thomson is the sort of person who sees what should be done and he will settle for nothing less. He is not interested in compromises, the bureaucratic way of things, or old-fashioned red tape. Politics, as some of his friends say he might have discovered, is often a case of not what should be done, but what can be done.

These days Thomson has no intention of standing for parliament again. No matter how hard the Liberal Party tried to keep him interested in running for office, he had reached the conclusion that he wasn't destined for political life after all. He felt disillusioned by what had happened, not only by the landslide that put John Cain's Labor Party into power, but also by the attitude of some Liberals who clearly refused to accept that they could lose. The Libs were going through a difficult phase in both the state and federal arenas (Labor won the federal election less than twelve months after their success in Victoria) and many observers thought it was time to accept the cyclical nature of the beast, take it on the chin, and plan for the future. Thomson has said that if he had been elected member for Prahran in 1982 the job would have received his utmost attention, whether in government or opposition, but the fact remains that he was not immediately prepared for the gruelling journey through another election campaign. History told him that very few governments in Australia had lost office after just one term, and that if he chose to run again he stood a strong chance of experiencing a similar defeat.

After his election loss, politics for Thomson became a room with the light switched off. He wanted time, time to assess the future in his own ticking of the clock. His political ambition ended, he needed something to stabilise the listing ship. His natural instinct was to fall completely, comfortably, unashamedly and some say selfishly, into the arms of an old friend — the game of golf. Some argued that it took an enormous force to drag him away from the game in the first place; now it would be almost impossible. While he'd been chasing votes in Prahran, Thomson noted with interest that his old golfing adversaries in the USA had been chasing glory — with much greater success — on a competitive, yet curiously little circuit known as the 'Seniors Tour'.

In 1978, NBC television in the USA covered a nostalgic event in Austin, Texas, called the 'Legends of Golf'. A tournament for golden names of the past, it appealed so much to sponsors that the world's biggest ever golfing purse of US$400,000 was up for grabs. It was a three-round best-ball affair and the low-key Australian duo of Peter Thomson and Kel Nagle picked up a healthy US$65,000 by finishing second, a stroke behind Sam Snead and Gardner Dickinson. Everyone thought it was nice, and rather special. The following year, when organisers decided the event should be limited to those big names over 50-years-of-age, the Legends took on another dimension. A six hole play-off won by the durable names of Roberto de Vicenzo and Julius Boros, in which every extra hole had offsetting birdies, truly caught lightning in a bottle. As old-timers sank one long putt after another and openly rejoiced in doing so, those watching on television and at the course loved every minute. All it needed was someone to remark that these veterans still had something to offer the world of golf and, more importantly, an ability to entertain. Pushed by US PGA Tour Commissioner Deane Beman, himself a successful former circuit player, in 1980 there were two events for those over-50, then five in 1981, and for the 1982 season, eleven Seniors tournaments were scheduled.

Having finished runner-up in the 1981 Legends of Golf with Kel Nagle, again by a stroke, Thomson was hoping that no matter what happened with his political career he might find the time to return in 1982. As it turned out the timing couldn't have been better. The thought of teeing it up once more against his old American friends lured him out of his post-election depression and he again turned up at Onion Creek in Texas, only this time his prelude had been politics, not golf. With a rather rusty swing it wasn't a great surprise that he and Nagle didn't win. What was surprising, however, was that Thomson chose to remain in the United States immediately after the Legends to play in the remaining eight events on the fledgeling Seniors Tour. Caught up in this dynamic new force Thomson did not give another serious thought to a career in politics. There were those who labelled him a sore loser; but a political career hadn't come off, so he simply slipped back into something he knew. For his part, Thomson knew that he was making the right decision.

By the start of October 1982, he'd played in nine events and although winless had amassed US$46,891 in prizemoney on the Seniors Tour. Alongside, his pal Kel Nagle had played in the same number of events for US$33,415. They were having a ball, but not because they were lining their pockets. At that stage, when Thomson was asked by an American journalist the reasons behind his late-in-life love affair with American golf, he replied matter-of-factly: 'You will always have regrets at not having done something in your life if you are a busy person, and when I had to decide on playing the international circuit in the 1960s as opposed to coming to America full-time, there was regret. But then I would have regretted not playing in Europe, or the Far East, wouldn't I, had I done it otherwise?'

The truth of the matter is that when Thomson set out to investigate this totally new phenomenon that was Seniors golf, he thought he would discover 'a lot of cantankerous old men kidding themselves they were still heroes', but what he found was a happy, exciting environment and a totally different life to the one he'd previously experienced in America. It may not be a great exaggeration to say that champions die twice and that, of the two deaths, retirement may seem the more excruciating pain. All the qualities that top-level sport demands — love of competition, desire to be recognised, dedication to task, ability to perform under stress — are precisely the attributes most affected by the realisation that the dreaded moment has arrived. After his unsuccessful foray into political life, Peter Thomson discovered that the game could go on; life for a professional golfer could be prolonged. Perhaps it was Billy Casper who best summed up the feeling for the codgers over-50 when he said: 'This isn't just a second chance for a career, it's a second chance for some of us to change our personalities … Like who? Well, me. I used to be known as a grouch and a grump. Look at me now. Wearing knickers and argyle plus fours and silly hats. And we get to meet some great fans who really appreciate us. I never thought I'd see the day.'

In 1983 the US PGA Seniors Tour expanded by seven tournaments to eighteen, and Thomson played in fifteen of them, and this time Mary came too — previously she hadn't been alongside and he had found it very lonely. America had also changed dramatically — it now had nice hotels instead of motels and they were seeing the most famous, glamorous and exclusive parts of the country, such as Rhode Island, Florida, California, Texas, Virginia, Arizona and Nevada, and not simply the golfing monuments. Thomson renewed acquaintances with all those old champions that had been at loggerheads all those years ago — Casper, Arnold Palmer, Gene Littler, Sam Snead, Julius Boros, Gay Brewer, Lee Elder, Miller Barber, Don January, Doug Ford, Ted Kroll, and international stars like Christy (white shoes) O'Connor, Harold Henning, Al Balding and, of course, Kel Nagle. Their children were all now off their hands; they all had a few dollars (not necessarily too many); they were now earning more money than they ever knew what to do with: they were treading upon the best courses in the best conditions; they were experiencing grassroots golf by playing with amateurs during each tournament; they did not have the pressure of making a halfway cut; they had lavish cocktail parties held specifically for them, silver service wherever they went, the finest hotel rooms and cars; everything was organised for them; they were accompanied by their wives or girlfriends; and they were seeing each other in a totally different light. Most importantly, they again felt the delicious stress of battle. In a nation famous for worshipping youth, it was clear that grey hair and bulging belts were trendy. For those professional golfers over 50-years-of-age, America in the mid-1980s was a marvellous place to be.

Also there in 1983 was Thomson's great chum, Guy Wolstenholme. Their friendship went back to the late 1950s when Thomson was first introduced to the English amateur on the British tour and they immediately found harmony in each other's whimsical sense of humour. In Thomson's eyes Wolstenholme was refreshing company and the tall man from Leicester duly became a constant companion and a regular member, alongside Bobby Locke, Kel Nagle and later Mike Wolveridge, of 'the gang'. Much to Peter's delight he discovered that Guy was as splendid a pianist as he was a golfer, and a familiar scene was acted out on many memorable evenings on the tour. The group, joined by maybe one or two others, would find a quiet corner of their hotel — a secluded place where the piano was usually parked to keep it out of the way — and there would be Wolstenholme, tinkling away with a little bit of 'Rustling in Spring' or the like, and the others would imbibe (except Kel), chat and maybe sing.

After Wolstenholme had finished sixth in the 1960 British Open, won by Nagle, Thomson convinced him to turn professional, and to try the fledgeling Far-East circuit, where he won a good share of prizes and events and became a popular member of the touring party. It seemed then only natural, again through Thomson's urging, that Wolstenholme set up his home in Melbourne and he eventually took out Australian citizenship. 'He was one of six children in his family,' says Thomson, 'and I think he was the last living in England. He had one brother in Johannesburg and a sister in Cleveland and the rest were scattered all over the world. He reckoned the family needed a representative in Australia!'

While resident in Melbourne, Wolstenholme won the Victorian Open four times, once in a tension-packed play-off over Arnold Palmer (when he later confessed to feeling 'like an Aunt Sally' because he sensed everyone wanted Arnie to win) and for the final time in 1980, again at the Metropolitan course.

After two decades of battling uphill with the red-blooded young power-players of the game, Wolstenholme, the witty, unpretentious fellow of guardsmanlike stature affectionately nicknamed 'Tally-Ho', now 50, took Thomson's advice and headed for the Seniors Tour. While his pedigree was not in the same class as his good friend, he played well enough in his first season to win almost US$100,000 and he sensed a new life opening up before him. Wolstenholme was planning to move to America with his wife Robin, and two young sons, James and Myles, and had selected a house on the east coast when he discovered he had cancer. Within the space of a year he had to have painful operations to fight the disease. In September 1984, moments after Thomson won his first tournament on the US Seniors Tour, the World Seniors Invitational at Quail Hollow Country Club, he and Mary were whisked away to the Charlotte-Douglas International Airport for a connecting flight to London where Wolstenholme had been taken to see his family. Earlier that day he'd wondered whether he would be able to make this important flight if he found himself in contention for the last round at the end, but with a police escort, complete with sirens and flashing lights, he and Mary were on board. The trip was to visit a dying Wolstenholme in a Nottingham hospital, and news of Thomson's first win was to brighten Guy's spirits considerably. It was a huge blow to the Thomsons to see their great friend in such a condition. Just a few weeks after Thomson's visit, Guy B. Wolstenholme died and his ashes were scattered over the course he revered most, Royal Dornoch in the very north of Scotland. International golf had lost one of its finest men.

It hit Peter Thomson as hard as the death of a close and dear friend would hit anybody, but he always tried to think of the good times they'd shared. Not one to display his emotions, people have remarked that in some strange way Wolstenholme's death stirred some old warhorse thoughts in Peter Thomson and rather than let it drag him down he used the memory of Guy to inspire him and carry him on.

It was no coincidence that in the twelve months following Wolstenholme's death, Thomson rediscovered his most ruthlessly competitive playing skills and started to attack the game with a new lease of life. In this mood he won a staggering nine Seniors events in 1985. He set a new record for tournament victories in a year (behind him on six victories in 1985 were Seve Ballesteros, Bernhard Langer and Tsuneyuki 'Tommy' Nakajima), and a record Seniors prizemoney haul of US$414,199. Incredibly, Thomson achieved a higher placing on the 1985 World Money List than any other Australian, and that includes Greg Norman. It prompted Don January, the leading career money winner on the Senior Tour, to remark: 'I've thought about calling the consulate to see if I can get Peter's green card pulled.' Another player overwhelmed by Thomson's resurgence was Sam Snead. 'Peter just played super golf,' he recalls. 'You can't win nine of anythin' without doing somethin' right. I remember at one tournament I said to him, "Hell, Peter, why can't you go back to Australia — don't you have enough money yet?" He just grinned and laughed at me and said he was plannin' on taking a few more bucks back! But he was determined though. I think he mighta been fired up by some guys sayin' he only won one tournament back in the fifties. He sure shut 'em up on that alright!'

Thomson himself tried, in his inimitable style, to play down the importance of his nine victories in one year by highlighting the shortened courses, the lack of quality, top-level opposition, the fact that most tournaments were played partly in the company of amateurs who spent between US$1,000 and US$5,000 to buy their way into the pro-am section of each event, and that tournaments were mostly three-round affairs and social gatherings as opposed to kill-or-be-killed championships. Seniors Tour officials were obviously and understandably enthusiastic, and indeed many excited veteran competitors joined them in the claim that their new baby might soon overtake the regular professional tour. Thomson wished to set them straight: 'The foolish suggestion that the Seniors Tour will overtake the regular one before very long, is something the professional golf scene should view with alarm,' he wrote for an American publication. 'It implies, not so much that the Seniors events are an attractive and surviving success, but that there is something distinctly unsatisfying about the regulars. It puts forth the notion that people inside and outside the sport are looking for something alternative and better. Time and again I hear, unfairly in my view, that the regular tour lacks colour and personalities, and that there is a certain grim monotony about its onward roll. I usually assume that people who say such things are excluding Greg Norman. I wonder if there has ever been a more exciting performer than him, unless it be the one and only Arnold Palmer. The regulars get a rough deal in many ways, but mostly it's an uncalled for comparison with their predecessors — those ageing stars of the newly founded Seniors circuit. I find the Big Tour enormously colourful. I also find the players who make it work a team of interesting characters, who put on an enthralling show worth paying to see. Shot for shot there is no comparison between the two tours. The juniors beat the oldies hands down. On the same courses, the scores are miles apart.'

Thomson's debut Seniors victory, his first in America since the Dallas Centennial twenty-eight years earlier, was typically Thomson. It came in the WBTV World Seniors Invitational at Quail Hollow in Charlotte, North Carolina, the venue for many years of the regular tour's Kemper Open. Over a course measuring 6,894 yards, he carded a seven-under-par total of 281 to hold off a belated charge from Arnold Palmer by a stroke. The American had previously made mention of his strong desire to capture the World Seniors title in the city where he had strong business and personal ties and on the course on which he had a home, and he swept home in 68, the best round of the tournament, with a birdie at the last hole from 15 feet to roaring support from the partisan crowd. As he stood on the final tee, Thomson led Palmer by a single shot, but he then drove into a fairway bunker. His second shot still left him 100 feet from the hole. He was equal to the challenge though, and from there managed to get down in two for a brilliant victory.

Three months later he snared his second win, this time in the prestigious PGA Seniors Championship, over the tough 6,520-yard PGA National Championship course at Palm Beach Gardens in Florida. He started with a superb 67, eventually totalled 286, and was the only player under par in a remarkable wire-to-wire performance. His 73 on the Friday brought an end to his run of eight consecutive sub-par rounds. The victory pushed him to third on the final Seniors order-of-merit for 1984 with US$255,000, ahead of Arnold Palmer and behind Don January and Miller Barber.

Before 1984 only a few of the leading veterans from other countries campaigned with any regularity on the Senior Tour (Nagle and Wolstenholme among them) and until that year Robert de Vicenzo was the lone non-American winner. After Thomson's first two victories, other foreigners suddenly showed interest in the new thirty-tournament schedule offering a phenomenal seven million dollars in purses. The fields were much stronger in 1985, but the urbane Australian continued on from where he'd finished the previous year — with victory. In March he withstood a dramatic, pressure-packed finish — worthy of any British Open — again to finish a stroke ahead of his old adversary, Palmer.

The tournament was one of the richest that year, the US$300,000 Vintage International at Indian Wells in California. No fewer than six players still had a chance as the event at the plush Vintage Club in the heart of the Palm Springs resort area climaxed. One was Palmer, who had lost the title in 1982 with a triple-bogey at the 16th. This time, Palmer tapped and missed an 18-inch par putt on the same hole. Thomson, playing alongside the American, quickly took advantage of the miscue, snatching a birdie at the 17th with a brilliant 8-iron tee shot and a six-foot putt. He was now ahead by two shots, but Palmer wasn't finished. He nailed a 4-wood second shot on the par-5 18th that bounded onto the green from 240 yards out and stopped just 12 inches from the cup for a certain eagle. With a grin, Palmer had thrown the pressure right back in Thomson's face. 'The ball was sitting nicely on the fairway,' he recalls, 'but one slip and I was in a play-off. I took my 4-wood.' Thomson countered superbly with a 225-yard shot that almost hit the flagstick. Now he needed to get down in two from 20 feet to keep Palmer at bay. He ran his first putt four feet past the cup, and safely holed the next. 'I was a bit worried about that one, but it went in.' Palmer tapped in to tie Billy Casper in second place and put his arm around the Australian in an affectionate hug. Thomson's scores were 69-73-69-69 for 280. That was seven-under-par, since three rounds, including the last two, were on the par-72 Mountain course and the other during the pro-am section on the par-71 Desert course. The first prize of US$40,000 was worth more than his five British Opens put together, 'but inflation takes care of that', he says.

Two weeks later he edged out Don January by a stroke in the awkwardly titled American Golf Carta Blanca Johnny Mathis Classic in Los Angeles. It was his fourth win in eight starts since September of 1984. Then in the first week of May there was victory in the Mony Senior Tournament of Champions at the resort of La Costa, north of San Diego. It was the second edition of the companion event to the long-running Tournament of Champions, engaging the Senior Tour winners of the previous twelve months in a separate competition from the one for the younger men of the regular circuit play. Same course, but tee positions made it 169 yards shorter at 6,742, a decision that Arnold Palmer, in particular, found distasteful. Even at that though, only three players — Thomson at 284 and Don January and Dan Sikes at 287 — broke par.

In the space of eight days in June Thomson won another two tournaments, the Champions Classic at Sparks in Nevada (a short distance from Reno) and the Senior Players Reunion Pro-Am in Dallas, Texas, beating the fields by two shots on both occasions. The tour had gone six weeks without let-up when the circus pulled into the Lafayette Country Club in Jamesville, New York, for the Mony Syracuse Classic in July. While several of the stars decided to take a break, Thomson had no intention of doing likewise. He had a sad reason for returning to Syracuse. He had used a local young man as his caddy in the tournament's first three years across town at the Bellevue Country Club and was shocked to learn shortly after the 1984 event that the boy, Mark Karpinski, had drowned. He immediately sent a sizeable contribution to a scholarship fund started in Karpinski's honour, but he wanted to win the tournament for Mark and did so, holding off challenges from Barber and Littler to post another two-stroke victory. 'When his mind is made up in such instances, he is the closest anyone can get to unbeatable,' said a Senior rival.

The following week Thomson lost a sudden-death play-off to Lee Elder at Newport, Rhode Island, then in August scored his seventh 1985 victory at Vancouver, one more than the record number set by Don January in 1983. An eighth came in September when he reeled off three consecutive rounds of 69 to win the United Virginia Bank Classic by four strokes at Richmond in Virginia. And then in October, fittingly at a place called Melbourne — in Florida — Thomson won the Barnett Suntree Senior Classic by a single stroke and he moved so far ahead on the Order of Merit that he could not be caught by anyone. He would leave this unfamiliar Melbourne with a bonus of US$125,000 for finishing on top. It had been some twelve months. Back home, as Thomson walked around at the Australian Open in November at Royal Melbourne, there was much congratulation but he always attempted to put his effort into some sort of perspective. 'I must stress that what I've been doing is playing with my own age group on shortened courses,' he would say. 'I'm as surprised as anybody that I won so often.'

But what about all that money? Surely it must have been satisfying. We all know what Billy Casper had to say about it — that the players are like a bunch of children locked in a lolly shop with the owner nowhere in sight. 'You just fill your pockets,' Casper grinned gleefully. For Thomson enjoyment was still the most important thing. When he was playing well he was happy in himself. When he was happy he would win or go close to it, and because of the affluence of the circuit, the prizemoney would naturally follow. 'I didn't need to go to the Seniors to win any money,' he replied. 'I would have gone there if the prizemoney was minimal. I went there for the friendships and the fun.'

Perhaps the Seniors year of 1985 filled a void in Thomson's life. Afterwards many of his detractors noticed that he had mellowed considerably; success in America, they said, knocked the chip from his shoulder. That charge does him less than justice; it was more a case that he was the happiest he'd been for some time and it showed. His family life was settled — his wife Mary was with him on the tour and had become a popular member of the gang. She loved the social interaction at night. The men would play during the day, the women would join them for parties and dinners at night and it seemed like one big party. Mary had felt the urge to do something useful during the day instead of tagging along to watch her husband compete. Before leaving Australia she organised a series of colour slides from the Tourism Commission and she would contact the local primary schools of the cities they visited to lecture the children about that big island country down under. The American kids loved it; their teachers were delighted by this display of diplomacy. Mary became a sort of unofficial ambassador.

Then, in 1985, the Thomsons' daughter Pan left her job and joined them on the Seniors tour, initially for a three-week holiday but she enjoyed the atmosphere and would partner Kel Nagle for parties and dinners on Kel's ladies ticket. To Peter, it all felt like home, and as he began to win more and more events, Pan became known by the other players on tour as his good luck charm, and Peter and Mary adored having her there with them. 'I had never been really close with Pan until then,' remembers Mary, 'because she was very much Daddy's girl, but we decided that it would be good for her to come and stay with us for a few weeks to see how it all worked. When it was time for her to go home, I would urge her to stay on for just another week. When we got to Dallas I'd talk her into Denver, and when we got to Denver I'd talk her into the next place, and so on.' Much to Peter's delight Mary did a lot of talking and Pan eventually came home with her parents in October. 'We had a completely different relationship going at the end of those six months and it was an enormous plus,' says Mary. It made the trip a thoroughly memorable one, and for Peter Thomson quite remote from the America of the 1950s. Never an outrageous dresser, Thomson began to wear brightly coloured 'American-style' golf attire (although never confusing the course with the catwalk as 'the playing peacock' Doug Sanders seemed to do). He seemed completely relaxed in all pink or apricot, or in checked trousers. His fellow veterans noticed that the car he drove around in the States bore personalised number plates: '5 TIMES'. He was having a ball.

For Thomson 1985 was always going to be a hard act to follow. No one knew this more than the man himself. To the surprise of many, he cut his schedule back and refused to commit himself as much as before. He was simply being honest to himself and to his future. He was nearing 60 and realised that he should devote his attention to his architectural business. In early 1986 he failed to reach anywhere near his form of the previous year. Then during a round on the tour he brought his club down, struck the tip of a buried rock beneath his ball, and tore the ligaments in his left wrist severely. It was almost a carbon-copy of an injury he'd sustained in Asia in 1968 and it required another plaster cast and a lengthy period of rest away from golf. 'It's fine now,' says Thomson, 'but I don't abuse it. I treat it very gently. It doesn't have the power that it used to have — I can't do the things that I used to — but then, these days it doesn't matter.'

The Seniors Tour was now growing bigger and bigger each year, with more and more name players joining to bolster the ranks. With this influx of a new breed of competitors, applying the same seriousness to tournaments as they had done in their prime, the happy-go-lucky Senior Tour suddenly seemed not so much fun any more. In Thomson's eyes the shine had gone from what was once a competition notwithstanding, but a friendly social one.

He eventually recovered from his wrist injury, although not completely, and returned for the occasional performance in America and to be reunited with those whose company he had enjoyed so much, but the fact remains that he never won another tournament there. In 1987 he finished 20th on the Seniors Order-of-Merit with US$117,184, and soon decided to play in only as many tournaments as was required for him to keep his player's ticket so that he could always go back to America whenever he wished to track down his old comrades, play a little with them, and maybe make a nice little earner for his troubles.

In 1988, Australia's bicentennial year, Thomson realised he was nearing the end of his competitive playing days. Something he'd always wanted to do before tossing it all in was to return to his many friends in Britain for a successful tilt at their now-flourishing Seniors titles. He'd finished runner-up to Englishman Neil Coles in the British PGA Seniors at Coventry in 1987, but came out at the conclusion to warn, tongue firmly in cheek, 'I shall return.' In fact Thomson was keen to play in both the British Seniors Open at Turnberry *and* the PGA at North Berwick in 1988, but he was told rather callously by US Tour commissioner Deane Beman that he would only be released from the US Seniors Tour for one of the events. Thomson chose the event at North Berwick, 'because I have always supported PGA tournaments'.

When Thomson arrived in Scotland in July he found several of his old friends dismayed by the condition of the course. For the previous two months the area had undergone a drought with only minimal rainfall; it all had a familiar ring to it for the visitor. The course authorities had been advised by agronomists against artificial watering in order to encourage the growth of the natural links grasses, and there was almost a total absence of greenery. One player described it as 'mid-summer in the Gobi desert', and another suggested he had not encountered such conditions since he fought in the battle of El Alamein! Whatever, it was a journey back to the old days for the Australian who could almost be seen rubbing his hands with delight. Defending champion Neil Coles, who was in fact on line for £1,000 bonus if he could achieve his fourth successive victory, could not hide his distaste for the course, saying that the pitch-and-run shot, which would be much in demand that week, had 'defeated me all my life', adding: 'If I had known what it was like here I would not have bothered to come.' Thomson, on the other hand, thought the whole experience was 'fun' and said he was glad he'd made the journey.

Surprisingly, in view of their pre-tournament statements, Coles started with an even-par 70, while Thomson, who putted poorly, opened with a dreadful 78, but said afterwards: 'I'll do better. I might even catch up by the end of the week.' That he did so is testimony to his fighting qualities. He came out next morning to leap into contention with a magnificent 67. The weather turned foul on the third day with an icy cold wind putting the thought in more than a few old brains that a scotch sitting by the fire would be a much more sensible pastime. Thomson ploughed delightfully through it all though and finished with rounds of 72–70 for a total of 287 and victory over South African Denis Hutchinson by two strokes.

That was the last time Thomson won. It could not be more appropriate that his final victory in his golfing career, the last in a procession of more than a hundred triumphs, would come on a hard, fast, links course in Scotland, home of his ancestors and a place where he felt such affinity. Somehow, ending his forty-year professional career with a win in the United States would not have seemed right.

C • H • A • P • T • E • R 9

Building an Empire

ACCORDING to the fire chief's report the blaze was officially brought under control at 6.50 a.m, Monday 9 February 1970, but by that time all that remained was the pro shop alongside the front of the dwelling. The clubhouse of the Royal Park Golf Club stood a blackened ruin. All trophies and photographs, all records of membership, competitions and committee meetings had gone up in smoke. Sadly for the members and the clubhouse manager in particular, the path to this tragedy was not a complicated one. The night before the manager, dutifully making certain all was done before he locked up after Sunday evening's post-competition gathering, had taken the embers from the club's old hot-water service and, believing them to be extinguished, pitched them in their usual heap beside the back door. Hours after he went home, the coals were brought to life by a night breeze and flames soon burnt the dry grass and began licking the weatherboard walls.

The tragedy brought Royal Park's most famous member, Peter Thomson, back to the club. After that blaze the club committee wanted to change the course and build a new clubhouse to their liking but disputes with the owners of the land, the Melbourne City Council, meant the committee and members chose to disband and start afresh on land at Tullamarine; where they started the Tullamarine Golf Club. The MCC took over the running of Royal Park and, retaining its name, opened the course to the public. Plans for a new clubhouse were drawn up and the Council also wanted to upgrade and redevelop the existing nine holes. In September 1970 they contacted South Pacific Golf Pty Ltd, international golf course architects, consultants and designers. One of the company directors was Peter Thomson; the Council knew that he and Royal Park went back a long way.

For Thomson and his partners (one of whom was old friend Walter Hadlee, the father of New Zealand's first cricketing knight, Sir Richard, and himself a former Test player) there was not much to do. 'We were invited to give an opinion on it, to see if it was worth putting money into it, and also to solve some serious problems,' he says. 'At the time the South Melbourne council was copping some law suits over people being hit by golf balls at Albert Park, and Royal Park was just as dangerous. We indicated a few changes and the city engineer made them.' Although Peter was happy to be casting his eyes over those friendly, familar fairways once more, it was completely an advisory role; more than anything it highlighted the fact that he no longer needed to *play* golf for his bread and butter. It was only appropriate that Royal Park should witness his life turning once more. While it was clear he still had many, many tournaments left him, Thomson was building a new life in course architecture. His company today represents a world leader in its field, a multi-million dollar practice under the banner of Thomson, Wolveridge and Associates.

Ask anyone in the street their idea of golf course architecture as an occupation and more often than not the answer would be that it is easy. Find a paddock, mow a square bit for a tee — a round bit a few hundred metres away for a green, and you're off and running. Do it eighteen times and there you are. You might even wish to incorporate a dam right in front of a green, or a hill, or a tree, or whatever. Simple. But golf course architecture is an art, a science and, big business. A century ago if someone had suggested a golf course could be built by completely altering the existing landscape they would have been locked in a padded cell. Today, in a world consumed by the game, architects are often obliged to move mountains, irrigate deserts, fill swamps and reclaim the sea. They are required to create a perfect playing surface in the shortest possible time, often involving many millions of dollars.

How does one cater for the long-hitting, birdie-devouring professional who expects nothing but the finest, and still keep the plodding club member or green-fee paying visitor satisfied? 'It involves many skills and gifts,' says Thomson. 'It is a tradesman job that produces a course that makes Greg Norman's knees shake. Almost anyone can do that. It is entirely another matter to design a course that is all things to all manner of golfers.'

In tennis there is no outsize court for the pros and another smaller one for children. Most cricket fields are the same size. Soccer pitches, basketball courts, baseball, football and rugby fields, squash, rowing, bowls, boxing, horse racing — they all have clearly defined and uniform boundaries. Only in golf does the quality (and quantity) of play begin with the man who designs the layout.

Michael Wolveridge is a debonair Englishman, who has lived at Mt Eliza, south of Melbourne, since 1970. Eight years younger than his partner, he is short and slender, has a thatch of wavy, greying hair and an infectious giggle which is heard often, due to his enthusiastic humour and lively character. In size, accent and blithe spirit, some say he provides a Dudley Moore to Thomson's Peter Cook. Both men have golf running through their veins and are passionate about its future. Wolveridge was a young lad of 17 when he first laid eyes on the newly-crowned British Open champion, Peter Thomson, who was paired with Peter Alliss in the final round of the 1954 Dunlop Masters at the Prince's course at Sandwich, Kent. As the riveted youngster watched Thomson putt out, and saw him receive the acclamation of the gallery, he could never have imagined that little more than a decade later their names would be as one, carving out some of the finest courses on the planet. In the end, as Thomson firmly believes, fate had its way.

As he watched that day in Kent, Wolveridge already had the distinction of being a scratch golfer. He grew up in Essex with a golf course literally on his back doorstep — 'I used to change my shoes at the kitchen steps, walk through our garden and onto the 18th fairway.' He was headed for an international amateur career and a university education at Cambridge until National Service intervened, and he found himself a radio operator in an RAF unit. 'My little role was to sit in the back of a jet called a Javelin,' he says, 'which was a great big delta wing fighter that made a hell of a noise and ran out of fuel after 55 minutes. We'd fly out over the North Sea and I'd be up the back twiddling with these knobs. I remember I once picked up "Housewife's Choice!" I must admit I treated it all rather lightly, and so did my superiors who wanted me to play golf on the Air Force team. When I made some chat about seriously learning the radar they said, "Oh come on, don't worry about that — we've got to play against Bomber Command and beat these fellows!" It was peacetime after all and we played a lot of golf.'

Once his two-year stint ended, Wolveridge had decided to toss in university for a career in professional golf. His father was appalled for he had expected young Michael to one day follow his footsteps to the heights at Mobil Oil. 'Well, you can forget about playing golf here,' he said to his son, firmly. 'If you want to play professional golf then you'd better go and do it somewhere else.' So Wolveridge was soon aboard 'one of my father's tankers' sailing from Holland to New Orleans and bound eventually for the Mid-Ocean Club in Bermuda, where it was arranged that he would start as an assistant to Archie Compston, runner-up in the 1925 Open Championship, and one of the outstanding personalities in British golf in the years between the two world wars. Since his glory days, Compston had headed for the warmer climes of Bermuda where he was to give lessons to famous pupils such as the Duke of Windsor and President Eisenhower. 'Archie was six-foot-four, and I'm a foot less than that in my spikes,' says Wolveridge. 'When he first saw me, he said, "Come on then, let's see how far you can hit the goddamn thing!" There he was looking down on me, this great big fellow wearing a dressing-gown. I hit a couple and looked up at him with an enthusiastically hopeful smile, and he said: "Jesus, I can spit further than that!" He wandered off laughing and chortling away and I was left alone on the tee, just myself and my feeble shots!'

Despite this inauspicious beginning, Compston took the youngster under his wing and twenty months later sent him on his way to America. In 1960 he won a pro-tournament in Mexico to earn his Tour Player's card and become the first Englishman to compete on the US Tour full-time. He also became the first foreign television golf commentator in America because 'I had a voice that they thought was rather interesting, I knew all the players, I knew the courses, and I rarely played on the last two days!' (This was well before the time of the legendary English commentator Henry Longhurst, who became famous in America for his work at the 16th hole of the US Masters, and whose career with the BBC was immortalised at St Andrews one day when he was commenting on an international match in which an American player was trailing rather badly. To liven up the telecast, the director cut to a view of the course showing an approaching train. 'And there,' said Longhurst, 'is the 3.25 from Dundee. I can even read its number — 3, 3, 4, 4, 3.' The director cut back to play, and Longhurst added, 'And if the American had started that way it would have been a damned less boring match!')

Although he played in a total of seventy-five events over four years on the US Tour, Wolveridge knew that through golf he could see the world and with that goal in mind he came to Australia in 1962 for the Open at Royal Adelaide. He finished in eighth place but, more importantly, at a cocktail party hosted by Dr Bill Ackland-Horman for all the foreign players and a few Australian stars, Wolveridge was introduced to Thomson. 'Peter was interested in a young man who would be playing from the UK,' recalls Wolveridge. 'There was no other Englishman in the field and it wasn't until the following year that Guy Wolstenholme came out to play. I met Peter and we fell into chatting and after a while he said, "So what are you going to do now?" and I said, "Well, I'm going to play in a couple more Australian events, and then I'm going back home to California." Then he said, "You ought to try the Far-East circuit. We're getting that going and I'm trying to get people from around the world there, and it's exciting. I'm sure this is in keeping with you wanting to see everything, with a sense of adventure." We hit it off nicely, and it wasn't long before the end of the week and we'd had dinner, that he invited me to join him in Melbourne for the summer.'

There was Wolveridge, sitting next to Thomson in his Aston Martin DB24, as they drove to Melbourne from Adelaide, with a marvellous opportunity to chat for several hours. 'We spoke about all sorts of things,' says Wolveridge. 'And hardly about golf at all. Our friendship really blossomed on matters of common interest, such as reading, writing, music, the world and its people and places. I've always retained a great admiration and respect for a very caring and delightful man, who coincidentally lived by many principles which I shared.' He spent three months with the Thomsons, playing golf with Peter almost daily. Wolveridge went back to America when the pro circuit started, but returned to Australia when the season ended, and again stayed with the Thomsons, joined this time by Guy Wolstenholme. They made a trip to New Zealand where Wolveridge learned of Thomson's staggering feats in their Open, and was introduced to the Australian's many friends on the other side of the Tasman. 'Those friendships,' he says, 'as so often was the case around the world, were to become my friendships too. I was persuaded in Christchurch by some dear friends of his to stay on and take up a job there at a club, and do something to help them with their golf. When I met a young lady there who was to become my wife, Gillian, I did stay.' Wolveridge stayed in New Zealand for two years, still playing events in America, Australia and Britain, but he feared he was becoming a 'hot-dog' player — the type that makes such an impression on the draw sheet that spectators, seeing this player's name among the next group coming through, say to themselves, 'I think it's time to go and get a hot dog.'

He played in the 1964 British Open at St Andrews, finishing far behind the winner, and the following week lined up in the French Open. In the first two rounds he was paired with a Yorkshireman named Bill Baker, who played off a two handicap. While the same could have been said of himself, Wolveridge realised that Baker was never going to give the title a shake, and sensed his partner's trip was not purely for the Open. Out of sheer inquisitiveness, he asked, 'What are you *doing* here?' Baker replied that he knew he didn't play so well, but he thought he'd play anyway, as he was in the area building a 36-hole golf course at Ormesson, just north of Paris for a chap called Commander John Harris, a noted English golf course architect. 'That sounds interesting,' said Wolveridge, and by the end of a round full of chat, dinner was planned for that evening. That meal proved to be a turning point in Wolveridge's life, and indirectly in Peter Thomson's too. 'It suddenly dawned on me that here was the elusive *something* that I had been looking for,' says Wolveridge. 'If I'd been a brilliant golfer, like Peter, it would have been all right, but to be out there, and just be one of the pack, was to lead to a waste of my time and education.' The more he thought about it, the more he realised his background was ideally suited to golf architecture, even though the thought had never previously crossed his mind. That French Open was Wolveridge's last tournament as a serious player. Over the next few weeks he contacted John Harris many times and with sheer persistence won him over. 'If I'm able to find more work,' said Harris, 'I'll make sure you get involved in some of it.' Commander Harris was a typically English upper-class gentleman whose manners were impeccable; his voice delightfully resonant and eloquent; educated in public schools then the navy, and deeply interested in golf, he eventually drifted into architecture, producing more than 250 new or remodelled courses in some twenty countries. Much to Wolveridge's delight, 'he had a great sense of humour and did all the pranks and those sort of things that were a part of public school life.'

To hear him tell it, it seems that chance, rather than natural talent and sheer hard work, has dictated the course of Wolveridge's remarkable career, but when Harris agreed to come to New Zealand in late 1965, he discovered that his protégé had been extremely busy. Wolveridge was not simply a golfer, but one who could also draw (in the late 1950s Wolveridge worked briefly for Walt Disney in London, drawing characters from *Alice in Wonderland* and *Wind in the Willows* for Mickey Mouse comics), write and certainly talk. Harris found a couple of jobs had been lined up and, greatly impressed, suggested to Wolveridge that they form a company if they could only find a big name to attract the eye of customers. Wolveridge pounced on the phone. He could think of no better name than Peter Thomson, whose immediate reaction was: 'What a great idea!'

As with Wolveridge, it simply hadn't dawned on Thomson that he was naturally suited to a career in golf course architecture. Just as he found when he first picked up a hickory-shafted golf club, Peter Thomson discovered course architecture to be a natural outlet for his imagination, intellect and philosophies. A deep traditionalist, he marvelled at the thought of designing and building a course *his* way — a course that might still be around years after he was gone. While his golfing schedule was hardly affected, Thomson was impressed by John Harris and plunged headlong into their new company, South Pacific Golf Pty Ltd.

Over the next two years a course at Wairakei in New Zealand was completed for the Tourist Hotel Corporation and in 1968 Wolveridge moved to Hong Kong and stayed over a year to design and build the Eden course for the Royal Hong Kong Golf Club. Harris remained in Europe, concentrating on the market there and in the West Indies, while

Thomson made full use of his contacts in Asia and the Pacific, expanding the practice further. They soon had offices in London, Christchurch and Melbourne. In 1970 Wolveridge took up residence in Melbourne to establish the Australian office with Thomson. In 1971 the group became the first to venture behind the iron curtain, commissioned by the Yugoslav government to design no less than ten courses to promote tourism. The following year another office opened in Nagoya, responding to an insatiable demand for golf in Japan and the Fujioka Country Club soon joined Wairakei, Royal Hong Kong and Bali Handara rated by British and American golf magazines among the top fifty Golf Courses in the World. Business was booming. South Pacific Golf no longer reflected their incredible success in just six years so the trio changed the name of the company to simply: Harris Thomson & Wolveridge. In early 1976 Peter and Michael were shocked to learn of the sudden death of Commander John Harris. The effect of his passing on the firm was negligible; as Thomson Wolveridge & Associates it continued to ride the world-wide boom. With competition demanding less and less of Thomson's time, they slipped comfortably into overdrive. Along with their established consultancy to leading private golf clubs, the pair placed a strong emphasis on courses as part of residential estates and tourist resort developments. With Harris no longer there, the strength of the partnership between Thomson and Wolveridge was given full rein. The work was a perfect vehicle for them both. It took them around the world many times and to lands that had previously never seen golf projects.

These days it is no less so. 'When somebody calls us and wants a golf course,' says Wolveridge, 'the first thing that happens is that we see the site. Then it becomes a land planning exercises. That's what I do. I plan the site and the land, and then Peter gets involved when it's time to actually design the golf course and we get to the detail of setting out the holes. Peter is an excellent sketcher and together we look at designing the layout. It's not simply a case of going in and moving earth from one place to another. We have to take everything into account from the natural lie of the land and its vegetation to the type of club or resort the developers are planning. Most of the time when we come up with a certain design, we've got a good reason for it. It might be traffic, or drainage, the *context* of a golf course, or because we've simply decided to ease up and give a player something easy. We might design something that has a player thinking, "Boy, I love this golf course" after he's had two 3s in a row, but then we might throw in something to really test him. All that is a part of golf. You're meant to enjoy it in some sort of way!'

For Thomson's part, sitting down at his desk with a blank piece of paper, a pencil and his imagination is just as exciting and challenging as

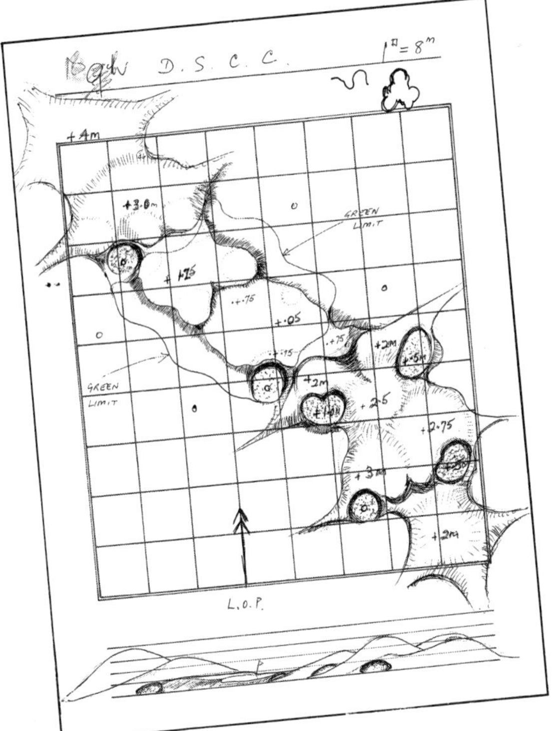

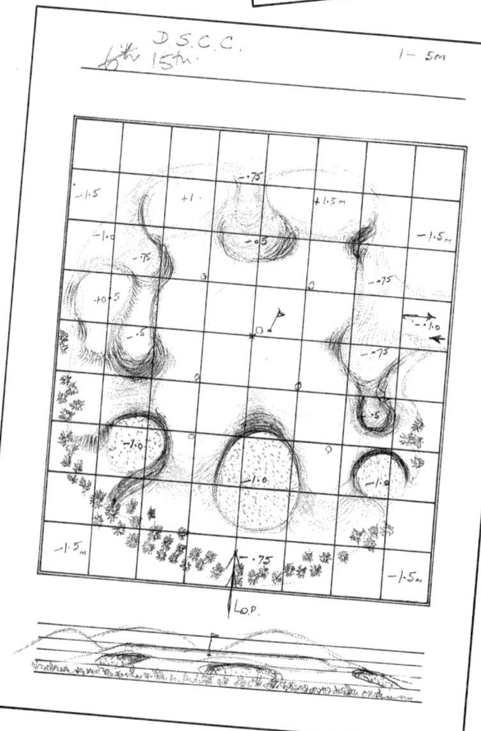

Sketches from Thomson for two greens at the Desert Springs Country Club in Alice Springs, Australia's first desert course. Designed and built by Thomson Wolveridge & Associates, it was opened in 1985. Note the point of view sketches at the bottom of each, and the L.O.P. (line of play).

any golf tournament was in his playing days. From his wealth of experience he pictures in his mind's eye a player coming to the hole he is about to sketch. What would that player be thinking? Are they angry? Are they having their best ever round? Whatever the case, Thomson decides, there must always be an element of *fear* — the golf course architect's main weapon. 'Fear is involved in every shot of the game,' he says. 'Let this be an elementary example: you are playing at a green with a medium-iron. There is out-of-bounds on the right, a great, deep bunker on the left. You look at these obstacles and, whether you like it or not, an element of fear comes into your mind. I might play that shot with the element reduced to one per cent — but never doubt it, I have fear in my mind too. Someone else on the other hand, not having the chance to play much golf, may have 50 per cent, or even more, of fear. Now the only sensible thing to do is to recognise the existence of these obstacles and to compromise over them. Have you the game to forget about them? If you haven't, or you are not quite sure you have, there is only one sensible thing to do and that is to skirt trouble. Play a shorter iron, take two to reach the green instead of one. There is always the chance that the second shot will put you close enough for the putt to go down; and even if it doesn't you have still spared yourself the agony and trouble which, as your mind tells you, an ill-played medium-iron shot might have landed you in.' It is through their understanding of fear that Thomson and Wolveridge know instinctively where to place their hazards (bunkers, creeks, lakes, trees, out-of-bounds fences), position their tees and greens, and carve out their fairways.

Characteristically, Thomson always falls back on the classic courses for his inspiration. The subtlety of angling the green and leaving the fairway wide open, as at St Andrews, gives them immense joy. After a visit to Britain in the 1980s, he wrote to Wolveridge, 'I have been stimulated to see these courses here again, not only Muirfield, but the other links like Nth Berwick, Gullane etc. I come to a striking conclusion that all hazards were positioned in the line of play, to be played *over* and that this provides for the most stimulating golf and the more attractive. I will keep some of these things on paper and show them (when I return).' Thomson is not fond of the architecture that has penal traps or water waiting to catch the sliced ball — it should be more difficult for a player to get to the green after a poor shot such as a slice or hook, but not impossible. He also disapproves of bunkers behind greens. In another letter to Wolveridge, this one from the USA, he wrote: 'The reverse facing trap at the back of every green is almost universal here — every one copying Jones [Robert Trent Jones]. Even Nicklaus does it ad nauseam. There is no such thing in nature or the classics and nor should there be. It is an abomination and the one thing that torments everyone. It is not so much the water — as the reverse traps on the beyond side — let's hammer the point and show the alternatives.'

Golf course architecture in America is a sore point with Thomson Wolveridge and Associates. 'I think some of the designs in America are quite dreadful,' says Wolveridge. 'This comes from the boom days when landscape gardeners were given the chance of doing golf courses as well as the clubhouse lawns and gardens. They'd plonk a lake between the tee and green of a par 3 and think it was marvellous. Then in the late 1970s they were colouring the lakes to give them a new appeal. Because America had so many marvellous players, the country became the focal point of the golfing boom, and I believe they've led golf up the garden path. It was that brilliant Scot Dr Alister Mackenzie who came up with a wonderful phrase that "Golf should offer pleasurable excitement" which is exactly what brings out the best in us all. But with water hazards, there's the despondency. Water is positive. You're either in it, or you're out of it. Golf is not positive. It's a game of chance. Water is unworthy of a noble game that should move forward, not be held up by reloading and hitting again.'

But what about the course Thomson and Wolveridge built for the Mirage resort at Port Douglas on the Queensland coast — doesn't that have water hazards in abundance? 'Well,' says Wolveridge, adopting a quizzical look, 'Port Douglas was a massive project built on mangrove swampland. The very nature of the beast meant that we were going to have big excavations because we had to get materials from somewhere, and big excavations there mean water. We tried so hard to put the water to the side — that's very much our style — but inevitably it intruded into some holes. In general, we succeeded at Port Douglas because we had a tortuous piece of land and although the water is prolific, a player is not asked to hurdle it. This philosophy comes from an appreciation of the origins of golf which Dr Mackenzie shared.

Dr Mackenzie also designed the famous Augusta National course, home of the US Masters — is a player not required to hurdle the water there? 'Of course he is, but Augusta was created around a creek, not a lake, and you could call the Swilcan Burn at St Andrews a sort of creek. The point is, you are required to take a drop on the other side of the creek to the green and chip over it, not simply throw another ball on the tee after driving into a lake. There are few things as nauseating in golf as having to play three from the tee after driving into a lake. We're all for creeks in our designs. I might add though that Mackenzie certainly made an exception when he called upon the biggest water hazard of them all to weave into the play at Cypress Point in California to create the most famous one shotter in the world, the spectacular 16th hole. But if playing that hole is not pleasurable excitement, I don't know what is!'

There is much to be discovered about Thomson himself, and his business, from examining the work of Dr Alister Mackenzie. Thomson has researched the man in detail and wrote a book, in collaboration with Wolveridge, called, *Dr Mackenzie's Golf Architecture*. 'Everyone has their likes and dislikes, favourites and hates,' Thomson has written. 'In regard to golf holes and courses, I have mine. They come from a lifetime of playing the game worldwide, but particularly they come from my early experience of playing the courses of my home city. In this I was very fortunate. Melbourne courses owe much to the influence of Dr Alister Mackenzie — a giant in the field of course architecture. He visited Australia twice in the 1920s and left an indelible stamp on every course he touched. His masterpiece in Australia is the West Course of the Royal Melbourne Golf Club, which even today is almost 100 per cent Mackenzie. But it wasn't only RM that benefited from his knowledge. Almost every course or hole constructed since his departure has some Mackenzie in it. In formative years then, my eye become accustomed to the Mackenzie look. I came to recognise the merit of his design. I became a believer in his philosophy of the game, as it applies to golf holes. He intended holes to be "enjoyable", "tempting", free from irritations and torment, and certainly "free from the humbug of lost balls". This was not just the Scotsman in him coming through. It makes the soundest commonsense — just as much today as it did more than half a century ago.'

So when Thomson and Wolveridge sit down together and design a course, or alter an existing hole, they try to fit the golf to the land in preference to shaping the land for the golf. They try to make it a memorable round for hero and hacker alike. If water is involved, there must always be a way around for those unwilling to attempt the carry and, for those who do, there must always be a reward waiting. Without the alternative route, golf becomes unfair; without the reward it is meaningless. Courses should be both easy and tough. There shouldn't be a hole out there that can't be birdied if a player uses his mind, and there shouldn't be one that can't be double-bogeyed if that player stops thinking.

One can easily get an impression that Thomson would love to be transported back in time, back to the days during the first world war when Mackenzie, an ordinary MD in his 40s based in Leeds and a chairman of the greens committee at Alwoodly Golf Club, chose to hang up his stethoscope in pursuit of golf course architecture. How Thomson would have enjoyed being at his side. 'Above all else,' he says. 'Mackenzie was a Scotsman, steeped in the ancient spirit of golf and its lore. He made himself an architect of golf trained at the cradle of the game and became an avowed disciple of the Old Course at St Andrews.

His splendid depiction of that famous links in 1926 is probably the m popular and printed golf course plan ever drawn. Mackenzie was excellent salesman and public relations man. He presented his clients or the day, together with his hole plans and putting green drawings, with a brochure containing a set of aphorisms of his own, prefaced by a striking photograph of himself in a kilt, jacket and sporran, touched with watercolour. On the subject of bunkers, he was impressive. Where one bunker strategically placed will do the job, don't build two. Where a bunker does not serve some purpose or strategy, fill it in or grass it over. Although brief and to the point, his philosophy answered everything. He observed that golf should be pleasurable, interesting and optionally challenging and as with all noted architects, he produced his best work when he was present to stand over the construction phase. The designer is always at the mercy of those who will interpret his drawings.'

And on this last point, Thomson Wolveridge & Associates are indeed fortunate. When they become involved in a project for a resort course, there is a team of associates: market researchers, botanists, irrigation experts, planners, architects, agronomists, engineers, surveyors and finally the men who control the machines that mould the golf course into shape. When they are required to make changes to an existing course at a private club, there are fewer involved but the project is of no less importance. Aside from all the massive resort and residential courses they've built in California, Washington, England, Indonesia, Tunisia, Singapore, Mauritius, Portugal, Spain, the West Indies, Italy, Scotland, France, Thailand, India and of course Japan, the business has made alterations and improvements to golf clubs as famous as Milan, Delhi, Auckland, Wellington, Pasatiempo and El Camino in California, Royal Hong Kong, Royal Madrid, Royal Calcutta, and in Australia the 'Royal family' of Sydney, Adelaide, Perth and Canberra, and others such as Lake Karrinyup in Perth, Kooyonga in Adelaide, the New South Wales, Sorrento, and on the sandbelt in Melbourne — Metropolitan, Kingston Heath and Thomson's 'home' course of Victoria.

At this last venue, in March 1989, Thomson had a chance to make history. His friends at Victoria had come to him with a problem. The 17th green, the place where a victorious young lad had shaken hands with many a defeated opponent in club or pennant competitions, was now an embarrassment. As it was a par-5 with a long, skinny green to aim at, a collection of four traps to the right of the green had claimed countless members in the past and many were finding it increasingly difficult to play from these bunkers and finish near the pin. Of far greater concern to the club was the fact that a large percentage of players, in trying to impart as much spin as possible, often caught the ball before the sand and flew it right over the green and the boundary fence, to the roofing tiles of the single storey homes on the other side. After many complaints and the odd broken window, the club decided to act. Thomson was to rectify the situation. Thomson had sat alone in the study of his Toorak home and sketched the solution. Once at Victoria he showed the sketch — a small, simple pencil drawing about the size of a paperback book cover, to the man in control of the bulldozer and seemingly within minutes the green and its bunkers were gone leaving a sea of rich, dark-grey soil. The sketch showed the slope of the green, a few trees and bunkers, a large mound at the rear of the green blocking out the view of the boundary fence and, significantly, a hollowed section of grassland at the front right where the bunkers in question had been. The hole now had a completely different perspective. Thomson decided that weak shots would now finish in the hollow, making escape easier, but the task of holing out equally as difficult, due to a severely sloping green. Strong shots would hit the mound at the back and be completely at the mercy of the slope. Whatever the case, the roofing tiles and windows would be preserved in future. Club officials wandered over occasionally to observe the work (Thomson yelled out: 'It's too late to back out now!' when he saw them coming). It wasn't only Thomson's presence demanding their attention. They marvelled at the man behind the wheel of the machinery. 'He's the Alex Jesaulenko of bulldozer drivers,' Thomson grinned, using the analogy of the champion Carlton footballer, in his obvious respect for the man nicknamed 'Spider', Norman Hazeldine. It harks back to Mackenzie's lesson that a golf course architect is only as good as those who interpret his drawings. By lunchtime, and operating with such precision that you'd think he was a little boy in a sandpit controlling the bulldozer from above, Hazeldine, stocky and silent, dressed in bottle-green work trousers and matching T-shirt, had all but shaped the new hole. He occasionally leapt from his cabin to examine Thomson's drawing wedged under the windscreen wiper of his ute, and to chat with the designer for a more detailed explanation, before gouging loads of soil in the 'dozer's giant claws and placing them like chess pieces. 'A job like this would take any other firm about a week,' said Thomson, as the 'dozer dragged a square net of chain, shaping the new green. 'But with "Spider" in the saddle they'll be sowing the new grass tomorrow!' Hazeldine and his fellow operators have performed similar magic at most of their proudest projects around the world and his brilliance trumpets loud and clear that their business is a team effort.

The world of course architecture noted with interest the announcement from 1982 Australian Open Champion Bob Shearer in October 1990, that he was quitting the international circuit in favour of a design apprenticeship with Thomson Wolveridge after negotiations with both men began during the British Open at St Andrews. But one expects Thomson will remain involved in the business in some capacity until the day he dies. As he says: "A golf course creates valuable land." In some cities they provide the only relief from industrial sprawl and residential areas. There are few complaints from environmentalists when it is announced a golf course is being built somewhere.

Thomson delves into numerous business enterprises — there have been sports stores, real estate ventures, shares in the old East Bros company (manufacturing golf clubs), even a cannery on the Mornington Peninsula exporting abalone shellfish to China and Japan, an idea that came to him whilst skin diving with a friend, and one that a thriving local industry today considers to be years ahead of its time. These days he is still involved in a company with an old friend which runs the local line of school buses in Warrnambool and of course he remains a contributor to the *Age* and ABC-TV golf telecasts, which despite the funding cutbacks in the area of live sport, will always call on him to add his unrivalled authority.

He has an interest in a hotel on the North Queensland coast at Cooktown and owns an apartment and house only a hundred or so kilometres south at Port Douglas. And he likes to keep his family close by. Wife Mary now travels with him constantly, eldest daughter Pan works for the Mirage resort at Port Douglas and Fiona is now Peter's personal secretary and office manager. Thomson has formed a partnership with an old Japanese friend and, as Kosaido-Thomson, is building hotel condominiums at Camden in New South Wales, surrounding a Thomson Wolveridge course. Fiona takes away most of the pressure by coping with the paperwork and organisation required for such a project, leaving him free to dabble in his various private interests while still making certain his many business connections are healthy and operating in capable hands.

'I will never leave Melbourne altogether, but probably spend the majority of my time at Port Douglas and come back to Melbourne for the summers, where the climate is nice and where my family and friends live.' He pauses, 'And I'll have plenty of things to keep me interested.' Thomson might be getting older, but he doesn't *feel* older — he just has a body that doesn't perform as well as it used to. Golf will remain his sport and he will continue to play social rounds with friends for fun, always finding some humour in it.

Those who know him well say there is not a finer partner — recently during a social four-ball Thomson told the joke about a group of super-veterans, over age 75, playing in a competition, all of them concerned that failing eyesight might pose the biggest worry to their event; they could see the ball and hit it from the first tee all right, but that's where the problems would start. While the oldies were all standing about wondering whether the tournament would come off, one senior citizen hobbled confidently to the tee with his secret weapon — a 75-year-old caddy he'd tracked down the night before. 'Okay, so you want to be my caddy,' said the super-veteran over a beer, 'But can you see?' The bespectacled bagman shot back with: 'Sir, I have the sight of young boy.' So the next morning, there was the hardened campaigner taking address on the first tee, and with a sweet crack he made contact with his ball. 'Brilliant shot!' exclaimed the enthusiastic old man carrying the bag while all heads turned to the caddy for news of the ball's direction. 'So come on — where did it go?' appealed the veteran who'd just hit. His caddy turned and with a vacant look, said: 'Umm ... Aah ... I forget.'

So the memorable rounds will continue for Thomson and so will his passion for golf and all that happens with it around the world. With each new British, US, and Australian Open champion, there will be Thomson — watching, observing, analysing and marvelling at the new young names taking hold of the game as he did. They will be required to perform some remarkable feats indeed if they hope to force their way into his top-twelve list of the best players he has ever seen, which is currently:

Seve Ballesteros	Jack Nicklaus
Julius Boros	Greg Norman
Ben Hogan	Arnold Palmer
Bobby Locke	Gary Player
Kel Nagle	Sam Snead
Byron Nelson	Tom Watson

Thomson's curriculum vitae reads like a logbook of someone desperate to keep themselves busy and their mind alert, active and interested. There are other sports that he enjoys watching, such as Australian Rules football, sumo wrestling in Japan and, of course, Test cricket. While an unashamed traditionalist and 'not too keen' on the coloured clothing and hit-and-run style of limited-overs fixtures, he finds modern Tests, 'most exciting, very professional and very efficient'. Along with Richie Benaud, another close Thomson friend is the former English Test cricketer, Colin Cowdrey. 'I've kept in touch with a great many cricketers both from Australia and England,' he says, 'because when I was in Britain and they were there playing for the Ashes, there would always be a few players wanting a game of golf.' Cricketers like Keith Miller, Bob Simpson, Ray Lindwall, Tom Graveney, Denis Compton, Brian Close and Peter Richardson would gladly reciprocate and doubtless were impressed by Thomson's ability with bat-and-ball in charity matches. Richardson, who opened the innings for England in 34 Tests, scoring over 2,000 runs, once recalled a match in Kent, pitting his own celebrity XI against another led by Cowdrey. Each side was a mixture of Test and county players and personalities from other fields, and Thomson managed to get a guernsey in Cowdrey's line-up. 'He was a hell of a player,' said Richardson. 'He made a superb century and we had to tell him to get out in the end. It was a charity match and he was hogging the crease!' Then, when Cowdrey's team was in the field, Thomson was asked if he would like to bowl. 'He came on and produced leg breaks — not cutters, but genuine finger spin,' said Richardson. 'Some of our younger players had never seen that type of bowling in their lives.' Thomson picked up two wickets, one of whom was the left-handed Richardson, bowled neck and crop through a gap between bat and pad. The golfer was an enthusiastic member of charity sides wherever he travelled, but began to scale down his celebrity appearances after a match in Kuala Lumpur in the 1970s. 'I've still got a bent finger from an injury I received in that match,' he says. 'I took a ball on the end of the finger when I was wicketkeeping and dislocated it.'

Aside from the interest in sport, Thomson remains a broadly cultured man, he reads widely and not simply topics that interest him. He wants to understand ideas he does not accept, and is not afraid to expose his own beliefs to critical analysis, usually in private. One of the first things you notice about his study — the place where he works, draws, thinks and writes — are the books: politics, art, travel, history, literature, sport, law, religion. He recently put down *The History of Europe*, which had absorbed his spare time for almost two years, to pick up Salman Rushdie's *The Satanic Verses*, mainly to see what all the fuss was about. Shakespeare, Tolstoy, Nietzsche, Koestler and Hemingway are among his favourites. 'I read what interests me,' he says. 'I'm fascinated by the lives of others, and by their discoveries. By true experiences.' Another noticeable thing about Thomson's study is the lack of golfing memorabilia, in fact, no trophies at all. On the wall is a framed photograph of Peter with Kel Nagle, an incidental snap taken during a Legends tournament in America. The only other thing suggesting that the man who works in this study has some connection to golf is a map of the Royal Melbourne course, presented to him during the Bicentennial Classic.

Thomson prefers to decorate his home with works of art. He once sold a painting of his own, of a group of Indian children, in an 'art-by-amateurs' exhibition, with proceeds donated to the Victorian Society for the Prevention of Cruelty to Children. He occasionally finds time to attend the opera, and enjoys classical music. 'The music I enjoy mainly are the romantics like Mahler, Wagner and Berlioz,' he says. 'I thrill to all the Mahler symphonies. I used to listen to classical music when I was a boy. In America, when I was touring it would be impossible to find it.

It's only in recent times that they've developed classical music stations. We didn't have tapes in those days and I certainly couldn't take my records with me, so I'd have to go without.' Another reason for his preference for playing elsewhere. 'Now I can listen to music any time I want; at home, in the car, and on my walkman.' Thomson is also fascinated by the progress made by his Japanese friends in the area of electronics and he wears an elaborate multi-function wrist watch. Everywhere he goes he carries a small Japanese AM/FM radio about the size of cigarette packet and as thin as an audio-cassette. Fully charged it can operate for around eight hours, and linked discreetly to his ear by a small plug he listens to whatever takes his fancy, often whilst in the company of friends or business associates. It gives rise to claims that he is in a world of his own and helps Thomson switch off and relax.

'He's not called "Placid Pete" for nothing,' says Wolveridge. 'I think his is an attitude that's very much in-built and I don't think I've ever found anyone who can just cruise along like he does. In setbacks in life he has always been exactly the same as when we've had a windfall. About the only difference would be that when we've had a windfall he can't stop himself from giving his hands a brisk, little rub — like a little field mouse that's just found a big acorn for winter storage! That's his little idiosyncrasy. Of course there are many, many people who find his complete balance irritating, and I often find myself the one getting mad for both of us because, quite frankly, I think he's hopeless at planning things. He's a dead loss — but he *gets* through it all beautifully — he deals with everything as it comes and there isn't much that fazes him, or rattles him.'

Thomson has often been approached to release his definitive coaching book. They soon discover it would be no more than a coaching pamphlet. Henry Longhurst was one of those who approached Thomson. In 1959 he wrote a fascinating article for *The Times* on Thomson's game. It remains just as logical and pertinent today.

> *How far away from the ball should you be?*
>
> Thomson often uses the expression 'measuring off', and he himself measures off quite deliberately before each shot. Stand relaxed, leaning slightly forward, with your knees slightly bent and the whole body in balance. Extend the left arm and the club in a straight line, not stiff as a ramrod, and you are now measured off. 'Picture in mind your position as you strike the ball and make final adjustments from that.' This applies to every club.
>
> *How do you grip the club?*
>
> Again, delightfully simple. Get set up right and you won't notice! Take it as you find it.

How hard do you hold onto the club

'Often,' says Thomson, 'you can actually see the tension in a man's hands. You should start with a light touch, barely enough to lift it off the ground, so that it feels heavy. It is just like using an axe. You lift it with a light grip, just enough to raise it, and it feels heavy. As you bring it down, your grip tightens without your thinking about it and reaches its tightest at the moment of impact.

'There is another likeness with golf. Using an axe, you do not hit with it; you accelerate it. That is exactly what you should do with a golf club.'

How do you start the club back?

'Well, you just draw it straight back. Never mind about what the books din into you about turns and pivots. Just draw it straight back as far as is comfortable and let nature take its course. Don't turn away; just draw it back — but keep your weight squarely on both feet and make sure you don't sway back with it yourself.'

Finally what Thomson describes as the key axiom in the golf swing, namely, to be behind the ball when you strike it — not all of you, maybe, but certainly your head. 'A plumb line from your nose as you strike the ball should hit the ground several inches behind it' — a sobering thought for us lurchers and swayers, to whom, as we heave forward, the ball so often appears to be moving rapidly backwards.

• • •

The position of the ball with the driver was simple. It was opposite the left foot. Where is it to be with the other clubs? Again there are no complications. His answer is, 'roughly an inch farther back for each club'.

This finds the ball midway between the feet with a 5-iron and about off the right heel with a 9-iron. With the driver you hit the teed-up ball an ascending blow, the clubhead having already passed its lowest point. With the short irons you hit it a descending blow, taking a good-sized divot after the ball.

How far away do you stand? Again the same principles apply throughout. You 'measure off', as before, with the left arm extended, and yourself poised and in balance, though naturally stooping a little more with the shorter clubs than you did with the driver.

Thomson also likes to have his feet progressively closer together as the shots become shorter. It all seems to fit into a very simple and intelligible pattern. As the shots become short enough to require judgment rather than power for their execution, he likes to open the stance slightly, drawing his left foot back a little.

For the short game his maxim, typically, is that one should always look for the simplest way. He describes the high wedge shot, which we so much admire when played by professionals, as, for most people, 'a form of lunacy'. The more you can picture a short approach as a kind of extended putt, he says, the better.

The ruin of most handicap players' short games comes from their efforts to hit the ball up. It is the golfer's job to hit it forward, the lofted club's job to hit it upward. It is an old professional trick, in trying to teach this to beginners, to put a lofted club into their hands and invite them to try to hit the ball along the ground into a bunker between them and the flag. They concentrate on hitting the ball forward, whereupon it sails over the bunker.

Thomson is a supremely good bunker player. Perhaps his finest exhibition of this art was when he won the Open at Lytham, where they have innumerable bunkers, of which he encountered at least his share. I have always remembered his remark afterwards that he had 'never seen such a beautiful sand'. He sincerely regards 'splashing' the ball out of the sand as the simplest shot in the whole game, if only because there is so much greater margin for error than with a similar shot off grass.

. . .

Thomson is also — again in an unostentatious and 'simple' way — a supremely good putter. I spent a long time drawing him out on the subject and from this I think three main points emerge. He does not think that the grip matters unduly — indeed, he used the words 'almost any grip will do' — but he has no doubt about his own method.

To initiate it, take a normal grip, then rotate your left hand to the left so that the back of it is at about 45 degrees to the ground; do likewise with your right hand to the right, and then stick your right thumb firmly on the shaft. He also reckons to stand with his eyes vertically over the ball. All this is common ground but there are many who might vastly improve by giving it a trial.

His second point interested me because I have so often referred to it as one of the main secrets of Bobby Locke's phenomenally successful putting and because it is something that we can all so easily do and, even when we mean to, so often don't. It is to carry out a sort of drill: in other words, to find a set of motions that suits our own particular eye and temperament and carry them out, without exception, every time we putt.

(*The Best of Henry Longhurst*, Collins, 1979, pp. 60–6.)

It is also Thomson's strongest belief that anyone who plays the game, and especially those who play it for a living, should need only one person to tell them how to play — and that is themselves. Thomson had to save himself from laughing out loud as he sat in the media tent at the 1990 British Open and listened to Payne Stewart as the American enthusiastically revealed the secrets of his success — an instructional coach, a mental coach, a dietitian and a fitness coach that followed him to tournaments and that he called, 'Team Stewart'. Thomson turned to a fellow scribe and joked, 'I wonder what kind of a career I could have had with such a team!' He will continue to offer advice to any of his brethren struggling with their game, young or old, but only to those who actively seek it. Even then he will only point them in what he considers to be the right direction and never offer a clear-cut opinion as to where they are falling down.

It is the same with the PGA. He says he will remain president, but only as a figurehead — an elder tribesman there for advice, to encourage and observe, and to show a deep interest until the day arrives when he can gracefully step aside and leave it all to the young lions of the professional game in Australia. 'I made a strong resolve not to be anybody's guru,' he says. 'I'm perfectly willing to give any young Australian the sort of advice I gave Ian Baker-Finch if they're interested enough to ask. I've helped a few youngsters in bits and pieces along the way, but I certainly don't go charging up to them and say, "Hey son, you'd better do this or you won't get anywhere" — I don't think any young player is going to get anywhere if he has to rely on someone else's brains.'

Incredibly, this policy was adhered to so rigidly that not even his own son received a word of coaching. It remains the clearest indication of Thomson's resolve. In the late 1960s and early 1970s, young Andrew Thomson caddied for his father in tournaments both in Australia and New Zealand and the thought of a career in golf crossed his mind many times. 'I used to play as much as I could,' says Andrew, 'and still do [to a handicap of 10], but by about the age of 16 it was clear I didn't have a genius for the game and the idea of following in Dad's footsteps just faded away. But I must say it became a matter of strange pride that I virtually taught myself the game. He never gave me any advice when it came to hitting a golf ball any better, so I observed him many, many times and taught myself how to play.' And that's exactly the way Thomson wanted it.

Like any young child Andrew was encouraged to become interested in his father's occupation, to the point where he was thrilled to be given permission to take the gleaming British Open trophy to junior school with him after his dad had brought it home in 1965. Off he went with the auld silver claret jug wrapped in a pillow and stuffed inside his school bag, hoping for a big reaction from his chums. 'At four that afternoon he burst in the front door dishevelled as usual,' recalls Thomson, 'but when he saw me he burst into tears. "What happened?" I asked. "The boys teased me," he said through his sobs. "One boy said his dad has eight cups. It was terrible." Cups are important to boys.' Mary Thomson believes that episode was a very good lesson for Andrew, as it immediately brought him back down to earth. Later, in his teen years he was persuaded to explore other careers and make up his own mind. Golf wasn't such a priority.

In Thomson's analysis, true greatness in anything — be it sport, business, music, the arts, politics or life itself — is not measured by the material yardstick and does not involve being better than anyone else. He believes greatness comes down to using skills, talents and capacities to the absolute maximum. In his view a great person is one who understands what his or her capacities are and then maximises what they've got. It all boils down to satisfaction within ourselves that we've done everything to the best of our ability. 'Sport is for pleasure, for amusement, for exercise, for fun,' he would always say. 'Golf is my sport as much as it is my business.' And his unique humour would always surface. It was golf after all, not brain surgery.

Once during the late 1970s in Japan, where he was accorded demigod status for his creation of numerous courses and tournaments, and where he was a key factor in the golfing boom. Thomson was invited by the sporting goods manufacturer Dunlop to display his skills at an exhibition. Nowhere was his influence more evident than at the venue for this little show, an enormous triple-decked driving range in downtown Tokyo. There the patrons might never have a chance to put their skills to the test on a proper course; for them, the range was the only game in town, even if they had to wait three hours to get on.

After the exhibition Thomson sat down in the small pro shop, and noticed that somebody's shots were travelling much further than anyone else's. He traced them back to a small cubicle and there saw a well-built Japanese man teeing up ball after ball, employing a rusty, awkward swing, but bashing each shot with a brute of a driver directly to the far precincts of the range. 'He's good,' said Thomson. 'Who is he?' The Japanese pro alongside him replied: 'He works at a factory nearby and comes here every day and has been doing that ever since we opened.' Thomson's curiosity was aroused so he wandered over for a closer look. After watching several more mighty drives he stepped forward, nodded a greeting, picked up another club and suggested the man hit a few with the 5-iron. The burly local had arrived after the exhibition and had no idea who this inquisitive foreigner was, but out of typical Japanese politeness, he bowed, leant his driver against the wall and proceeded to try the 5-iron. To Thomson's complete surprise he couldn't get the hang of it at all and each duffed, topped and foozled shot trickled down amongst the failures at the front. At the earliest opportunity the man grabbed his driver back and resumed booming his shots out to the perimeter fence. 'The only club he ever uses is the driver,' said the pro to Thomson as they made their way back to the shop. 'He has never had the opportunity of playing on a golf course and probably never will. This is the sole enjoyment he gets out of the game.' It was his idea of heaven. Why should anyone want to ruin his fun by placing him on the first tee in the final round of a British Open?

It might all be contained in the little rhyme printed on the business card of that globe-trotting Australian, Joe Kirkwood, the man whose name was soaked up by an eager young lad in short pants at Royal Park all those years ago:

> Tell your story of hard luck shots,
>   Of each shot straight and true;
> But when you are done, remember, son,
>   Nobody cares but you.

Epilogue

MAKING a success of golf is not composed of perfecting by repetitive practice, but of understanding how to compete. The former assists the latter but it doesn't assure it. Amongst us there are practising addicts. With one or two exceptions these people are chasing something different in life. Target practice doesn't make you a good guerilla.

Competing and winning has to be in your make-up before you start. You don't learn it. You just bring it out.

Succeeding, it goes without saying, is more important to some people than others. Competition with other people for certain goals may even be a little show of insecurity, like young monkeys scrambling for peanuts. For some it is a desperate effort to win recognition from the rest of the tribe, or to gain power and status. With golf, since there are huge prizes at stake, it can be a chase after financial wealth. Nobody would say in this day and age there is anything wrong with this. Everyone amongst us whatever activity he engages in, must be chained to the same wheel.

Duties are demanding. You have duties to your parents, your children, your spouse and the human race. Your life is consumed fulfilling these obligations. It is a lucky quirk of fate if you can carry these out while doing something you love at the same time. Millions of people hate their work and no one blames them, but although I have seen countless golfers tangled up in a furious hate of their environment, I have never come across one who didn't really like what he was doing. (I don't see many of the unsuccessful ones giving it up to pursue something else.)

But it is not all as easy as it looks. Golf doesn't select the people who play it. Most of us are misfits who have drifted into at an early age, when our narrow view of the world showed nothing else. Why then should some of us be blamed for not coming out on top? Indeed why should those who win be acclaimed? For being more desperate than the rest?

Golf playing is not an art at which one can demonstrate one's gifts. It is a craft, a trade, a profession, prize-fight, all in one. The total picture when we are all set loose is a circus of performers at each other's throats. It is not for the meek and mild. Whatever their inheritance will be, it will not include golf championships. But even if man doesn't succeed, for whatever reason, playing golf can be a unique education for him. (If, that is, he can keep his eyes and mind open.) It is a lesson in human relationships, human idiosyncrasies and failings. It is a broad picture of life itself.

P. W. THOMSON

Peter Thomson's Tournament Victories

1947	Australasian Foursomes Shield (with H.R. Payne)
1948	Victorian Amateur Championship
1949	Victorian Close (amateur)
1950	New Zealand Open, New Zealand Masters
1951	Australian Open, New Zealand Open, Victorian Close (as a professional)
1952	Mobilco tournament (S. Africa), 1,000 Guineas (S. Africa), Victorian PGA
1953	New Zealand Open, New Zealand PGA, Victorian PGA
1954	OPEN CHAMPIONSHIP, World Cup (with K.D.G. Nagle), British PGA Matchplay, Ampol tournament
1955	OPEN CHAMPIONSHIP, New Zealand Open, Pelaco, Speedo, Caltex, Wiseman's (S. Africa) tournaments
1956	OPEN CHAMPIONSHIP, Dallas Centennial, Pelaco
1957	Yorkshire Evening News
1958	OPEN CHAMPIONSHIP, Dunlop, Daks (UK), Pelaco
1959	World Cup (with K.D.G. Nagle), New Zealand Open, Italian Open, Spanish Open, Pelaco, Coles, Caltex (NZ)
1960	Yorkshire Evening News, New Zealand Open, German Open, Hong Kong Open, Daks and Bowmaker tournaments (UK), Wills Masters, Adelaide Advertiser
1961	British PGA Matchplay, Yorkshire Evening News, Dunlop Masters, Esso Golden (UK), New Zealand Open, NSW Open
1962	Piccadilly tournament, Martini International (UK), Yomiuri Open (Jap.)
1963	Indian Open, Lakes Open
1964	Philippines Open
1965	OPEN CHAMPIONSHIP, New Zealand Open, Hong Kong Open, Daks tournament (UK), Caltex and Metalcraft tournaments (NZ)
1966	British PGA Matchplay, Indian Open, Caltex (NZ), Wills Masters (NZ)
1967	Australian Open, Australian PGA, British PGA Matchplay, Alcan International (UK), Hong Kong Open
1968	Dunlop Masters (UK), Victorian Open, South Australian Open
1969	Chunichi Crowns (Jap.), Sax Altman tournament
1970	Martini International
1971	New Zealand Open, Dunlop tournament (Jap.)
1972	Australian Open, Wills tournament, Chunichi Crowns, Pepsi tournament (Jap.)
1973	Victorian Open
1976	Indian Open, Pepsi tournament (Jap.)
1984	WBTV World Seniors Invitational, PGA Seniors Championship
1985	Vintage International, American Golf Carta Blanca Johnny Mathis Classic, Mony Senior Tournament of Champions, Champions Classic, Senior Players Reunion Pro-Am, Mony Syracuse Classic, Du Maurier Champions, United Virginia Bank Seniors, Barnett Suntree Classic
1988	British PGA Seniors

Peter Thomson's British Open Record

Year	*Finish*	*Course*	*Score*	
1951	T-6th	Royal Portrush	70–75–73–75	293
1952	2nd	Royal Lytham & St Annes	68–73–77–70	288
1953	T-2nd	Carnoustie	72–72–71–71	286
1954	1st	Royal Birkdale	72–71–69–71	283
1955	1st	St Andrews	71–68–70–72	281
1956	1st	Hoylake, Liverpool	70–70–72–74	286
1957	2nd	St Andrews	73–69–70–70	282
1958	1st	Royal Lytham & St Annes	66–72–67–73	278
1959	T-23rd	Muirfield	74–74–72–74	294
1960	T-9th	St Andrews	72–69–75–70	286
1961	7th	Royal Birkdale	75–72–70–73	290
1962	T-6th	Royal Troon	70–77–75–70	292
1963	5th	Royal Lytham & St Annes	67–69–71–78	285
1964	T-24th	St Andrews	79–73–72–75	299
1965	1st	Royal Birkdale	74–68–72–71	285
1966	T-8th	Muirfield	73–75–69–71	288
1967	T-8th	Hoylake, Liverpool	71–74–70–72	287
1968	T-24th	Carnoustie	77–71–78–75	301
1969	T-3rd	Royal Lytham & St Annes	71–70–70–72	283
1970	T-9th	St Andrews	68–74–73–74	289
1971	T-9th	Royal Birkdale	70–73–73–69	285
1972	T-31st	Muirfield	71–72–74–77	294
1973	T-31st	Royal Troon	76–75–70–73	294
1974	–	Royal Lytham & St Annes	79–81	
1975	–	Carnoustie	73–75–81	
1976	–	Royal Birkdale	75–79	
1977	T-13th	Turnberry	74–72–67–73	286
1978	T-24th	St Andrews	72–70–72–76	290
1979	T-27th	Royal Lytham & St Annes	76–75–72–74	297
1984	–	St Andrews	72–73–76	

Conversion table

1 inch	=	2.54 cm	1 cm	=	0.39 in.
1 foot	=	30.5 cm	1 m	=	3.28 ft
1 yard	=	0.914 m	1 m	=	1.09 yd
1 mile	=	1.61 km	1 km	=	0.62 mile

Index of Names